JOURNAL FOR THE STUDY OF THE OLD TESTAMENT SUPPLEMENT SERIES

66

Editors
David J A Clines
Philip R Davies

JSOT Press
Sheffield

SECRETS

OF THE

TIMES

Myth and History in
Biblical Chronology

Jeremy Hughes

Journal for the Study of the Old Testament
Supplement Series 66

For my parents

Published by JSOT Press
JSOT Press is an imprint of
Sheffield Academic Press Ltd
The University of Sheffield
343 Fulwood Road
Sheffield S10 3BP
England

Typeset at the Oxford University Computing Service
Printed in Great Britain
by Billing & Sons Ltd
Worcester

British Library Cataloguing in Publication Data available

ISSN 0309-0787
ISBN 1-85075-178-1

PREFACE

This book is a revised version of a doctoral thesis which was submitted to the Faculty of Oriental Studies of Oxford University in 1986. I originally planned to write a short monograph on the chronology of the Priestly stratum of the Pentateuch, but this evolved to become a full-length study of Biblical chronology and went on to displace a projected thesis on the more intractable question of the Hebrew verbal system. One consequence of these circumstances was that I came to the historical chronology of Israel and Judah via the mythical chronology of antediluvian times, and only began to dabble in matters of historical chronology because the mythical chronology of the early books of the Bible seemed to provide an answer to problems in the chronology of Kings. Scholars who have previously considered these problems have normally travelled in the opposite direction, from historical chronology to Biblical chronology, without considering the possibility that the chronology of Kings might not be a straightforward species of historical chronology after all.

In writing this study I have benefited greatly from the advice and assistance of others. I am especially indebted to my thesis supervisor, Professor James Barr, for arousing my interest in Biblical chronology (initially through his paper on Ussher and Biblical chronology), and for offering helpful criticisms of my own work as it developed. I was also fortunate in being supervised, for two terms, by Dr Terence Fenton and Dr Sebastian Brock, who offered their own constructive criticisms; and I am further indebted to Dr Stephanie Dalley, who read most of the chapters in their thesis stage and offered helpful advice on Assyrian and Babylonian chronology, and to Professor John Baines for advice and guidance in matters of Egyptian chronology. Dr John Day and Dr John Barton examined the thesis and made helpful and detailed criticisms.

The original thesis was written while I was a junior research fellow at Merton College, Oxford. It was then revised during my time as Kennicott Fellow at the Oriental Institute in Oxford; and as the final tasks of indexing and proof-checking are being completed I am currently Pusey and Ellerton Fellow at the Oriental Institute. I am indebted to the trustees of the Kennicott and Pusey and Ellerton Funds for a generous subsidy towards the cost of publication. I am also grateful to Sheffield Academic Press, for their patience in waiting for the book to be completed; to my family (for the same reason!); and to Jennifer Baines, for helping me meet this objective by typesetting the book at the Oxford University Computing Service.

Oxford   Jeremy Hughes
January 1990

CONTENTS

ABBREVIATIONS

1. Modern reference works

ABC	A. K. Grayson, *Assyrian and Babylonian Chronicles* (New York, 1975)
AcOr(D)	*Acta Orientalia*, ediderunt Societates Danica etc.
AfO	*Archiv für Orientforschung*
AION	*Annali dell'Istituto Orientale di Napoli*
AJBA	*Australian Journal of Biblical Archeology*
AJSL	*American Journal of Semitic Languages and Literatures*
ANET	J. B. Pritchard (ed.), *Ancient Near Eastern Texts relating to the Old Testament* (3rd ed. with supplement, Princeton N. J., 1969)
AnOr	Analecta Orientalia
AOT	H. F. D. Sparks (ed.), *The Apocryphal Old Testament* (Oxford, 1984)
ARAB	D. D. Luckenbill, *Ancient Records of Assyria and Babylonia* (Chicago, 1926/7)
AS	Assyriological Studies
AUSS	*Andrews University Seminary Studies*
BA	*Beiträge zur Assyriologie und Semitischen Sprachwissenschaft*
BASOR	*Bulletin of the American Schools of Oriental Research*
BHS	K. Elliger and W. Rudolph (edd.), *Biblia Hebraica Stuttgartensia*
BibOr	*Bibbia e Oriente*
BJRL	*Bulletin of the John Rylands Library*
BZAW	Beihefte zur *Zeitschrift für die Alttestamentliche Wissenschaft*
CBQ	*Catholic Biblical Quarterly*
CIS	*Corpus Inscriptionum Semiticarum*
CT	*Cuneiform Texts from Babylonian Tablets in the British Museum*
DBS	*Dictionnaire de la Bible, Supplément*
DZGW	*Deutsche Zeitschrift für Geschichtswissenschaft*
EB	*Encyclopaedia Biblica*
GCS	Die Griechischen Christlichen Schriftsteller der Ersten Jahrhunderte

GK	A. E. Cowley, *Gesenius' Hebrew Grammar, as edited and enlarged by E. Kautzsch* (2nd ed., Oxford, 1910)
GM	*Göttinger Miszellen*
HTR	*Harvard Theological Review*
HUCA	*Hebrew Union College Annual*
IDB	*The Interpreter's Dictionary of the Bible*
IEJ	*Israel Exploration Journal*
JANES	*Journal of the Ancient Near Eastern Society of Columbia University*
JAOS	*Journal of the American Oriental Society*
JBL	*Journal of Biblical Literature*
JCS	*Journal of Cuneiform Studies*
JDT	*Jahrbücher für Deutsche Theologie*
JEA	*Journal of Egyptian Archeology*
JNES	*Journal of Near Eastern Studies*
JPT	*Jahrbücher für Protestantische Theologie*
JSOTS	*Journal for the Study of the Old Testament* Supplement Series
JTS	*Journal of Theological Studies*
KAI	H. Donner and W. Röllig, *Kanaanäische und Aramäische Inschriften* (3 vols., 3rd ed., Wiesbaden, 1971–6)
KB	E. Schrader (ed.), *Keilinschriftliche Bibliothek* (6 vols., Berlin, 1889–1915)
MVAG	*Mitteilungen der Vorderasiatisch (-Ägyptischen) Gesellschaft*
Or	*Orientalia*
OTP	J. H. Charlesworth (ed.), *The Old Testament Pseudepigrapha* (2 vols., London, 1983/5)
OTS	*Oudtestamentlische Studien*
RA	*Revue d'Assyriologie et d'Archéologie Orientale*
RB	*Revue Biblique*
RE	*Revue d'Égyptologie*
RLA	*Reallexikon der Assyriologie und Vorderasiatischen Archäologie*
SC	Sources Chrétiennes
SH	*Scripta Hierosolymitana*
ST	*Studia Theologica*
STT	O. R. Gurney, J. J. Finkelstein, and P. Hulin, *The Sultantepe Tablets* (2 vols.; London, 1957, 1964)
SVT	Supplements to *Vetus Testamentum*
TLZ	*Theologische Literaturzeitung*
TSBA	*Transactions of the Society of Biblical Archeology*
TUAT	O. Kaiser (ed.), *Texte aus der Umwelt des Alten Testaments* (Gutersloh, 1982–)
VT	*Vetus Testamentum*
WO	*Die Welt des Orients*

ZAW	*Zeitschrift für die Alttestamentliche Wissenschaft*
ZDMG	*Zeitschrift der Deutschen Morgenländischen Gesellschaft*
ZDPV	*Zeitschrift des Deutschen Palästina-Vereins*
ZWT	*Zeitschrift für Wissenschaftliche Theologie*

2. *Ancient texts*

2.1 Hebrew Bible (Old Testament)

Gn	Genesis
Ex	Exodus
Lv	Leviticus
Nu	Numbers
Dt	Deuteronomy
Js	Joshua
Ju	Judges
Ru	Ruth
1-2S	1-2 Samuel
1-2K	1-2 Kings
1-2C	1-2 Chronicles
Ezr	Ezra
Ne	Nehemiah
Est	Esther
Jb	Job
Ps	Psalms
Pr	Proverbs
Qo	Qoheleth
Sg	Song of Songs
Is	Isaiah
Je	Jeremiah
La	Lamentations
Ezk	Ezekiel
Dn	Daniel
Ho	Hosea
Jl	Joel
Am	Amos
Ob	Obadiah
Jn	Jonah
Mi	Micah
Na	Nahum
Hb	Habbakuk
Zp	Zephaniah
Hg	Haggai
Zc	Zechariah
Ma	Malachi

2.2 Apocrypha and Pseudepigrapha

1-2 Esd	1-2 Esdras
Jub	Jubilees
LAB	*Liber Antiquitatum Biblicarum*
1-4M	1-4 Maccabees
TLev	Testament of Levi
Tmos	Testament of Moses

2.3 Rabbinic literature

SOR	*Seder Olam Rabba*

2.4 Classical texts

Ant	Josephus, *Jewish Antiquities*
Ap	Josephus, *Against Apion*
War	Josephus, *Jewish War*

2.5 Akkadian texts

Adn Cal	Adadnirari III, Calah Slab
Adn Rim	Adadnirari III, Rimah stele
Adn Sab	Adadnirari III, Saba'a stele
Adn SH	Adadnirari III, Sheikh Hammad stele
Ash PrC	Ashurbanipal, Prism C
Ep Chr	Eponym Chronicle
Esrh NinAF	Esarhaddon, Nineveh Prisms A and F
Esrh NinB	Esarhaddon, Nineveh Prism B
Sg AC	Sargon II, Ashur Charter
Sg Cal	Sargon II, Calah Prism
Sg Cyl	Sargon II, Cylinder Inscription
Sg Kh	Sargon II, Khorsabad annals
Sg LD	Sargon II, Large display inscription
Shl 5	Shalmaneser III, Ashur text 5 (Basalt Statue)
Shl 22	Shalmaneser III, Ashur text 22 (annal fragment)
Shl 32	Shalmaneser III, Ashur text 32 (marble slab)
Shl 33	Shalmaneser III, Ashur text 33 (Black Obelisk)
Shl Bull	Shalmaneser III, Bull Inscription
Shl Kurb	Shalmaneser III, Kurba'il statue
Shl Mon	Shalmaneser III, Monolith Inscription
Sn B1-3	Sennacherib, Bull inscriptions 1-3
Sn Bell	Sennacherib, Bellino Cylinder
Sn Neb	Sennacherib, Nebi Yunus inscription
Sn Pr	Sennacherib, Prisms
Tgl An	Tiglathpileser III, Annals
Tgl Iran	Tiglathpileser III, Iran stele

Tgl K1	Tiglathpileser III, 'Kleinere Inschrift 1'
Tgl K 3751	Tiglathpileser III, tablet K3751
Tgl ND 400	Tiglathpileser III, tablet ND 400
Tgl ND 4301 +	Tiglathpileser III, tablet ND 4301 + ND 4305 + ND 5422 + K 2649 (+) ND 5419

3. *General abbreviations*

1QIs^a	Qumran Isaiah Scroll a
A	Septuagint, Codex Alexandrinus
AM	Anno Mundi
aut.	autumn calendar
B	Septuagint, Codex Vaticanus
E	Elohistic stratum of the Pentateuch
ET	English translation
J	Yahwistic stratum of the Pentateuch
Jos.	Josephus
Jul.	Julian calendar
L	Septuagint, Lucianic recension
LXX	Septuagint
LXX^A	Septuagint, Codex Alexandrinus
LXX^B	Septuagint, Codex Vaticanus
LXX^D	Septuagint, Codex Cottonianus
LXX^L	Septuagint, Lucianic recension [Judges: KZgln(o)w, (d)ptv; Samuel-Kings: bor(c$_2$)e$_2$]
LXX^M	Septuagint, Codex Coislinianus
LXX^N	Septuagint, Codex Venetus
MT	Masoretic Text
N	Septuagint, Codex Venetus
Nis.	Nisan calendar
P	Priestly stratum of the Pentateuch
SP	Samaritan Pentateuch
spr.	spring calendar
T. b.	Babylonian Talmud

1

INTRODUCTION

Chapter 14 of the second book of Esdras (also known as 4 Ezra) describes how the Jewish scriptures, which had (supposedly) been lost in the destruction of the first temple, were subsequently rewritten under Ezra's inspired dictation. This produced a total of ninety-four books of sacred scripture, comprising twenty-four books that were to be published openly—and which presumably correspond to the twenty-four books of the Hebrew Bible—and seventy books that were intended for restricted circulation among the wise. This distinction between esoteric and non-esoteric scripture is said to go back to Moses, who had received the original copies of the scriptures on Mount Sinai. God describes his revelation to Moses as follows: 'I kept him with me many days. And I told him many wondrous things, and showed him the secrets of the times and declared to him the end of the times. Then I commanded him, saying, "These words you shall publish openly, and these you shall keep secret"' (2 Esd 14.3–6).

The secrets of eschatological chronology ('the end of the times') evidently held some fascination for the author of 2 Esdras, but they were presumably one of the subjects which Moses was prohibited from publishing openly, since eschatological revelations are notably absent from the canonical books of Moses (the Pentateuch), and the only Biblical book which shows much interest in eschatological chronology is the book of Daniel. But the Pentateuch and other Biblical books do contain a significant amount of chronological information which is historically orientated rather than eschatological in that it is concerned with the past rather than the future. So also does the book of Jubilees, which presents a rewritten account of events from creation to the exodus, and claims to contain revelations which Moses received during the forty days which he spent on Mount Sinai. The book of Jubilees is characterized by a distinctive jubilee chronology, in which the 'secrets of the times' are revealed as a chronological scheme of fifty 49-year jubilees from creation to the settlement in Canaan. It is clear from the schematic nature of this figure that the chronology of Jubilees is mythical rather than historical in purpose: it was not primarily conceived as a historical framework for the events which it describes, but is an essentially mythical expression of the belief that history is ordered according to a divine plan. The central thesis of this book is that this is equally true of Biblical chronology, except that I shall qualify this by arguing that parts of the chronology of the Bible originated as a historical chronology which was later 'mythicized' by Biblical writers.

The schematic nature of Biblical chronology has been recognized by previous scholars, though it has been largely ignored by twentieth-century scholarship. Julius Wellhausen noted a century ago that Judean regnal years stated in Kings add up to a round total of 430 years for the period from the foundation of the temple in Solomon's fourth year to its destruction by Nebuchadrezzar, and that a 50-year period of exile (from 587 BC to *c.* 538 BC) makes an overall total of 480 years which mirrors the 480 years assigned to the period from the exodus to the foundation of the temple (1K 6.1). Or again: according to the Masoretic text of the Bible (which underlies almost all English translations) there are exactly 290 years from the birth of Abraham to the entry into Egypt (Gn 21.5; 25.26; 47.9). If we add this to the figure of 430 years for Israel's stay in Egypt which is given in Exodus 12.40, plus 480 years from the exodus to the foundation of the temple, it is apparent that Biblical chronology (as preserved by the Masoretic text) assigns a round duration of 1200 years to the period from Abraham to the foundation of the temple. It is interesting to note that Archbishop Ussher contrived a similar round duration of 1000 years for the period between the *completion* of the temple and the birth of Christ. Ussher's chronology (which was widely printed in the margins of English Bibles until recent times) also incorporated a 4000-year interval from creation to the birth of Christ, which is why—in Ussher's scheme—the world was created in 4004 BC (the birth of Christ is commonly dated to 4 BC, which was the year in which Herod the Great died).[1]

1. See Barr 1984.

One reason why modern Biblical scholarship has been inclined to overlook the schematic nature of Biblical chronology may be that it is, in a way, rather embarrassing. Modern Biblical scholarship is largely historical in outlook, and considerable effort has been devoted to establishing a reliable chronological framework for the history of the Israelite and Judean kingdoms. If the chronological data on which this framework is based should turn out to be mythical rather than historical this might be regarded as undermining part of the basis of modern Biblical scholarship. It could be worse than this: if the chronology is mythical rather than historical, the same might also be true of the narrative which contains this chronology. In which case Biblical scholarship may be seriously misguided in its preoccupation with historical fact rather than mythical meaning.

There is, I think, a sense in which the last statement is true. But in the case of Biblical chronology there is also evidence which suggests that it is wrong to draw a sharp antithesis between history and myth. The two chapters which follow are mainly concerned with the mythical character of Biblical chronology from Genesis through to Kings, but chapters four and five contain a reconstruction of the historical chronology of the Israelite and Judean kingdoms which is based on chronological data from the book of Kings. I am not trying to build castles out of sand. The basis for my historical reconstruction of Israelite and Judean chronology is to be found in the fact that certain features of the chronology of Kings—including internal discrepancies between reign lengths and synchronisms—provide evidence to suggest that the chronology of Kings was adapted from an earlier non-schematic chronology. This part of Biblical chronology is outwardly mythical, but it is also based on an originally historical chronology.

I should perhaps explain my use of the term 'myth'. Many Biblical scholars avoid using this term in relation to the Bible because they argue that myths are stories about the gods, and that Biblical religion, by recognizing only one God, is therefore inherently non-mythical. This is, in my view, a simplistic definition of myth. A more adequate description would be to say that myth is fiction which is used to express truth. In arguing that Biblical chronology is essentially mythical, I am saying that it uses historical fiction to express ideological beliefs. The most fundamental of these beliefs, which motivated Ussher just as it motivated the original Biblical chronologers, is the belief that there is a divine plan behind human history.

2

THE PRIESTLY CHRONOLOGY OF THE WORLD

2.1 Pre-Abrahamic Chronology

The Priestly stratum of the Pentateuch (P) shows a marked interest in chronology that is conspicuously absent from the other main Pentateuchal strata. In Genesis this chronological information is mostly presented in genealogical form: P contains a complete genealogy from Adam to Jacob which incorporates chronological information such as the age at which each ancestor fathered a successor (henceforth referred to as his age of begetting), his total lifespan and/or the number of his remaining years after fathering a successor, and in some instances his age at the time of important events such as the flood. This information offers us a comprehensive chronology of world history, by which the lives of Israel's and mankind's ancestors, and certain key events such as the flood and Abraham's migration, are datable in years from the world's creation. Priestly chronology is essentially a relative chronology: the flood is dated in relation to Noah's lifespan, and Noah's lifespan is dated in relation to that of his father, which in turn is dated in relation to that of *his* father, and so on. But because this relative chronology has a fixed point in Adam's creation, which is contemporaneous with the creation of the world, it can also be converted into an absolute chronology of world history. It is obvious that the crucial figures from which this absolute chronology is derived are the ages of begetting: the birth date of an ancestor (in years from creation) is simply the sum of his predecessors' ages of begetting. Any increase in these ages would necessarily result in a longer chronology, while any decrease would correspondingly shorten the chronology—so the Septuagint, with ages of begetting for most of Abraham's ancestors that are significantly greater than those of the Masoretic Text, also has a considerably longer pre-Abrahamic chronology.

The table on the opposite page presents the chronological data of the Masoretic text (MT), Samaritan Pentateuch (SP), and Septuagint (LXX) for the period from Adam to Abraham. This reveals a high degree of textual variation between these different textual witnesses; but it is clear from the nature of this variation that differences between MT, SP, and LXX result, for the most part, from systematic alteration rather than accidental corruption of the original Priestly figures. Despite assertions to the contrary by some scholars (e.g. De Vries 1962:581) it is far from obvious that the original figures are preserved in MT, and it is quite possible that none of the three main textual witnesses has preserved them. It is therefore necessary that any discussion of Priestly chronology should begin with an evaluation of the available textual evidence.[1]

The pre-Abrahamic chronology of P is preserved in two genealogical lists comprising Genesis 5.1–28, 30–32; 7.6; 9.28–29, and Genesis 11.10–26, 32. As these lists are almost identical in form, and run consecutively from Adam to Terah, it is likely that they once formed an independent Priestly document that was only subsequently incorporated into the Priestly Pentateuchal history;[2] confirmation of this may be seen in the fact that the genealogy uses

1. Compare the discussion of textual variants by Klein (1974). For a recent claim that MT has preserved the original chronological figures see Larsson (1983), who argues that all chronological differences between MT and LXX are explicable as rationalizing alterations in LXX. Larsson's faith in the chronological data of MT is based on his acceptance (and advocacy) of the chronological theories of Stenring (1966), who thought that MT contained a cryptic chronology which involved three different calendars and was intelligible only to the initiated. But it cannot be said that Larsson has provided an adequate defence of MT. One serious objection is that Larsson tacitly adopts the inferior LXX figure of 187 years for Methuselah's age of begetting, without even mentioning the strongly attested variant figure of 167 years. The latter figure, which is almost certainly original (see p. 14n.), is actually a serious embarrassment to Larsson's thesis that LXX figures are rationalizing alterations of MT's supposedly original figures, for it results in Methuselah's having survived the flood in LXX chronology, despite not having been included in Noah's ark.

2. 'Pentateuchal history' is intended as a neutral term for any account approximately covering the series of events described in the Pentateuch: 'Priestly Pentateuchal history' (or 'Priestly history') may therefore be interpreted as 'Priestly source' or as 'Priestly redaction of the Pentateuch' according to one's literary-historical assessment of the Priestly stratum. The point at issue is discussed further in section 3 of this chapter.

Chronological Data: Genesis 5–11

		MT	LXX	SP
(Gn 5.3)	Adam	130+800 = 930	130+800 = 930	230+700 = 930
(Gn 5.6)	Seth	105+807 = 912	105+807 = 912	205+707 = 912
(Gn 5.9)	Enosh	90+815 = 905	90+815 = 905	190+715 = 905
(Gn 5.12)	Kenan	70+840 = 910	70+840 = 910	170+740 = 910
(Gn 5.15)	Mahalalel	65+830 = 895	65+830 = 895	165+730 = 895
(Gn 5.18)	Jared	162+800 = 962	62+785 = 847	162+800 = 962
(Gn 5.21)	Enoch	65+300 = 365	65+300 = 365	165+200 = 365
(Gn 5.25)	Methuselah	187+782 = 969	67+653 = 720	167+802 = 969
(Gn 5.28)	Lamech	182+595 = 777	53+600 = 653	188+565 = 753
(Gn 5.32)	Noah	500	500	500
(Gn 7.6; 9.28)	age at flood	600+350 = 950	600+350 = 950	600+350 = 950
(Gn 11.10)	Shem	100+500 (= 600)	100+500 = 600	100+500 (= 600)
(Gn 11.10)	flood to Arpachshad	2	2	2
(Gn 11.12)	Arpachshad	35+403 (= 438)	135+303 = 438	135+430 (= 565)
(Gn 11.13)	Kenan	—	—	130+330 (= 460)
(Gn 11.14)	Shelah	30+403 (= 433)	130+303 = 433	130+330 (= 460)
(Gn 11.16)	Eber	34+430 (= 464)	134+270 = 404	134+370 (= 504)
(Gn 11.18)	Peleg	30+209 (= 239)	130+109 = 239	130+209 (= 339)
(Gn 11.20)	Reu	32+207 (= 239)	132+107 = 239	132+207 (= 339)
(Gn 11.22)	Serug	30+200 (= 230)	130+100 = 230	130+200 (= 330)
(Gn 11.24)	Nahor	29+119 (= 148)	79+ 69 = 148	79+129 (= 208)
(Gn 11.26)	Terah	70 205	70 145	70 205

Column 1: age of begetting (etc.).   Column 2: remaining years of life.   Column 3: total lifespan.
Unstated totals are given in parentheses.

an unusual form of numerical syntax which appears to be unattested elsewhere in P (or in any other part of the Hebrew Bible), whereby units and tens with an enumerated noun are followed by hundreds with the enumerated noun repeated.[3] This document, which in Genesis 5.1 is titled 'The Book of the Generations of Adam' (and which I shall refer to from now on as 'The Book of Generations'), will necessarily have been divided into antediluvian and postdiluvian sections when it was combined with the flood narrative as part of P's primaeval history.

Antediluvian and postdiluvian sections of the Book of Generations are roughly symmetrical in that the first section (from Adam to Noah) contains ten genealogical entries, while the second section (from Shem to Terah) contains nine entries (ten in LXX). Both sections use identical phraseology, stating each ancestor's age of begetting and the number of his remaining years (in Noah's case, remaining years after the flood), besides noting the birth of additional children. The antediluvian section also states total lifespans (which are not stated for postdiluvians other than Terah, except in SP) and includes a concise statement of death, or in Enoch's case a statement about his translation to heaven, which is also included in SP's and LXX's postdiluvian entries. The genealogical entry on Terah is anomalous in that it omits a statement on the number of remaining years, which is included in all other antediluvian and postdiluvian entries, but includes (in all text forms) a total lifespan and statement of death.[4]

---

3. The closest parallel to this construction is found in Numbers 2.16, 31, where hundreds with an enumerated noun are followed by units and tens with the enumerated noun repeated. Elsewhere P repeats the enumerated noun after each element in a compound numeral, or writes it once only after the entire compound numeral (the construction in Genesis 47.28, where units with an enumerated noun are followed by tens and hundreds with the enumerated noun repeated is an anomalous exception). It should be noted, however, that there are also significant syntactic similarities between the Priestly genealogies of Genesis 5–11 and other Priestly strata. Despite detailed differences in numerical syntax it is only within these genealogies and in other Priestly passages (including 1 Kings 6.1: see below) that an enumerated noun is repeated after separate elements of a compound numeral (GK § 134h). Another shared feature is the use of מאת (the construct form of מאה, 'hundred'), which occurs only four times outside P (Est 1.4; Qo 8.12; Ne 5.11; 2C 25.9).

4. The statement on Terah's total lifespan differs slightly from statements on antediluvian lifespans in that it omits כל ('all') from before ימי תרח ('the days of Terah')—in the absence of a statement on Terah's remaining years there was no

The various textual pluses found in SP and/or LXX are probably secondary from a textual point of view, since it is difficult to see why MT and LXX would have omitted postdiluvian lifespans if these were originally present in the Biblical text, whereas their presence in SP is easily accounted for as the result of secondary harmonization with the form of antediluvian entries; the same is true of the statement of death which SP and LXX include in their postdiluvian entries. On the other hand the fact that these elements are included in Terah's genealogical entry in all text forms might indicate that they were originally included in all postdiluvian entries of the original Book of Generations, but were subsequently omitted in the course of the redactional process by which this was incorporated into the Priestly history. Equally, the fact that remaining years are not stated in Terah's entry may well be because these were omitted during the same redactional process. The possibility that these elements were present in the literary prehistory of the Biblical text does not of course affect their textually secondary nature in SP and LXX.

The extra member of LXX's postdiluvian genealogy (Kenan) is clearly secondary, since he borrows his name from the fourth antediluvian ancestor, and his age of begetting and remaining years are borrowed from Shelah, whom he precedes in LXX's post-diluvian genealogy. The insertion of Kenan does in fact produce a greater formal symmetry between antediluvian and postdiluvian sections of the genealogy, with the result that both sections contain ten entries and the last ancestor in each section has three sons (Shem, Ham, Japheth; and Abraham, Nahor, Haran).[5] However, the formal symmetry produced by this insertion is gained at the expense of an underlying symmetry of ten generations from Adam to Noah and ten generations from Shem to Abraham, in which Abraham's position as the twentieth generation from creation undoubtedly underlines his climactic significance in the genealogy. The apparent lack of formal symmetry in the original genealogy may simply be a secondary consequence of this underlying

need to emphasize that the following numeral represented Terah's total lifespan as opposed to his remaining lifespan.

5. This is in contrast to other ancestors who father an unspecified number of sons and daughters in addition to their named successor. The ages of begetting ascribed to Noah and Terah are presumably the ages at which they each fathered their eldest son and successor, and need not be taken to imply that their respective offspring were born in a single year (as triplets).

symmetry between generations; but one should also consider the
possibility that the formal asymmetry of the Book of Generations
in its present form (in MT and SP) may be purely redactional in
origin. It is tempting to suppose that this document may originally
have included genealogical entries on Abraham, Isaac, and Jacob,
which were subsequently omitted when the Book of Generations
was incorporated into the Priestly history (formal differences of
expression prevent us from finding the original continuation of the
Book of Generations in existing genealogical notices on the
patriarchs, though it could well have provided the chronological
information contained in these notices). If this were in fact the
case, we should then have a genealogical document which
originally contained twenty-two genealogical entries symmetri-
cally divided between eleven antediluvian generations (Adam to
Shem) and eleven postdiluvian generations (Arpachshad to Jacob).
This suggestion is also supported by the fact that there appears to
be an intentional parallelism between Noah (tenth generation) and
Abraham (twentieth generation), who both father 'a multitude of
nations' (Gn 10; 17.5) and are also recipients of divine covenants,
and between Shem (eleventh generation) and Jacob (twenty-
second generation), respective ancestors of the Semitic peoples and
of the nation of Israel.

Textual variation between MT, SP, and LXX over ages of
begetting is found in the case of all ancestors from Adam to Nahor
apart from Noah and Shem; but only in the case of Methuselah and
Lamech is there disagreement between all three text forms. In all
other cases variation between the three text forms involves only
two figures differing by 100 years, or by 50 years in the case of
Nahor. The three-way variation in ages of begetting ascribed to
Methuselah and Lamech also involves a 100-year difference, but
this is supplemented by further differences of 20 years in
Methuselah's case $(X \sim X + 100 \sim X + 120)$ and of 29 and 35 years in
Lamech's case $(X \sim X + 129 \sim X + 135)$. Variation in ages of
begetting is thus essentially reducible to two sets of figures. The
higher set is consistently given in LXX, whereas MT generally
gives the lower set, three exceptions being Jared, Methuselah, and
Lamech. SP, on the other hand, consistently gives the lower set of
figures for the antediluvian period and the higher set of figures for
the post- diluvian period.

The existence of two distinct sets of figures for ages of begetting is most naturally explained as deriving from two textual traditions, one containing the higher set of figures and consequently presenting a long chronology for the pre-Abrahamic period, and another containing the lower set and thus presenting a short chronology.[6] The first of these textual traditions appears to be preserved in LXX and to a partial extent in MT and SP, while the second is partially preserved in MT and in SP, which may therefore be viewed as conflations of the two traditions: evidence of the conflate nature of MT and SP in this respect is provided by the fact that Jared, Methuselah, and Lamech have incongruously high ages of begetting in MT, while SP's postdiluvian ages of begetting are incongruously high in relation to its antediluvian ages of begetting. One important consideration in deciding which of the two sets of figures is likely to be original is that Abraham's disbelief that he might father a child at 100 years of age (Gn 17.17, P) is hardly consistent with the higher set of figures, according to which his recent ancestors had fathered children at ages well in excess of this. It is therefore probable that the lower set of figures is original and that the higher set of figures is secondarily derived from these; further detailed evidence for this conclusion is given below (see p. 16). From this we may conclude that the original ages of begetting for Genesis 5 are preserved in SP (and to a large extent in MT), and that MT has preserved the original ages of begetting for Genesis 11 (similarly Jepsen 1929).[7]

The following table sets out the pre-Abrahamic chronologies of MT, SP, and LXX. AM stands for Anno Mundi ('year of the world').

6. This explanation contrasts with Klein's attempt to explain chronological variation between MT, SP, and LXX within the framework of Cross's local text theory. According to Klein (1974) we have to suppose that postdiluvian ages of begetting were raised prior to the differentiation of an earlier 'Palestinian-Egyptian' text form into local 'Palestinian' and 'Egyptian' texts, thus affecting SP and LXX, which are allegedly of Palestinian and Egyptian origin, but not MT, which supposedly originated in Babylonia. We must then assume that the raising of *antediluvian* ages of begetting in the textual tradition behind LXX occurred subsequently to this differentiation into Palestinian and Egyptian texts, leaving SP unaffected, and that the similar raising of three antediluvian ages of begetting in the textual tradition behind MT is entirely unrelated. If one accepts these rather unobvious assumptions it is clear that some kind of accommodation can be reached between the textual data and Cross's theory, but this hardly supports Klein's conclusion that his study 'provides further evidence for three distinct local texts of the Pentateuch.' My own interpretation of the evidence points, in precisely the opposite direction, to the conflation of *locally coexisting* textual traditions.
7. But see p. 22f. for a minor modification to this conclusion.

	MT	SP	LXX
Adam	1–930 AM	1–930 AM	1–930 AM
Seth	130–1042 AM	130–1042 AM	230–1142 AM
Enosh	235–1140 AM	235–1140 AM	435–1340 AM
Kenan	325–1235 AM	325–1235 AM	625–1535 AM
Mahalalel	395–1290 AM	395–1290 AM	795–1690 AM
Jared	460–1422 AM	460–1307 AM	960–1922 AM
Enoch	622–987 AM	522–887 AM	1122–1487 AM
Methuselah	687–1656 AM	587–1307 AM	1287–2256 AM
Lamech	874–1651 AM	654–1307 AM	1454–2207 AM
Noah	1056–2006 AM	707–1657 AM	1642–2592 AM
Shem	1556–2156 AM	1207–1807 AM	2142–2742 AM
Flood	1656 AM	1307 AM	2242 AM
Arpachshad	1656/8–2094/6 AM	1307/9–1745/7 AM	2242/4–2807/9 AM
Kenan			2377/9–2837/9 AM
Shelah	1691/3–2124/6 AM	1442/4–1875/7 AM	2507/9–2967/9 AM
Eber	1721/3–2185/7 AM	1572/4–1976/8 AM	2637/9–3141/3 AM
Peleg	1755/7–1994/6 AM	1706/8–1945/7 AM	2771/3–3110/2 AM
Reu	1785/7–2024/6 AM	1836/8–2075/7 AM	2901/3–3240/2 AM
Serug	1817/9–2047/9 AM	1968/70–2198/2200 AM	3033/5–3363/5 AM
Nahor	1847/9–1995/7 AM	2098/2100–2246/8 AM	3163/5–3371/3 AM
Terah	1876/8–2081/3 AM	2177/9–2322/4 AM	3342/4–3447/9 AM
Abraham	1946/8– AM	2247/9– AM	3312/4– AM

Differences between the overall chronologies of MT, SP, and LXX are primarily the result of differences in ages of begetting rather than differences in total lifespans, but some account should also be taken of the latter, as these may have significant consequences within the different overall chronologies. In the case of antediluvian lifespans there is substantial agreement between all three text forms. LXX antediluvian lifespans are identical with those of MT except in the case of Lamech (LXX: 753 years; MT: 777 years), where LXX's figure is more probably original, since it is partially supported by SP (653 years) and is less obviously symbolic; MT's figure appears to have resulted from modifications designed to produce a symbolic association with the number 7 (see below). The three cases where SP differs from LXX in its antediluvian lifespans, namely Jared (SP: 847 years; LXX: 962 years), Methuselah (SP: 720 years; LXX: 969 years) and Lamech (SP: 653 years; LXX: 753 years), clearly result from secondary adjustments in SP. LXX is supported by MT in the case of Jared and Methuselah, while in all three instances the Samaritan figure has the effect of placing the ancestor's death in the exact year of the flood (see previous table);[8] had SP contained the same antediluvian lifespans as LXX the three ancestors who conveniently die in the year of the flood would all have outlived it despite their not being included in the ark (LXX's chronology actually has precisely this effect in the case of Methuselah). Given that the three places where SP differs from LXX in its antediluvian lifespans may be explained as chronological corrections in SP, while the one place where MT differs from LXX may be viewed as a symbolically motivated alteration in MT, there is a strong case for thinking that LXX has preserved the original antediluvian lifespans in all cases (similarly Klein 1974). A corollary of this, taken with our earlier conclusion that SP has preserved the original antediluvian ages of begetting, is that Jared, Methuselah, and Lamech did in fact outlive the flood in the original Priestly chronology (see below, p. 27f.).

This conclusion helps to explain why MT, or the textual tradition behind MT, adopted increased ages of begetting for precisely the same three antediluvians. Any increase in an ancestor's age of begetting necessarily increased the date of subsequent events fixed in relation to that figure while leaving the date of his death unaffected (since this was determined by his total lifespan). Thus a 100-year increase in Jared's age of begetting increased the date of the flood by 100 years, and so reduced the period by which Jared survived the flood in the original chronology. Methuselah's age of begetting might also have been increased by 100 years (following the textual tradition behind LXX), and this increase, coupled with the 100-year increase in Jared's age of begetting, would have ensured that Jared died well before the flood. However, an increase of 135 years in Lamech's age of begetting (in line with the textual tradition behind LXX), coupled with a 100-year increase in Methuselah's age of begetting, was insufficient to prevent Methuselah from surviving the flood. MT, or the textual tradition behind MT, resolved this problem by adding a further 20 years to Methuselah's age of begetting, while subtracting 6 years from Lamech's increased age of begetting (alterations to Lamech's figures are discussed in the following

---

8. We are doubtless intended to infer that they died just before the start of the flood (rather than that Noah abandoned his father, grandfather, and great-great-grandfather to drown in the flood).

paragraph). This had the effect of placing Methuselah's death in the same year as the flood, a few years after Lamech's death, and a number of LXX manuscripts subsequently borrowed MT's figure for Methuselah in order to resolve their own problems in this respect.[9] The coincidence between the year of Methuselah's death and the year of the flood in MT's chronology, and similar coincidences in the case of Jared, Methuselah, and Lamech in SP's chronology, seem to have resulted from application of the minimum adjustment that would ensure that these ancestors died before the start of the flood; according to Genesis 7.11 the flood began on the 17th (LXX: 27th) day of the 2nd month, which leaves a period of 1 month and 17 (or 27) days in which these various deaths may be assumed to have occurred. One further point which should be made is that although the textual traditions behind SP and MT both corrected the original chronology's failure to ensure that Noah's ancestors had all died before the start of the flood, these corrections had significantly different effects: the overall chronology was unaffected in SP whereas the modifications reflected in MT increased this chronology by 349 years. Other evidence (discussed in chapter 6) suggests that this increase may represent a deliberate revision of the original overall chronology in the textual tradition behind MT.

The most extensive adjustments to antediluvian chronology appear to have been directed at Lamech's figures. If we assume that LXX, as in other antediluvian entries, has preserved Lamech's original lifespan (753 years), and that SP, as in other antediluvian entries, has preserved Lamech's original age of begetting (53 years), it follows from this that Lamech's remaining years must originally have numbered 700, possibly reflecting an association with the number 7 that is clearly evident in MT's lifespan of 777 years (and which is doubtless connected with the fact that Lamech's namesake in Genesis 4 is 7th from Adam, and

9. '187 years' is the corrected reading of LXX[A], and is also attested in LXX[DM] and some minuscules. But according to Berlin Papyrus 911, LXX[A] (original reading), and other minuscules, Methuselah's age of begetting is '167 years'. There is little doubt that this second figure is the original LXX reading (cf. Wevers' edition of Genesis in the Göttingen Septuagint), for it is hard to account for on any other hypothesis, whereas '187 years' is explicable as a borrowing from MT or the textual tradition behind MT, which is a familiar feature of LXX textual history. We may also note that '167 years' resembles previous LXX ages of begetting in being 100 years greater than SP's figure.

claims the right to 77-fold vengeance). The textual tradition
behind LXX presumably reduced Lamech's remaining years from
700 to *600 in order to compensate for a 100-year increase in
Lamech's age of begetting (compare the 100-year increase in ages
of begetting ascribed to other antediluvians in LXX's genealogy),
but subsequently seems to have made a further adjustment,
increasing Lamech's age of begetting by 35 to 188 years while
correspondingly reducing Lamech's remaining years by 35 to 565
years. This adjustment was not required for purposes of chronological harmonization: without it Lamech would have died in the
year of the flood, and its presence is not enough to prevent
Methuselah from surviving the flood by 14 years. It is therefore
likely that the originators of this chronology had other reasons
adding 35 years at this point (see p. 238f).

MT's figures show enough similarity to those of LXX to
suggest that they are derived from the latter, with MT dependent
on the textual tradition behind LXX at this point. Starting with
the figures found in LXX the textual tradition behind MT
apparently increased Lamech's remaining years by 30 to 595 years,
while reducing Lamech's age of begetting by 6 to 182 years, thus
adding 24 years to Lamech's total lifespan so as to produce the
obviously symbolic total of 777 years. One reason for this
somewhat complex adjustment (the same lifespan could have been
achieved by a straightforward addition of 24 to Lamech's remaining years) was doubtless that it resulted in the figures for Lamech's
age of begetting and remaining years being themselves multiples of
seven.

Postdiluvian lifespans from Shem to Nahor are stated explicitly
only in SP, but SP's stated lifespans are with two exceptions
identical with the lifespans presupposed by MT's figures. SP's
total lifespan for Eber (404 years) is partially supported by LXX
(presupposing 504 years), and should probably be preferred to the
total lifespan presupposed by MT (464 years; see below for further
discussion). On the other hand MT is supported by LXX in the
case of Terah (MT, LXX: 205 years), while SP's figure of 145 years
is explicable as a secondary modification based on the exegetical
supposition that Abraham will not have left Haran until after his
father's death (cf. Acts 7.4): Abraham is said to have been 75 when
he left Haran (Gn 12.4), and Terah is said to have been 70 when he
fathered Abraham (Gn 11.26), so that on SP's chronology

Abraham left Haran in the same year as his father's death. This exegetical assumption was apparently based upon the fact that Abraham's migration is narrated immediately after a statement on Terah's death (Gn 11.32), but it should be noted that this statement belongs to Terah's genealogical entry in the Book of Generations, and it is in the nature of these genealogical entries that information on each ancestor is self-contained, and is not arranged in strict chronological sequence with information on other ancestors (Adam's death, for example, occurs long after Seth has fathered Enosh). SP's chronological adjustment of Terah's lifespan so as to place Terah's death in the same year as Abraham's migration resembles its earlier adjustment of antediluvian lifespans placing the deaths of Jared, Methuselah, and Lamech in the same year as the flood.

The postdiluvian lifespans presupposed by LXX are 100 years greater than those given by SP for ancestors from Eber to Serug, and slightly more than 100 years greater with Arpachshad and Shelah. A natural explanation for this is that the textual tradition behind LXX raised postdiluvian ages of begetting by 100 years but did not trouble to adjust remaining years so as to retain total lifespans that were unstated. (By contrast, in the antediluvian section of the Book of Generations, where lifespans are stated explicitly, the textual tradition behind LXX did adjust remaining years so as to retain the original lifespans.) SP, or the textual tradition behind SP, also raised postdiluvian ages of begetting by 100 years, but in this case since total lifespans *were* stated explicitly, the increase was compensated for by a corresponding reduction in the number of remaining years. It should be noted that this explanation depends upon the lower set of figures for ages of begetting being original and thus provides further evidence that this is in fact the case. On the opposite assumption that the higher set of figures is original one might suppose that the textual tradition behind MT increased postdiluvian remaining years (as compared with SP's supposedly original figures) to compensate for a reduction in postdiluvian ages of begetting, even though postdiluvian lifespans are not stated in MT; but one would then be at a loss to explain why the textual tradition behind LXX, which on this assumption has (like SP) preserved the original ages of begetting, should also have increased the remaining years of postdiluvian ancestors.

It was suggested above that SP's lifespan for Eber (404 years), which is partially supported by LXX (presupposing 504 years), is to be preferred to the lifespan presupposed by MT's figures (464 years). This difference results from a difference in the stated number of remaining years, but it is not immediately obvious why MT should have 430 as against LXX's 370 and SP's 270 (i.e. 370 reduced by 100) for Eber's remaining years. Nor is it immediately clear why LXX has 430 versus MT's 403 and SP's 303 (i.e. 403 reduced by 100) for Arpachshad's remaining years, 330 versus MT's 403 and SP's 303 (403 reduced by 100) for Shelah's remaining years, and 129 versus MT's 119 and SP's 69 (119 reduced by 50) for Nahor's remaining years. Apart from compensatory adjustments of 100 or 50 years in SP's remaining years there is no obvious reason why any of the three text forms should have deliberately modified these figures, since they have no significant effect on the overall chronology and there is no discernible numerical symbolism that might have motivated such alterations. We may therefore assume that textual variation in these four instances is probably the result of accidental corruption, especially since the absence of total lifespans (except secondarily in SP) will presumably have made postdiluvian remaining years more easily susceptible to corruption than antediluvian figures.

In the case of Nahor's remaining years MT's figure (119 years) is probably original, since LXX's figure (129 years) can be explained as resulting from partial assimilation to Nahor's age of begetting (29 years in the original Priestly genealogy), or as incorporating a misplaced textual variant to Nahor's age of begetting (79 years in LXX's chronology). On the other hand it is probable that Arpachshad and Shelah did not originally share the same number of remaining years, as happens in MT and SP, since the genealogies of Genesis 5 and 11 generally tend to avoid assigning identical figures to successive ancestors (exceptions being Kenan II and Shelah in LXX, where Kenan has simply borrowed Shelah's figures, and the lifespans of Peleg and Reu, which are discussed below). One further clue which may help us in evaluating the textual evidence at this point is that elsewhere the remaining years of postdiluvian ancestors decrease steadily from Shem to Nahor (exceptions such as Eber's remaining years in MT are almost certainly secondary). This being the case we may probably assume that Arpachshad's remaining years originally

numbered 430 (as in LXX) while Shelah's remaining years
originally numbered 403 (as in MT). The corruption of Arpachshad's remaining years from 430 to 403 in the textual tradition
behind MT and SP (with 403 later reduced to 303 in SP) is then
explicable as an accidental assimilation to the number of Shelah's
remaining years, facilitated by the graphic similarity of '3' (שלש)
and '30' (שלשים). In the textual tradition behind LXX the reverse
process seems to have occurred, so that 403 was initially replaced
by *430 as the number of Shelah's remaining years through
accidental assimilation to the number of Arpachshad's remaining
years; the further reduction of *430 to 330 (which presumably
occurred before the insertion of Kenan, whose remaining years
also number 330) probably results from partial assimilation to
Eber's 370 remaining years. MT's figure of 430 for Eber's
remaining years (versus LXX's figure of 370 years and SP's 270
years) is probably related to these developments, since it has all the
appearance of being a misplaced textual variant to 403 as the
number of Arpachshad's or Shelah's remaining years. One
significant result of preferring 430 as the original number of
Arpachshad's remaining years is that Arpachshad's original lifespan works out at 465 years (his original age of begetting being 35
years, as in MT), which is exactly half Adam's lifespan: the first
postdiluvian not inappropriately had a lifespan which was exactly
half that of the first man, thereby underlining Arpachshad's
position as the first man of a new age inaugurated by the flood.

There is, however, a rather curious discrepancy over the date of
Arpachshad's birth, which according to Genesis 11.10 occurred in
Shem's 100th year, 2 years after the flood. Since we are told that
Noah was 500 years old when he fathered Shem, Shem's 100th year
ought to be Noah's 600th year, and since the flood is dated to
Noah's 600th year (Gn 7.6), Arpachshad ought on this evidence to
have been born in the same year as the flood and not 2 years after
this event. In accounting for this discrepancy it has frequently
been suggested that the phrase '2 years after the flood' is a
secondary addition (e.g. Skinner [2]1930:231f.), although no plausible explanation has ever been given to account for its insertion.
This suggestion is almost certainly correct, since it is hardly likely
that the original Priestly writer would have created or tolerated so
glaring a discrepancy with such serious consequences for the
overall chronology: as the text stands, all absolute dates in the

period after the flood may be worked out to two alternative possibilities varying by a difference of 2 years (see table on p. 7). A probable explanation of this anomaly is suggested below (p. 22f.).

It may be helpful at this point if I summarize the main conclusions of the previous discussion. These are:

1. That the original antediluvian ages of begetting are preserved in SP, and to a large extent also in MT (this conclusion will later have to be modified slightly).
2. That MT has preserved the original postdiluvian ages of begetting.
3. That the original antediluvian lifespans are preserved by LXX and also, with the single exception of Lamech's lifespan, by MT.
4. That MT's figures for postdiluvian remaining years are original except in the case of Arpachshad and Eber, where LXX has preserved the original figures.

The crucial figures through which the overall chronology is expressed are the ages of begetting, and here we have seen that variation between MT, SP, and LXX may be explained relatively simply as a development from two earlier textual traditions, one of which (preserved in LXX) contained ages of begetting that were mostly 100 years higher than those given by the other tradition (which has been partially preserved in both MT and SP). Since we have also seen that there are good reasons for thinking that the higher set of figures was secondarily derived from the lower set, we may plausibly reconstruct the original chronology of Genesis 5–11 by adding together the lower set of figures as these are preserved in MT and SP. The following table sets out these figures together with dates of birth which have been calculated from them. (There is an inconsistency here, which I shall return to shortly: the postdiluvian figures include a 2-year interval between the flood and the birth of Arpachshad, even though I have argued that the phrase '2 years after the flood' is a secondary addition to the text.)

	Age of begetting (etc.)		Date of birth (etc.)
Adam	130: SP, MT	(230: LXX)	1 AM
Seth	105: SP, MT	(205: LXX)	130 AM
Enosh	90: SP, MT	(190: LXX)	235 AM

Kenan	70: SP, MT	(170: LXX)	325 AM
Mahalalel	65: SP, MT	(165: LXX)	395 AM
Jared	62: SP	(162: LXX, MT)	460 AM
Enoch	65: SP, MT	(165: LXX)	522 AM
Methuselah	67: SP	(167: LXX, 187: MT)	587 AM
Lamech	53: SP	(188: LXX, 182: MT)	654 AM
Noah	500: SP, MT, LXX		707 AM
age at flood	600: SP, MT, LXX		
Shem	100: SP, MT, LXX		1207 AM
Flood	2: SP, MT, LXX		1307 AM
Arpachshad	35: MT	(135: LXX, SP)	1309 AM
Shelah	30: MT	(130: LXX, SP)	1344 AM
Eber	34: MT	(134: LXX, SP)	1374 AM
Peleg	30: MT	(130: LXX, SP)	1408 AM
Reu	32: MT	(132: LXX, SP)	1438 AM
Serug	30: MT	(130: LXX, SP)	1470 AM
Nahor	29: MT	(79: LXX, SP)	1500 AM
Terah	70: MT, SP, LXX		1529 AM
Abraham			1599 AM

It will be seen that on this chronology the flood occurs in 1307 A(nno) M(undi) and Abraham is born in 1599 AM. Neither date is particularly remarkable at first glance, but the second figure is one year short of a schematic total of 1600 years. The significance of this fact becomes clear when it is seen that Priestly chronology uses a dating system known as 'postdating', which was also used for regnal chronology in Mesopotamia and late pre-exilic Judah (see p. 179f.). Under this system, as it applied to regnal years, the first part of a king's reign from accession to the following new year was not counted in chronological reckoning (having already been assigned to that king's predecessor), and the first chronological year of a king's reign began with the new year following his accession. The same principle may also be applied to chronological periods other than reigns. Thus the first year of a person's life may for chronological purposes be dated from the new year following his birth, and some such system clearly underlies Priestly chronology, where the detailed chronology of the flood in relation to Noah's age clearly presupposes that each year of Noah's life began at the start of a calendar year (note for instance Genesis 8.13: 'In the 601st year, in the first month, on the first day of the month the waters had dried from the earth.').[10] Consequently Abraham was born in the year 1599 AM, but Abraham's first year was the year 1600 from creation. 1600 is 40 times 40, a perfect square of one of the most commonly occurring round numbers in Biblical literature.

The relevance of postdating to Priestly chronology has not been pointed out previously to my knowledge. Jepsen (1929) argued for essentially the same pre-Abrahamic chronology, but attempted to date Abraham's actual birth to 1600 AM. In order to achieve this result he argued that we should allow 1 year for the duration of the flood (compare Genesis 7.11 and Genesis 8.14), and then proceeded to date Arpachshad's birth 2 years after *the end of* the flood, which brings us down to 1310 AM instead of 1309 AM. By the same token, however, Noah's total lifespan should be 951 years instead of 950 years: 600 years to the start of the flood (Gn 7.6), 1 year for the flood's duration, and 350 years after the flood (Gn 9.28)! Fortunately, the realization that Priestly chronology is based on postdating makes this kind of arithmetic unnecessary. It may also be noted that the overall chronology reconstructed by Klein (1974) is 35 years longer than the reconstruction presented above. This is because Klein gives 88 years rather than 53 years as Lamech's age of begetting, with the result that 1600 AM loses its significance, and Abraham is born insignificantly in either 1632 or 1634 AM, depending on whether one counts the 2-year period from the flood to the birth of Arpachshad.

10. Theoretically it is also possible that Priestly chronology could have been based on some other system of synchronizing years of life with calendar years. One such system was antedating, which was practised in both the Israelite and Judean kingdoms until the latter went over to postdating. Under this dating system the first chronological year of a king's reign was counted from the new year preceding his accession, and consequently overlapped with the last regnal year of his predecessor's reign. A modified form of antedating, in which the incomplete final year of a king's reign was discounted for chronological purposes (thereby removing 1-year overlaps between successive reigns) is attested in Egyptian chronological literature and was also used in a late revision of the synchronisms given in Kings (see p. 93f.). In its modified form, antedating is quite similar to postdating: as applied to Priestly chronology it would mean that Adam lived 130 complete years and fathered Seth in the 131st (incomplete) year of his life, which would also have been the first year of Seth's life. But there are minor ways in which this system is incompatible with Priestly data. For example, the statement that Noah was 600 years old when the flood started (Gn 7.6) clearly does not mean that Noah had lived for 600 complete years (and the flood occurred in his 601st year), since Genesis 7.11 dates the start of the flood to the 600th year of Abraham's life.

This brings us back to the paradox admitted above: that the calculations which date Abraham's first year to 1600 AM depend upon inclusion of the 2-year interval between the flood and Arpachshad's birth, although the phrase '2 years after the flood' creates serious chronological ambiguity and is therefore unlikely to be original. One would also expect the original Priestly chronology to have equated Arpachshad's first year with the first year of postdiluvian history, just as Adam's first year was also the first year of world history, and if we ignore the 2-year interval referred to in Genesis 11.10 this is indeed the case—Arpachshad is born in Shem's 100th year and Noah's 600th year, which is also the year in which the flood occurred. We are therefore faced with the dilemma that the period of 2 years between the flood and the birth of Arpachshad is necessary to the chronology and yet is almost certainly secondary. And the only way out of this dilemma that I can see is to suppose that this 2-year interval is actually a chronological correction made after 2 years had fallen out of antediluvian chronology through some process of textual corruption, when it was noticed that the remaining figures no longer added up to the correct totals required by Priestly tradition. In other words, the original chronology had dated the flood to 1309 AM, with Arpachshad's birth occurring in the same year and Abraham's birth occurring 290 years later in 1599 AM; but the loss of 2 years from antediluvian chronology meant that the flood and Arpachshad's birth now fell in the year 1307 AM, and Abraham was born in 1597 AM, a date of no significance. The insertion of 2 years between the flood and Arpachshad's birth subsequently restored the correct birth dates of Arpachshad and Abraham, but whoever was responsible for this correction evidently failed to notice the resultant discrepancy between Arpachshad's birth date (on this reckoning) and Shem's age of begetting.

Indirect evidence in support of this hypothesis is provided by the book of Jubilees, which contains an absolute chronology expressed in jubilees, weeks, and years, whereby 1 jubilee is equivalent to 7 weeks, and 1 week equals 7 years. Jubilees' antediluvian chronology agrees for the most part with SP's antediluvian chronology (see table on p. 7), apart from a few obvious textual corruptions. But Jubilees does not in fact agree with SP in its date for the flood. According to Jubilees 5.22–23 Noah constructed the ark in the 5th year of the 5th week of the

*27th jubilee[11] (i.e. 1307 AM, the year of the flood in SP's chronology), but did not in fact enter the ark until the 6th year (1308 AM). However, the text of Jubilees is repetitive and somewhat confused at this point, and it is likely that 'in the 6th year' is a secondary addition, without which Jubilees 5.22f. agrees with SP in dating the flood to 1307 AM.[12] There is also a rather interesting discrepancy between Jubilees 5.22f., with or without its secondary accretions, and Jubilees 6.17–18, which states that Noah and his sons observed the Feast of Weeks for 7 jubilees and 1 week of years (= 350 years) after the flood, but that previously it had been celebrated in heaven for 26 jubilees and 5 weeks of years (= 1309 years) from creation till the days of Noah. This second passage clearly presupposes that the flood occurred in 1309 AM, with Noah and his sons celebrating the Feast of Weeks for the first time in the following year, and this is precisely the date which I have argued was given in the original Priestly chronology. The discrepancy between Jubilees 5.22f. in its earlier form (in which the flood was dated to 1307 AM) and Jubilees 6.18 incidentally provides an explanation for the insertion of 'in the 6th year' in Jubilees 5.23, since this insertion may plausibly be regarded as an attempt to harmonize this discrepancy. On the harmonizer's chronology the flood began in 1308 AM, God's covenant with Noah was made in the 3rd month of 1309 AM (Jub 6.1f.), and the Feast of Weeks (being a covenant-*renewal* festival according to Jubilees 6.17) was first

11. '22nd jubilee', which is the reading of all existing manuscripts, is clearly impossible, and Charles (1902:47) is doubtless correct in emending this to '27th jubilee'.
    12. As evidence for secondary accretions in Jubilees 5.23 we may note that Noah is twice said to have entered the ark; note also the curious statement that Noah's entry occurred 'on the new moon of the 2nd month till the 16th (day).' The following translation of Charles's Ethiopic text brackets out the apparently intrusive material in this verse.
    'And he entered {in the 6th (year) thereof} in the 2nd month {on the new moon of the 2nd month till the 16th (day), and he entered}, he and all that we brought him, into the ark, and the Lord shut it from the outside on the 17th evening.'
The first expansion is discussed below, while the second probably originated as a misplaced chronological note on the previous verse, and originally stated that God commanded Noah to build an ark 'on the new moon of the *first* month (cf. Jub 6.25)—when this was inserted in its present position 'first' was naturally altered to '2nd' (the flood began in the second month), while the curious phrase 'till the 16th (day)' was apparently added to make it clear that there was no delay between Noah's entry and God's shutting the ark: it actually took Noah 16 days to enter the ark (presumably because of difficulties in handling large numbers of animals)!

celebrated by Noah in the following year, 1310 AM. There is little doubt, however, that in Jubilees 6.18 the institution of the covenant was originally conceived as having coincided with Noah's first celebration of this festival, since the 350 years during which Noah and his sons are said to have celebrated the Feast of Weeks correspond to the 350 years that Noah lived after the flood according to Genesis 9.28; in the revised chronology Noah must be supposed to have lived for 351 years after the flood.

The harmonized chronology of Jubilees 5.22f. was also less than successful in one other respect. Given that Noah first celebrated the Feast of Weeks in 1310 AM, 350 years from and including 1310 AM brings us to 1659 AM as the year of Noah's death, in which case since Noah is said to have lived a total of 950 years (Jub 10.16; Gn 9.29) he must evidently have been born in 709 AM. Now Jubilees 4.28, relating the birth of Noah, omits to tell us the exact date of Noah's birth, stating only that it occurred in the same week of years in which Lamech married, this being the 3rd week of the 15th jubilee (701–707 AM). But even this degree of vagueness, which is untypical of birth notices in Jubilees, cannot conceal the fact that there is a discrepancy between this verse and Jubilees 6.18, which implies a date of 709 AM for Noah's birth. On the other hand Jubilees 4.28 is in agreement with SP's total of 707 years to the birth of Noah, and the same is true of Jubilees 4.33, which dates Shem's birth to the 3rd year of the 5th week of the 25th jubilee (1207 AM). The book of Jubilees evidently reflects two incompatible antediluvian chronologies, one of which (found in Jubilees 4.28, 33, and also underlying Jubilees 5.22f.) agrees with the chronological totals of SP, while the other (found only in Jubilees 6.18) apparently preserves the original Priestly chronology.

It is this second Jubilees chronology which is clearly of major interest. The existence in Jubilees of two incompatible antediluvian chronologies is most naturally explained on the assumption that Jubilees has undergone a chronological revision bringing it into line with the antediluvian chronology which is given by SP (and which also underlies the chronologies of MT and LXX). In the course of this revision the date originally given for the flood in Jubilees 5.22f. was reduced by 2 years, as were the birth dates of Shem, Ham, and Japheth, and also (in a seemingly vaguer fashion) the birth date of Noah, but Jubilees 6.18 was apparently overlooked and consequently remained unaltered. The original Priestly chronology was therefore 2 years higher than SP's chronology and Jubilees' revised chronology from the birth of Noah or earlier, whereas the textual tradition which underlies existing texts of Genesis and which also underlies the text of Genesis used in revising Jubilees has lost 2 years in its chronological totals down to Noah. Theoretically it is possible that this resulted from two separate losses of a single year, but it is simpler to assume that the age of begetting ascribed to one of Noah's predecessors has been reduced by 2 years.

The textual evidence of Jubilees allows us to form a strong suspicion of where this reduction is likely to have occurred. It was noted above that Jubilees 4.28 is uncharacteristically vague about the exact date of Noah's birth. Jubilees 4.27 is, however, even more anomalous in that it gives us no date at all for Lamech's birth. Prior to Methuselah chronological information is given in a stereotyped form, stating the week of years in which an ancestor married and the exact year in which he fathered his successor. But from Methuselah on, all antediluvian chronological notices giving an ancestor's date of marriage and his son's date of birth are anomalous in one way or another. Thus the date of Methuselah's marriage is given to the exact year, instead of to within a week of years, while no date is given for the birth of his son Lamech. Lamech's marriage is dated normally (to within a week of years), but the date at which he fathered Noah is stated to within a week of years, instead of to the exact year. Finally, the date of Noah's marriage is given to the exact year instead of to within a week of years. These anomalies may plausibly be taken as providing evidence that the revision of Jubilees' antediluvian chronology necessitated the alteration of chronological notices associated with Methuselah, Lamech, and Noah but left previous notices unaffected.[13] In other words, Jubilees' original antediluvian chronology has been preserved down to Methuselah's birth in 587 AM but has thereafter been reduced by 2 years, which can only mean that Jubilees' revised chronology was based on a text of

13. The outright omission of Lamech's birth date and the rather vague indication of Noah's birth date may suggest that this revision was carried out somewhat carelessly; but these rather clumsy devices should possibly be seen as the work of a later harmonizer, who was attempting to conceal the discrepancy between the revised chronology and Jubilees 6.18 (overlooked in the original revision). If this suggestion is correct then only the unusually precise dating of Methuselah's and Noah's marriages to the exact year may be taken as evidence for the earlier revision.

Genesis in which 2 years had been lost from Methuselah's age of begetting. Since SP reflects the same antediluvian chronology as Jubilees in its revised form (disregarding later accretions in Jubilees 5.23), we may therefore reconstruct Methuselah's original age of begetting by adding 2 years to SP's figure, which means that Methuselah was 69 when he fathered Lamech according to the original Priestly chronology. The corruption of '69 years' to '67 years' apparently reflects graphic confusion of תשע ('9') and שבע ('7').

This corruption of Methuselah's original age of begetting will inevitably have created a discrepancy between the new figure for Methuselah's age of begetting and the figures given for his total lifespan and remaining years, which was presumably resolved by the addition of 2 years to the figure for Methuselah's remaining years.[14] Given that Methuselah's original lifespan was probably 969 years, as in MT and LXX, it therefore follows that his remaining years will originally have numbered 900. Since the remaining years ascribed to Lamech, Enoch, and Jared (Methuselah's successor and two immediate predecessors) were also round numbers in the original chronology (see p. 14f. on the original number of Lamech's remaining years), and since the same is true of Adam, Shem, and Serug, this provides significant support for reconstructing '69 years' as Methuselah's original age of begetting.

The restoration of Methuselah's original age of begetting resolves our previous dilemma over the phrase '2 years after the flood', which may now be disregarded as a secondary chronological correction. The following table incorporates these modifications to our reconstruction of the original Priestly chronology, and presents what are probably the original Priestly figures for the ages and lifespans of Abraham's ancestors, together with the absolute chronology which these figures presuppose. The first three columns ('Priestly figures') present ages of begetting (and Noah's

14. Theoretically it is of course also possible that the loss of 2 years from Methuselah's age of begetting could have been compensated for by the removal of 2 years from his total lifespan rather than by the addition of 2 years to his remaining years, but it is inherently more probable that the total lifespan was left unaltered. It is worth noting that the textual tradition behind LXX compensated for its increase in antediluvian ages of begetting by a corresponding reduction in its figures for remaining years, so retaining the original antediluvian lifespans, and the same is true of SP in the postdiluvian period: stated lifespans were not altered unless there was a strong reason for doing so.

age at the start of the flood) followed by remaining years and total lifespans, while the right-hand columns give actual dates of birth (and the date of the flood) followed by postdated lifespans. With the exception of Methuselah's age of begetting, the ages of begetting in this table are identical with those in the table on p. 19f. Antediluvian lifespans are identical with those given by LXX and also (except in Lamech's case) by MT, while postdiluvian lifespans are mostly identical with those presupposed or stated in MT and SP.

	Priestly figures	Priestly chronology
Adam	130 + 800 = 930	1 AM (1–930 AM)
Seth	105 + 807 = 912	130 AM (131–1042 AM)
Enosh	90 + 815 = 905	235 AM (236–1140 AM)
Kenan	70 + 840 = 910	325 AM (326–1235 AM)
Mahalalel	65 + 830 = 895	395 AM (396–1290 AM)
Jared	62 + 900 = 962	460 AM (461–1422 AM)
Enoch	65 + 300 = 365	522 AM (523–887 AM)
Methuselah	69 + 900 = 969	587 AM (588–1556 AM)
Lamech	53 + 700 = 753	656 AM (657–1409 AM)
Noah	500	709 AM (710–1659 AM)
age at flood	600 + 350 = 950	
Shem	100 + 500 (= 600)	1209 AM (1210–1809 AM)
flood		1309 AM
Arpachshad	35 + 430 (= 465)	1309 AM (1310–1774 AM)
Shelah	30 + 403 (= 433)	1344 AM (1345–1777 AM)
Eber	34 + 370 (= 404)	1374 AM (1375–1778 AM)
Peleg	30 + 209 (= 239)	1408 AM (1409–1647 AM)
Reu	32 + 207 (= 239)	1438 AM (1439–1677 AM)
Serug	30 + 200 (= 230)	1470 AM (1471–1700 AM)
Nahor	29 + 119 (= 148)	1500 AM (1501–1648 AM)
Terah	70(+ 135) = 205	1529 AM (1530–1734 AM)
Abraham		1599 AM (1600– AM)

The most curious feature of this reconstructed chronology may be seen in the fact that it allows Jared, Methuselah, and Lamech to survive the date of the flood, although they are not listed among the occupants of the ark. As has been noted, the various chronological adjustments by which MT and SP avoid this situation provide inescapable evidence that this was indeed the

case in the original Priestly chronology. There are two ways in
which this apparent oversight may be accounted for. Firstly, it has
already been argued that the genealogies in Genesis 5 to 11 form an
originally independent document which was secondarily incorporated into the Priestly history, and it is the latter which describes
the occupants of the ark as Noah, his sons, his wife, and his sons'
wives (Gn 7.13). So it is possible that the original author of the
genealogical chronology in Genesis 5 and 11 did not see any
problem in the fact that this chronology allowed three of Noah's
ancestors to survive the flood; he may have assumed that Noah
would naturally have taken his father and other living ancestors
into the ark along with the rest of his family. A second,
complementary way of explaining the matter is that the Priestly
chronologist who produced the Book of Generations may have
been constrained by having to work with an existing set of lifespans
and an existing chronological framework in which the length of
time from creation to the flood was already specified. It will be
shown below that Abraham's first year, 1600 AM, is in fact part of a
wider chronological framework, and that the 290 years from the
flood to Abraham are paralleled by 290 years from Abraham's birth
to the entry into Egypt, so we may reasonably conclude that the
genealogical chronology of the Book of Generations was contrived
to fit into this wider framework. It is also inherently probable that
the author of this document utilized an existing genealogy, which
may also have included total lifespans: a genealogy of precisely this
type occurs in Exodus 6.16f., where total lifespans, but not ages of
begetting, are given for the three generations from Levi to Amram.

There is also internal evidence which suggests that the
genealogical chronology of the Book of Generations was constructed from an earlier genealogy containing total lifespans. A glance at
the original figures in the table given above shows that round
numbers are fairly infrequent among total lifespans, but are rather
more common as ages of begetting or remaining years; there are in
fact only three ancestors (Seth, Reu, and Nahor) with ages of
begetting and remaining years that are both unround numbers.
The infrequency with which round numbers occur as total
lifespans, in contrast to their frequency as ages of begetting or
remaining years, clearly calls for some explanation, and is most
plausibly taken as an indication that the total lifespans given in the
Book of Generations originated independently of ages of begetting;

and that the latter were created secondarily either by selecting an appropriate round number as the ancestor's age of begetting or by subtracting a round number of remaining years from an ancestor's lifespan. Thus antediluvian ages of begetting for ancestors from Mahalalel to Lamech have all the appearance of having been derived from their total lifespans by subtracting a round figure (round hundreds in the case of Jared, Enoch, Methuselah, and Lamech) so as to produce ages of begetting in the vicinity of 60 years. On the other hand the ages of begetting ascribed to Adam, Enosh, and Kenan are themselves round numbers which decrease progressively from 130 years (Adam) to 70 years (Kenan), while Noah and Shem have round ages of begetting of 500 and 100 years respectively. Within the antediluvian section of this genealogy Seth's age of begetting is the only age of begetting which is neither a round number itself nor the result of subtracting a round number from the associated total lifespan. We may expect, however, that some numerical adjustment will have been necessary to produce the required chronological total, and it is probable that Seth's age of begetting was further modified for this reason.

In the case of postdiluvian ancestors these two methods of creating ages of begetting appear to have been used alternately. Thus Shelah, Peleg, Serug, and Terah (13th, 15th, 17th, and 19th from Adam) are assigned round ages of begetting of 30 years each, or 70 years in Terah's case, whereas Arpachshad and Eber (12th and 14th from Adam) have unround ages of begetting in the vicinity of 30 years, and a round number of remaining years. Likewise Reu and Nahor (16th and 18th from Adam) have unround ages of begetting in the vicinity of 30 years, but in their case the number of remaining years is also an unround figure. The absence of round figures for these last two ancestors probably results from adjustments designed to achieve the required total of 290 years from Arpachshad to Abraham: in Nahor's case we might have expected an age of begetting of *28 years, leaving *120 remaining years, while in Reu's case we might have expected *29 years, leaving *210 remaining years (note, however, that this would have broken the descending sequence of remaining years from Arpachshad to Nahor, which may have provided an additional reason for adjusting Reu's figures). It is worth noting, incidentally, that Reu has the same lifespan as his father Peleg, although the author of the Book of Generations otherwise avoided assigning the same figures

to successive generations, and took care to distinguish Peleg's and
Reu's ages of begetting and remaining years. The fact that this is so
possibly reflects a wordplay on the names Peleg ('one half') and
Reu ('another').

Within the overall sequence of ages of begetting it may be noted
that Shem, and particularly Noah, are ascribed incongruously high
figures, presumably because the author of the Book of Generations
wished to restrict the number of Noah's offspring who would be
alive at the time of the flood (according to the flood story only
Noah and his three sons, with respective wives, were included in
the ark). The flood itself was dated late in Noah's life, thereby
minimizing (though not eliminating) the number of ancestors who
might otherwise have outlived it. Any attempt to resolve this issue
by adjusting total lifespans would have fundamentally altered the
significance of these figures. In the original genealogy primaeval
lifespans remained roughly stable at around 900 years during the
antediluvian period (Noah's lifespan is actually 20 years longer
than Adam's) and were then dramatically halved within two
generations, decreasing steadily thereafter. By contrast SP's
adjusted lifespans show a steady decline from Adam to Nahor,
broken only by Noah's lifespan of 950 years, which is unusually
high in this context. The original lifespans reflect a belief that
primaeval longevity remained undiminished throughout the antediluvian period and was then drastically reduced at the time of the
flood (Genesis 6.3 seems to indicate that the Yahwist shared this
belief, while having a less exaggerated notion of primaeval
longevity).

2.2 *Post-Abrahamic Chronology*

The Book of Generations (in its present form) ends with the birth
of Abraham, but P continues to give the same kind of chronological
information down to the time of Jacob. We are informed of
Abraham's age on his migration from Haran (Gn 12.4), his age at
the birth of Ishmael (Gn 16.6), his age when God made a covenant
with him (Gn 17.1), his age—and Ishmael's age—at circumcision
(Gn 17.24–25), his age at the birth of Isaac (Gn 21.5), his total
lifespan (Gn 25.7), and his wife's total lifespan (Gn 23.1).
Subsequently we are told Ishmael's lifespan (Gn 25.17), Isaac's age

on marrying Rebecca (Gn 25.20), Isaac's age at the birth of Jacob
and Esau (Gn 25.26), and Isaac's total lifespan (Gn 35.28). We are
also told Esau's age on marrying his Hittite wives (Gn 26.43),
Jacob's age on entering Egypt (Gn 47.9), Jacob's remaining years
in Egypt (Gn 47.28), and Jacob's total lifespan (ibid.). Oddly,
however, we are not told Jacob's age on marrying Leah and
Rachel, nor Jacob's age on fathering his various children.
Consequently although we are given Joseph's age on entering
Egypt (Gn 37.2), his age on entering Pharaoh's service (Gn 41.46),
and his total lifespan (Gn 50.22, 26), these ages are apparently
unrelated to any overall chronology; at least P in its present form
does not provide us with the necessary chronological information
for relating Joseph's ages to a wider chronological framework,
although they look as if they ought to belong within a framework of
this kind.

It is possible that we can link chronological data on Joseph with
other chronological data on the basis of information given in
non-Priestly strata of Genesis. Thus Genesis 45.6 provides us with
the information that Joseph's brothers made their second visit to
Egypt during the 2nd year of the famine. If we add 7 years of
plenty and assume that the first year of plenty began with the year
following Joseph's appointment by Pharaoh, it follows that Joseph
was 39 when his brothers made their second visit to Egypt, having
been 30 years old when he was appointed to Pharaoh's service (Gn
41.46). If we also assume that the brothers returned with their
father in the same year that they made their second visit we may
conclude that Joseph was 39 when his father entered Egypt, and
since we are told that Jacob was 130 years old when he entered
Egypt (Gn 47.9) it follows that he was 91 when Joseph was born.
Those who believe that P is not an independent Pentateuchal
source may see this as an instance where the Priestly stratum
presupposes information given in non-Priestly strata. But on this
interpretation P is being uncharacteristically indirect in presenting
its chronology at this point,[15] and it is also difficult to believe that P

15. The fact that Sarah's lifespan (Gn 23.1) is related to P's overall chronology
only through Abraham's (unspoken) allusion to her age as well as his own age in
Genesis 17.17 could perhaps be cited as a partial parallel. But lifespans *are*
sometimes unrelated to any overall chronology (as in Exodus 6.16f.), whereas in
Joseph's case we are confronted with a whole series of chronological figures whose
present relationship to P's chronology is much more tenuous than is the case with
Sarah's lifespan.

would have presented this information in such a way that its interpretation depended on the reader making two unsupported assumptions. Were it not the case that the first year of plenty began in the year following Joseph's appointment, or that Jacob travelled to Egypt in the same year that the brothers returned from their second visit, the inferred chronology would clearly be invalid. As a matter of fact, the chronology of Jubilees supports the second assumption (compare Jubilees 42.20 and Jubilees 45.1), but allows a one-year gap between Joseph's appointment and the first year of plenty (Joseph is appointed in 2162 AM—compare Jubilees 40.11–12 and Jubilees 36.1f.—and the seven years of famine begin in 2171 AM (Jub 42.1); subtracting 7 from this date brings us to 2164 AM for the first year of plenty.)[16] In view of these uncertainties it is more probable that P originally did state the age at which Jacob fathered Joseph (and his various other children) and that this information was omitted during the redactional process by which P was incorporated into the Pentateuch. This presupposes of course that P is an independent Pentateuchal source and not merely a redactional stratum.

Whatever the uncertainties in chronological data associated with Joseph it is clear that P's genealogical chronology never extended beyond the death of Joseph (in its present form it cannot be traced with any certainty beyond the death of Jacob). But P's chronology does not end at this point; it simply ceases to be expressed within a genealogical framework. A Priestly note in Exodus (Ex 12.40–41) gives the number of years that Israel spent in Egypt (or according to SP and LXX the number of years spent in Canaan and Egypt), and so continues the chronology from the time that Jacob entered Egypt (or in SP and LXX from the time that Abraham entered Canaan). The same chronology also extends beyond the end of the Pentateuch, being continued by a post-Deuteronomistic note in 1 Kings 6.1, which gives the number of years which elapsed between the exodus and the foundation of the Jerusalem temple. The figure of 480 years given in MT's text of 1

16. It must be said that there are major problems with Jubilees' postdiluvian chronology, but Jubilees does in fact present a fairly consistent chronology for the period following Joseph's descent into Egypt. Note also that in Jubilees 46.1 Joseph is said to have lived for 10 weeks of years after the children of Israel entered Egypt, in which case seeing as he lived 110 years in all (Jub 46.3; Gn 50.22) he was 40 and not 39 on that occasion (this agrees with chronological information in the Testament of Levi, TLev 12.5, 7).

Kings 6.1 is typical of Priestly numerical schematism (discussed below), and also uses a form of numerical syntax, whereby an enumerated noun is repeated after separate elements of a compound numeral, which is otherwise unattested outside P (see above, p. 8n.). There is therefore little doubt that this verse, which is in any case at variance with Deuteronomistic chronological data in Judges and Samuel (p. 61), should be seen as a Priestly addition within the book of Kings.[17]

There is textual unanimity between MT, SP, and LXX over the various chronological figures that are associated with patriarchs from Abraham to Joseph. The more important of these are summarized in the following table, in which the first column of figures gives ages of begetting (or ages at other specified events) followed by remaining years (where stated) and total lifespans.

(Gn 21.5; 25.7)	Abraham	100	175
(Gn 12.4)	age at migration	75	
(Gn 17.24)	age at circumcision	99	
(Gn 25.26; 35.28)	Isaac	60	180
	Jacob	—	
(Gn 47.9, 28)	age on entering Egypt	130 + 17 = 147	
	Joseph	—	
(Gn 37.2; 50.22, 26)	age on entering Egypt	17	110

Simple addition of Abraham's and Isaac's ages of begetting, plus Jacob's age on entering Egypt, gives a total of 290 years for the period between Abraham's birth and Jacob's entry into Egypt, and if we then subtract Abraham's age on migrating to Canaan we are left with a period of 215 years during which the patriarchs lived in Canaan. This last figure is exactly half the time which Israel spent in Egypt according to MT's text of Exodus 12.40 ('the length of time that the children of Israel dwelt in Egypt was 430 years'). There is, however, a significant chronological disagreement at this point between MT on the one hand and SP and LXX on the other, since according to SP and LXX the figure given in Exodus 12.40 represents not only the time spent in Egypt but the time spent in

17. This was noted already by Burney (1903:61), but has generally been overlooked in more recent Biblical scholarship—Noth ([ET]1981:18f.) asserts baldly that the verse is 'generally and rightly attributed to a "Deuteronomistic editor".' Burney points to further evidence of Priestly redactional activity in 1 Kings 6.11–13 and 1 Kings 8.1–11.

Canaan and Egypt, which is evidently intended to incorporate the
215 years that the patriarchs spent in Canaan; thus in SP's and
LXX's chronology the time spent in Egypt itself is only 215 years,
which is half MT's stated figure.[18] The secondary nature of SP's
and LXX's chronology in this instance is obvious from the fact
that reference to the period spent in Canaan before the entry into
Egypt is quite irrelevant to a chronological note on the exodus.

Nevertheless it is easy to see why the original Priestly
chronology came to be modified at this point, for there is a clear
discrepancy between P's chronological total of 430 years in Egypt,
and the Priestly genealogy in Exodus 6.14–25, giving four generations from Levi to Moses (Levi, Kohath, Amram, Moses). Even
with the relatively high lifespans ascribed to Levi (137 years),
Kohath (MT, SP: 133 years; LXX: 130 years), and Amram (MT:
137 years; SP, LXX^A: 136 years; LXX^B: 132 years)[19] this genealogy

18. Note, however, that LXX^B, unlike other LXX manuscripts, gives '435 years'
as the time spent in Canaan and Egypt. This is probably not the original LXX
reading (Demetrius, who generally follows LXX's chronology, allows 430 years for
the time spent in Canaan and Egypt), and it is almost certainly not the original
Priestly figure.

19. Kohath's original lifespan is probably 133 years, as in MT and SP, since
LXX's figure of 130 years is explicable through a common type of numerical
corruption involving the omission of units from compound numerals (see p. 109). In
Amram's case the available textual evidence might be thought to favour 136 as the
original figure, with MT's figure of 137 years being explicable as an assimilation to
Levi's lifespan. However, the lifespans given in Exodus 6 form part of a sequence of
lifespans extending from Jacob to Aaron, which is characterized by the recurrence
of 3 and 7 as the unit-element of a compound numeral and also by its fairly
consistent use of the numerical construction 'units + tens + hundreds + noun' (the
construction used in Genesis 47.28 is 'units + noun + tens + hundreds + noun', but
this is unparalleled in any other chronological notice and may reflect accidental
dittography of the enumerated noun).

(Gn 47.28)	Jacob	147
(Ex 6.16)	Levi	137
(Ex 6.18)	Kohath	133 (MT, SP) ∼ 130 (LXX)
(Ex 6.20)	Amram	137 (MT) ∼ 136 (SP, LXX^A) ∼ 132(LXX^B)
(Nu 33.29)	Aaron	123

Once Amram's lifespan is seen within the context of this sequence of lifespans it is
not so clear that MT's figure is less original than that of SP and LXX^A. In the
context of this series it is tempting to suppose that his original lifespan was actually
*127 years (giving the descending sequence 147, 137, 133, *127, 123), and became 137
in the textual tradition behind MT through partial assimilation to Kohath's and
Levi's lifespans. In this case SP's and LXX^A's figure of 136 may have been derived
from '137 years' in order to redifferentiate between Levi's and Amram's lifespans,
while LXX^B's figure of 132 years possibly reflects a deliberate attempt to restore a

is obviously incompatible with a chronology which allows 430 years for the period in Egypt.[20] This discrepancy was almost certainly absent from the original Priestly history, for Exodus 6.14–30 is an obviously secondary addition, which interrupts the narrative continuity between Exodus 6.13 and Exodus 7.1 (both P). It is unlikely, however, that the genealogy of Exodus 6 is a late invention; more probably it is actually rather older than P's chronology, but was discarded by the Priestly historian because it conflicted with this chronology. Whoever was responsible for inserting Exodus 6.14–30 may have been unaware of the discrepancy with P's chronology (or did not consider it important), but it evidently did not escape the notice of later chronologists, and in the textual traditions behind SP and LXX the problem was resolved by extending the 430 years spent in Egypt to include a previous period of 215 years in Canaan. The Samaritan Tolidah Chronicle and the Hellenistic Jewish chronographer Demetrius subsequently provided genealogical chronologies based on this scheme;[21] and it is worth noting that their creation of a genealogical

decreasing sequence of lifespans (this must necessarily have preceded the accidental reduction of Kohath's lifespan to 130 years).

20. According to Exodus 7.7 (P) Moses was 80 years old when he first confronted Pharaoh, and since this is supposed to have happened during the final year of Israel's stay in Egypt there are 350 (430 - 80) years remaining to be accounted for over three generations. If we assume that Joseph was 39 or 40 when Jacob entered Egypt (see p. 31f.) Levi must evidently have been over 40 on that occasion, which means that 40 + years of Levi's age of begetting elapsed before the entry into Egypt. The genealogy in Exodus 6 cannot therefore be reconciled with P's chronology unless one is prepared to assume that Levi, Kohath, and Amram fathered their respective children at an average age of 130 years ($3 \times 130 - 40 = 350$). The discrepancy between years and generations is made even worse if one takes account of the fact that Genesis 46.11 (possibly a later addition to P) includes Kohath among the children of Israel who originally entered Egypt; this leaves us with only two generations spanning 350 years, which is impossible on any set of calculations.

21. See Bowman 1977:47 for a translation of the relevant passage in Tolidah, but ignore Bowman's notes on the chronology: Bowman unfortunately supposes that the figures given by Tolidah represent total lifespans, whereas in fact they represent ages of begetting from Adam to Amram and priestly ministries thereafter. The ages of begetting which Demetrius (2.19) and Tolidah ascribe to Jacob, Levi, Kohath, and Amram are as follows:

	Demetrius	Tolidah
Jacob	87	87
Levi	60	52
Kohath	40	71
Amram	78	52

It is interesting to note that Demetrius and Tolidah are in agreement over Jacob's chronology for this period, on the basis of an existing chronological framework and an existing genealogy giving total lifespans, is precisely analogous with the way in which I have suggested the Book of Generations was composed. It should also be noted that the reduction of the period in Egypt from 430 years to 215 years in SP's and LXX's chronology created a further discrepancy with Genesis 15.13, according to which the oppression in Egypt was to last 400 years, a round total which was probably based on the Priestly figure of 430 years. This last verse is part of a late insertion (Gn 15.13–16) which within the space of four verses succeeds in incorporating the original discrepancy between years and generations, with verse 16 stating that the fourth generation would return from Egypt.

Further chronological variation between MT and LXX concerns the number of years that are said to have elapsed between the exodus and the foundation of the temple (1K 6.1). Here LXX reads '440 years' in place of MT's '480 years', but there is little doubt that 480 years is the original figure.[22] Priestly chronology allows 290 years from the birth of Abraham to the entry into Egypt (compare the 290 years which elapse between the birth of Arpachshad and the birth of Abraham according to the original postdiluvian ages of begetting, given by MT). If we then add the 430 years spent in

age on fathering Levi. On the other hand, they give completely different ages of begetting for Levi, Kohath, and Amram, and it should be noted that Demetrius's figure for Amram represents Amram's age at the birth of Moses, whereas Tolidah's figure represents Amram's age at the birth of Aaron. If we add 80 years to Demetrius's ages of begetting for Levi, Kohath, and Amram, and 83 years to Tolidah's figures (since according to Exodus 7.7 these were the respective ages of Moses and Aaron in the last year of Israel's stay in Egypt) this produces a total of 258 years in each case. Since both sources agree that Jacob was 87 when he fathered Levi, the latter must evidently have been 43 when he entered Egypt (cf. Demetrius 2.17), Jacob being 130 years old on that occasion according to Genesis 47.9. 258 years from the birth of Levi to the exodus, minus the 43 years that Levi lived in Canaan, leaves exactly 215 years for the time that Israel spent in Egypt.

22. LXX's figure of 440 years was possibly derived by reckoning 40 years priestly ministry to each of the 11 priestly generations from Aaron to Zadok in 1 Chronicles 5.29f., (cf. Montgomery and Gehman 1951:143). But in all probability the genealogy of 1 Chronicles 5.29f. is itself based on the original Priestly figure of 480 years (Koch 1978:438f.). 1 Chronicles 5.36 says of Azariah the son of Johanan: 'it was he who (first) served as priest in the temple which Solomon built in Jerusalem'—but this note almost certainly referred originally to *Azariah the son of Ahimaaz*, who was the grandson of Zadok (according to this genealogy) and 13th in line from Aaron. This results in a total of 12 generations from the exodus to the foundation of the temple (assuming that this occurred at the start of Azariah's ministry).

Egypt (according to the original text of Exodus 12.40, as preserved in MT), the total number of years from the birth of Abraham to the exodus is 720 years. Finally the addition of 480 years from the exodus to the foundation of the temple (following MT) gives us a round total of 1200 years from Abraham to the temple, which neatly complements the 1600 years of the original pre-Abrahamic chronology. These various figures evidently reflect a numerical schematism based on multiples of 40, with 480 (12 × 40), and modifications of 480 involving the addition/subtraction of 50 and division by 2, playing a prominent role in this schematism: 430 years is 480 minus 50, 215 is half 430, and 290 is half 480 plus 50.[23]

In the light of these remarks on Priestly numerical schematism it is striking that in MT the total number of Judean regnal years from the foundation of the temple to its destruction by Nebuchadrezzar is exactly 430 (see table on p. 57).[24] It is difficult to believe that this is merely coincidental, when we have already seen evidence of Priestly redactional activity in the chronological note in 1 Kings 6.1, and a more probable conclusion is that the regnal chronology of Kings has been deliberately adjusted in order to produce this result.

Consideration of LXX's chronology for the first temple period is less straightforward than might be expected. An initial problem is posed by the fact that the original LXX text of Kings is preserved only in 1 Kings 2.12 to 1 Kings 21, having elsewhere been replaced, in non-Lucianic manuscripts, by the Kaige recension,

23. 12 and 40 are common schematic numbers: there are 12 tribes of Israel, Israel wanders for 40 years in the wilderness, Moses spends 40 days on Mount Sinai etc. 40 years was considered to be the typical duration of adult life (Nu 32.13), and is therefore used as an ideal figure for periods of ministry or rule: Moses was a prophet for 40 years, David and Solomon reigned for 40 years each, and so on. Schematic Biblical numbers typically fall into one (or more) of two categories. Some numbers (10, 100, 1000, and multiples) are simply round decimal figures. Others (such as 12 and 7) have calendrical associations: 12 is the number of months in a year and 7 is the number of days in a week. 365 (the number of days in a solar year) is occasionally used as a schematic number: Enoch lives for 365 years, and there are also 365 years from the flood to Abraham's migration. Similarly, 52 (the number of weeks in a solar year) is used as a schematic figure in postbiblical literature.

24. There are 434 Judean regnal years from Solomon's accession to the exile, and the temple was founded in Solomon's 4th year (1K 6.1, 37), leaving 430 years from the foundation of the temple to its destruction (in the 11th year of Zedekiah's reign). Note that in a postdated chronology the first year of the temple's existence begins with the first new year after its foundation.

whose chronology is largely identical with MT's chronology. Fortunately this problem may be overcome by using chronological data from Lucianic manuscripts, which do not incorporate the Kaige recension, for in view of the fact that Lucianic figures are generally the same as the original LXX figures in non-Kaige sections, it is reasonable to suppose that the Lucianic text (LXX^L) has also preserved the original LXX chronology in places where the original LXX text is no longer extant.[25] Judean regnal years in LXX^L are, as it happens, identical with those of MT except in the case of Abijam (1K 15.2) and Jehoram (2K 8.17). In Abijam's case LXX^L agrees with LXX^B (containing a non-Kaige text at this point) in giving 6 years in contrast to MT's figure of 3 years, while for Jehoram LXX^L gives 10 years in place of MT's figure of 8 years.[26] LXX^L's chronology is thus 5 years longer than MT's, giving a period of 435 years from the foundation of the temple to its destruction. This figure is untypical of Priestly numerical schematism, and might therefore be regarded as secondary, but it is also possible that in this instance LXX has preserved evidence of an earlier, *pre-Priestly* chronology (see following chapter). However, the chronology given by LXX also shows signs of having been secondarily modified to bring it into line with the Priestly total of 430 years for the first-temple period. LXX contains two chronological notices on Rehoboam's reign, the second of which (1K 14.21) agrees with MT in ascribing Rehoboam a reign of 17 years. But in LXX^B's text of 1 Kings 12.24a (not present in MT) Rehoboam is said to have reigned for only 12 years, which is probably the original LXX figure at this point,[27] though it is

25. See Shenkel 1968:10f. Lucianic manuscripts in Kings are b, o, r, c_2, e_2 (r is fragmentary, containing 2 Kings 1.19–4.31; 10.3–11.15; 12.4–17.37; 18.9–19.24). However, c_2 contains its own idiosyncratic chronology, based on an eclectic conflation of Lucianic and non-Lucianic data, and is thus a secondary witness to Lucianic chronology. In the present study, Lucianic chronological data for Samuel and Kings are generally taken from Lucianic manuscripts excluding c_2.

26. LXX^{AB} have '40 years' for Jehoram's reign length, but this is probably a secondary modification of '8 years' (LXX^N and most minuscules).

27. '12 years' is also cited by Origen as being the LXX reading in 1 Kings 12.24a (Rahlfs 1904:78). By contrast, LXX^L and most other manuscripts which include this verse (it is omitted in LXX^A and other hexaplaric manuscripts) read '17 years', as in 1 Kings 14.21. But this is easily explained as a secondary harmonization. LXX^L and a few non-Lucianic manuscripts show similar harmonization with regard to Rehoboam's accession age: in 1 Kings 12.24a LXX^B and other manuscripts give '16 years' as Rehoboam's accession age, whereas in 1 Kings 14.21

certainly not the original Biblical figure for Rehoboam's reign (it is in conflict with all existing synchronisms between Israelite and Judean reigns). This alternative figure for Rehoboam's reign is 5 years lower than MT's figure, and thus cancels out the additional 5 years which LXX ascribes to Abijam and Jehoram. We therefore have two alternative LXX chronologies for the first-temple period, one of which ascribes Rehoboam a reign of 17 years and gives a total of 435 years, while the other ascribes Rehoboam a reign of only 12 years to produce a total of 430 years.

Direct evidence of Priestly chronology ends with the destruction of the temple by Nebuchadrezzar in 587 BC,[28] but there is indirect evidence which allows us to trace it for 50 years beyond this point. According to Ezra 3.8f. the second temple was founded in the second month of the year following the return of exiles from Babylon, which in turn is dated in Ezra 1 to Cyrus's first year. Since Cyrus's first year in Babylon was 538 BC, the second temple was (on this dating) founded in 537 BC, exactly 50 years after the destruction of the first temple in 587 BC. If we add this figure to the 430 years of the first temple's existence we arrive at a total of 480 years from the first temple's foundation to the foundation of the second temple. And since this total is exactly parallel to the 480-year period from the exodus to the foundation of the first temple (1 K 6.1), there can be little doubt that it belongs to the same scheme of Priestly chronology.

This schematic pattern of 2 × 480 years centred on the foundation of the first temple was pointed out in the last century by Wellhausen (1875:621), though Wellhausen referred to the second 480-year period as having lasted from the foundation of Solomon's temple to the end of the Babylonian exile. In my view, the book of Ezra's date for the foundation of the second temple provides what is in some ways a more appropriate end-point, and also has the advantage of being exactly 50 years (instead of 49 years) after the first temple's destruction; but there is probably also an intentional parallelism between the exodus from Egypt (480 years before the foundation of the first temple) and the return from

the figure given is '41 years'; LXX[L] and some non-Lucianic manuscripts have '41 years' in both places.

28. Scholars are divided over whether the fall of Jerusalem is to be dated to 587 or 586 BC, but there are strong arguments for preferring the first alternative (see below, p. 229f.)

Babylon (479 years after the first temple's foundation). This is less asymmetrical than it seems, for the foundation of the second temple one year after the return from exile is directly paralleled by the erection of the tabernacle one year after the exodus from Egypt (Ex 40.17). This produces an interesting chiastic symmetry: the foundation of the first temple comes 480 years after the exodus and 479 years before the return from exile; but it is also 479 years after the erection of the tabernacle, and 480 years before the foundation of the second temple.

The absence of direct Biblical evidence specifying a period of 50 years from the first temple's destruction has already been noted. But it must also be remarked that some scholars (e.g. Rowley 1950:90; Bimson [2]1981:75f.) have argued that the absence of a specific Biblical reference to this 50-year period, or to a 480-year period from the foundation of the first temple, offers grounds for doubting the reality of the schematic pattern noted by Wellhausen. This argument is not convincing. The pattern discovered by Wellhausen is only part of a wider schematic chronology, which shows a similar parallelism of 2 × 290 years from the flood to the entry into Egypt, centring on the birth of Abraham. And it may be noted that there is no specific note on either of these 290-year periods; the Priestly writer(s) presumably expected readers to add up the relevant figures for themselves.[29] Secondly, the fact that the 50-year period from the first temple's destruction to the foundation of the second temple is not directly referred to in the Bible hardly disproves the reality of this schematism, since the Priestly scheme of world chronology may originally have existed independently of the various Biblical books which now incorporate parts of this chronology. Finally, lest it be argued that post-exilic Judeans could not have known the true length of the exile, attention may be drawn to Josephus's assertion, in *Against Apion* 1.154, that the 50-year period between the destruction of the temple in Nebuchadrezzar's 18th year and its refoundation in Cyrus's 2nd year, is recorded in Jewish books ($\tau\alpha\hat{\imath}\varsigma$ $\dot{\eta}\mu\epsilon\tau\acute{\epsilon}\rho\alpha\iota\varsigma$ $\beta\acute{\imath}\beta\lambda\iota\varsigma$), which

29. In point of fact, Priestly chronological totals are *never* stated when they can be derived from other figures. The only cases in which chronological totals are explicitly given (the 430-year period in Egypt and the 480-year period from the exodus to the temple) are cases where this information cannot be derived in this way: there is no genealogical chronology for the period in Egypt, and chronological notices found in Judges and Samuel do not provide a complete chronology for the exodus-temple period.

are thereby claimed to demonstrate agreement with Berossus's chronology of the Neobabylonian empire. In view of Josephus's previous insistence that there are only twenty-two 'justly accredited' Jewish books covering the period from creation to Artaxerxes (*Ap* 1.38f.), this statement could be taken to imply the existence of variant Biblical texts in which a reference to this 50-year period had been incorporated; but it is probably safer to assume that Josephus was dependent on non-Biblical Jewish traditions at this point (having possibly failed to notice that the 50-year period which he referred to lacked direct Biblical support).[30] Later Jewish tradition reckoned 52 years for the Babylonian exile (*SOR* 27) and 70 years as the interval between the destruction of the first temple and the foundation of the second temple, with this event dated in the 2nd year of *Darius* (*SOR* 28; cf. Zc 1.12). But significantly, this 20-year increase in the period from the first temple's destruction to the foundation of the second temple was compensated for by a 20-year decrease in the period from the foundation of the first temple to its destruction, thereby preserving the original Priestly total of 480 years from the foundation of the first temple to the foundation of the second temple.[31]

It should be clear by now that Priestly chronology is not simply the chronology of P (the Priestly stratum of the Pentateuch), but that the latter is based on an independently existing Priestly chronology and necessarily presents only part of that chronology. Priestly chronology beyond the time covered by P is incorporated

30. Bimson (²1981:75f.) is incorrect in his assertion that 'the biblical tradition for the length of the Exile was that it lasted seventy years (Jer 25:11; Zech 1:12).' There is a single Biblical text, unmentioned by Bimson, which sets the length of the exile at 70 years (2 Chronicles 36.21; the previous verse refers to the prophecies of Jeremiah). However, the Jeremiah passages which refer to a period of 70 years (Je 25.11; 29.10) ascribe this to the total duration of Babylonian domination, which followed Nebuchadrezzar's victory at Carchemish in 605 BC ('the 4th year of Jehoiakim': Je 25.1; 46.2). Finally, the 70 years referred to in Zechariah 1.12 are apparently counted from the destruction of Jerusalem (in 587 BC), but extend as far as the early years of Darius's reign (Zc 1.1), some two decades after Ezra's date for the return from exile.

31. See *Seder Olam Rabba* 11, where the period from the settlement to the exile is given as 850 years, i.e. 440 years from the settlement to the foundation of the temple plus 410 years from the foundation of the temple to the exile (this second figure was achieved by incorporating two overlaps into MT's regnal chronology; see pp. 100, 105). It is also worth noting that *Seder Olam Rabba* is historically correct in allowing an 18-year interval from Cyrus's first year to the 2nd year of Darius, although this information is not contained in any Biblical text.

into the book of Kings through Priestly chronological revision, but the chronology of Kings ends with the Babylonian exile, and a final period of 50 years from the temple's destruction to its later refoundation was apparently never incorporated into the Biblical text, presumably because suitable accounts of postexilic history (such as Ezra-Nehemiah) did not exist during the Priestly school's literary lifespan.

The following table sets out the more important original Priestly figures for post-Abrahamic chronology, together with the absolute chronology which is implied by these figures. The left-hand part of the table ('Priestly figures') gives ages of begetting (etc.), remaining years (if stated in the Biblical text), and total lifespans for Abraham, Isaac, and Jacob, followed by the various stated and unstated totals which continue this chronology down to the foundation of the second temple (unstated totals are bracketed and the inferred period of 50 years from the destruction of the first temple is additionally starred). Apart from the 50-year period from the destruction of the first temple to its refoundation all figures in this part of the table are identical with figures given by MT or with unstated totals that are derived from figures given by MT. The right-hand part of the table ('Priestly chronology') gives actual dates of birth, foundation dates, or dates of other specified events followed by postdated lifespans (or other specified periods). It should be noted that the post-exodus period has not been postdated: the exodus occurred during the new-year period on the 14th day of the first month, and Priestly chronological notice on the post-exodus period invariably count the year in which the exodus occurred as the first year of the post-exodus period.[32] Non-application of postdating in this particular instance also means that we cannot calculate the date of the exodus simply by adding 430 years to the date at which Israel entered Egypt, for if the exodus is equated with the first year of the post-exodus period it must obviously have occurred in the year following the final year of Israel's stay in Egypt. According to the figures given below, the first year of Israel's stay in Egypt began with the new year of 1890

---

32. Thus the tabernacle is erected 'in the 2nd year' (Ex 40.17), meaning the year after the exodus, and Aaron dies at the age of 123 'in the 40th year of the departure of the Israelites from the land of Egypt' (Nu 33.38–39)—according to Exodus 7.7 Aaron was 83 years old when he first confronted Pharaoh (in the year preceding the exodus).

AM; the 430th year of Israel's stay in Egypt was therefore 2319 AM, and the date of the exodus is 2320 AM.

	Priestly figures		Priestly chronology
Abraham	100	175	1599 AM (1600–1774)
age at migration	75		1674 AM
age at circumcision	99		1698 AM
Isaac	60	180	1699 AM (1700–1879)
Jacob	—		1759 AM (1760–1906)
age on entering Egypt	130 + 17 = 147		1889 AM
period in Egypt	430		1889 AM (1890–2319)
exodus to first temple	480		2320 AM (2320–2799)
first temple to exile	(430)		2799 AM (2800–3229)
exile to second temple	*(50)		3229 AM (3230–3279)
second temple			3279 AM (3280–)

2.3 *Priestly ideology and the date of P*

The tables of pre-Abrahamic and post-Abrahamic chronology set out at the end of the last section and on p. 27 present a critical reconstruction of Priestly chronology from the creation of the world to the foundation of the second temple. This original chronology was evidently subjected to various deliberate modifications (and a few accidental alterations) in the different textual traditions, and we have seen that none of the three main textual witnesses has in fact preserved the original Priestly scheme. Fortunately, these modifications and alterations appear to have been comparatively limited in extent, so that it is possible to reconstruct the original chronology with a high degree of probability from existing textual evidence. It is worth noting that, apart from minor alterations to Arpachshad's and Eber's remaining years, MT appears to have consistently preserved the original Priestly figures for postdiluvian chronology from the birth of Arpachshad to the destruction of the first temple. On the other hand SP is clearly our best witness to the original antediluvian chronology (adjustments to the lifespans of Jared, Methuselah, and Lamech do not materially affect the overall chronological framework), and LXX sometimes preserves original Priestly figures which have been altered in MT and SP.

Chronological Data: Genesis – Kings

		MT	
(Gn 5.3)	Adam	130 + 800	= 930
(Gn 5.6)	Seth	105 + 807	= 912
(Gn 5.9)	Enosh	90 + 815	= 905
(Gn 5.12)	Kenan	70 + 840	= 910
(Gn 5.15)	Mahalalel	65 + 830	= 895
(Gn 5.18)	Jared	*162 + 800*	= 962
(Gn 5.21)	Enoch	65 + 300	= 365
(Gn 5.25)	Methuselah	*187 + 782*	= 969
(Gn 5.28)	Lamech	*182 + 595*	= *777*
(Gn 5.32)	Noah	500	
(Gn 7.6; 9.28)	age at flood	600 + 350	= 950
(Gn 11.10)	Shem	100 + 500 (	= 600)
(Gn 11.10)	flood to Arpachshad	*2*	
(Gn 11.12)	Arpachshad	35 + *403* (	= *438*)
(Gn 11.13)	Kenan	—	
(Gn 11.14)	Shelah	30 + 403 (	= *433*)
(Gn 11.16)	Eber	34 + *430* (	= *464*)
(Gn 11.18)	Peleg	30 + 209 (	= *239*)
(Gn 11.20)	Reu	32 + 207 (	= *239*)
(Gn 11.22)	Serug	30 + 200 (	= 230)
(Gn 11.24)	Nahor	29 + 119 (	= *148*)
(Gn 11.26)	Terah	70	205
(Gn 21.5; 25.7)	Abraham	100	175
(Gn 12.4)	age at migration	75	
(Gn 17.24)	age at circumcision	99	
(Gn 25.26; 35.28)	Isaac	60	180
	Jacob		
(Gn 47.9, 28)	age on entering Egypt	130 + 17	= 147
	Joseph		
(Gn 37.2; 50.26)	age on entering Egypt	17	110
(Gn 41.46)	age on entering		
	Pharaoh's service	30	
(Ex 12.40)	Israel in Egypt	430	
	Israel in Canaan		
	and Egypt	—	
(1K 6.1)	Exodus to temple	480	
(Kings)	1st temple period	(430)	

SP	LXX	(Priestly)
130 + 800 = 930	230 + 700 = 930	130 + 800 = 930
105 + 807 = 912	205 + 707 = 912	105 + 807 = 912
90 + 815 = 905	190 + 715 = 905	90 + 815 = 905
70 + 840 = 910	170 + 740 = 910	70 + 840 = 910
65 + 830 = 895	165 + 730 = 895	65 + 830 = 895
62 + 785 = 847	162 + 800 = 962	62 + 900 = 962
65 + 300 = 365	165 + 200 = 365	65 + 300 = 365
67 + 653 = 720	167 + 802 = 969	69 + 900 = 969
53 + 600 = 653	188 + 565 = 753	53 + 700 = 753
500	500	500
600 + 350 = 950	600 + 350 = 950	600 + 350 = 950
100 + 500 = 600	100 + 500 (= 600)	100 + 500 (= 600)
2	2	—
135 + 303 = 438	135 + 430 (= 565)	35 + 430 (= 465)
—	130 + 330 (= 460)	—
130 + 303 = 433	130 + 330 (= 460)	30 + 403 (= 433)
134 + 270 = 404	134 + 370 (= 504)	34 + 370 (= 404)
130 + 109 = 239	130 + 209 (= 339)	30 + 209 (= 239)
132 + 107 = 239	132 + 207 (= 339)	32 + 207 (= 239)
130 + 100 = 230	130 + 200 (= 330)	30 + 200 (= 230)
79 + 69 = 148	79 + 129 (= 208)	29 + 119 (= 148)
70　　145	70　　205	70　　205
100　　175	100　　175	100　　175
75	75	75
99	99	99
60　　180	60　　180	60　　180
130 + 17 = 147	130 + 17 = 147	130 + 17 = 147
17　　110	17　　110	17　　110
30	30	30
(215)	(215)	430
430	430	—
—	440	480
—	(430/435)	(430)

The table on pp. 44–5 sets out the original figures of Priestly chronology alongside the existing figures of MT, SP, and LXX, and uses italics to highlight differences from the original Priestly figures. The original figures in Genesis 5 to 11 translate into a chronology in which the birth of Abraham is dated 1599 years after the creation of the world, 290 years after the flood and the birth of Arpachshad. In the postdating system used by Priestly chronologists, Arpachshad's first year (the first year of post-diluvian history) is 1310 AM, and Abraham's first year is 1600 AM. Further information in the Priestly stratum of the Pentateuch continues this chronology to the eve of Israel's entry into Canaan, the two major events of this period being the entry into Egypt in 1889 AM, 290 years after the birth of Abraham, and the exodus, which is dated to the new year of 2320 AM following a period of 430 years spent in Egypt (1890–2319 AM). A Priestly note in 1 Kings 6.1, and Priestly revision of the regnal chronology of Kings, subsequently extend this chronology as far as the exile: the temple is said to have been founded in the 480th year from the exodus, which is 2799 AM (the temple's first year is therefore 2800 AM), and a total of 430 Judean regnal years from the temple's foundation to its destruction places the destruction of the temple in 3229 AM. Finally a period of 50 years, which is only indirectly attested in the Bible, extends this chronology to the foundation of the second temple in 3279 AM.

The two key dates in this chronological scheme are quite obviously Abraham's first year, 1600 AM, and the first year of the Jerusalem temple, 2800 AM, each date being the product of round numbers which recur throughout Biblical literature (1600 equals 40 times 40, and 2800 is 70 times 40). Overall symmetry suggests that we should probably infer a total era of 3999 years, within which the first year of the Jerusalem temple stands midway between Abraham's first year and the first year of a new era (4000 AM).[33] The present era of history divides into a pre-Abrahamic age lasting 1599 years and a post-Abrahamic age of 2400 years' duration, with

33. An era of 4000 years is attested in several postbiblical texts. According to *Liber Antiquitatum Biblicarum* 28.8, the present world will exist for 4000 years (a variant reading has 7000 years). Similarly, the Testament of Moses calculates 4250 (2500 + 1750) years from creation to the Messiah (TMos 1.2; 10.12). Finally, the Babylonian Talmud reports that the 'school of Elijah' reckoned 4000 years from creation to the Messiah and a further 2000 years for the Messianic age (T. b. *Abodah Zarah* 9a; T. b. *Sanhedrin* 97b).

Priestly Chronological Schematism

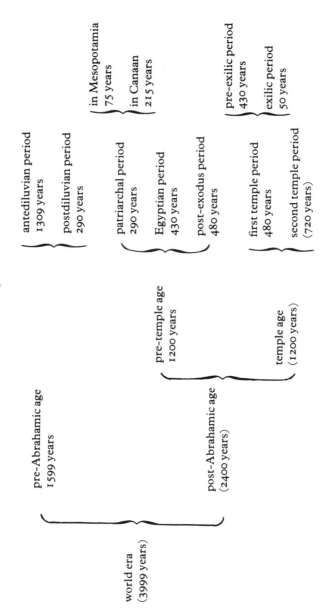

post-Abrahamic history subdivided into pre-temple and temple ages each lasting 1200 years.[34] Each age is itself subdivided into smaller periods of history. Thus the pre-Abrahamic age divides into antediluvian and postdiluvian periods lasting 1309 and 290 years respectively. The pre-temple age divides into patriarchal, Egyptian, and post-exodus periods lasting 290, 430, and 480 years respectively, with the patriarchal period further subdivided into 75 years in Mesopotamia (before Abraham's migration) and 215 years in Canaan. Finally the temple age divides into first-temple and second-temple periods of 480 and 720 years, with the first-temple period subdivided into a pre-exilic period of 430 years and an 'exilic' period of 50 years (a period of 50 years from the destruction of the first temple to the foundation of the second temple, a year after the return from exile). There is a striking symmetry between the final period of one age and the first period of the following age. Thus the postdiluvian period, which is the final period of the pre-Abrahamic age, lasts for 290 years and is followed by a patriarchal period of 290 years. Similarly the post-exodus period, which is the final period of the pre-temple age, lasts for 480 years and is followed by a first-temple period of 480 years. The chiastic symmetry of these last two periods—the exodus and the erection of the tabernacle occur 480 and 479 years before the foundation of the first temple, while the return from exile and the foundation of the second temple occur 479 and 480 years after the first temple's foundation—has been pointed out earlier (p. 39f.).

There is an obvious correlation between this chronology and the ideology of P. The two most important elements after creation in P's ideology are the person of Abraham and the priestly cult. Abraham is the father of the Israelite nation, and the Israelite nation, through Abraham, is God's chosen people. This is spelt out in Genesis 17 (P), where God makes a covenant with Abraham to be Abraham's God and the God of his descendants through Isaac,

34. The 1599 years of pre-Abrahamic history should doubtless be seen as a close approximation of 1600 years, just as 1309 years (the duration of antediluvian history) is a close approximation of 1310 years, and 3999 years (the present era) is a close approximation of 4000 years. The unrounded nature of these numbers is simply an accidental consequence of the fact that there is no year nought in Hebrew chronology (and no numeral nought in the ancient Hebrew numerical system): the pre-Abrahamic age runs from 1 AM to 1599 AM and has a duration of 1599 years, while the pre-temple age runs from 1600 AM to 1799 AM and has a round duration of 1200 years.

and to give them the land of Canaan in perpetuity; in return Abraham and his descendants are required to adopt circumcision as a sign of the covenant. Abraham is therefore central to Israel's self-awareness in Priestly ideology, since it is to Abraham that Israel owes its existence and its relationship with God. The priestly cult is only slightly less central. It is not the basis of Israel's relationship with God, but it is fundamentally important as a means of regulating and maintaining that relationship. The ideological importance which P attaches to Abraham and the cult is highlighted in Priestly chronology by the fact that the birth of Abraham and the foundation of the temple each stands at the start of a new age of history. It may be noted that the events at Sinai are not ascribed the same chronological prominence as is given to Abraham and the temple, despite the considerable amount of space which P devotes to these events. However, the central Sinai events described by P are the construction of the tabernacle, which is essentially a scaled-down version of the temple in tent form, and the subsequent institution of the priesthood and cult, which prefigures the later temple cult.

The ideological presuppositions reflected in Priestly chronology are thus in direct opposition to the view of Cross (1973:318) that 'the covenant at Sinai was the climax to which the entire Priestly labour had been directed.' In Cross's opinion the absence from P of any narrative of the Sinai covenant ceremony is a 'stunning omission', proving that P is a redactional stratum which presupposes the JE narrative and which never existed as an independent source. In fact, however, Priestly references to a covenant at Sinai are conspicuous by their absence, and the Sinai covenant actually has no place in Priestly ideology. As far as P is concerned the only covenant between God and Israel was the covenant made with Abraham, which is expressly designated as an 'eternal covenant' between God and Abraham and Abraham's descendants 'throughout their generations' (Gn 17.7). Thus when God promises Moses that he will deliver Israel from Egypt and bring them to Canaan, this is because he has remembered his covenant with Abraham, Isaac, and Jacob (Ex 6.2–9), and not because he intends to replace that covenant with a new covenant at Sinai. The covenant which is referred to several times in the conclusion to the Holiness Code (Leviticus 26) is *not* the Sinai covenant (as Cross supposes) but the covenant made with

Abraham and Abraham's descendants (Lv 26.42); and the reference in Leviticus 26.45 to 'the covenant with the forefathers whom
I brought out of the land of Egypt' does not imply a separate
covenant made at Sinai, any more than the reference in verse 42 to
'my covenant with Jacob and my covenant with Isaac' refers to
separate covenants made with Jacob and Isaac.

Recognition that the Sinai covenant has no place in Priestly
ideology demolishes the central pillar of Cross's thesis that P is
merely a redactional stratum of the Pentateuch, and Cross's
arguments may actually be turned on their head to show that it is
most unlikely that P is merely a redactional stratum. Cross is struck
by the absence of any covenant ritual in P's account of the
institution of the Abrahamic covenant, and comments that the
covenant ritual of Genesis 15 (traditionally ascribed to J) must be
assumed to have served this purpose (Cross 1973:319n.). But this
overlooks the crucial fact that as far as P is concerned cultic ritual
simply did not exist before the institution of the cult at Sinai: P
consistently avoids making any reference to sacrifice or ritual in
the pre-Mosaic period (it is J and not P which makes the
distinction between clean and unclean animals at the time of the
flood). Thus in contrast to Cross's claim that P presupposes the
covenant ritual of Genesis 15, that account is actually in direct
contradiction to P's presuppositions. Nor is it the case that P
presupposes J's story of primaeval human rebellion, and that P's
reference to human corruption at the time of the flood, or indeed
the entire Priestly cult with it function of providing atonement for
sin, is otherwise inexplicable (Cross 1973:306f.). On the contrary P
appears to have deliberately avoided mythicizing sin as an
inheritance from the dawn of history, thereby maintaining the full
personal responsibility of each individual for his own sinful
actions. Unless one shares Cross's incredulity at P's omission of
elements which are in fact inconsistent with Priestly ideology there
is no reason to accept Cross's conclusion that P never existed as an
independent Pentateuchal source. Indeed P's careful omission of
these elements argues rather strongly that P *was* an independent
source, and that it was intended as an alternative to the JE
narrative rather than as a supplement to that narrative.[35]

35. Tengström (1982) is one of a number of Biblical scholars who have been
persuaded by Cross's arguments. Similar views have also been expressed independently by Rendtorff (1977:112–142), who concentrates on discontinuities in the

The Priestly scheme of chronology may also have significant implications for the date at which P was composed, for the fact that P makes use of a chronology which extends to the foundation of the second temple clearly excludes a date of composition earlier than the post-exilic period, and rules out the possibility that the Priestly source (as we may now refer to it) was composed before or during the Babylonian exile.[36] This conclusion cannot be avoided by postulating a post-exilic updating of an earlier chronology: the symmetry between the 480-year period from the exodus to the foundation of the first temple and the 480-year period from the foundation of the first temple to the foundation of the second temple (paralleling the symmetry in length between postdiluvian and patriarchal periods) shows that the second 480-year period is integral to the chronology and was not simply tacked on at a later date. Another point which should be taken into account is that if the Book of Generations is an originally independent document we must also allow an interval of time between the creation of the Priestly chronological system and the composition of P.

These conclusions might also be taken a stage further, since there is reason to question the historicity of the book of Ezra's account of the foundation of the second temple. According to this account the second temple was founded under the leadership of Joshua and Zerubbabel in the 2nd year of Cyrus (537 BC). However, according to chronological notices in the book of Haggai (Hg 1.1, 15) work on the second temple was started under the leadership of Joshua and Zerubbabel in the 2nd year of *Darius* (520 BC), and there is no hint of any previous attempt to rebuild the temple. Similarly Zechariah, in a vision dated towards the end of Darius's 2nd year (Zc 1.7), is assured that Zerubbabel, having laid

Priestly stratum as evidence that P is not a continuous narrative source (though these could also have resulted from redactional omissions), but ignores narrative continuities in P which point to the opposite conclusion. On the subject of Priestly chronology, Rendtorff denies that there is any connection between the chronological notices of P and the ideological views expressed in other Priestly texts: 'Auch zwischen den chronologischen Notizen einerseits und den theologischen Texten andererseits bestehen kaum Beziehungen.' (Rendtorff 1977:141).

36. A pre-exilic dating is favoured by most Israeli scholars (following Kaufmann [ET] 1960:175–200); most non-Israeli scholars date P in the exilic or post-exilic period. However, those who have dated the (main redaction of the) Priestly source in exilic or post-exilic times have generally argued that P also contains material that is considerably earlier in date (the core of the Holiness Code is almost certainly pre-exilic).

the temple's foundation, will also complete the temple (Zc 4.9). The book of Ezra harmonizes this picture of events with its own account by claiming that the original construction work was halted as a result of hostility on the part of neighbouring communities (Ezr 4.4–5), and was not resumed until the second year of Darius's reign (Ezr 4.24–5.2). But this is scarcely convincing, since Haggai sees the failure to rebuild the temple as due to self-interest on the part of the Jews, who are said to be more concerned with their own affairs than with the state of Yahweh's temple, and neither Haggai nor Zechariah make any mention of hostility from neighbouring communities. In all probability the book of Ezra is simply reading back into an earlier period the hostility which the post-exilic Judean community certainly experienced in later times; and it is in fact striking that this hostility is illustrated with events said to have occurred during the reigns of Xerxes (486–465 BC) and Artaxerxes (465–424 BC)—the author of Ezra 1–6 apparently confused Darius I (522–486 BC), in whose reign the temple was rebuilt, with Darius II (424–405 BC), who reigned a century later.[37] On this evidence it might be argued that the book of Ezra's account of an initial attempt to rebuild the temple during the reign of Cyrus is a historical fabrication, based upon a fictitious date that was invented by Priestly chronologists to fit in with their schematic chronology of world history. This would then imply that the Priestly scheme of world chronology was not created until some considerable time after the actual foundation of the second temple in the 2nd year of Darius.

There is, however, one other piece of evidence to be taken into account, which supports the historicity of Ezra's date for the foundation of the second temple. This is provided by the text of an Aramaic letter found in Ezra 5.7–17, and purporting to have been written by officials of Darius, which reports that Jewish elders who

---

37. This confusion supports Williamson's suggestion that Ezra 1–6 was written in the early Hellenistic period (Williamson 1983:29), two centuries after the events which it describes; similar chronological confusion is also reflected in the book of Daniel, whose scheme of four Persian kings for the entire duration of the Persian empire (Dn 7.6; 11.2) apparently telescopes the reigns of Darius I, II, and III, Xerxes I, II, and III, and Artaxerxes I, II, and III, besides leaving out Cambyses and Arses, who are not mentioned elsewhere in the Bible. Williamson also argues persuasively that Ezra 4.6–6.18 does not constitute an independent Aramaic source, but was written by the final author of Ezra 1–6, who worked directly from the original Aramaic documents which occupy most of this section.

were asked to produce authorization for their involvement in rebuilding the Jerusalem temple responded by claiming that it had been authorized by a decree of Cyrus in the first year of his reign; in the course of this reply it is stated that the foundations of the temple had already been laid by Sheshbazzar, the first governor of Judah appointed by Cyrus (Ezr 5.13–16). The basic authenticity of the Aramaic letters found in Ezra 1–6 is generally accepted, and this document may therefore be seen as independent confirmation of an attempt to rebuild the temple early in the reign of Cyrus (although it is worth noting that the letter contradicts the book of Ezra's own account by asserting that this initial foundation was the responsibility of Sheshbazzar, not Zerubbabel). For some reason or other—perhaps because of economic difficulties which are alluded to in Haggai 1.6 and 2.15f.—this initial attempt was abandoned and the main rebuilding work was not begun until the reign of Darius.

In view of this last piece of evidence, it is reasonable to conclude that Ezra 3.8f. is historically correct in dating the initial foundation of the second temple to the 2nd year of the return from exile (the 2nd year of Cyrus's reign). It follows that the Priestly scheme of world chronology could have been created at any time after this event, although it may still be argued that this is more likely to have happened when the temple was actually completed than during the period in which the construction work was suspended (one would not expect the foundation of a non-existent temple to have been invested with great chronological significance). There is therefore no essential reason why the (main redaction of the) Priestly source cannot be given a comparatively early date in the post-exilic period (late 6th or early 5th century), so long as we allow sufficient time for the Priestly scheme of world chronology to to have been incorporated into originally independent documents such as the Book of Generations.[38]

---

38. There are linguistic arguments against dating P in the late post-exilic period, for although there are undoubtedly some affinities between the language of P and Late Biblical Hebrew (see Polzin 1976:85f.), there are also significant differences which suggest that P is earlier than texts written in Late Biblical Hebrew. Differences between the language of P and Late Biblical Hebrew are emphasized by Hurvitz (1976), who believes (with other Israeli scholars) that P is pre-exilic in date. In furtherance of this viewpoint Hurvitz has also published an interesting, but one-sided, comparison of the language of P and that of Ezekiel (Hurvitz 1982), which claims to prove that P is linguistically earlier than Ezekiel and therefore

pre-exilic. However, it must be said that some of Hurvitz's comparisons are of dubious validity, and his overall conclusions are weakened by his refusal to discriminate between original and secondary material in Ezekiel. Other complicating factors in the attempt to provide a linguistic dating of P are the fact that the P source utilizes earlier Priestly documents, and may also have been written in a deliberately archaic style which was intended to enhance its authority as ancient torah.

3

THE DEUTERONOMISTIC CHRONOLOGY OF ISRAEL

3.1 *Pre-Priestly Chronological Schematism*

The Deuteronomistic History (Deuteronomy to Kings) contains various chronological notices for the period from the exodus to the Babylonian exile. However, the chronology found in the Masoretic text of Kings is not the original Deuteronomistic chronology, but has been modified to reflect the Priestly total of 430 years from the foundation of the temple to the Babylonian exile (see p. 37f.). By contrast, chronological notices in Judges and Samuel are inconsistent with Priestly chronology, and are in fact bypassed in the Priestly chronological scheme by the chronological note in 1 Kings 6.1. Chronological notices in Judges and Samuel may therefore be taken to represent a pre-Priestly chronology, and evidence of pre-Priestly chronology may also have been preserved in the Septuagint text of Kings, whose chronology of the monarchic period is rather imperfectly harmonized with the Priestly total of 430 years from the foundation of the temple to its destruction (see p. 38f.).

Deuteronomistic chronology in Judges and Samuel may have escaped Priestly schematization, but it is nevertheless highly schematic. This is shown by the repeated occurrence of 40-year periods. In 1 Samuel 4.18 Eli is said to have judged Israel for 40 years, and in 2 Samuel 5.4 David is said to have reigned for the same length of time. In Judges the periods of tranquillity following Mesopotamian, Canaanite, and Midianite oppressions are each assigned a duration of 40 years (Ju 3.11; 5.31; 8.28), while the period of tranquillity following the Moabite oppression is said to have lasted 80 (2 × 40) years (Ju 3.30). Similarly the period of Philistine oppression is put at 40 years (Ju 13.1), while the period of

Canaanite oppression and the period of Samson's rule are both said to have lasted 20 (40 ÷ 2) years (Ju 4.3; 15.20; 16.21). The same overt schematism continues into the beginning of Kings, where David is again said to have reigned for 40 years (1K 2.11), and Solomon is ascribed the same figure (1K 11.42), but subsequent chronological notices are less obviously schematic, and only one Israelite or Judean king after Solomon is ascribed a reign of 40 years (2K 12.2: the king in question is Joash of Judah).

Chronological schematism in Judges and Samuel is also reflected in the overall totals gained by adding together the various lengths of time specified in individual chronological notices (see table opposite). On MT's figures the period from the settlement to the death of Eli works out at exactly 450 years. This calculation disregards the (unspecified) period of time between the settlement and the death of Joshua and those of his generation (Ju 2.8f.); but there is in fact a Biblical precedent for this, since in Judges 11.26 Jephthah claims that for 300 years from the settlement the Ammonites had failed to dispute Israel's transjordanian territory: if one adds together the various periods of time given in MT's text of Judges as far as the start of the Ammonite oppression (i.e. the point at which the Ammonites first laid claim to this territory) the resulting total is 301 years, which is within a year of Jephthah's stated figure.

Chronological figures in LXX[BMN] for the period preceding the Ammonite oppression are identical to those of MT; but in LXX[AL] the total number of years for this period is 311—these manuscripts read '50 years' in place of '40 years' in Judges 3.11. The discrepancy between LXX[AL]'s total and Jephthah's reference to 300 years is one reason for preferring '40 years' as the original reading in Judges 3.11, and the secondary nature of LXX[AL]'s figure is also clear from the fact that it lacks the 40-year schematism which characterizes all other periods of tranquillity. '50 years' may nevertheless be the original *Septuagint* reading, and may be explained as a chronological correction designed to compensate for the loss of 10 years later in the chronology.[1] Eusebius tells us that the LXX text of his day lacked the chronological notice on Elon's 10-year rule in Judges 12.11–12 (Helm [2]1956:60a), so that it is not unreasonable

---

1. Bodine (1980) argues that LXX[A] and LXX[L] are better witnesses to the original LXX text of Judges than LXX[B], which contains the Kaige recension, or LXX[MN], which contain a mixed text showing Kaige influences.

Chronological data: Judges – Kings

(Ju 3.8)	Mesopotamian oppression	8 years	
(Ju 3.11)	Period of tranquillity	40 years	(LXX^{AL}: 50)
(Ju 3.14)	Moabite oppression	18 years	
(Ju 3.30)	Period of tranquillity	80 years	
(Ju 4.3)	Canaanite oppression	20 years	
(Ju 5.31)	Period of tranqillity	40 years	
(Ju 6.1)	Midianite oppression	7 years	
(Ju 8.28)	Period of tranquillity	40 years	
(Ju 9.22)	Abimelech	3 years	
(Ju 10.2)	Tola	23 years	
(Ju 10.3)	Jair	22 years	
(Ju 10.8)	Ammonite oppression	18 years	
(Ju 12.7)	Jephthah	6 years	(LXX^{BMN}: 60)
(Ju 12.9)	Ibzan	7 years	
(Ju 12.11)	Elon	10 years	(*LXX: —)
(Ju 12.14)	Abdon	8 years	
(Ju 13.1)	Philistine oppression	40 years	
(Ju 15.20; 16.31)	Samson	20 years	
(1S 4.18)	Eli	40 years	(LXX: 20)
(1S 7.15)	Samuel	—	
(1S 13.1)	Saul	2 years	(LXX^{BMN}: —)
(1K 2.11)	David	40 years	
(1K 11.42)	Solomon	40 years	
(1K 12.24a)	Rehoboam	—	(LXX^B: 12)
(1K 14.21)	Rehoboam	17 years	
(1K 15.2)	Abijam	3 years	(LXX^{BL}: 6;
(1K 15.10)	Asa	41 years	LXX^A: 16)
(1K 22.42)	Jehoshaphat	25 years	
(2K 8.17)	Jehoram	8 years	(LXX^L: 10;
(2K 8.26)	Ahaziah	1 year	LXX^{AB}: 40)
(2K 11.4)	Athaliah	7 years	
(2K 12.2)	Joash	40 years	
(2K 14.2)	Amaziah	29 years	
(2K 15.2)	Uzziah	52 years	
(2K 15.33)	Jotham	16 years	
(2K 16.2)	Ahaz	16 years	
(2K 18.2)	Hezekiah	29 years	
(2K 21.1)	Manasseh	55 years	
(2K 21.19)	Amon	2 years	
(2K 22.1)	Josiah	31 years	
(2K 23.31)	Jehoahaz	3 months	
(2K 23.36)	Jehoiakim	11 years	
(2K 24.8)	Jehoiachin	3 months	
(2K 24.18)	Zedekiah	11 years	

to suppose that the addition of 10 years to the original figure in Judges 3.11 was intended to correct a chronology in which 10 years had been lost through the omission of Judges 12.11–12.[2] A second instance of textual variation over chronological figures between LXX^{AL} and LXX^{BMN} occurs in Judges 12.7, where there is little doubt that LXX^{AL} have preserved the original LXX figure for Jephthah's rule (6 years, as in MT); LXX^{BMN}'s figure of 60 years (ἐξήκοντα ἔτη) may be explained as having resulted from partial assimilation of ἕξ ('6') to τεσσαράκοντα ('40') in the previous verse. The original LXX total for the period covered by Judges (from the settlement to the death of Samson) was therefore identical with MT's total (410 years), although it was arrived at through slightly different figures. However, in 1 Samuel 4.18 virtually all LXX manuscripts apart from a few minuscules give 20 years in place of MT's figure of 40 years for Eli's rule; the original LXX total to the death of Eli was therefore 430 years, as against 450 years in MT.

Deuteronomistic chronology breaks off with the death of Eli. The latter is succeeded by Samuel, but, oddly, no figure is given for the duration of Samuel's rule. There are also notorious problems with the chronological notice on Saul's reign (1 Samuel 13.1, which is lacking in LXX^{BMN}), but the chronology is taken up again with clear notices on the reigns of Ishbosheth (2S 2.10) and David (2S 5.4), and continues thereafter down to the exile. On MT's figures the period from David's accession to the exile lasts for 474 years (see table on p. 57); but this total reflects Priestly manipulation of regnal years in the period from the foundation of the temple and is therefore secondary. On the other hand, we have seen that LXX's figures for this period are only partially harmonized with Priestly chronology. If we ignore this partial harmonization (by disregarding the 12-year figure for Rehoboam's reign in 1 Kings 12.24a in favour of the 17-year reign length in 1 Kings 14.21), and take the original LXX figures, which are preserved in LXX^{BL} as far as 1 Kings 21 and in LXX^{L} thereafter,[3]

---

2. This is presumably a case of parablepsis through homoiarchon, a scribe's eye having jumped from 'and there judged Israel after him' in verse 11 to the same phrase in verse 13. The presence of Judges 12.11–12 in almost all existing LXX manuscripts (q is the only manuscript cited in the Cambridge Septuagint which omits these verses) is doubtless the result of later recensional activity: the Syro-hexaplar marks the passage as a hexaplaric addition.

3. See discussion on p. 37f.

the total period from David's accession to the exile is 479 years; if we then read *"11 years' in place of '10 years' in 2 Kings 8.17, as is required by LXX^L's chronological synchronisms (see p. 129f.), the total period is exactly 480 years, which is a transparently schematic number. Within this overall period the division of the kingdom occurs 400 years before the Babylonian exile, and 267 years before the fall of Samaria in the 6th year of Hezekiah's reign (2K 18.10); the northern kingdom is thus assigned a duration which (in whole figures) is exactly two-thirds that of the kingdom of Judah. Taken as a whole, the pre-Priestly chronology of Kings is no less schematic than the chronology of Judges and Samuel, even if this schematism is less apparent in individual chronological notices.

In view of the schematic similarity which exists between the Deuteronomistic chronology of Judges and Samuel and the Deuteronomistic chronology of Kings, it is worth taking a fresh look at the curious break in this chronology which occurs with the death of Eli. It has long been recognized that there is something seriously wrong with the chronological notice on Saul's reign (1S 13.1: 'Saul was a year old when he became king, and he reigned 2 years over Israel.'), but the absence of any chronological notice for Samuel's rule is really no less remarkable. 1 Samuel 7.15 is virtually identical in form with chronological notices in Judges ('and X judged Israel for Y years', Ju 10.2, 3; 12.7, 9, 11, 14; 15.20), but instead of a specific figure for the length of Samuel's rule we find only the vague phrase 'all the days of his life', which is in any case inconsistent with the fact that Samuel is depicted as having abdicated in favour of Saul (1 Samuel 12 contains his abdication speech). In view of the fact that Deuteronomistic chronology runs continuously from the settlement to the death of Eli (and is even extended 20 years into Samuel's rule by the chronological note in 1 Samuel 7.2) it is difficult to believe that it did not at one time include a figure for Samuel's rule, which was later replaced by the (somewhat inappropriate) phrase 'all the days of his life'.

In Saul's case it is patently obvious that a figure for Saul's accession age has dropped out (or been removed) from before שָׁנָה ('year'), since בֶּן שָׁנָה ('a year old') is quite nonsensical. Nor is what follows very much better, for '2 years' (שְׁתֵּי שָׁנִים) is hardly long enough for all the events of Saul's reign, which occupy two-thirds of the first book of Samuel. Furthermore, שְׁתֵּי שָׁנִים is a unique expression for '2 years', which is normally expressed by the dual

form שְׁנָתַיִם (Gn 11.10; 41.1; 45.6; 2S 14.28; 1K 15.25; 16.8; 22.52;
2K 15.23 etc.) or else by שְׁתַיִם שָׁנִים (2S 2.10; 2K 21.19 // 2C 33.21).[4]
The textual corruption of Saul's figures, when viewed in conjunction with the disappearance of Samuel's figures, is unlikely to have
occurred through simple mischance (as is often supposed), and we
may therefore suspect that Saul's original figures were deliberately
suppressed.[5] The textual tradition behind LXX evaded the
chronological problems of 1 Samuel 13.1 by omitting the entire
verse (though it has been secondarily restored in LXX^L and
hexaplaric manuscripts).[6]

This raises the obvious question of why anyone should have
wanted to suppress the original chronology at this point. And there

___

4. Cf. Driver (²1913:97). יום ('day') behaves similarly: '2 days' is normally
expressed by the dual יוֹמַיִם (Ex 16.29; 21.21; Nu 9.22; 11.9; Ho 6.2), or else by יָמִים
שְׁנַיִם (2S 1.1; 2C 21.19). There is in fact only one other instance where a time noun
which is morphosyntactically indefinite is preceded by a construct form of
שְׁתַיִם/שְׁנַיִם, and this is שְׁנֵי חֳדָשִׁים ('2 months') in Judges 11.38 (where there is also a
variant שְׁנַיִם חֳדָשִׁים).

5. Despite analogies with Mesopotamian scribal practice it is not really very
likely that the author of this verse originally left the figures blank, with the intention
of filling them in at a later date when he had obtained the necessary information.
This was suggested by Wellhausen (1871:79f.), who argued that the original author
of the book of Samuel omitted to provide a chronological notice for Saul, and that
this omission was subsequently filled by a later scribe who no longer knew the
actual figures. (שׁתי '2' originated, according to Wellhausen, as an accidental
dittography of the first three letters of שָׁנִים 'years'.) More recently Buccellati
(1963:29) has drawn attention to examples of numerical omissions in Mesopotamian literature, which he suggests were left blank because the scribe did not know the
correct figures at the time of writing; see also the additional note by Grayson
(1963:86, 110) concerning the absence of a figure for Tiglathpileser III's reign in
the Babylonian Chronicle (also commented on in Grayson 1975:72f.). But it is
unlikely that these analogies have any relevance to 1 Samuel 13.1; the author
responsible for the chronological material of Judges and Samuel was doubtless
ignorant of the number of years that Saul reigned, but he was almost certainly
equally ignorant of how many years Samson or Eli had 'ruled', and this did not
prevent him from inventing schematic figures in the absence of any historical
evidence. This observation carries less weight if we suppose, with Wellhausen, that
the notice on Saul was supplied by a later scribe. But this simply raises the question
of why the original chronologist should have omitted chronological notices on Saul
and Samuel in a chronology which otherwise runs consecutively from the
settlement to the exile.

6. This omission probably reflects scribal suppression of an obviously corrupt
text; see McCarter 1980:222 and compare the similar omission of a corrupt
chronological notice in LXX's text of Jeremiah 27.1 (discussed below, p. 86n.). It
is unlikely (*contra* Wellhausen 1871:79f.) that LXX preserves a more original form
of the text.

is one suspect, or group of suspects, with a very obvious motive. Even with what is left of the original Deuteronomistic chronology there is clearly an irreconcilable discrepancy between this chronology and the Priestly figure of 480 years from the exodus to the foundation of the temple (1K 6.1), for if we add 40 years in the wilderness plus a 5-year period of conquest[7] to the 430 (LXX) or 450 (MT) years from the settlement to the death of Eli, and then add 40 years for David's reign plus the first 4 years of Solomon's reign (prior to the foundation of the temple), we have a total which already exceeds 500 years without taking account of Samuel and Saul.[8] Thus it was clearly in the interests of the Priestly school to suppress the earlier Deuteronomistic chronology by excising chronological information on Samuel and Saul. This simple expedient failed to remove all trace of the discrepancy between Deuteronomistic and Priestly chronology, but it succeeded in making this discrepancy rather less obvious, and (more importantly) it had the effect of making it impossible to calculate the period from the exodus to the temple on the basis of Deuteronomistic chronological notices—and why should anyone attempt this now impossible task when the Priestly chronologists had supplied a very clear and convenient chronological notice on this period in 1 Kings 6.1?

For modern scholars the task of reconstructing the original Deuteronomistic chronology in disregard of 1 Kings 6.1 is clearly a matter of considerable interest, which may not be entirely impossible despite the activities of Priestly chronologists. It may have been possible for the Priestly school to see that their version of Samuel and Kings was promulgated as the official text, but the suppression or alteration of deviant texts could not have been achieved so easily, and we have already seen that LXX has preserved evidence of pre-Priestly chronology in Kings. The

---

7. The 45-year period mentioned in Joshua 14.10. apparently comprises 40 years in the wilderness plus 5 years' conquest.

8. There have inevitably been numerous attempts to harmonize this discrepancy: see Moore 1895: viiif. and Rowley 1950:90f. for a representative selection, to which one should add Noth [ET]1981:18f. and Richter 1964:132f. (Richter's solution is endorsed in two recent commentaries on Judges—Boling 1975:23 and Soggin 1981:10f.) All such attempts depend upon the selective omission of certain figures from the overall total (thus following the same approach as *Seder Olam Rabba* 11–15), and stem from a failure to recognize that two distinct chronological systems are involved.

situation in this instance is less fortunate: no existing Biblical text preserves the original figures for Samuel's and Saul's periods of rule, but in Saul's case two Lucianic manuscripts and a few other Greek minuscules give 30 years as his age at accession.[9] This *may* be no more than a guess, but it is also possible that it represents a genuine proto-Lucianic reading derived from a Hebrew text in which Saul's age had escaped Priestly suppression.

The possible survival of Saul's age at accession in a few LXX manuscripts does little to help in recovering the original chronology of this period, but evidence for a possible reconstruction may be found outside the Hebrew Bible. In the book of Acts (13.21) the apostle Paul tells us quite plainly that Saul was king for 40 years, and this agrees with Josephus's reckoning in *Antiquities* 6.378. The Acts passage is also of further interest in that it specifies a period of 450 years from the settlement to the accession of Saul (verses 19 to 20), which is roughly in line with LXX's version of Deuteronomistic chronology (430 years to the death of Eli).[10] The figures given in Acts might of course be rough estimates, based perhaps on Deuteronomistic chronology as preserved in LXX and supplemented by guesswork. However, in view of the fact that Acts 13 agrees with Josephus in ascribing 40 years to Saul there is a reasonable case for thinking that it may have derived its figures, directly or indirectly, from a Biblical text form—also available to Josephus or one of his sources—in which the durations of Samuel's and Saul's periods of rule were still preserved. Acts' total of 450 years to Saul's accession evidently presupposes a figure for Samuel's rule, but this cannot be deduced simply by subtracting LXX's total of 430 years to the death of Eli and assigning the difference of 20 years to Samuel, since we do not know that the hypothetical Biblical text underlying Acts 13 necessarily contained the same chronology as LXX to the death of Eli. In any case, 20 years cannot have been the original Biblical figure for Samuel's

9. Marcus (in Thackeray and Marcus 1934:357n.) and Wacholder (1974:65n.) are incorrect in stating that LXX[L] gives '30 years' as the duration of Saul's *reign*.

10. The passage is not entirely clear about when this 450-year period terminated, but since the reference to this period is preceded by a reference to 40 years in the wilderness and followed by a reference to the 40-year reign of Saul, it is reasonable to equate the 450 years in which '(God) gave (Israel) their land as an inheritance' (verse 19) with the period in which 'he gave them judges until (and including) Samuel the prophet' (verse 20; the book of Samuel depicts Samuel as the last of the judges who ruled Israel before the institution of the monarchy).

term of office, since 1 Samuel 7.2 mentions a 20-year period which occurred during the first part of Samuel's rule. According to this passage 20 years elapsed between the time that the ark was brought to Kiriath-jearim and Israel's victory over the Philistines at Mizpah. Since the ark was taken to Kiriath-jearim some 7 months after its capture by the Philistines (1S 6.1), and since Eli died immediately after hearing of the ark's capture (1S 4.18), it follows that this 20-year period is more or less equivalent to the first 20 years of Samuel's rule.

Clearer evidence in Samuel's case is to be found in *Antiquities* 6.292, where the duration of Samuel's rule is given as 30 years. If we add this figure to MT's total of 450 years to the death of Eli, we arrive at the highly interesting total of 480 years from the settlement to the end of Samuel's rule, balancing the 480 years of Deuteronomistic chronology from David's accession to the exile; 40 years for Saul's reign (*Ant* 6.378; Acts 13.21) then brings this to a round total of 1000 years for Israel's existence in Canaan. In view of the neatness with which Josephus's figures slot into Deuteronomistic chronology there is a pretty strong case for thinking that they once formed part of this chronology and are ultimately derived from a Biblical text which gave precisely these figures for Samuel's and Saul's periods of office.

Josephus's evidence is actually a little less straightforward than I have suggested. In the first place, it should be noted that *Antiquities* 6.31 paraphrases 1 Samuel 7.15–17 without giving any indication of Samuel's period of office beyond the vague phrase 'and he administered much good justice for a long time', which appears to be based on 'and Samuel judged Israel all the days of his life' in MT and LXX. Similarly *Antiquities* 6.95f. paraphrases 1 Samuel 13.2f. without prefacing a chronological notice on Saul's reign, and since the notice on Saul's reign in 1 Samuel 13.1 is also omitted in LXX this suggests that Josephus is dependent on LXX or a text form resembling LXX at this point. However, even if Josephus used LXX or a similar text form as his main narrative source, this does not exclude the possibility that he also consulted other Biblical text forms or used chronological sources which were based on variant text forms—in *Antiquities* 5.359 Josephus agrees with MT in assigning Eli a rule of 40 years rather than 20 years as in LXX.

A more serious consideration which must be taken into account in using Josephus's figures for Samuel and Saul is that Josephus himself clearly does not intend the 30 years of Samuel's rule and the 40 years of Saul's reign to be taken consecutively. He is actually quite explicit on this point: Samuel is said to have ruled for 12 years by himself and for 18 years with Saul (*Ant* 6.292), while Saul is said to have reigned for 18 years during Samuel's lifetime and for 22 years after Samuel's death (*Ant* 6.378). Now it could be thought that this seriously undermines my earlier argument that Josephus has preserved authentic evidence of pre-Priestly chronology at this point, for by Josephus's own reckoning the combined duration of Samuel's and Saul's terms of office was 52 years, and not 70 years as I have supposed. But in fact this is not a serious difficulty. Josephus, as I noted above, was apparently familiar with a Biblical text which stated (as do MT and LXX) that Samuel judged Israel 'all the days of his life'; and since Samuel lived well into Saul's reign according to the Biblical account, Josephus would have been forced to conclude that Samuel's term of office overlapped with Saul's reign, even if the source from which he derived his figures made no mention of any overlap. Alternatively, if Josephus derived these figures from secondary chronological sources which included an overlap then the same argument applies to the way in which these sources interpreted the figures provided by their own source of chronological information. Since the overlap of Samuel's and Saul's terms of office is thus explicable as a secondary exegetical adjustment, we may reasonably regard the individual totals of Samuel's and Saul's terms of office as the primary data from which the chronology presented by Josephus was originally constructed. It is hardly fortuitous that these totals come out as schematic round numbers that are typical of Deuteronomistic chronological data, and the fact that this schematism is disguised in *Antiquities* by a chronological overlap of 18 years actually strengthens the case for believing that these figures were derived from Biblical texts, in as much as it would appear to exonerate Josephus (or his source) from the charge of having simply invented suitably schematic figures for Samuel and Saul.

One further complication in Josephus's evidence should also be considered. Although Josephus gives 40 years as the duration of Saul's reign in *Antiquities* 6.378, elsewhere in *Antiquities* (10.143) he cites a figure of 20 years for Saul's reign. And while it might be thought that this is no more than an approximation for the 22 years that Saul is said to have reigned after Samuel's death in *Antiquities* 6.378, the context (giving regnal years down to the exile) shows clearly that it is actually intended as an exact figure. Similar chronological inconsistencies occur elsewhere in Josephus and may probably be attributed in part to an eclectic use of conflicting chronological sources. It is therefore natural to wonder where the figure of 20 years for Saul's reign was originally taken from. 20 years is in fact a rather interesting figure when it is placed in the context of LXX's chronology. It was noted earlier that this allows 430 years (instead of MT's 450 years) for the period from the settlement to the death of Eli; if we then add 30 years for Samuel's rule (as in *Antiquities* 6.292) plus 20 years for Saul's reign (following *Antiquities* 10.143) the resulting total is exactly 480 years from the settlement to the end of Saul's reign, balancing the 480 years from David's accession to the exile, and the addition of 40 years in the wilderness once again produces an overall total of 1000 years.[11] There is therefore a reasonable case for thinking that the 20 years of *Antiquities* 10.143 may also be ultimately derived from a Biblical text giving this figure as the duration of Saul's reign. In this case '40 years' and '20 years' will have existed as Biblical variants for the length of Saul's reign, just as the same variation exists between MT and LXX over the duration of Eli's term of office. The variant figures are in each instance explicable as belonging to different overall chronologies.

In trying to reconstruct Deuteronomistic chronology as it existed before it was altered by Priestly chronologists we have now ended up with two alternative Deuteronomistic chronologies, and this leaves us with the task of deciding which of these alternatives is original. Here it seems to me that it is more likely that a chronology covering Israel's existence in the land of Canaan was later extended to include a period of 40 years from the exodus to the settlement, than that a 1000-year scheme which originally extended from the exodus to the exile was later restricted to the post-settlement period. A second consideration which leads to the same conclusion is that a chronology which distinguishes Saul's

---

11. This total disregards the 5 years of conquest which are alluded to in Joshua 14.10 (see p. 61n.), as well as the unspecified interval between the conquest and the death of Joshua, which is also disregarded in Jephthah's reference to a period of 300 years from the settlement to the Ammonite oppression.

reign from a preceding 480-year period of judges and a following 480-year period of Davidic kings has more in common with the Deuteronomistic History's picture of events than one in which Saul's reign is included within the first 480-year period of judges: the book of Samuel stresses the point that Saul's kingship marked a major new development in the history of Israel, while at the same time emphasizing the transitional nature of Saul's kingship. For these reasons, therefore, the most probable conclusion is that Deuteronomistic chronology originally presented a 1000-year scheme for Israel's existence in Canaan, and that this was later modified to include 40 years in the wilderness by halving the periods of rule ascribed to Eli (MT: 40 years; LXX: 20 years) and Saul (Acts 13.21, *Ant* 6.378: 40 years; *Ant* 10.143: 20 years).

MT's figure of 2 years for the duration of Saul's reign was dismissed earlier as being unoriginal and linguistically anomalous. But there is an interesting similarity between this figure and Josephus's figure of 22 years for the duration of Saul's reign after the death of Samuel (*Ant* 6.378). It is sometimes supposed that a numeral may have dropped out of the Hebrew text from before or after ושתי ('and 2'), and restoration of ועשרים ('and 20') before ושתי would produce an exact agreement with *Antiquities* 6.378. But this is improbable on two accounts. In the first place Hebrew numerals above 10 require a following commonly-enumerated noun such as שנה ('year') to be singular, not plural (we therefore need שנה rather than שנים in this passage). Here it could of course be argued that since numerals from 2 to 10 require plural forms of all classes of noun, an original שנה would probably have been altered to שנים if '22 years' had been reduced to '2 years'. More seriously, however, עשרים ושתי is simply not a possible way of expressing '22' in Biblical Hebrew, which requires עשרים ושתים, since compound numerals of this kind invariably contain the absolute form of the numeral '2'. There is, in any case, an indirect chronological agreement between MT and Josephus without our emending the text of 1 Samuel 13.1: on Josephus's alternative reckoning of 20 years for Saul's entire reign (*Ant* 10.143) the duration of Saul's period as sole ruler works out at exactly 2 years (20 years minus 18 years when Samuel was alive), and the Latin text of *Antiquities* 6.378 actually gives precisely this figure, thereby harmonizing *Antiquities* 6.378

with *Antiquities* 10.143 and with MT's text of 1 Samuel 13.1.[12]

The indirect nature of this agreement between MT and Josephus makes it unlikely that either is directly dependent on the other, and it is of course intrinsically unlikely that MT is dependent on Josephus at this point. A more probable inference is that Josephus's and MT's figures for Saul are independently derived from an earlier Jewish calculation which estimated an 18-year overlap between Samuel's and Saul's terms of office, and was itself based on Biblical texts that assigned 30 years to Samuel and 40 or 20 years to Saul. This chronology probably also underlies the figures given in *Seder Olam Rabba* chapter 13, where Saul is said to have reigned for 2 years (= 20–18 years), as in MT, and Samuel is ascribed a period of 12 years (= 30–18 years). It is striking that *Seder Olam Rabba* and MT both cite figures which originally represented periods of sole rule as if they represented the entire durations of Saul's or Samuel's terms of office; *Seder Olam Rabba* even adopts a new 1-year overlap between Samuel's 12-year rule and Saul's 2-year reign, thus producing a total of 13 years for Samuel and Saul together. This elimination of the previous 18-year overlap (and creation of a new 1-year overlap) is possibly explained by *Seder Olam Rabba*'s interpretation of the 20 years of 1 Samuel 7.2: in this interpretation the 20-year period which is mentioned in this verse is taken to represent the entire period during which the ark remained at Kiriath-jearim, so that if one subtracts the 7 years of David's reign in Hebron (2S 2.11), which preceded his conquest of Jerusalem and transfer of the ark, one is

12. Marcus (in Thackeray and Marcus 1934:357n.) cites a suggestion by S. Rappaport that '2 years' is the original reading in *Antiquities* 6.378, and that a Christian scribe later altered the Greek text to read '22 years' so as to produce a total reign of 40 years in conformity with Acts 13.21. This is unlikely for the following reason: in *Antiquities* 8.61 Josephus specifies a round total of 592 years for the period from the exodus to the foundation of the temple, and the various figures which Josephus gives for this period add up to 591½ years only if Saul is ascribed *22* years of sole rule. (See appendix B for a table of chronological data given by Josephus. Josephus omits Tola, who reigned for 23 years according to MT and LXX, from his narrative, and also omits to give any figure for Abdon [MT and LXX: '8 years']; on the other hand Shamgar, who is not assigned any figure in MT and LXX, is assigned 1 year's rule, and 18 years anarchy—which evidently includes 8 years of Mesopotamian oppression—is said to have followed Joshua's death. Josephus's chronology from the death of Joshua to the death of Eli is therefore 20 years shorter than MT's chronology for the same period, and thus arrives by a different route at the same total as is produced by LXX's chronology.)

left with only 13 years for the combined periods of Samuel's and
Saul's rule. MT's figure of 2 years for Saul may therefore be
based on the chronological calculations given in *Seder Olam
Rabba*, which in turn appear to derive from a chronological
reckoning used by Josephus. In this case the calculations concerning Samuel and Saul in *Seder Olam Rabba* are presumably
earlier than the composition of this work, which is traditionally
ascribed to Rabbi Jose ben Halaphta of the second century AD.
There is, however, some reason to think that MT's figure of 2
years is a fairly late addition to the text: the phrase שְׁתֵּי שָׁנִים is
(as was noted earlier) an abnormal way of expressing '2 years' in
Biblical Hebrew, but it is perfectly acceptable in post-Biblical
(Mishnaic) Hebrew, in which שָׁנִים and שְׁתִּים are always used in
their construct forms when they precede an enumerated noun
(Segal 1927:194f.).

There are a number of similarities between the original
Deuteronomistic chronology of Israel and the Priestly chronology of the world. Deuteronomistic periodization of history is
not essentially different in nature from Priestly periodization,
even if there is a significant difference of scale. Both chronologies work with 480 as a basic chronological unit and have
overall schemes which are constructed from 1000-year periods:
1000 years for the history of Israel in the land of Canaan, or
4000 minus 1 years for duration of the present world era. But
there is also a significant difference: Priestly chronology is
forward-looking as well as backward-looking (the second temple
is founded 720 years before the year 4000), whereas Deuteronomistic chronology covers an age which has ended (the pre-
exilic history of Israel). This presumably reflects the differing
historical situations in which the two chronologies were created:
the Priestly chronology of world history is self-evidently post-
exilic in origin (p. 51), so the Babylonian exile is no more than
an interlude in this chronology; by contrast the Deuteronomistic
chronology of Israel was almost certainly produced during the
exilic period, and the Babylonian exile is therefore the end-point
of this chronology.

3.2 *Deuteronomistic chronology: formation and development*

3.2.1 *Judges and Samuel*

The fact that the Deuteronomistic scheme of Israelite chronology ends with the Babylonian exile raises the question of its literary-historical relationship to the Deuteronomistic History. The latter in its present form is certainly exilic (with minor post-exilic modifications), but there are persuasive reasons for thinking that an original edition was first produced in pre-exilic times. Evidence for this view was presented over a century ago by A. Kuenen, who noted that some passages in the Deuteronomistic framework of Kings presuppose the Babylonian exile while others reflect a pre-exilic situation (see Mayes 1983:3), but this evidence was later dismissed by Noth ([ET]1981:139n.) on the grounds that passages which reflect a pre-exilic situation may be explained as source material used by an exilic historian. More recently, however, F. M. Cross's study of thematic tensions in the book of Kings (Cross 1973:274–289) has presented strong additional evidence that the original edition of the Deuteronomistic History was composed during the reign of Josiah (or shortly thereafter), and this view has been supported in detailed studies by Nelson (1981) and Mayes (1983).[13] This raises the obvious question of what kind of chronology (if any) can have existed in the original

13. Mayes' study is an important contribution to understanding the redactional development of the Deuteronomistic History, but in two cases it may be argued that Mayes has underestimated the original Deuteronomistic Historian's contribution by ascribing Deuteronomistic material to pre-Deuteronomistic stages of redaction. Unlike Mayes I am not persuaded by H. Weippert's arguments for a pre-Deuteronomistic edition of Kings covering the period from Jehoshaphat and Joram to the fall of Samaria (Weippert 1972). Weippert argues that the framework formulae of Kings fall into several distinct groups, one of which covers the period from Jehoshaphat and Joram to Ahaz and Hoshea, while a second extends backwards to the division of the kingdom and forwards to the time of Josiah. But there is actually considerable variety in framework formulae for this period, and this variety does not obviously resolve itself into the two groups claimed by Weippert (cf. Nelson 1981:31. Mayes notes a degree of overlap between these hypothetical groupings though he understates the extent of this overlap). One may also question Mayes' acceptance of Richter's view that the framework passages in Judges are pre-Deuteronomistic (Richter 1964); the stereotyped nature of these passages and their use of the Deuteronomistic phrase 'did what was evil in the sight of Yahweh' suggests rather that they are to be ascribed to the (original) Deuteronomistic historian.

Deuteronomistic History; a pre-exilic edition of this history clearly cannot have contained a chronology which runs from the settlement to the exile, nor can we suppose that an exilic chronologist merely extended an original chronology which ended with the reign of Josiah, for the Babylonian exile is self-evidently an integral part of the overall chronological scheme outlined above. There are, as I see it, two possible answers to this question: either the exilic chronologist inherited an earlier chronology which he then modified to produce his overall scheme of 1000 years of Israelite history, or else he simply invented a chronology where none had previously existed.

These possibilities are not necessarily mutually exclusive. In the case of Kings there are good reasons for thinking that the exilic chronologist modified an existing chronology based on historical records (see following section of this chapter). However, there is no reason to suppose that the original Deuteronomistic History contained any chronology for the period preceding David's accession; it is certainly unlikely that historical records were available for this period (none are ever cited). Also, the overt schematism of the chronology of Judges and Samuel, in contrast to the less obvious schematism of the chronology of Kings, suggests that this probably originated as the straightforward invention of an exilic chronologist who created it as a schematic counterpart to the schematized (but originally non-schematic) chronology of Kings.

There are in fact a number of internal indications that the chronology of Judges and Samuel has been secondarily inserted. In the first place, the chronological notices of Judges and Samuel are quite easily detached from their contexts: note for instance Judges 3.8, 'and the Israelites became subject to Cushan-Rishathaim {for 8 years}', or Judges 3.11, 'and the land was quiet {for 40 years}' (compare the use of similar phrases, without a time reference, in Joshua 11.23, 14.15, and 2 Kings 11.20). It is also quite easy to envisage an earlier form of the list of 'minor judges' in Judges 10.1–5 and 12.7–15 which gave only the relative order of these judges without specifying their period of office: 'and X arose after him and judged Israel {for Y years}', or 'and X judged Israel after him ... {and he judged Israel for Y years}' (compare the notice on Shamgar's rule in Judges 3.31, which informs us that Shamgar followed Ehud without stating the length of his rule). The fact that these notices are easily detachable from their contexts does not of course prove of itself that they are secondary, but the fact that some of these notices are not only detachable but also fit awkwardly in their contexts points strongly in this direction. One example of this is Judges 10.8, 'and the Ammonites shattered and crushed the Israelites that year {for 18 years}', where the juxtaposed time phrases 'that year' and 'for 18 years' appear to require two different interpretations of the verbs 'shattered and crushed': either the Ammonites 'defeated' the Israelites 'that year' or they 'oppressed' them 'for 18 years'. Similarly Jephthah's rhetorical question in Judges 11.26 makes better sense (and is stylistically improved) if we omit 'for 300 years': 'when Israel settled/{dwelt} in Heshbon and its villages and in Aroer and its villages {for 300 years}, why did you not recover them at/{during} that time?' (Would the Ammonites' claim to these territories have been strengthened in Jephthah's eyes if they had only waited say 50 or 100 years before taking them?) A final example that may be cited is 1 Samuel 7.2: 'from the time that the ark came to rest in Kiriath-jearim the days multiplied {and became 20 years}, and the whole house of Israel lamented after Yahweh.' Here the bracketed time phrase is curiously expressed, and a specific time reference comes awkwardly after the indefinite period implied by 'the days multiplied' (i.e. a long time passed; cf. Genesis 38.12, 'the days multiplied and Judah's wife Bath-Shua died').

There are other tensions between chronology and narrative. According to Deuteronomistic chronology the Philistine oppression lasted for 40 years and was followed by a period of 20 years when Samson was judge over Israel. By contrast the narrative of Judges and Samuel describes the period of Philistine oppression as having lasted right through Samson's and Eli's lifetimes. This tension is highlighted in Judges 15.20, which states that Samson judged Israel 'in the time of the Philistines for 20 years.' The first temporal phrase states clearly that Samson's period as judge occurred *during* the Philistine oppression, but this was manifestly not the view of the Deuteronomistic chronologist who supplied the reference to 20 years: even if we follow LXX in allowing Eli only 20 years' rule there is simply no way that Samson's rule of 20 years plus Eli's rule of 20 or 40 years and another 20 years from the return of the ark to Samuel's victory over the Philistines can possibly be fitted into a period of Philistine domination lasting 40 years.[14] A second and more fundamental discrepancy between narrative and chronology is that the latter numbers the years of Israel's settlement from the period of Mesopotamian oppression, completely ignoring the time of 'Joshua and the elders' referred to in Joshua 24.31 and Judges 2.7–10. Discrepancies of this kind are hard to account for if it is thought that the chronology of Judges and Samuel was an integral part of the original Deuteronomistic History, whereas they are readily explicable if this chronology was secondarily inserted into the original narrative.

It was noted earlier that much of the chronology of Judges and Samuel is characterized by an overt numerical schematism based on the figure 40, but it should also be remarked that this overt schematism is not uniformly distributed among the various chronological notices of Judges and Samuel. Three types of chronological period are referred to in these notices: periods of tranquillity (Ju 3.11, 30; 5.31; 8.28), periods of oppression (Ju 3.8, 14; 4.3; 6.1; 10.8; 13.1), and periods of rule (Ju 9.22; 10.2, 3; 12.7, 9, 11, 14; 15.20; 16.31; 1S 4.18). Of these three types only the first is invariably characterized by overt 40-year schematism: three periods of tranquillity lasting 40 years and one period lasting 80 years produce an overall total of 200 years.

(1) Ju 3.11	Period of tranquillity		40 years
(2) Ju 3.30	Period of tranquillity		80 years
(3) Ju 5.31	Period of tranquillity		40 years
(4) Ju 8.28	Period of tranquillity		40 years
	total		200 years

Other types of chronological period are less overtly schematic. Among periods of oppression there are only two instances of overtly schematic numbers, and the overall total is 111 years.

---

14. Noth ([ET]1981:21f.) resolved this discrepancy by claiming that the chronological notices for Samson and Eli are secondary additions. The resultant loss of 60 years from Deuteronomistic chronology then allowed him to arrive at a total of 481 years from the exodus to the foundation of the temple, which is only 1 year off the supposedly Deuteronomistic [Priestly] figure of 480 years in 1 Kings 6.1 (a hypothetical 1-year overlap between David and Saul is invoked to take care of this remaining discrepancy).

(1) Ju 3.8	Mesopotamian oppression	8 years
(2) Ju 3.14	Moabite oppression	18 years
(3) Ju 4.3	Canaanite oppression	20 years
(4) Ju 6.1	Midianite oppression	7 years
(5) Ju 10.8	Ammonite oppression	18 years
(6) Ju 13.1	Philistine oppression	40 years
	total	111 years

Note, however, that although this list is less overtly schematic than the last, there is an interesting form of schematic parallelism between the first and second three periods, which is more obvious if they are juxtaposed as in the following table.

(1) 8 years	(4) 7 years
(2) 18 years	(5) 18 years
(3) 20 years	(6) 40 years

This shows an unmistakable parallelism between the second and fifth periods, each lasting 18 years, and between the third and sixth periods, lasting for 20 and 40 years respectively, but there is a rather less precise parallelism between the first and fourth periods of 8 and 7 years respectively. Now it may be that the Deuteronomistic chronologist never intended the two series of oppressions to be in perfect chronological parallelism; but it is also possible that the period of Mesopotamian oppression was originally reckoned to have lasted for 7 years like the Midianite oppression, and that *'7 years' in Judges 3.8 was later corrupted to '8 years' through partial assimilation to '18 years' in Judges 3.14 (six verses later). There is no direct textual evidence to support this suggestion, but there are two interesting consequences that may count in its favour. Firstly the total number of years works out at a round figure of 110 years, which is comparable to the round total of 200 years for periods of tranquillity. Secondly, and more importantly, the total number of years from the settlement to the start of the Ammonite oppression now comes to exactly 300 years, which is the precise figure stated by Jephthah in Judges 11.26. It could of course be argued that for Jephthah's rhetorical purposes an inexactitude of 1 year was hardly of great importance, and this would be a reasonable argument were it not for the fact that (on previous evidence) the figure of 300 years was inserted into its present context by the Deuteronomistic chronologist and should therefore be interpreted in the same way as other numbers inserted by this chronologist, i.e. *as an exact figure.*[15]

Overt schematism is also relatively uncommon in chronological notices on periods of rule. Within the book of Judges only Samson's rule of 20 years and (possibly) Elon's rule of 10 years are overtly schematic.

(1)	Ju 9.22	Abimelech	3 years
(2)	Ju 10.2	Tola	23 years
(3)	Ju 10.3	Jair	22 years
(4)	Ju 12.7	Jephthah	6 years
(5)	Ju 12.9	Ibzan	7 years
(6)	Ju 12.11	Elon	10 years
(7)	Ju 12.14	Abdon	8 years
(8)	Ju 15.20; 16.31	Samson	20 years
		total	99 years

One conclusion which might be drawn from the absence of overt schematism in the first seven notices of this list (one round number in seven is hardly very significant) is that the figures in these notices are in fact historical (cf. Soggin 1981:198–199), in which case the list of so-called minor judges in Judges 10.1–5 and 12.7–15 must presumably be based on an authentic historical document, although it also incorporates obviously legendary statements such as 'he had thirty sons who rode on thirty asses, and they had thirty cities ...' (Ju 10.4; cf. 12.9, 14). It must be said, however, that the fact that a set of numbers is not overtly schematic does not of itself prove that it is historically authentic—not all antediluvian life-spans are schematic round figures, for example. Furthermore, if I am right in suggesting that the Mesopotamian oppression may have been accidentally increased from 7 to 8 years then it follows that the chronology must elsewhere have been reduced by 1 year in

15. There is one further piece of evidence which can be cited in support of this suggestion. According to the Biblical Antiquities of Pseudo-Philo (*LAB* 27.16), 'Kenaz' ruled Israel for 57 years after the death of Joshua. This corresponds to 8 years of Mesopotamian oppression and 40 or 50 years of tranquillity during which *Othniel* the son of Kenaz ruled Israel according to the Biblical text. Now it is possible that the number found in Pseudo-Philo is textually corrupt (there are other instances where this is certainly the case), but if it is not corrupt there is a strong inference that Pseudo-Philo's Biblical text had *'7 years' and not '8 years' as the duration of the Mesopotamian oppression.

order to preserve the overall schematism of 480 years to the accession of Saul. In view of the fact that remaining periods of oppression are characterized by a schematic parallelism which would have been destroyed by a 1-year reduction (as would the overt schematism of periods of tranquillity), this reduction can only have occurred in one of the periods of rule. In which case the periods of rule stated in Judges will originally have totalled 100 years, which is an obviously schematic total.

We can perhaps be rather more specific about where a reduction of 1 year might have occurred, since the fact that the original 300-year total for the period from the settlement to the start of the Ammonite oppression was not restored shows that this reduction cannot have occurred in any of the periods of rule preceding the Ammonite oppression. The periods of rule ascribed to Elon and Samson may also be excluded by the fact that they are schematic round numbers, and this leaves us with the periods of rule ascribed to Jephthah, Ibzan, and Abdon as three possible candidates. There is no immediately obvious way of deciding between these three possibilities. However, the addition of 1 year to Jephthah's rule produces an interesting schematic pattern whereby the first and fourth periods of rule total 10 years, the second and fifth total 30, and the third and seventh also total 30.

$$
\begin{array}{ll}
(1) \quad 3 \text{ years} + (4) \; {}^*7 \text{ years} = {}^*10 \text{ years} \;\Big\} & {}^*40 \text{ years} \\
(2) \; 23 \text{ years} + (5) \quad 7 \text{ years} = \quad 30 \text{ years} \;\Big\} &
\end{array}
$$

$$
\begin{array}{ll}
\qquad\qquad (6) \; 10 \text{ years} \;\Big\} & \\
(3) \; 22 \text{ years} + (7) \quad 8 \text{ years} = \quad 30 \text{ years} \;\Big\} & 40 \text{ years}
\end{array}
$$

$$
\qquad (8) \quad 20 \text{ years} \qquad\qquad\qquad 20 \text{ years}
$$

$$
\qquad\qquad\qquad\qquad\qquad \text{total} \quad {}^*100 \text{ years}
$$

It must be said that there is no real textual evidence to support this suggestion,[16] which stands (or falls) together with my earlier suggestion that the period of Mesopotamian oppression was accidentally increased by 1 year; if that suggestion is accepted— and the existing discrepancy between Jephthah's reference to 300

16. A single Lucianic minuscule (v) does give '7 years' (ζ' ἔτη) as the duration of Jephthah's rule, but this is almost certainly a corruption of '60 years' (the reading found in other Lucianic manuscripts) resulting from graphic confusion of ξ' ('60') and ζ' ('7').

years from the settlement and an actual total of 301 years is a
significant argument in its favour—then Jephthah's period of rule
is most likely to have been reduced to compensate for this increase,
since restoration of a year to Jephthah's rule also restores an overall
schematic pattern which is comparable with the schematic pattern
which exists in the case of periods of oppression.

These arguments (if accepted) show that the chronology of
Judges and Samuel may be more schematic than is immediately
apparent. In addition to the overt 40-year schematism which
characterizes a number of individual notices, and the overall
480-year schematism of the period from the settlement to the
accession of Saul, it also appears that different series of chronological notices have their own overall schematism, and that periods
of oppression and periods of rule are characterized by internal
schematic patterning. The disguised schematism of these last two
series possibly reflects a desire to avoid ascribing overtly schematic
numbers to less significant periods of Israel's history, in order to
highlight the significance of those periods to which schematic
numbers *are* attached; i.e. Samson's 20-year rule was judged to be
of greater significance than Tola's 23-year rule, while the particular seriousness of the Canaanite and Philistine oppressions was
underlined by their schematic durations of 20 and 40 years
respectively. This suggestion naturally requires us to take note of
the consistent 40-year schematism which characterizes periods of
tranquillity; and the obvious conclusion is that the schematic
durations of these periods were intended to highlight the importance of the 'deliverers' (Othniel, Ehud, Shamgar, Deborah, and
Gideon) who ruled Israel during these times. In point of fact the
four periods of tranquillity in Judges 3–8 probably belong to the
same chronological series as the periods of rule in Judges 9ff.;
formal differences between periods of tranquillity and periods of
rule are explicable as a secondary result of the way in which
Deuteronomistic chronology was secondarily inserted into the text
of Judges and Samuel. In this connection it may be noted that five
deliverers are associated with periods totalling 200 (5 × 40) years,
and that the 80-year period of tranquillity following the Moabite
oppression, which contrasts with the 40-year periods of tranquillity following other oppressions, is explained by the fact that two
successive deliverers, Ehud and Shamgar, are associated with this
period. But it is also obvious that the reference to Shamgar has

been secondarily inserted into the text at Judges 3.31 in order to extend the chronology at this point, for the statement that Israel lapsed into apostasy after the death of Ehud (Ju 4.1) obviously leaves no room for Shamgar's (40-year) rule (and therefore points to an earlier form of the text in which Judges 4.1 followed directly after Judges 3.30). The notice on Shamgar's rule may originally have belonged to the list of minor judges in Judges 10.1–5 and 12.7–15.

3.2.2 *Kings*

The chronology of Judges and Samuel finds its direct continuation in the chronology of Kings, where 480 years from the settlement to Saul, and 40 years for the reign of Saul, are balanced by a pre-Priestly total of 480 years from David to the exile. The chronology of Kings is less overtly schematic than the chronology of Judges and Samuel, but it is not without its own internal schematism. This is most apparent in the period from the division of the kingdom to the Babylonian exile. In the pre-Priestly form of this chronology (in which Abijam and Jehoram reign for 6 and *11 years respectively, and which is therefore 6 years longer than MT's chronology), the period from the division of the kingdom to the Babylonian exile lasts exactly 400 years, with the fall of Samaria in Hezekiah's 6th year (2K 18.10) coming 267 years after the division of the kingdom, or two thirds of the way through this period. This, however, is only one of a series of schematic dates which are assigned to significant events in the history of the Israelite and Judean kingdoms.

The book of Kings, despite its synchronistic chronology of the two kingdoms, gives specific dates for very few events other than the accession, or death, of a particular monarch, so that those events which are provided with specific dates must evidently have been regarded as particularly significant. Within the period from the division of the kingdom to the fall of Jerusalem there are ten such year-dates, as listed below.

1K 14.25	5th year of Rehoboam	: Shishak attacks Jerusalem
2K 12.7	23rd year of Joash	: inauguration of temple repairs; Hazael attacks Jerusalem
2K 17.6	9th year of Hoshea	: capture of Samaria

2K 18.9	4th year of Hezekiah	
	= 7th year of Hoshea	: Shalmaneser attacks Samaria
2K 18.10	16th year of Hezekiah	
	= 9th year of Hoshea	: capture of Samaria
2K 18.13	14th year of Hezekiah	: Sennacherib invades Judah
2K 22.3	18th year of Josiah	: discovery of lawbook; reform
2K 23.23	18th year of Josiah	: Passover celebration
2K 25.1	9th year of Zedekiah	: Nebuchadrezzar attacks Jerusalem
2K 25.2	11th year of Zedekiah	: capture of Jerusalem

It may be noted that the majority of these dates relate to foreign attacks, and that those which do not, or are less directly connected with foreign attacks (e.g. 2K 12.7), relate to important religious matters such as the inauguration of temple repairs and Josiah's reform. None of these dates is obviously schematic when taken in isolation, but clear evidence of chronological schematism emerges once they are translated into year-dates from the division of the kingdom using pre-Priestly Judean reign lengths. This is shown in the following table.

Year 5	Shishak attacks Jerusalem (5th year of Rehoboam)
Year 131	inauguration of temple repairs (23rd year of Joash); Hazael attacks Jerusalem
Year 265	Shalmaneser attacks Samaria (4th year of Hezekiah)
Year 267	capture of Samaria (6th year of Hezekiah)
Year 275	Sennacherib invades Judah (14th year of Hezekiah)
Year 365	Josiah's reform (18th year of Josiah)
Year 398	Nebuchadrezzar attacks Jerusalem (9th year of Zedekiah)
Year 400	capture of Jerusalem (11th year of Zedekiah)

The most immediately striking feature of this list is the high proportion of dates which turn out to be multiples of 5. Out of a total of eight year-dates (two of ten year-dates in the previous list duplicate other dates in that list), five are multiples of 5 and two (years 267 and 398) are not themselves multiples of 5 but are directly related to other dates that are. (Given the 3-year durations of the final sieges of Samaria and Jerusalem it was clearly impossible that the dates for both the beginning and end of each siege should be multiples of 5.) The only real exception to this numerical schematism is therefore the 23rd year of Joash, which corresponds to the 131st year from the division of the kingdom. It should be noted, however, that this date is identical with that given for Jehoahaz's accession (2K 13.1: בשנת עשרים ושלש שנה ליואש) and may have been inadvertently assimilated to the latter; confirmation of this suggestion is provided by the the fact that the date in question uses a form of numerical syntax which is regularly used with accession dates but is not normally used for other specific dates in Kings.[17] There is unfortunately no real textual evidence for the original date at this point, but either the *27th year of Joash's reign or the *17th year of Joash's reign, corresponding to years 135 and 125 from the division of the kingdom, are possible candidates; the latter produces an interesting chronological pattern whereby Sennacherib's invasion 125 years before the fall of Jerusalem is mirrored (150 years earlier) by Hazael's attack on Jerusalem 125 years after the division of the kingdom, while Josiah's reform, instituted after the discovery of the 'book of the law' was reported during temple repairs, is dated 240 years after Joash first inaugurated the temple-repair programme. There is of course no way of knowing whether this pattern really existed in an earlier form of the chronology; but whatever date was originally given in 2 Kings 12.7, the fact that Sennacherib's invasion is dated 275 years after the division of the kingdom (and 125 years before the fall of Jerusalem) while Josiah's reform is dated 365 years after the division of the kingdom (35 years before the fall of Jerusalem) is certainly evidence for some form of schematism. We should also take note of the 10-year interval between Shalmaneser's attack on Samaria in Hezekiah's 4th year and Sennacherib's invasion of Judah in Hezekiah's 14th

---

17. Accession dates (and dates of death) in Kings invariably follow the syntactic form (A) שנת + cardinal (+ שנה)—the last element occurs with numbers over 20 and is optional with numbers over 10—whereas other specific dates, apart from two external synchronisms with Nebuchadrezzar's reign (2K 24.12; 25.8), normally follow the construction (B) שנה/שנת + ordinal (with article) for numbers up to 10, and (C) cardinal + שנה for numbers over 10. A fourth construction (D) שנה + cardinal (with article), is essentially the same as construction B adapted for numbers over 10 (the Hebrew series of ordinals ends at this point). There is only one instance, apart from 2 Kings 12.7, where the first construction is used for a non-accession date in Kings, and this is in 2 Kings 18.10, which dates the capture of Samaria in Hezekiah's 6th year = Hoshea's 9th year. In the last example the unusual numerical syntax contrasts strikingly with that used in the previous verse, and may therefore be an indication that this (second) date for the capture of Samaria has been secondarily inserted.

year; in reality these events were separated by over 20 years.[18]

The schematic nature of the chronology of Kings clearly reduces its historical value for modern scholarship (as the last example illustrates), but it does not necessarily follow that the chronology of Kings is historically worthless. The chronology in its present form reflects the work of an exilic chronologist who created the chronology of Judges and Samuel, but this does not mean that the chronology of Kings is the free invention of that chronologist. Given the synchronistic nature of Kings' presentation of Israelite and Judean history from the division of the kingdom to the fall of Samaria it is difficult to conceive of the book of Kings in a form which did not contain some kind of chronology for the period of the divided monarchy: the synchronistic principle behind the book of Kings' arrangement of its material, whereby the reigns of Israelite and Judean kings are described in chronological order of accession, clearly presupposes a synchronistic chronology of Israelite and Judean reigns. Thus in contrast to the chronology of Judges and Samuel, which is structurally inessential and appears to have been secondarily inserted into the original narrative, the synchronistic chronology of Kings is structurally essential and must therefore have existed, in some form or other, in the original (pre-exilic) edition of the Deuteronomistic History. It is also reasonable to expect that this edition will have continued Judean chronology beyond the end of the northern kingdom, when

18. It is worth asking whether this schematic chronology has also left traces in other Biblical books which were subject to Deuteronomistic editing, the most obvious example being the book of Jeremiah. One date in Jeremiah which has generated considerable discussion is the date given for the start of Jeremiah's ministry (Je 1.2). Many scholars feel that the 13th year of Josiah's reign is too early, since the majority of oracles deal with events in the reigns of Josiah's successors (the only oracle which is explicitly dated to Josiah's reign, Jeremiah 3.6ff., is probably not by Jeremiah at all), and one view, which has no support in the Biblical text, is that this is really the date of Jeremiah's birth (Holladay 1986:1). But if we look at this in the context of dates in the book of Kings, the 13th year of Josiah's reign is actually the 360th year from the division of the kingdom. There is another point which all but proves the schematic nature of the date in Jeremiah 1.2: within the chronology of Kings there are 40 years from the 13th year of Josiah's reign to the fall of Jerusalem in the 11th year of Zedekiah's reign, which is precisely the period of Jeremiah's ministry as stated by Jeremiah 1.2. According to these dates, Jeremiah, like Moses, has a ministry of 40 years, but whereas Moses's ministry ended with Israel's entry into Canaan, Jeremiah's ministry ended with Israel's exile to Babylon. It has often been noted that there are literary parallels between Jeremiah's call to be a prophet (Je 1) and the call of Moses in Exodus 3.

it was no longer necessary for synchronistic presentation of material, as it would be curious if the chronology was simply broken off at that point; and it may be remarked that David's accession was probably a more logical starting point for the original chronology than the division of the kingdom. The exilic chronologist who created a schematic chronology of Israel's existence in the land of Canaan must therefore have inherited a pre-schematized chronology of Israelite and Judean history from the division of the kingdom (or from David's accession), which he subsequently modified to produce his own schematic chronology of this period.

Further evidence that the exilic chronologist took over and modified an existing chronology is provided by the fact that reign lengths and regnal synchronisms given by Kings clearly presuppose no less than three different dating systems, one of which is actually incompatible with Deuteronomistic chronological schematism. This may be illustrated from chronological data for the early period of the divided monarchy down to Jehu's revolt. There are, however, a number of preliminary points which must be made. Firstly, despite some assertions to the contrary (which are usually motivated by a desire for greater leeway in harmonizing apparent discrepancies in the chronology of Kings), it is reasonably certain that Israel and Judah both used essentially the same (autumn new year) calendar at this period (see p. 166f.), so that Israelite and Judean years may be safely equated for present purposes. Secondly it is also reasonable to assume that when it is said that 'X slept with his fathers and Y his son (or brother) became king in his place' (1K 14.20, 31; 15.8, 24, 31; 16.6, 28; 22.40, 50; 2K 1.17; 8.24 etc.) this means that the second king acceded to the throne *after* his father's (or brother's) death, and it is presumably self-evident that an assassin who is said to have killed his predecessor and become king in his place (1K 15.28; 16.10 etc.) must likewise have become king *after* his predecessor's death; the theories of Biblical scholars for whom these assumptions are not self-evident, and who suppose that some kings acceded to the throne before the the death of their predecessors (as coregents etc.) are discussed below (p. 98f.). Finally it is surely logical to suppose that while a king may have acceded to the throne in the year preceding his first official regnal year (see below), it is rather unlikely that he will have done so in the year following his first official regnal year.[19]

The table given below incorporates these fairly basic assumptions in outlining MT's chronology for the reigns of Abijam and Asa and their Israelite contemporaries. In this and in following tables regnal years are listed in vertical columns, and attested synchronisms between Judean and Israelite regnal years are indicated by bold print; 'd' and 'ac' stand for 'death' and 'accession'. The data on which this table and other tables in the rest of this chapter are based are listed in the following chapter (p. 123f.).

Abijam	**ac** 1	**18**	Jeroboam
	2	19	
Asa	3/ **ac**	**20**	
	1	21	
	2	22/**ac** 1	Nadab
	3	**d**2/**ac** 1	Baasha
	4	2	
	5	3	
	~	~	
	25	23	
	26	**ac** 1/24	Elah
	27	ac 1/**ac**/2	Zimri/Omri
	~	~	
	37	11	
	38	12/**ac** 1	Ahab

19. Contrast Andersen (1969:73f.), who suggests that official proclamation of a king's accession was made at the first new year's festival after the death of his predecessor, and argues that מלך ('become king') sometimes refers to this event rather than to the actual point at which a king assumed royal power, although his regnal years were nevertheless counted from the year in which he assumed royal power and not from his official accession. But there is no evidence that מלך, in an inchoative sense, ever refers to anything other than the actual point at which a king assumed power: the chronological data which Andersen cites in support of his hypothesis (e.g. the fact that Abijam's accession is synchronized with Jeroboam's 18th year, although Rehoboam, who came to the throne shortly before Jeroboam, is ascribed a reign of only 17 years) are all capable of a simpler explanation than Andersen proposes (see below). Neither is there any evidence that official proclamation of a king's accession was normally deferred until the first new year of his reign; from the accounts of the accessions of Solomon, Jehu, and Joash (1K 1.38f.; 2K 9.4f.; 11.9f.) it would appear that proclamation of a king's accession was actually one of the first events of his reign.

	39	2
	40	3
Jehoshaphat	ac/41	**4**

This table illustrates two significantly different ways in which regnal years may be counted: Asa's first regnal year is reckoned as the year following his accession year, while the first regnal year of Asa's Israelite contemporaries is the same year as their accession year, and there is also an overlap between the last regnal year of one Israelite king and the first regnal year of his successor. Note that Asa's first year cannot be identified with his accession year (= Jeroboam's 20th year), since in that case his 2nd year would be identical with Jeroboam's 21st year, and Nadab (whose accession is dated to Asa's 2nd year) would consequently have succeeded his father before the latter had vacated the throne. Conversely Nadab's first year can only be identified with his accession year (= Asa's 2nd year), in view of the fact that he is said to have died after a reign of 2 years in Asa's 3rd regnal year, and the same is true of the reigns of Nadab's successors (these are incompatible with MT's synchronisms unless they are counted inclusively from the year of accession, and unless this also corresponds to the last regnal year of the previous king). We therefore have evidence for two distinct dating systems, one (used in dating Asa's reign) in which the first regnal year is counted as the year following a king's accession year, and a second (used to date the reigns of Asa's Israelite contemporaries) in which the first regnal year is identified with a king's accession year and there is an overlap between this and the last regnal year of the previous king.

A third dating system may be seen to underlie Omri's accession date, which is disregarded in the table given above. According to 1 Kings 16.23, Omri became king in Asa's 31st year and reigned for 12 years; but since his predecessor (Zimri) is said to have become king in Asa's 27th year and to have reigned for only 7 days (1K 16.15) this apparently leaves 4 years unaccounted for. It is true that according to 1 Kings 16.21–22 Zimri's death was followed by an armed struggle between supporters of Omri and supporters of Tibni, and we might therefore suppose that Omri's accession was delayed for 4 years because of civil war (although the text of Kings suggests a much shorter conflict), but this suggestion runs against

the fact that in MT's chronology Omri is succeeded by Ahab 12
years (inclusively) from Asa's *27th* year (1K 16.29, dating Ahab's
accession to Asa's 38th year). Those who wish to harmonize MT's
chronological data by positing a 4-year period of civil war must
therefore argue that although Omri did not become undisputed
ruler until Asa's 31st year he nevertheless counted the 4 years of
civil war in his own regnal total, and they should then explain why
Omri's accession date was not also put back to the start of the civil
war. However, although the synchronism in 1 Kings 16.23 cannot
easily be fitted into the chronological scheme displayed in the
previous table, it fits perfectly into an alternative scheme in which
the accession year of each Israelite king is counted as the year
following the last regnal year of his predecessor.[20] This is
illustrated in the following table.

Asa		ac	20	Jeroboam
		1	21	
		2	22	
		3	ac1	Nadab
		4	2	
		5	ac1	Baasha
		~	~	
		25	21	
		26	22	
		27	23	
		28	24	
		29	ac1	Elah
		30	2	
		31	ac/**ac1**	Zimri/Omri

The same dating system also underlies Abijam's accession date.
Rehoboam is said to have reigned for 17 years (1K 14.21) before
being succeeded by Abijam in Jeroboam's 18th year (1K 15.1).
Since Rehoboam and Jeroboam came to power at virtually the
same time (Jeroboam's accession occurred shortly after Rehoboam's), Abijam's accession year necessarily follows Rehoboam's
last regnal year on this dating.

20. This was noted by Wellhausen (1875:614), but has generally been
overlooked in more recent studies, which usually postulate a 4-year period of civil
war between Omri and Tibni; two exceptions are Miller 1967:282 and Andersen
1969:81.

Rehoboam	I	I	Jeroboam
	~	~	
	17	17	
Abijam	ac I	**18**	

Differences between the three dating systems outlined above may be illustrated with a sequence of two hypothetical reigns dated according to each of the three systems.

(A)		(B)		(C)	
	I		I		I
	2		2		2
	3/ac		3/ac I		3
	I		2		ac I
	2		3		2
	3				3

Here it can be seen that in each of the first two systems the accession year of a new king is also the last year of his predecessor, whereas in the third system the accession year of a new king follows the last regnal year of his predecessor—which might seem to run counter to the common-sense assumption that a king will normally have acceded to the throne in the same year as, and shortly after, the death of his predecessor. On the other hand, the first and third systems agree in that the first year of the second king follows the last year of his predecessor, whereas in the second system the first year of the second king is identical with the last year of his predecessor. Finally the second and third systems both identify the accession year of the second king with his first regnal year, whereas the first system distinguishes between the year of accession and the first regnal year.

The first system is in fact the dating system used in Babylonia and Assyria during the first millennium BC. Under this system, generally known as 'postdating', the first year of a king's reign was not counted in that king's regnal total but was designated as his *rēš šarrūti* (literally 'beginning of reign'), and the first official year of reign began with the new year following a king's accession. The same system was evidently used in Judah in late pre-exilic times (see p. 179f.): this is the only dating system by which Biblical data on the reigns of Josiah's successors can be correlated with Babylonian historical evidence, and direct Hebrew equivalents of *rēš šarrūti* are found in four chronological notices associated with

Jehoiakim and Zedekiah, although two of these (Je 27.1; 28.1) are textually suspect and should therefore be disregarded as evidence of postdating.[21]

(Je 26.1)	בראשית ממלכות יהויקים	'in the beginning of the
(Je 27.1)	בראשית ממלכת יהויקם	reign of Jehoiakim'
(Je 28.1)	בראשית ממלכת צדקיה	'in the beginning of the
(Je 49.34)	בראשית מלכות צדקיה	reign of Zedekiah'

Assuming that these expressions are correctly interpreted as technical equivalents of *rēš šarrūti*, the close similarity between the Hebrew and Akkadian expressions may not unreasonably be taken to indicate that Judah borrowed the postdating system from Babylonia or Assyria.

Postdating contrasts with antedating, whereby a king's first regnal year is antedated to the new year preceding his accession and is therefore identical with his accession year. This system is known to have been used in Egypt (except during the New Kingdom, when regnal years were reckoned from the actual date of accession to each anniversary of that event) but it has the effect of creating an overlap between the last regnal year of one king and the first regnal year of his successor, as in the second of the three

---

21. LXX lacks Jeremiah 27.1 (which is obviously corrupt since the following narrative refers to events in the reign of *Zedekiah*) and has 'in the 4th year of Zedekiah king of Judah' in place of MT's 'in that year, in the beginning of the reign of Zedekiah, in the 4th year' in Jeremiah 28.1. A few Hebrew manuscripts along with the Syriac and Arabic versions have 'Zedekiah' instead of 'Jehoiakim' in 27.1, but this is almost certainly a secondary correction (note that the designation 'son of Josiah', which occurs in this verse, is more commonly used of Jehoiakim than Zedekiah: Je 1.3aα; 22.18; 25.1; 26.1; 35.1; 36.1; 9; 45.1; 46.2 [Jehoiakim]; Je 1.3aβ; 37.1 [Zedekiah]). MT's text of Jeremiah 27.1 probably results from assimilation to the date in 26.1; the original text presumably had 'in the 4th year of Zedekiah king of Judah' (cf. 28.1). This corruption also serves to explain MT's text of 28.1, which appears to have arisen through a conflation of *'in that year, in the 4th year of Zedekiah king of Judah' (cf. LXX) and the date now found in 27.1 (but with 'Jehoiakim' corrected to 'Zedekiah'). Tadmor's claim that ראשית ממלכת and its variants refer only to the early years of a king's reign in a general sense and do not have the specific meaning of *rēš šarrūti* in Babylonian texts (Tadmor 1965:353n.) cannot therefore be argued on the basis of Jeremiah 28.1. It should also be noted that the date given in Jeremiah 49.43, which according to Tadmor must also be interpreted in a general sense, relates to the prophecy itself and not to its fulfilment; besides, the events of 596 BC (Zedekiah's 2nd year), when the king of Elam retreated in the face of Nebuchadrezzar's army (*ABC* 5.rev.16–20), can hardly be viewed as more than a partial fulfilment of this prophecy.

dating systems noted earlier, thereby complicating the addition of successive reigns through the need to subtract 1 year for each overlap.[22] Egyptian chronologists resolved this problem by adopting the convention that a ruler's last unfinished year was to be excluded from his regnal total; thus Amenemhet I, whose date of death is given in the Story of Sinuhe as 'Year 30, 3rd month of Inundation, day 7' is ascribed only [2]9 regnal years in the Turin Canon (Gardiner 1945:22). Or taking a hypothetical example, a king who dies in the 4th year of his reign will under this system be credited with only 3 regnal years.

1

2

3

d(4)/ac1

2

3

It is obvious that this last scheme bears a rather close similarity to the third Biblical dating system illustrated earlier, and proof that the two systems are indeed identical is provided by LXX's chronology for the reigns of Abijam and Asa. LXX agrees with MT in ascribing Rehoboam a reign of 17 years and in dating Abijam's accession to Jeroboam's 18th regnal year; Abijam's first

---

22. The basic study of Egyptian dating systems is Gardiner 1945. Note that the New Kingdom method of counting regnal years from the actual date of accession effected a divorce between regnal years and calendar years, with the paradoxical result that 'Year 6, 3rd month of Inundation, day 23' might fall 364 days later than 'Year 6, 3rd month of Inundation, day 24' (see Gardiner 1945:23; this would be the case if day 24 was an accession anniversary). This confusing system was later abandoned with a return to antedating, either at the start of the Saite dynasty (Gardiner 1945:28) or during the Third Intermediate Period, between the end of the New Kingdom and the beginning of the Saite dynasty (Gardiner 1961:71). Theoretically the same system might also have been used in Israel or Judah, but there is no evidence to suggest that it was. Under this method of dating a king who died in his 3rd regnal year would actually have reigned 2 complete years and a fraction of a year, and a series of reigns which ended in the 3rd regnal year would presumably average out at $2\frac{1}{2}$ actual years. Given a series of reigns stated in round figures it would therefore be necessary to add or subtract half a year from each reign—depending on whether reign lengths were originally rounded up or down—in order to calculate overall totals. As applied to the chronology of Kings this simply creates a progressively worse series of discrepancies between reign lengths and synchronisms.

regnal year is thus equivalent to Jeroboam's 18th regnal year, as in MT's chronology, and his 6th regnal year must therefore correspond to the 23rd year of Jeroboam's reign (Abijam is ascribed a 6-year reign in LXX's chronology, and Asa's accession is dated to the 24th year of Jeroboam's reign). One might therefore suppose that Abijam's death will have occurred in Jeroboam's 23rd year, but LXX[BL] actually date Abijam's death to Jeroboam's 24th regnal year (1K 15.8; this synchronism is not given in MT). This obviously presupposes that Abijam died in the 7th year of his reign, although as in the Egyptian dating system described above, this final incomplete year is not included in his regnal total.

Abijam	**ac**1	**18**	Jeroboam
	2	19	
	3	20	
	4	21	
	5	22	
	6	23	
Asa	**d**(7)/**ac**1	**24**	

This modified form of antedating is essentially the converse of postdating, in which the incomplete *initial* year of a king's reign is excluded from his regnal total, and both systems may therefore be described as 'non-inclusive' dating systems. However, unlike postdating, non-inclusive antedating could only be applied retrospectively for the obvious reason that one would not normally be able to identify the final year of a king's reign until after that reign had ended; thus it is only in secondary chronological literature, as opposed to contemporary documents, that non-inclusive antedating exists as a third possibility alongside postdating and inclusive antedating.[23] The following table is a modified version of the table given on p. 85, which illustrates the differences between these various dating systems using our hypothetical sequence of two 3-year reigns.

23. Tadmor (1962:271–272) is, to my knowledge, the only scholar who has previously noted the relevance of non-inclusive antedating to the chronology of Kings, though he does not mention LXX's chronology of the reigns of Abijam and Asa in this connection.

Postdating	Inclusive Antedating	Non-inclusive Antedating
I	I	I
2	2	2
3/ac	3/ac I	3
I	2	(4)/ac I
2	3	2
3		3

The juxtaposition of all three dating systems in the chronology of Kings is one of the most striking features of this chronology, and stands in contrast to the rather more consistent use of postdating in Mesopotamia and inclusive or non-inclusive antedating in Egypt (where inclusive antedating was used in contemporary documents and non-inclusive antedating in secondary chronological literature). Admittedly, antedating was discontinued in Egypt during the New Kingdom in favour of a different dating system, and it is not unreasonable to suppose that similar changes of dating practice could have occurred in Israel and Judah. However, the repeated alternation of different dating systems in the chronology of Kings is most unlikely to have originated in this way. In MT's version of Judean chronology we have a switch from (non-inclusive) antedating to postdating on Asa's accession (as illustrated by previous tables), followed by a change to (inclusive) antedating for the reigns of Jehoram and Ahaziah, which is shown in the following table (note that since Ahaziah and Joram were both killed during Jehu's coup d'état, Ahaziah's first, and last, regnal year is necessarily equivalent to Joram's 12th and last year).

Jehoshaphat	ac	4	Ahab
	I	5	
	2	6	
	~	~	
	12	16	
	13	17	
	14	18	
	15	19	
	16	20	
	17	21	
	18	22	
	19	I	Ahaziah

	20	2	
	21	1	Joram
	22	2	
	23	3	
	24	4	
Jehoram	25/**ac**1	**5**	
	2	6	
	3	7	
	4	8	
	5	9	
	6	10	
	7	11	
Ahaziah	**ac**1/8	**12**	

This table disregards MT's accession synchronisms for Ahaziah of Israel and his successor, Joram, since these are inclusively antedated, whereas other chronological data in MT clearly presuppose a non-inclusive dating system—postdating or non-inclusive antedating—for the reigns of Ahaziah and Joram; also disregarded are MT's alternative accession dates for Joram (2nd year of Jehoram) and Ahaziah of Judah (11th year of Joram), as these belong to a different chronological system (which is more or less the same as LXX's chronology). The remainder of MT's data expresses a coherent chronological scheme, in which Ahaziah of Judah's reign is inclusively antedated and the same is apparently true of Jehoram's reign. (Theoretically one might shift Jehoshaphat's regnal years back 1 year, in which case Jehoshaphat's reign would be inclusively antedated, and Jehoram's reign non-inclusively antedated.)

Irregular alternation between antedating and postdating also continues after Jehu's revolt,[24] although contemporary changes in dating practice can hardly have occurred with this degree of frequency.[25] The alternation of different dating systems in the

24. See table on p. 141f. The majority of reigns during this period are non-inclusively antedated, but postdating is presupposed by accession synchronisms for Jeroboam II, Menahem, Ahaz, and Hezekiah.

25. Tadmor (1962:268–269) argues that the alternation of antedated and postdated reigns does not in fact reflect the use of different dating systems, but is the result of historically plausible departures from standard dating practice which allegedly occurred whenever a king's accession fell on a date close to the new year. In his view Israelite and Judean reigns were regularly antedated throughout the period of the divided monarchy, but a king who came to the throne shortly before the new year might decide to disregard the short interval between his accession and

chronology of Kings must therefore be attributed to various stages of chronological reworking, and here it may be noted that of the three dating systems found in this chronology, one (inclusive antedating) is fundamentally incompatible with a chronological scheme, such as the Deuteronomistic and Priestly chronologies, in which reign lengths are simply added together (under this system of dating, two consecutive 3-year reigns total 5 years, not 6). This basic discrepancy between Deuteronomistic chronology and one of the dating systems evidenced in Kings is a clear indication that the exilic Deuteronomistic chronologist took over and schematized an existing chronology; traces of inclusive antedating in the chronology of Kings may be regarded as vestiges of this original chronology, whereas instances of non-inclusive dating (postdating or non-inclusive antedating) which occur in alternation with inclusive antedating may be attributed to chronological reworking by the exilic Deuteronomistic chronologist or by later chronologists.

Further evidence that the chronology of Kings has undergone various stages of reworking is provided by the fact that MT and LXX present radically different chronologies for the period up to Jehu's revolt. The following table presents LXX's chronology for the period from Jehoshaphat's accession to Jehu's revolt, and may be compared with the table on p. 89f., which gave MT's chronology for the same period.[26]

the new year, and postpone his first regnal year until the start of the coming year. No evidence is offered to support this assertion, but the fact that Tiglathpileser III counted his first regnal year from the new year *preceding* his accession (on 13th Iyyar 745 BC) is cited as evidence for the converse possibility that in a society where reigns were normally postdated a king who came to the throne shortly after the new year might antedate his first regnal year to the beginning of that year. The two situations are not really comparable, however, since regnal dating was one of the ways in which a new king asserted his authority and it would therefore be surprising if a king were to postpone his first regnal year in the absence of the postdating convention of a zero accession-year, whereby the beginning of a king's reign could be used for dating purposes even though his first regnal year was counted from the following new year. Besides, Tiglathpileser's accession date (13th Iyyar) was not particularly close to the Babylonian new year (1st Nisan), and the fact that Tiglathpileser predated his first regnal year to the new year before his accession is more probably a consequence of the fact that he came to power after a period of anarchy which began during the previous year (according to the Eponym Chronicle the year preceding Tiglathpileser's accession was marked by a revolt in the Assyrian capital).

26. For reasons explained earlier (p. 37f.), LXX^L is taken as our main witness

Jehoshaphat	**ac**	**11**	
	1	12	
	2	**ac**1	Ahab
	~	~	
	22	21	
	23	22	
	24	**ac**1	Ahaziah
	25	2	
Jehoram	**1(2)**	**ac**1	Joram
	2	2	
	3	3	
	4	4	
	(**ac**)5	**5**	
	6	6	
	7	7	
	8	8	
	9	9	
	10	10	
Ahaziah	**ac**1	**11**	
Athaliah	1	12	
	2	**ac**1	Jehu

LXX's synchronism for Jehoram's accession (5th year of Joram: 2K 8.16) is identical with MT's accession synchronism and fits perfectly within the chronological scheme expressed by MT, but is obviously incompatible with LXX's own chronology. Conversely, however, MT's variant synchronism for Joram's accession (2nd year of Jehoram: 2K 1.17) conflicts with MT's chronology but is identical with LXX's accession synchronism and (nearly) agrees with LXX's chronology (it actually agrees perfectly with LXX's chronology up to this point if Jehoram's reign is inclusively antedated, but is incompatible with LXX's chronology beyond this point unless Jehoram's reign is extended by 1 year).[27] Similarly MT's variant synchronism for Ahaziah of Judah's accession (11th year of Jehoram: 2K 9.29) is incompatible with MT's chronology but agrees with LXX's chronology. The same is also true of MT's synchronism for Omri's accession (31st year of Asa), as can be seen if we extend our previous chronological table back to the beginning of Omri's reign.

to LXX's original chronology.

27. This is why Jehoram's original reign length has been reconstructed as *11 years rather than 10 years; see p. 130 for further discussion.

Asa	31	ac I	Omri
	~	~	
Jehoshaphat	41/ac	11	

All this clearly points to a degree of conflation of different chronological schemes in both MT and LXX. However, the fact that LXX's reign lengths for Abijam and Jehoram were not replaced by the Priestly figures found in MT might lead us to suppose that the dominant pattern of synchronisms found in LXX would be more original than the dominant pattern of synchronisms in MT. In fact the reverse appears to be the case: MT preserves many more instances of inclusive antedating than LXX,[28] and the secondary nature of LXX's pattern of synchronisms is also obvious from the fact that in LXX's chronology Ahaziah of Judah dies 1 year before Joram of Israel, and Jehu's accession is dated to the 2nd year of Athaliah's rule (according to 2 Kings 9f., Jehu assassinated both Joram and Ahaziah in close succession, and Athaliah seized power in Judah in the aftermath of this revolt). The chronology found in LXX should therefore be seen as a secondary reworking of Deuteronomistic chronology, in which synchronisms based on inclusive antedating and some synchronisms based on postdating were replaced by synchronisms presupposing non-inclusive antedating. This revision incorporated pre-Priestly figures for the reigns of Abijam and Jehoram, but was probably a post-Priestly development, since there is reason to think that it also incorporated Priestly data in its Israelite chronology of the early monarchic period (see p. 133f.). It is important to note that this revision is also represented in large sections of MT's chronology. For most of the early monarchic period MT and LXX contain radically different chronologies, and evidence of non-inclusive antedating is restricted to LXX's chronology; but during the short period up to (and including) Abijam's accession, and again after Jehu's revolt (or, more specifically, after Joash's accession) MT and LXX have virtually identical chronologies, and non-inclusive antedating predominates in both. These facts are easily accounted for: the chronological

28. Inclusive antedating is reflected in MT's accession dates for Nadab, Baasha, Elah, Zimri, Ahab, Ahaziah of Israel, Joram, Jehoram, Ahaziah of Judah, and Joash; only Nadab's and Baasha's accessions are dated this way in LXX (see tables on p. 125f. and p. 141f.).

revision reflected in LXX's chronology of the divided monarchy was also incorporated into the textual tradition behind MT *wherever it did not conflict with Priestly figures for Judean reign lengths*; thus the period in which MT's chronology diverges from LXX's chronology begins with the reign of Abijam and ends shortly after the death of Jehoram—the two Judean kings whose reign lengths were altered by Priestly chronologists.

We have now identified four stages of development behind existing versions of the chronology of Kings:

1. An original chronology incorporated into the pre-exilic edition of the Deuteronomistic History.
2. Deuteronomistic schematization of this chronology during the Babylonian exile.
3. Priestly adaptation of this Deuteronomistic schematized chronology.
4. A later revision of the chronology using non-inclusive antedating.

It is natural to ask where the original chronology was derived from. This question is fairly easy to answer on a superficial level: there can be little doubt that the Deuteronomistic historian derived most of his factual evidence for the monarchic period, including chronological data, from the two sources which are cited throughout Kings, 'the book of the chronicles of the kings of Israel' and 'the book of the chronicles of the kings of Judah' (ספר דברי הימים למלכי ישראל/יהודה). What is less certain, however, is whether these sources are to be regarded as official records or as literary compositions based on official records, and whether they contained reign lengths *and* synchronisms or reign lengths without synchronisms.

It is not my intention to enter into a detailed discussion of these matters, but there are a number of general points that are worth making. Firstly, one may question the usual assumption that the chronicles of the kings of Israel and Judah were literary compositions based on official records rather than original records. This assumption *may* be correct, but it is usually founded either on a priori judgements about the type of evidence that might have been available to the Deuteronomistic historian, or else on inferences drawn from material in Kings which is probably derived from these sources but may have been heavily reshaped by the Deuteronomistic historian. With one exception all Biblical references to 'chronicles' which are not merely stereotyped citation formulae clearly denote some kind of official record. Two of these occur in Esther, where we are told that a state execution for treason was included in 'the book of chronicles' (ספר דברי הימים: Est 2.23); and that King Xerxes, having turned to this 'book of chronicle records' (ספר הזכרנות דברי הימים) as a cure for insomnia, learnt how Mordecai had given information leading to the arrest of those involved (Est 6.1).[29] Outside of Esther we have one reference to a 'book of chronicles' which is apparently a genealogical document of some kind (Ne 12.23), and another reference in 1 Chronicles 27.24, stating that certain census figures were not entered 'in the account of the chronicles of King David' (במספר דברי הימים למלך דויד).[30] With the exception of Nehemiah 12.23 these passages clearly refer to an official court record similar to the Egyptian 'daybook', which is described by Van Seters (summarizing an unpublished study by Redford) as being 'the precisely dated daily record of activity in important institutions such as the court, the temple, the courts of law, and the necropolis.'[31]

The second question raised above concerns the origin of synchronisms between Israelite and Judean chronology: should we assume that the (original) Deuteronomistic historian took over reign lengths and synchronisms from his historical sources, or did these contain only reign lengths, from which the Deuteronomistic historian constructed his own synchronistic chronology? The issue is not of great importance for the present study. It is certainly possible that Israelite-Judean synchronisms are the work of the Deuteronomistic historian and did not exist in his sources. But it is also entirely possible that the latter derived both reign lengths and synchronisms from the chronicles of Israel and Judah: following

29. A third reference in Esther to 'the chronicles of the kings of Media and Persia' (10.2) is merely a stereotyped citation formula modelled after those in Kings.

30. מספר ('account') is probably a corruption of ספר ('book') by assimilation to the previous word, המספר ('the number'); cf. *BHS*.

31. Van Seters 1983:293. However, Van Seters goes on to assert that 'none of the Egyptian examples suggests a work containing a summary of the principal deeds of a series of kings, or even of each king, *such as the biblical references* [in Kings] *seem to indicate*' (my italics). This last remark is questionable: the book of Kings gives its own summary of the principal deeds of each king, and refers to the chronicles of the kings of Israel or Judah for further information about these, but there is nothing to suggest that these chronicles were themselves merely summaries of royal achievements.

the discovery of the Babylonian Chronicle series, in which Assyrian and Elamite reigns are synchronized with Babylonian chronology in precisely the same way that Israelite reigns are synchronized with Judean chronology (and vice versa) it is no longer possible to argue that nationalistic sentiments would necessarily have been opposed to sychronistic dating during the period of the divided monarchy (Wellhausen 1875:608–610). On balance, the fact that the state records of either kingdom will have had frequent cause to refer to relations (friendly or hostile) with the other kingdom increases the likelihood that some form of synchronistic dating existed from a comparatively early date.

The creative processes which produced the chronology of Kings are therefore significantly different from the creative processes behind the chronology of Judges and Samuel, and this has certain obvious implications for the study of Israelite and Judean history. The chronology of Judges and Samuel is a purely fictitious chronology which was constructed during the exile as part of a 1000-year scheme for Israel's existence in Canaan; as such it has no more historical validity than the antediluvian chronology of Genesis, and it is entirely fanciful to imagine that one can use it to calculate the date of the exodus or any other event in Israel's history. However, the chronology of Kings is a fictionalized, rather than a wholly fictional chronology, which originated in a historical chronology based on historical chronicles but was subsequently schematized by both Deuteronomistic and Priestly chronologists. Such a chronology is obviously not a reliable source of historical information, but it may nevertheless *contain* reliable information alongside fictionalized and unreliable data.

4

THE ORIGINAL CHRONOLOGY OF THE BOOK OF KINGS

4.1 *Problems and Solutions*

Discrepancies between the chronology of Kings and ancient near eastern historical chronology have been a source of puzzlement to Biblical scholars ever since the discovery and decipherment of ancient near eastern texts first drew attention to the problem. This discovery, however, merely compounded the difficulties already presented by the existence of serious internal discrepancies in Biblical chronology. On MT's figures Judean regnal years from the division of the kingdom to the fall of Samaria add up to 261 years (or 250 years if allowance is made for 1-year overlaps produced by inclusive antedating), while Israelite reigns for the same period add up to only 241 (or 226) years. This overall discrepancy results from various smaller discrepancies in the chronology of the two kingdoms, but there are also other discrepancies which do not affect the overall totals, including a number of striking cases where conflicting accession dates are given for the same king. Did Joram become king in the 18th year of Jehoshaphat (2K 3.1), or in the 2nd year of Jehoram (2K 1.17)? Did Hoshea come to the throne in the 20th year of Jotham (2K 15.30)—although the latter reigned for no more than 16 years according to 2 Kings 15.32—or in the 12th year of Ahaz (2K 17.1)? A third problem, to be set alongside the existence of internal discrepancies and external conflict with historical chronology is the considerable degree of textual disagreement over basic chronological data—resulting at times in radically different Biblical chronologies for the same period of history.

It will be obvious to those who have followed the arguments of the previous chapter that these different types of discrepancy are precisely what one would expect of a chronology which has undergone no fewer than three major revisions, two of which (the Deuteronomistic and Priestly revisions) were aimed at producing schematic totals within a larger framework of schematic chronology. It would be more surprising if the chronology of Kings in its various schematized and re-edited forms did not conflict with historical chronology, and it would also be surprising if these various stages of re-editing had not resulted in a number of internal discrepancies and textual variations. Conversely, however, the very existence of these discrepancies and contradictions offers us the possibility of recovering some part at least of the original chronology, and this chapter and the chapter which follows are largely devoted to this end. To set this in a wider perspective we may begin by looking at several alternative approaches to the problems outlined above.

One such approach, originating in pre-critical scholarship but influential to the present day, argues (or assumes) that some or possibly all of these discrepancies and contradictions are more apparent than real, and that scholarly effort should therefore be devoted to the task of harmonizing these apparent discrepancies. Since we are confronted with a significant overall discrepancy between Israelite and Judean reign lengths, two fairly obvious harmonizing devices are to suppose that Israelite chronology contains a number of gaps (or interregna), and is therefore longer than it seems, or else that Judean chronology contains a number of overlaps (coregencies etc.), and is therefore shorter than it appears. Either or both of these hypotheses may then be used to harmonize various lesser discrepancies; Ussher's scheme of Biblical chronology incorporated both.

The subsequent discovery that the chronology of Kings not only contained (apparent) internal discrepancies but was also (apparently) incompatible with ancient near eastern historical chronology did not deter exponents of this approach, but it certainly made their task much more difficult; and one important consequence has been that recent studies have largely had to abandon the use of interregna, as these tend to exacerbate the discrepancy between the chronology of Kings and historical chronology.[1] Two external synchronisms between the chronology

---

1. A few cases still survive. The 4-year period of civil war which is often invoked to explain the 4-year discrepancy between Omri's accession date and the death of his predecessor (see p. 83f.) is sometimes described as an interregnum, but since

of Kings and Assyrian chronology are provided by Ahab's participation in the battle of Qarqar in 853 BC and the Assyrian capture of Samaria in 723 or 722 BC. The historical interval between these events is 130 or 131 years, yet Israelite reign lengths from Ahaziah (Ahab's successor) to Hoshea (the last Israelite king) add up to 157 years if non-inclusively dated, or 148 years if inclusively antedated. Israelite chronology is clearly too long by historical standards, and can only be harmonized with historical chronology if we postulate a number of chronological overlaps in the form of coregencies or rival kingships. And since Judean reign lengths for this period are considerably in excess of Israelite reign lengths it will obviously be necessary to postulate a still greater number of overlapping years in the Judean chronology of Kings if this is to be harmonized also.

The use of chronological overlaps as a harmonizing device has been championed most notably by E. R. Thiele (1951, ²1965, ³1983), whose views have proven surprisingly influential across a wide spectrum of Biblical scholarship; but the overlap hypothesis has also been adopted to varying degrees by almost all who have attempted to reconstruct a historical chronology of Israel and Judah. Those who have made extensive use of this device—positing at least four overlaps (other than 1-year overlaps produced by inclusive antedating)—include J. Lewy (1927), Coucke (1928), Vogelstein (1944), Thiele (1951, ²1965, ³1983), Schedl (1962a), Tadmor (1962), Pavlovský and Vogt (1964), and Jepsen (1964); others, who have invoked overlaps more sparingly, include Wellhausen (1875), Kugler (1922), Begrich (1929a), Mowinckel (1932), Albright (1945), and Andersen (1969).[2] There is, however,

Omri's 12-year reign is nevertheless calculated from the start of this 4-year period there no gap in Israelite chronology at this point. A 2-year interregnum during the siege of Samaria is sometimes posited in order to harmonize a putative discrepancy between Israelite and Assyrian chronology—thus Wellhausen (1875:630), Lewy (1927:15f.), Begrich (1929a:103), Albright (1945:22), and Tadmor (1962:287). Finally, those who accept the date given in 2 Kings 18.10 for the capture of Samaria (6th year of Hezekiah) are also faced with a deficit of 2 to 3 years in Judean chronology beyond this point; Jepsen (1964:38) suggests the possibility of a 3-year interregnum after the death of Hezekiah as one way of resolving this.

2. In a recent study of the chronology of Kings, Hayes and Hooker (1988) deny that coregencies existed in Israel and Judah. But their chronology still contains several overlaps, since they argue that certain kings (Baasha, Asa, Joash, Amaziah, and Azariah) abdicated before their death, and that the regnal years of these kings continued to be counted after they had abdicated.

little or no direct Biblical evidence for the existence of overlapping reigns, and a number of scholars apparently regard the device as self-validating: it is possible to harmonize discrepancies in the chronology of Kings by hypothesizing overlaps; therefore these overlaps must have existed.

The hypothesization of overlaps in Biblical chronology has a long history, and it may therefore be appropriate to start by looking at a claimed 15-year overlap between Amaziah and Azariah, which was posited in traditional Jewish exegesis (*SOR* 19) and has since been adopted in essentially the same form by Lewy (1927:12f.), Vogelstein (1944:19), Tadmor (1962:282), and Jepsen (1964:38).[3] Biblical evidence for this theory rests on three verses. Firstly the statement that Azariah recaptured Elath 'after the king slept with his fathers' (2K 14.22) is taken to indicate that Azariah became king (and conducted military campaigns) *during* his father's lifetime. A second piece of evidence is provided by 2 Chronicles 25.27, which states that a conspiracy was formed against Amaziah 'shortly after (מעת אשר) he turned away from Yahweh': Amaziah's apostate adoption of Edomite gods (2C 25.14f.) preceded his defeat by Jehoash of Israel, so Amaziah must therefore have been deposed soon after that encounter, which presumably preceded Jeroboam's accession to the Israelite throne in Amaziah's 15th year (2K 14.23). 2 Kings 14.17, which states that Amaziah 'lived for 15 years after the death of Jehoash', offers a final piece of evidence: the fact that Amaziah is said to have *lived* (rather than *reigned*) for 15 years after Jehoash is supposedly an indication that he was deposed after his defeat by Jehoash and spent the last 15 years of his life as a private citizen.

This is hardly strong evidence. The statement that Azariah recaptured Elath 'after the king slept with his fathers' is neutral in regard to whether Azariah became king before or after the death of his father:[4] a Judean crown prince might presumably have been entrusted with military expeditions before he was yet king (just as Nebuchadrezzar was entrusted with military command during the

---

3. Variations involving an overlap of around 25 years have also been proposed (Thiele [3]1983:119., Schedl 1962a:97, and Pavlovský and Vogt 1964:331f.).

4. The phrase in question is quite probably a secondary addition, which appears to have been prompted by the fact that the statement on Azariah's recapture of Elath is (unusually) separated from the main account of his reign and could therefore suggest that Azariah's recapture of Elath preceded his accession.

last years of Nabopolassar's reign; *ABC* 4; 5). And 2 Kings 14.17 says nothing about Amaziah's status during the last 15 years of his life; if he was in fact deposed shortly after his defeat by Jehoash it is extraordinary that the book of Kings fails to mention this event. Besides, the notion that Amaziah reigned for only 14 years before he was deposed is in contradiction to the statement in 2 Kings 14.1 that Amaziah reigned for a total of 29 years, and Amaziah's ultimate assassination is somewhat curious if he had already been deposed 15 years earlier. Those who hold this view must also explain why 2 Kings 14.21 describes Azariah's accession as having followed the assassination of Amaziah; one rather drastic solution, proposed by Pavlovský and Vogt (1964:331), is to transpose verses 21 and 22 after verse 15 (similarly Thiele [3]1983:119), which amounts to an admission that the text as it stands is in direct contradiction to their adopted theory. This leaves us with the fact that 2 Chronicles 25.27 posits a close temporal connection between Amaziah's apostasy against Yahweh and the conspiracy which removed him from the throne. But since the Chronicler has almost certainly invented this apostasy as a theological explanation for Amaziah's defeat and later assassination one can hardly use this as historical evidence: the direct chronological connection between apostasy and assassination is simply a reflection of the direct theological connection posited by the Chronicler.[5]

A hypothetical overlap which rests on even flimsier evidence may be seen in the theory that Pekah reigned for 10 years in Gilead while Menahem was on the throne in Samaria.[6] Circumstantial evidence adduced by Thiele is as follows.

5. The theory of a 15-year overlap between Amaziah and Azariah was rightly criticized by Begrich (1929a:51–52), but was subsequently adopted by Jepsen in his revision of Begrich's chronology. This is not the only instance where Begrich offers pertinent criticism of views later adopted by Jepsen. It is also worth noting that although Jepsen took over many elements of Begrich's chronology, the theoretical basis of his own reconstruction was radically different: Begrich based his chronology on a complex reconstruction of different chronological systems which he believed were reflected in the textual evidence of MT and ancient translations (and which supposedly antedate the composition of Kings), whereas Jepsen—like Thiele—is primarily concerned to harmonize the maximum number of chronological data in MT.

6. See Thiele [2]1965:124f., [3]1983:129f., and Tadmor 1962:285; Lewy (1927:18f.) and Vogelstein (1944:19) propose a similar overlap but date the start of Pekah's rival kingship in the reign of Jeroboam.

1. It is one way of harmonizing the chronological data.
2. The fact that Shallum, whom Menahem deposed, is called 'the son of Jabesh' (2K 15.13) could indicate that he had Gileadite associations, Jabesh being a place name in Gilead; and Menahem's murder of Shallum might therefore have resulted in Gileadite support for a rival kingship to Menahem's.
3. Pekah did in fact have the help of fifty Gileadites in deposing Menahem's successor (2K 15.25).
4. The fact that Menahem paid tribute to Tiglathpileser III in order to gain Assyrian support for his reign (2K 15.19) indicates a degree of political insecurity that could have been occasioned by Pekah's rival kingship in Gilead.
5. During his reign in Gilead Pekah might have embarked on a policy of friendship with Syria on his northern border, and so laid the groundwork for the later Syro-Ephraimite alliance (2K 16.5f.).
6. The 'son of Tabeal' whom the Syro-Ephraimite alliance wished to place on the Judean throne (Is 7.6) was possibly a Transjordanian, for one 'Ayanur the Tabelite', who is mentioned in an Assyrian letter found at Nimrud, is said by Albright to have a name which is typical of the desert fringes of Palestine and Syria.
7. The fact that Hosea refers to 'Ephraim' alongside 'Israel' (Ho 5.5; 11.12; and elsewhere) is proof that two separate kingdoms existed in the north.[7]

These are the only arguments which Thiele offers in support of the theory of a rival Gileadite kingship, and they are a transparently inadequate basis for this theory. As far as Menahem's political insecurity is concerned there is little doubt that this was occasioned not by any hypothetical rival kingship in Gilead, but by the non-hypothetical presence of Tiglathpileser in western Syria. Assyrian royal annals repeatedly illustrate the fact that prompt payment of tribute was expected of all local rulers who had the misfortune to be in the vicinity of an Assyrian military expedition, whether or not they were previously vassals of Assyria; those who refuse to comply with Assyrian expectations are usually deposed. 2 Kings 15.19f. fits this picture exactly: Menahem is forced to pay

7. This curious argument appears in the third edition of Thiele's book. Most Biblical scholars see this as a straightforward case of synonymous parallelism (also found in Jeremiah 31.9).

tribute in order to maintain his position (verse 19) and secure the departure of Assyrian forces (verse 20); nothing is said of any rival Gileadite kingship. The possibility that Pekah could have exercised a rival kingship during Menahem's reign is in any case precluded by the fact that he is described as the 'personal adjutant' (שָׁלִישׁ) of Menahem's son and successor, Pekahiah (2K 15.25), since it is hardly credible that Pekahiah would have employed his father's political rival as his own personal adjutant, conveniently allowing the latter to depose him shortly after his accession.[8]

Neither of the two hypothetical overlaps discussed above can be described as a coregency in the normal sense of the word; but it is these which are usually invoked for the purpose of creating chronological overlaps. Now it is commonly supposed that two coregencies are explicitly attested in the Bible, since Solomon's accession is said to have occurred while David was still alive (1K 1.32f.), and Jotham is said to have assumed power after his father Azariah had contracted leprosy (2K 15.5f.). Taking Solomon's accession first it may be noted that none of our main difficulties with the chronology of Kings is in any way helped (or worsened) by the possible existence of a chronological overlap at this point; but the explicit attestation of even a single coregency might nonetheless help to justify the hypothesization of other coregencies where this is chronologically convenient. Actually the Biblical account offers little support for this. Solomon's accession took place while David was still alive, but this was at a time when David was already on his deathbed, and in response to an abortive attempt by Adonijah to secure the throne for himself in anticipation of David's death. This provides a fitting conclusion to the 'succession narrative' in 2 Samuel, but it is hardly to be interpreted as a typical picture of normal succession procedures; and it is also obvious that the coregency, if such it was, cannot have lasted for very long. It is doubtful, however, that Solomon's accession while David lay on his deathbed can be meaningfully described as a coregency. David gives instructions that Solomon is to be appointed as his successor, not as his coregent: 'then he shall enter (the palace) and sit upon my throne, and it is he who will be king in my place' (1K 1.35).

8. Thiele offers the following midrashic explanation (²1965:125): 'In the interests of joint resistance against Assyria, Pekah could have made his peace with Pekahiah at Menahem's death ... and been rewarded with a high military command by Samaria under the new king.'

The other passage which is widely believed to demonstrate the existence of coregencies actually provides significant disconfirmation of their existence. Contrary to what is often asserted, 2 Kings 15.5f. does not describe a coregency between Azariah and Jotham following Azariah's contraction of leprosy. What is actually described is a form of vice-regency in which Jotham took charge of affairs of state on Azariah's behalf but did not actually become king until Azariah's death. According to 2 Kings 15.5, Azariah 'dwelt in isolation quarters while Jotham the crown prince (בן המלך) was in charge of the palace, governing (שפט) the people of the land.' Only after Azariah's death did Jotham actually succeed to the throne (2K 15.7): 'and Azariah slept with his fathers, and they buried him with his fathers in the city of David, and Jotham his son became king in his place.' This procedure has close Mesopotamian parallels, since it was Mesopotamian practice for the crown prince to take charge of state affairs in his father's absence. One notable instance occurred during Nabonidus's extended absence in Tema, when (as administrative documents of the period indicate) affairs at Babylon were in the hands of the crown prince, Belshazzar. And although one Mesopotamian version of events states that Nabonidus 'entrusted the kingship' to Belshazzar,[9] it is clear that this did not involve an actual coregency, since the latter is invariably referred to as 'crown prince' (*mār šarri*, literally 'king's son' but often used in this more specialized sense) and never as king in contemporary documents.[10] Jotham, like Belshazzar, is also described as 'crown prince' rather than 'king' during his father's lifetime (בן המלך is the direct Hebrew equivalent of *mār šarri*), but Belshazzar unlike Jotham, never actually succeeded his father (being prevented by Cyrus's conquest of Babylon) and is therefore not included in Babylonian kinglists. This has serious implications for those who use coregencies as a device for harmonizing the chronology of Kings. 2 Kings 15.5f. is the one clear situation in Kings that might have called for a coregency, with Azariah being unable to carry out his royal duties, and yet the text of Kings plainly indicates that a coregency was not created. This must make

9. The Verse Account of Nabonidus 2.20 (= ANET p. 313).

10. This is in contrast to the fact that Belshazzar is regularly titled 'king' in the book of Daniel, which is apparently unaware of Nabonidus's existence; the latter appears to have been conflated with Nebuchadrezzar in Jewish traditions incorporated in Daniel—hence the historically erroneous idea that Nebuchadrezzar was Belshazzar's father (Dn 5.2 etc.).

it extremely doubtful that coregencies ever existed as a possible form of government in Israel or Judah. Finally the fact that Belshazzar is not included in Mesopotamian kinglists is evidence that years of vice-regency were not counted in Mesopotamian regnal chronology and are hardly likely to have been counted in Judean reign lengths (this being the obvious escape route for those who are determined to have a chronological overlap between Azariah and Jotham).[11]

Other alleged cases of coregencies in Biblical chronology are even less convincing, but it is perhaps worth noting one other example that is commonly cited. The Jewish chronicle *Seder Olam Rabba*, in contrast to most modern chronologists, does not postulate a coregency between Azariah and Jotham, but it does posit a 7-year overlap between Jehoshaphat and Jehoram. This is deduced from the fact that Joram of Israel's accession is dated in the 2nd year of Jehoram according to 2 Kings 1.17, but in the 19th year of Jehoshaphat (*sic*: *SOR* 17; MT and ancient translations have '18th year') according to 2 Kings 3.1. *Seder Olam Rabba* 17 explains this by saying that Jehoshaphat was originally destined to die at Ramoth Gilead, but was subsequently given 7 extra years, which were also counted in his son's reign (apparently because this was originally destined to begin 7 years earlier); Jehoram's 2nd year was therefore identical with Jehoshaphat's 19th year, although he did not properly begin to reign until the 5th year of Joram of Israel (2K 8.16).[12] This hypothetical overlap has since been taken over by a number of modern chronologists, although its midrashic explanation is dropped in favour of a straightforward coregency

11. Almost all modern chronologists have taken the existence of a coregency between Azariah and Jotham for granted, although Wellhausen (1875:633f.) and Mowinckel (1932:162) admit that this was not the view of the author, or redactor, of Kings. Thus Albright (1945:21n.) speaks of Jotham's '*attested* coregency with his father' (his emphasis), and Jepsen (1964:38) writes: 'Nun ist für Jotham eine lange Mitregentschaft anerkannt (sie ist ja ausdrücklich bezeugt).' Only Andersen (1969) avoids this assumption, though he subsequently follows Thiele in postulating a 4-year overlap between Jotham and Ahaz (see p. 112).

12. This 7-year reduction in Jehoram's actual reign is also reflected in *Seder Olam Rabba*'s total of 155 years from the foundation of the temple to its repair in the 23rd year of Joash (*SOR* 18). Coupled with a 15-year reduction in Amaziah's reign (see above), this brings the Judean regnal total from the division of the kingdom to the fall of Samaria down to 239 years instead of 261 years, which is roughly in line with Israelite chronology for the same period.

between Jehoshaphat and Jehoram. According to Thiele (³1983:
99f.) Jehoram became coregent in the 17th year of his father's reign
and succeeded him as sole ruler in the 5th year of Joram's reign.
Direct Biblical evidence for this theory is allegedly provided by 2
Kings 8.16 (Thiele ³1983:55, 1974:174), which apparently states
that Jehoram became king 'in the 5th year of Joram the son of
Ahab, king of Israel, *while Jehoshaphat was king of Judah*
(ויהושפט מלך יהודה).' However, this last phrase is omitted in
most LXX manuscripts (though it reappears, translated differently,
in LXXᴬᴮᴸ), and is almost certainly a dittography of בן) יהושפט)
מלך יהודה ('(son of) Jehoshaphat, king of Judah') within the
same verse. Besides, on Thiele's own interpretation the date given
in 2 Kings 8.16 marks the start of Jehoram's sole reign, *not* his
alleged coregency, so it is difficult to see how 2 Kings 8.16 offers
evidence of this coregency; it is obviously nonsensical to say that
Jehoram became sole ruler while his father was still king.[13] Thiele
confronts this problem by arguing that 'while Jehoshaphat was
king of Judah' is misplaced, and 'should properly have gone with a
synchronism of the commencement of Jehoram's coregency, which
began before Joram's accession in Israel' (Thiele ³1983:199). Other
modern chronologists who posit a coregency between Jehoshaphat
and Jehoram include Coucke (1928:1252), Begrich (1929a:109f.),
Schedl (1962a:98), Tadmor (1962:290f.), and Jepsen (1964:41).

One final and more general point which may be made
concerning the use of hypothetical overlaps to harmonize discrepancies between the chronology of Kings and the historical
chronology of the ancient near east is that it bears a suspicious
resemblence to the fundamentalist device of using hypothetical
gaps in order to harmonize discrepancies between the chronology
of Genesis and scientific chronology of the earth. Neither
procedure has any justification in the Biblical text, and the best that
can be said is that they represent highly unobvious ways of
interpreting Biblical chronology. As far as Kings is concerned it
must be said that if modern chronologists are right in hypothesizing chronological overlaps then the chronology of Kings is
seriously defective in its failure to state their existence: a
chronology which presents a series of reign lengths while omitting

13. The same objection applies to Lewy's use of this verse as evidence for a
coregency (Lewy 1927:21), although in Lewy's chronology Jehoram became
sole ruler during Jehoshaphat's lifetime.

to provide the crucial information that some of these reign lengths overlap, and by how much, is by itself virtually useless and can only be accounted for through ignorance or incompetence on the part of its author(s). Those scholars in conservative circles who have welcomed Thiele's chronological harmonizations may be less happy to accept this logical corollary.

The hypothesization of chronological overlaps is only one device in the harmonizer's toolkit, though it is certainly the most important. Other devices, such as ad hoc arrangements of different calendars and different dating systems, will be discussed in the following chapter; they are less widely accepted and are in any case used for fine tuning rather than major adjustments.[14] However, despite all the resources at their disposal no one has yet succeeded in harmonizing all the discrepancies in the chronology of Kings while accepting the historical constraints of ancient near eastern chronology. All recent reconstructions, including Thiele's, have therefore had to accept that some of the chronological data of Kings are simply erroneous, and the remainder of this section is devoted to a consideration of differing ways in which scholars have sought to account for this.

The most obvious way in which erroneous chronological data may be accounted for is through (accidental) textual corruption; but scholars have generally tended to adopt this explanation rather sparingly. Some of the reasons for this reluctance are stated by Begrich (1929a:63f.). Numerical corruption is relatively common in Greek and Latin textual traditions, but this is primarily because Greek and Latin texts commonly use numerical symbols (letters of the Greek and Roman alphabets) instead of writing numbers out in full, and the accidental alteration, duplication, or omission of a

---

14. One device which hardly merits discussion is Vogelstein's practice of inventing imaginary eras for the purposes of chronological harmonization. Here are two examples:

 1. An era of Hezekiah's reform (Vogelstein 1944:3) is posited in order to harmonize the statement that Samaria fell in Hezekiah's 6th year (2K 18.10) with the statement that Sennacherib invaded Judah in Hezekiah's 14th year (2K 18.13; according to Assyrian evidence more than 20 years separated these events): the second date is taken to mean the 14th year from Hezekiah's reform.
 2. An era of Assyrian rule (Vogelstein 1944:20) is posited in connection with Ahaz's accession date: according to Vogelstein the statement that Ahaz became king in Pekah's 17th year (2K 16.1), which is 733 BC in Vogelstein's chronology, really means that Ahaz's first year under Assyrian rule was Pekah's 17th year (his actual accession was some years earlier).

single symbol is thus sufficient to introduce a major corruption. There is, however, no evidence that numerical symbols were used in Hebrew literary texts from pre-Mishnaic times (although they are attested in certain non-literary texts such as ostraca and on weights), and there is therefore no reason to suppose that the numbers of the Hebrew Bible have not been fairly accurately transmitted as a rule. This is particularly likely to be the case with sets of interrelated numbers such as reign lengths and synchronisms, whereas a greater degree of corruption may naturally be expected in sets of unrelated figures.

Most scholars would nevertheless allow that some numerical corruptions could have occurred, and some would go further than others in this respect. Thus Schedl (1962a:91f.) posits a series of 'Zehnerverschreibungen', corruptions involving the addition of 10 or 20 years to the original figure: Ahaz originally came to the throne in the *7th (> 17th) year of Pekah and reigned for *6 (> 16) years; Pekah reigned for *10 (> 20) years, and Ahaz's successor Hezekiah became king at the age of *5 (> 25). However, when Pavlovský and Vogt (1964:337) adopted Schedl's corrections, they rejected his explanation of how the original numbers came to be altered. In their view this resulted from a series of deliberate chronological corrections by a later editor, who failed to recognize the existence of a 10-year coregency between Jotham and Azariah.

Numerical corruption on a more extensive scale was posited by Albright (1945:20f.), who argued that all Judean reign lengths from Athaliah to Ahaz—with the possible exception of Jotham's reign length—were textually corrupt, and that the same was true of various other Israelite and Judean reign lengths. On the other hand Albright also spoke of the 'astonishing accuracy' with which the numbers were transmitted after they had been incorporated in Kings (p.19), so that one can only suppose that they were transmitted with astonishing inaccuracy previous to that point. Even allowing for the possibility that numerical symbols could have been used in non-literary sources behind the chronology of Kings, numerical corruption on this scale seems improbable. The notion that oral tradition may ultimately be responsible for some of this corruption (n. 26) is also improbable, for there is no evidence or likelihood that regnal chronology was ever transmitted in this fashion.

It may be helpful to look at a few clear instances of textual corruption in a series of figures that is indirectly related to the chronology of Kings. Comparison of Judean accession ages in Kings and Chronicles reveals two numerical variants in the Hebrew text of Chronicles: Ahaziah is said to have been 42 rather than 22 when he became king (2C 22.2 : 2K 8.26) and Jehoiachin is said to have been 8 rather than 18 at his accession (2C 36.9 : 2K 24.8). In both instances the figure in Kings is to be preferred. Ahaziah cannot have been as old as 42 when he became king, if his father was 32 at his accession and reigned for *11 years (2K 8.17; 2C 21.5).[15] And Jehoiachin cannot have been only 8 years old when he became king if he was exiled *with his children* 3 months (or 3 months and 10 days) later (2K 24.8; 2C 36.9; Je 22.28). In Jehoiachin's case the corruption of '18' to '8' has resulted from the omission of עשרה ('10'), and thus belongs to a class of numerical corruptions (omission of tens in compound numerals) which is well attested in the Septuagint textual tradition: for instance LXX^A assigns Joram a reign of only 2 years in 2 Kings 1.18a, but agrees with other LXX manuscripts in reading '12 years' in 2 Kings 3.1. The corruption of '22 years' to '42 years' in 2 Chronicles 22.2 is a little more complex; but here LXX presents a third variant, '20 years', and MT's figure appears to represent a conflation of '20 years' and '22 years'. Similar conflation of variant figures is attested in the fact that LXX^i ascribes Abijam a reign of '6 and 3 years' in 1 Kings 15.2, whereas most other LXX manuscripts have either '6 years' or '3 years', but it must be said that this type of numerical corruption does not appear to be at all common in Greek manuscripts. By contrast, the variant '20 years' for Ahaziah's accession age represents one of the commonest types of numerical corruption in the Septuagint textual tradition (the omission of units from compound numerals): thus Jehoshaphat's accession age is reduced from 35 to 30 in LXX^{AN} in 2 Chronicles 20.31, while Manasseh's accession age is reduced from 12 to 10 in c_2e_2 in 2 Kings 21.1.

Pavlovský and Vogt's alternative explanation of Schedl's 'Zehnerverschreibungen' introduces a second way in which scholars have attempted to account for apparently erroneous data: these could have originated in erroneous calculations by the author of

15. MT gives '8 years' for Jehoram's reign length in both Kings and Chronicles, but I have argued elsewhere that this is a Priestly modification of the original figure; see pp. 37f., 58.

Kings, or by one of his predecessors, or by later editors. This explanation has proven to be popular with scholars of different persuasions, although conservative scholars have generally preferred to lay the blame on later editors rather than the author of Kings. For example, Thiele (^{2}1965:118–140, ^{3}1983:136–137), observing that chronological data which is problematic to modern scholars 'might well have provided similar problems to scholars of old, including late compilers of the Old Testament canon' (^{2}1965:133), posits a well-intentioned but misguided editor, 'a man who was deeply concerned about truth but did not understand all the truth' (^{2}1965:140). This ancient scholar, who evidently anticipated modern historical criticism by some two millennia, apparently noticed that certain parts of the chronology of Kings appeared to be 12 years in advance of their correct historical date, and therefore introduced what he thought were appropriate corrections. The problem, according to Thiele, was that this later editor was unaware of Jotham's 12-year coregency and Pekah's 12-year rival kingship.

Scholars of less conservative persuasions than Thiele have more readily taken the view that miscalculations in the chronology of Kings could have originated with the author of Kings or one of his predecessors. One widely adopted theory is that the author of Kings (or his predecessor) had access to sources containing Israelite and Judean reign lengths, but that he was forced to work out some or all of the synchronisms between Israelite and Judean chronology for himself, and in doing so he either failed to take account of coregencies,[16] or based his calculations on textually corrupt reign lengths.[17]

The problem with all these proposals is that they presuppose the existence of chronological overlaps or of extensive textual corruption, and are therefore vulnerable to the various arguments advanced earlier against these two hypotheses. A different miscalculation theory, put forward by Andersen (1969:91–107), is less seriously affected by this objection (it involves a single overlap, which is probably inessential) and therefore deserves more detailed consideration. Further reason for considering this theory is that it lies at the heart of Andersen's reconstruction of Israelite and

16. Wellhausen 1875:633f.; Begrich 1929a:109f.; Tadmor 1962:270; Jepsen 1964 45f.; Pavlovský and Vogt 1964:337.

17. Wellhausen 1875:630f.; Albright 1945:18f.

Judean chronology, which is adopted in a number of recent histories and Biblical commentaries.[18]

Andersen proposes a long series of scribal corrections and miscalculations radiating out from an initial alteration in Hezekiah's reign length. His starting point is Azariah's accession date (27th year of Jeroboam: 2K 15.1), which because it conflicts with all other chronological data in Kings is normally regarded as a textual error. Andersen does not consider this possibility; in his view the date must obviously represent a secondary calculation, and since it cannot be satisfactorily related to previous accession dates it must therefore have been calculated by counting backwards from Jotham's accession in Pekah's 2nd year (2K 15.32). There are, however, only 29 years between Jeroboam's 27th year and Pekah's 2nd year if we count up Israelite years on a non-inclusive dating system, and Andersen infers that Azariah, who is ascribed a reign of 52 years in 2 Kings 15.2, must therefore have reigned for only 29 years originally. This in turn necessitates an alteration in Jeroboam's reign length. On Andersen's reckoning Amaziah died in Jeroboam's 16th year,[19] which is therefore to be regarded as the original date of Azariah's accession. And since there are considerably more than 29 years from Jeroboam's 16th year (Azariah's original accession date) to Pekah's 2nd year (Jotham's accession date), Andersen accordingly reduces Jeroboam's reign from 41 to 32 years.

Why then were the reigns of Azariah and Jeroboam lengthened from their original durations? Andersen argues that this occurred in several stages. Following a 9-year increase in Jeroboam's reign (stage 1), and the subsequent alteration of Azariah's accession date, Azariah's reign was initially lengthened by 11 years (stage 2) in order to remove an 11-year discrepancy between Israelite and Judean chronology in the period from Jeroboam's accession to the

18. Two recent histories which use this chronology are Herrmann 1975 and Jagersma 1982; it is also adopted by Jones (1984) in his recent commentary on Kings. However, reservations are expressed by Herrmann (1975: 189,253) and Jones (1984:24), although the latter is incorrect in stating that Andersen's dates for Jehoash of Israel are incompatible with Assyrian evidence that Jehoash paid tribute in 796 BC: this reflects a confusion on Jones's part between Jehoash of Israel (who reigned from 799 to 784 BC according to Andersen) and his Judean namesake (836–797 BC in Andersen's chronology).

19. This date, which is calculated from Jeroboam's accession in Amaziah's 15th year, is dependent on Andersen's claim that Israelite and Judean kings officially acceded to the throne in their 2nd regnal year; see above, p. 82n.

2nd year of Pekah. Stage 3 occurred when a scribe noted the existence of a 12-year gap between Amaziah's death and Azariah's (secondarily calculated) accession date, and decided to remedy this discrepancy by adding 12 additional years to Amaziah's reign, which had the unintended effect of creating a 12-year surplus in Judean chronology. This leaves the 9-year increase in Jeroboam's reign length (stage 1) to be accounted for, and Andersen defers his explanation in order to take account of chronological problems relating to Azariah's and Jeroboam's successors.

The major historical problem in Israelite chronology for this period is Pekah's 20-year reign, which Andersen reduces to 12 years. Judean chronology presents a greater number of problems. Andersen starts from the fact that Sennacherib's campaign of 701 BC is dated to Hezekiah's 14th year in 2 Kings 18.13, and accordingly identifies Hezekiah's first year with 715/4 BC on an autumn calendar. This in turn necessitates a 4-year increase in Ahaz's reign length (16 years according to 2 Kings 16.2), since the latter was already on the throne in 734/3 BC (at the start of the Syro-Ephraimite war), and also requires a 10-year reduction in Hezekiah's reign (29 years according to 2 Kings 18.2), since Manasseh's accession is to be dated to 697/6 BC if we count back from Josiah's death in 609 BC using a non-inclusive dating system.[20] Andersen also reduces Jotham's reign from 16 to 8 years, having previously arrived at 741/0 BC as the date of Azariah's death.

At this point Andersen, uncharacteristically, resolves the 4-year discrepancy in Ahaz's reign length by adopting Thiele's theory that Jotham was deposed 4 years before his death, but continued to be regarded as the legitimate king in anti-Assyrian circles, who therefore dated the start of Ahaz's reign from Jotham's death in 730/29 BC. However, he is not prepared to follow Thiele in positing coregencies for Jotham and Hezekiah. The 10-year discrepancy in Hezekiah's reign length originated (according to Andersen) when the story of Hezekiah's illness (2K 20) was secondarily attached to the account of Sennacherib's campaign of 701 BC. This prophetic legend, in which Yahweh promises to add 15 years to Hezekiah's life, is itself undated but could reasonably be linked to the events of 711 BC, when Sargon put down a rebellion in Ashdod. However, once the story had been secondarily appended to the account of

---

20. In Andersen's opinion postdating and the spring new year calendar were adopted at the start of Manasseh's reign (Andersen 1969:100f.)

Sennacherib's campaign in Hezekiah's 14th year, the promise of 15 additional years necessarily required that Hezekiah's reign be extended from *19 to 29 (14 + 15) years. This 10-year increase over Hezekiah's original reign length then resulted, according to Andersen, in Hezekiah's accession being put back by 10 years, and a new accession date (3rd year of Hoshea) was accordingly calculated by counting 10 years back from the end of Ahaz's reign. It should be noted that these alterations to Hezekiah's reign length and accession date were in reality rather illogical: if, as Andersen claims, the scribe responsible for these corrections avoided lowering Hezekiah's death by 10 years (this being the obvious consequence of not raising his accession date) because he knew that Hezekiah had in fact died 5 years after Sennacherib's campaign, why did this scribe not correct the promise of 15 additional years to a promise of 5 additional years? This would then have obviated any need to alter Hezekiah's original reign length and accession date.

Whatever reasoning lay behind it, the alteration of Hezekiah's accession date led to a string of further alterations by a series of muddle-headed correctors. Initially it created a 10-year overlap between Ahaz and Hezekiah, which was subsequently corrected by lowering Hoshea's accession from Ahaz's 5th year to Ahaz's 12th year. (Why not Ahaz's 15th year? Andersen's explanation is that the corrector was influenced by 2 Kings 15.30, in which Hoshea's accession was—in Andersen's opinion—originally dated to Jotham's 12th year.) This then created a 7- or 8-year gap in Israelite chronology between Pekah's last year and Hoshea's accession, which contributed to a 9-year surplus in Judean chronology from Azariah's accession to Ahaz's 12th year. A scribe who noticed this surplus attempted to rectify matters and inappropriately added 9 years to Jeroboam's reign, thereby creating an 11-year surplus in *Israelite* chronology from Jeroboam's accession to the 2nd year of Pekah; a later corrector therefore added 11 years to Azariah's reign, which was subsequently increased by a further 12 years when it was (mistakenly) supposed that this would resolve a discrepancy between Azariah's accession date (secondarily calculated after the addition of 9 years to Jeroboam's reign length) and the end of Amaziah's reign. This last increase necessitated further alterations in the accession dates of Azariah's Israelite contemporaries, which ultimately resulted in a 12-year gap between Jeroboam's last year and Zechariah's accession date. All this did nothing to resolve the

gap in Israelite chronology between Pekah and Hoshea, which was
finally filled by the addition of 8 years to Pekah's reign, only to be
recreated when an apparently incompetent corrector proceeded to
lower Ahaz's accession by the same amount, and thereby also
created a second 8-year gap between Jotham and Ahaz. This
second gap was removed by the addition of 8 years to Jotham's
reign, but at this point the correction process abruptly ended,
leaving the chronology of Kings in its present condition. Andersen
does not speculate on whether the correctors finally gave up the
struggle or were overtaken by the restraints of canonization.

It will be clear from this (simplified) summary that Andersen's
reconstruction of this crucial period of Israelite and Judean
chronology is based upon an extremely complex literary-historical
hypothesis, which posits an elaborate series of corrections and
miscalculations, and requires us to ascribe a high degree of
incompetence to their hypothetical perpetrators. The complexity
and inherent implausibility of this hypothesis should therefore be
set against the apparent simplicity of Andersen's chronology in
certain other respects noted by Herrmann (1975:188f.) and others;
these include the absence of coregencies and the assumption that
both kingdoms used the same calendar and dating system during
the period of the divided monarchy.[21]

Twentieth-century study of the chronology of Kings has largely
followed the three basic approaches outlined above, in which
chronological discrepancies are either explained as textual corruptions or chronological miscalculations, or explained away by
various methods of chronological harmonization. However, all
these approaches miss one significant fact about the chronology of
Kings: in its present form this chronology is transparently
schematic. This was pointed out in the last century by Wellhausen
(1875:621n.), who observed that Judean regnal years from Solomon's 4th year (when the temple was founded) to the exile total
430, and that 430 plus 50 years from the foundation of the temple to
the end of the exile are balanced by an identical period of 480 years
from the exodus to the foundation of the temple (1K 6.1).
Wellhausen did not in this article draw any explicit connection
between this schematism and the historical inaccuracy of the

---

21. Herrmann (1975:188) is incorrect in stating that Andersen presupposes a
single calendar and dating system throughout the entire monarchic period (see
p. 112n.).

chronology of Kings. A year later, however, in a review of *The Assyrian Eponym Canon* by George Smith, Wellhausen remarked that Judean reign lengths in Kings 'bis zu einem gewissen Grade systematisirt sind' (Wellhausen 1876:54) and that there was therefore no doubt that historical preference should be given to Assyrian chronological data.

Wellhausen's observation that Judean chronology was 'to some extent systematized' was carried a good deal further by Krey (1877), who argued in a short but influential article that *Israelite* chronology displayed an elaborate internal schematism within an overall schematic total of 240 years, and soon afterwards discovered evidence of internal schematism in Judean chronology as well (see Wellhausen 1878:265). Krey's theories were fully endorsed, with minor modifications, by Wellhausen (ibid. and additional note to Krey's article), but they are not in fact very convincing. The 240-year total for Israelite chronology required that the 7 months ascribed to Zechariah and Shallum be counted as a whole year and that Elah's 2-year reign be omitted (Wellhausen preferred to deduct 2 years from Baasha's reign), and these arbitrary adjustments are also crucial to the alleged internal schematism, for it is only on this basis that Israelite chronology divides into two periods comprising 96 (8 × 12) years before Jehu's revolt and 144 (12 × 12) years after Jehu's revolt. The claimed internal schematism of Judean chronology is even less impressive, as it consists of nothing more than a demonstration that one may arbitrarily divide MT's Judean reign lengths into groups of approximately 20, 40, or 80 years: Rehoboam and Abijam, 20 years; Asa, 41 years; Jehoshaphat, Jehoram, Ahaziah, and Athaliah, 40 years; Joash, 40 years; Amaziah and Azariah, 81 years; Jotham, Ahaz, and Hezekiah (to the fall of Samaria), 38 years; Hezekiah (from the fall of Samaria), Manasseh, and Amon, 80 years; Josiah, Jehoahaz, Jehoiakim, and Jehoiachin (to release from detention), $79\frac{1}{4}$ years. It is to be noted that this alleged internal schematism cuts across the overall schematism of 480 years from the foundation of the temple to the end of the exile, and that the 40 years ascribed to Jehoshaphat, Jehoram, Ahaziah, and Athaliah is dependent on Athaliah being assigned 6 years instead of the 7 years implied by 2 Kings 11.4 (Athaliah's reign terminates 'in the 7th year').

A detailed refutation of Krey's theories was provided by Kamphausen (1883:7–15, 50–76), who demonstrated their arbitrary nature by making similar numerical play with French reign lengths. However, Kamphausen did not dispute the existence of the 960-year schematism noted by Wellhausen, although he considered it possible that the second 480-year period (from the foundation of the temple to the end of the exile) had originated through an accidental sequence of scribal corruptions (p. 54n.). Alternatively, and more plausibly, he conceded that a limited number of Judean reign lengths might have been deliberately altered by post-exilic scribes in order to achieve this schematic total (p. 53).

In contrast to Kamphausen's reluctant admission that post-exilic scribes might have deliberately altered a number of Judean reign lengths to produce the chronological schematism noted by Wellhausen, Begrich (1929a: 14–16) categorically denied that any such schematism existed. It was, he thought, curious that the book of Kings should end with Jehoiachin's release from detention if its alleged chronological schematism extended to the end of the exile. However, the conclusive disproof in Begrich's eyes was the fact that the second 480-year period claimed by Wellhausen pre-supposes the consecutive addition of Judean reign lengths, which is contrary to evidence that earlier reigns were dated inclusively and therefore require the subtraction of 1-year overlaps for each successive reign; the fact that consecutive addition produces this apparent schematism, with 480 years from the foundation of the temple to the return from exile mirroring the 480-year period from the exodus to the foundation of Solomon's temple was dismissed by Begrich as an odd coincidence. This is scarcely convincing. The schematic pattern of 2 × 480 years from the exodus to the return from exile (or, rather, to the foundation of the second temple) has been discussed earlier (p. 39f.); and I have noted that this pattern is only part of a wider schematic chronology which contains a similar pattern of 2 × 290 years from the flood to the entry into Egypt, and that it also possesses a chiastic symmetry whereby the exodus and the erection of the tabernacle occur 480 and 479 years before the foundation of the first temple, while the return from exile and the foundation of the second temple occur 479 and 480 years after the foundation of the first temple. This can hardly be dismissed as a coincidence; and in any case Begrich's objections fail to take account of the basic force of Kamphausen's observation that the chronology of Kings might have been secondarily altered in the post-exilic period. Whatever dating method was originally used by the author of Kings or his predecessors is quite irrelevant to the way in which post-exilic scribes totalled Judean reigns; given Begrich's own belief that postdating replaced antedating in the later period of the Judean monarchy (Begrich 1929a:93, 126),[22] one would naturally expect that post-exilic scribes would have counted reigns non-inclusively.[23] The possibility that later editors used a different dating system from that used by contemporary chronologists was clear enough to Kugler (1922:161–162), who argued that the 480-year period from the foundation of the temple to the end of the exile was the creation of a post-exilic editor; this editor, in contrast to the original author of Kings, presupposed postdating, and also held a 'mystical' belief in the periodic recurrence of important historical events. However, Kugler was unwilling, for theological reasons, to accept that this post-exilic editor had deliberately falsified the chronology; in his view the person responsible for this schematism was merely attempting, in the absence of historical evidence, to restore a number of figures which had been accidentally corrupted.

Studies of the chronology of Kings written since 1929 almost invariably refer to Begrich (1929a) for discussion of studies written before that date, and Begrich's rejection of Wellhausen's views on the schematic nature of Judean chronology has consequently gained uncritical acceptance in most subsequent scholarship.[24] One scholar who did not accept Begrich's objections was Mowinckel, whose own study of the chronology of Kings (Mowinckel 1932) is for this reason one of the more significant studies produced during

22. According to Begrich, postdating was adopted in Judah at the start of Ahaz's reign.

23. Begrich's failure to take account of the possibility that later editors may have operated with different dating systems from those used by earlier chronologists vitiates much of his own reconstruction: many of the alleged discrepancies between reign lengths and synchronisms which Begrich discovers, and on which his reconstruction depends, stem from his attempt to impose a uniform dating system (inclusive antedating or postdating) on all chronological data for a given historical period.

24. It should be noted that Begrich failed to distinguish between Wellhausen's original observation that Judean reigns had been schematized to produce a 480-year total for the period from the foundation of the temple to the return from exile, and his subsequent endorsement of the theories of Krey; this confusion is further compounded by the fact that Begrich mistakenly credits Krey with having first drawn attention to the 2 × 480 year pattern noted by Wellhausen (Begrich 1929a:11).

the present century.[25] Mowinckel recognized that the 480-year period (430 + 50 years) from the foundation of the temple was clearly artificial, and that a number of Judean reign lengths must have been deliberately altered to produce this result (p. 167f.). He also followed Wellhausen in rejecting the arbitrary invention of coregencies for harmonistic reasons, although like Wellhausen he accepted the existence of a coregency between Azariah and Jotham. However, while Wellhausen had dismissed Israelite-Judean synchronisms as secondary and of no historical value, Mowinckel believed that the synchronisms were an original feature of the chronology and were therefore of considerable importance, especially as they were less easily altered than reign lengths and might therefore preserve evidence of a pre-schematic form of the chronology (p. 170f.).

Mowinckel's recognition of the importance of synchronisms in reconstructing a pre-schematic form of the chronology of Kings represented an important advance on previous studies.[26] There are, however, a number of shortcomings in Mowinckel's study, most obviously in his use of textual evidence. On the one hand Mowinckel rejected the important chronological variants given by Josephus—which had been utilized by Lewy (1927)—roundly asserting that Josephus 'hat weder eine hebräische Textrezension noch die Septuaginta benutzt, sondern eine midraschisch erweiterte griechisch geschriebene Quelle, die die alexandrinische Schulweisheit und nur indirekt die Septuaginta (G) wiedergab' (p. 163); but on the other hand he was prepared to adopt minority readings that are attested in a handful of Septuagint minuscules and are far more likely to represent secondary corrections (or corruptions) than original LXX variants.[27] One should also take

25. Contrast Albright's statement that Mowinckel's study 'contains a number of excellent points, but does not represent any general development of theory' (Albright 1945:17).

26. Mowinckel (1932:163) tells us that he reached his conclusions on the value of Israelite-Judean synchronisms independently of Lewy (1927:7f.), who had argued for their originality from the presence of synchronistic dating in the Babylonian Chronicle. It is a pity that Lewy was (apparently) unaware of Wellhausen's observations on the schematic nature of Judean chronology, for he was close to Mowinckel's position in arguing that reign lengths may sometimes have been rounded off secondarily, and that synchronisms were therefore of greater historical value (Lewy 1927:9).

27. The worst example of this is Mowinckel's claim that '20 years', which is attested in 2 Kings 15.17 in two (non-Lucianic) minuscules, is the original

issue with Mowinckel's claim that the narrative order of reigns in the book of Kings derived 'aller Wahrscheinlichkeit nicht von dem [Redaktor des deuteronomistischen Geschichtswerkes], sondern von der Quelle' (p. 165), and that historical reconstructions of Israelite and Judean chronology should therefore preserve this sequence; Mowinckel offers no evidence for this assertion, and the fact that MT and LXX present different sequences for the early period of the divided monarchy is clear evidence that chronological revisers were perfectly capable of altering the narrative sequence of Israelite and Judean reigns to fit in with their revised chronologies. Finally it is to be noted that Mowinckel, like Wellhausen, mistakenly regarded the Priestly schematism of 480 years from the foundation of the temple to the end of the exile (and the foundation of the second temple) as a Deuteronomistic construction, and thereby overlooked the existence of an earlier and genuinely Deuteronomistic schematism of 480 years from David's accession to the exile.

Mowinckel's study of the chronology of Kings had little impact on subsequent research, which continued to disregard evidence of chronological schematism in Kings, and the same fate later befell a study by Wifall (1968), which argued that the original chronology of Kings was artificially constructed within a schematic total of 480 years from Saul to the exile, but which is referred to by Jagersma (1982:126) as having merely argued that postdating was used in both kingdoms from the death of Solomon. Even this is inaccurate, however: Wifall makes no comment on whether postdating or antedating was used officially by either kingdom; his argument is rather that the original compiler of Kings presupposed postdating when he constructed his chronology.

Wifall's study is significant in two respects: Wifall is one of the

Deuteronomistic figure for Menahem's reign length (Mowinckel 1932:245). It is not at all clear to me why Begrich, on whose list of variants Mowinckel depends, chose to cite this particular variant but omitted other (equally insignificant) variants. For example, Menahem's reign is given as '12 years' in one other minuscule (c_2), which is close to Mowinckel's figure of 13 years for Menahem's *actual* reign length, but this variant is omitted by Begrich, who also omits to mention that Pekahiah reigned for 12 years according to LXX[N] and 12 minuscules listed in the Cambridge Septuagint, and that Pekah reigned for 28 years according to six minuscules, or 30 years according to c_2. The mass of secondary variants at this point in the chronology is almost certainly the result of diverse attempts to harmonize a number of serious internal discrepancies between reign lengths and synchronisms.

few scholars since Mowinckel to have argued that the chronology of Kings is fundamentally schematic, and he is also one of
the first scholars to have recognized the importance of Lucianic
chronological data. However, Wifall's reconstruction of the original chronology of Kings and its subsequent modifications is
built upon shaky foundations. In the first place, Wifall confuses
postdating, whereby a king accedes to the throne in the year
before his first official year, and other non-inclusive dating
systems (such as non-inclusive antedating) in which a king's
accession year is identical with his first regnal year. This is clear
from his remarks on p. 329: 'the synchronisms in II Reg
18_{9-12}—4 Hezekiah equals 7 Hoshea and 6 Hezekiah equals 9
Hoshea—presuppose that Hezekiah came to power in the fourth
year of Hoshea. However, the synchronism in II Reg 18_1 (MT)
gives Hezekiah 3 Hoshea ... The implied reading of the siege
account of II Reg 18_{9-12}—Hezekiah 4 Hoshea—is the synchronism expected by postdating.' On the contrary, the synchronisms
in 2 Kings 18.9–12 presuppose no more than that Hezekiah's first
year is equivalent to Hoshea's 4th year, and the synchronism in 2
Kings 18.1 (Hezekiah becomes king in Hoshea's 3rd year) is
precisely the synchronism one would expect if Hezekiah's reign
is postdated: Hezekiah becomes king in the year preceding his
first regnal year.

This is not an isolated misunderstanding on Wifall's part.
Wifall bases his reconstruction of the original Deuteronomistic
chronology primarily on the Lucianic minuscule c_2, whose chronology is fundamentally different from that of other Lucianic
manuscripts. However, c_2 does not reflect postdating, as Wifall
supposes, but a quite different dating system which is superficially
similar to non-inclusive antedating, except that in this system a
new king accedes to the throne in the year after the death of his
predecessor (in non-inclusive antedating a king accedes to the
throne in the same year as the death of his predecessor, but this
year is deducted from the first king's total). c_2's data for the reign
of Abijam and the accession of Asa are given below.

> 1K 15.1–2   Abijam becomes king in Jeroboam's 18th year and
>   reigns for 3 years.
> 1K 15.8   Abijam dies in Jeroboam's 20th year.
> 1K 15.9   Asa becomes king in Jeroboam's 21st year.

This may be tabulated as follows (contrast my earlier table of LXX^{BL}'s chronology for the same period on p. 88).

Abijam	**ac**1	**18**	Jeroboam
	2	19	
	d3	**20**	
Asa	**ac**1	**21**	

The artificiality of the dating system reflected in this chronology is evident from the fact that unless Abijam and successive kings regularly died on new year's eve there must inevitably have been a gap of several days or months between their death and the accession of their successor.[28] The chronology of c_2 has no analogies with chronological practice in either Mesopotamia or Egypt, and is simply a late reworking of Lucianic chronology that has also incorporated a certain amount of non-Lucianic data (in the original Lucianic chronology Abijam reigns for 6 years, not 3). It cannot therefore be used as a key to the original Deuteronomistic chronology.

The present study continues the approach of Wellhausen and Mowinckel. The evidence for a 960-year schematism centred upon the foundation of the Solomonic temple—480 years from the exodus to the foundation of Solomon's temple plus 480 years from the foundation of Solomon's temple to the foundation of the second temple—is (in my view) incontrovertible, and must obviously reflect deliberate modifications to the chronology of Kings in post-exilic times. However, this schematism is not the work of a Deuteronomistic redactor, as Wellhausen and Mowinckel supposed, but is rather to be ascribed to Priestly circles, who sought to create a world chronology from creation to the foundation of the second temple. Underlying this Priestly schematism is an earlier schematic pattern of $480+40+480$ years from the settlement to the Babylonian exile, which is still largely preserved in Judges–Samuel and in the Septuagint chronology of Kings, and which may reasonably be ascribed to the exilic Deuteronomist (or Deuteronomistic school) who revised the original (pre-exilic)

28. The artificial nature of this system has previously been noted by Thiele (1951:186) and Shenkel (1968:28). Shenkel points out that Thiele was mistaken in thinking that Septuagint chronology (apart from c_2) reflects this dating system; but Shenkel is himself mistaken in thinking that Septuagint chronology reflects postdating (it actually reflects non-inclusive antedating for the most part).

Deuteronomistic History. Behind *this* schematism are traces of an earlier chronology, such as synchronisms which reflect inclusive antedating and are therefore incompatible with the non-inclusive reckoning of later schematizers.

It is this original chronology, apparently based on authentic historical records, which must obviously be of primary interest to historians. However, the task of reconstructing this original chronology is dependent on our ability to penetrate behind successive stages of schematization and re-editing. In this respect the variant chronological data of the Septuagint and Josephus can provide important evidence; while additional evidence is provided by internal discrepancies in the chronology of MT and other textual witnesses, in so far as these discrepancies are attributable to the inadequate re-editing of earlier data or to the secondary incorporation of earlier data from unrevised manuscript families. Both types of evidence are considered in the remaining sections of this chapter, which attempt to reconstruct what one can of the original chronology on an essentially literary-historical basis; the following chapter uses external historical evidence to supplement this internal reconstruction and translate it into a historical chronology of the Israelite and Judean kingdoms. I have also made limited use of historical evidence in the present chapter in order to identify schematized data and distinguish these from variant data which may be non-schematic, but I have avoided using historical evidence in this chapter as a basis for reconstructing the original chronology.[29]

4.2 *Internal evidence of pre-schematic chronology*

4.2.1 *From the division of the kingdom to Jehu's revolt*

The chronology of the early period of the divided monarchy has been the subject of some discussion in recent years, partly as a result of renewed interest in textual criticism. At present this

29. There is nothing to be gained by maintaining a completely rigid separation of (internal) literary-historical evidence and (external) historical evidence: the existence of external discrepancies between the chronology of Kings and historical chronology is the result of internal chronological schematization, and it is therefore reasonable that these discrepancies should be used to help identify chronological data that may have been modified for schematic purposes.

discussion is largely polarized into two camps, with one side (Thiele 1951:167–203, 1974; Gooding 1970; Green 1983; Hayes and Hooker 1988:15) claiming that MT has preserved the original chronology, while the opposing camp (Miller 1967; Shenkel 1968) asserts that LXX has preserved the more original chronology. My own view is that both sides are mistaken: LXX's reign lengths for Abijam and Jehoram are more original than MT's (Priestly) figures (see p. 58f.), but LXX's synchronisms reflect a late chronological revision that is largely absent from MT's chronology of this period (see p. 93f.).[30] Neither text preserves the original chronology of Kings, or even the original schematized version of this chronology; but evidence from both texts is crucial to any attempt to reconstruct the original chronology. We may therefore begin by listing the chronological data of MT and LXX[BL].[31] Note that LXX[B] and LXX[L] present largely identical data for most of 1 Kings, but from 1 Kings 22, where the original LXX text is replaced by the Kaige recension in LXX[B] and other non-Lucianic manuscripts, LXX[B]'s chronology is virtually identical with MT's chronology (the only notable exception being Jehoram's reign length).

1K 12.24a   Rehoboam reigns for 12 (B) / 17 (L) years.
1K 14.20   Jeroboam reigns for 22 years (MT).
1K 14.21   Rehoboam reigns for 17 years.

30. This is virtually the opposite of Miller's position. Miller (1967) argues that LXX[L]'s synchronisms are with one exception (1K 15.9) more original than MT's, but at the same time he rejects LXX[BL]'s figure of 6 years for Abijam's reign (p. 281n., where we are told that 'some of the recensions [!] expand Abijah's reign from three to six years'), and is unaware of LXX[L]'s figure of 10 years for Jehoram's reign (ibid.: 'with the exception of the reigns of Abijah and Pekahiah, the regnal periods recorded in the Septuagint agree with those recorded in the masoretic text.'). This rather serious oversight in respect of Jehoram's reign length would appear to indicate that Miller is dependent on Burney's table of chronological variants (Burney 1903:xliif.), for Burney, who probably relied upon Lagarde's reconstruction of the Lucianic text (Lagarde 1883), gives the Lucianic figure for Jehoram's reign as 8 years. This figure is indeed found in two closely related Lucianic manuscripts that are subsumed under the siglum 'b' in the Cambridge Septuagint; but the true Lucianic reading ('10 years') is given by all other Lucianic manuscripts (oc_2e_2).

31. This list also includes a single variant from Josephus (*Ant* 8.312); Josephus's chronological data for the early divided monarchy are otherwise identical with data in MT (see appendix B), although it must be said that Josephus gives relatively few accession dates for this period.

1K 14.25   Shishak attacks Jerusalem in Rehoboam's 5th year.

1K 15.1–2   Abijam becomes king in Jeroboam's 18th year and reigns for 3 (MT) / 6 (BL) years.

1K 15.8   Abijam dies in Jeroboam's 24th year (BL).

1K 15.9–10 Asa becomes king in Jeroboam's 20th (MT) / 24th (BL) year and reigns for 41 years.

1K 15.25   Nadab becomes king in Asa's 2nd year and reigns for 2 years.

1K 15.28   Nadab is killed in Asa's 3rd year.

1K 15.33   Baasha becomes king in Asa's 3rd year and reigns for 24 years.

1K 16.6   Elah becomes king in Asa's 20th year (BL).

1K 16.8   Elah ⟨becomes king in Asa's 26th year and (MT)⟩ reigns for 2 years.

1K 16.10   Elah is killed in the 27th year of Asa (MT).

1K 16.15   Zimri ⟨becomes king in Asa's 27th (MT) / 22nd (L) year and⟩ reigns for 7 days (MT, L) / years (B).

1K 16.23   Omri (MT, L, Jos.) / Zimri (B) becomes king in Asa's 31st (MT, BL) / 30th (Jos.) year and reigns 12 years.

1K 16.28a   Jehoshaphat becomes king in Omri's (L) / Zimri's (B) 11th year and reigns for 25 years.

1K 16.29   Ahab becomes king in Asa's 38th (MT) / Jehoshaphat's 2nd (BL) year and reigns for 22 years.

1K 22.41–2 Jehoshaphat becomes king in Ahab's 4th year and reigns for 25 years (MT,B).

1K 22.52   Ahaziah of Israel becomes king in Jehoshaphat's 17th (MT,B) / 24th (L) year and reigns for 2 years.

2K 1.17   Joram becomes king in Jehoram's 2nd year (MT)

2K 1.18a   Joram becomes king in Jehoshaphat's 18th (B) / Jehoram's 2nd (L) year and reigns for 12 years.

2K 3.1   Joram ⟨becomes king in Jehoshaphat's 18th year and (MT,B)⟩ reigns for 12 years.

2K 8.16–17 Jehoram becomes king in Joram's 5th year and reigns for 8 (MT) / 10 (L) / 40 (AB) years.

2K 8.25–6   Ahaziah of Judah becomes king in Joram's 12th (MT,B) / 11th (L) year and reigns for 1 year.

2K 9.29   Ahaziah of Judah becomes king in Joram's 11th year ⟨and reigns for 1 year (L)⟩.

2K 10.36   Jehu reigns for 28 years ⟨becoming king in Athaliah's 2nd year (L)⟩.

This may be tabulated as follows.

1. MT

Judah			Israel
Rehoboam	I	I	Jeroboam
	~	~	
	17	17	
Abijam	**ac**I	**18**	
	2	19	
Asa	3/**ac**	**20**	
	I	21	
	2	22/**ac**I	Nadab
	3	**d**2/**ac**I	Baasha
	4	2	
	~	~	
	24	22	
	25	23	
	26	**ac**I/24	Elah
	27	ac I/**ac**/**d**2	Zimri/Omri
	28	2	
	29	3	
	30	4	
(30$^{Jos.}$)**31**		5(**ac**)	(Omri)
	32	6	
	33	7	
	34	8	
	35	9	
	36	10	
	37	11	
	38	12 /**ac**I	Ahab
	39	2	
	40	3	
Jehoshaphat	**ac**/41	**4**	
	I	5	
	~	~	
	11	15	
	12	16	
	13	17	
	14	18	
	15	19	
	16	20	
	17	(**ac**I/) 21	(Ahaziah)
	18	(**ac**/2) 22	(Joram)

	19	1	Ahaziah
	20	2	
	21	1	Joram
	22	2	
	23	3	
	24	4	
Jehoram	25/**ac**1	**5**	
	2	6(**ac**)	(Joram)
	3	7	
	4	8	
	5	9	
	6	10	
(Ahaziah)	(**ac**)7	**11**	
Ahaziah /Athaliah	1/**ac**1/8	**12**/1	Jehu

2. LXX

Rehoboam	1	1		Jeroboam
	~	~		
	17	17		
Abijam	**ac**1	**18**		
	2	19		
	3	20		
	4	21		
	5	22		
	6	23		
Asa	**ac**1/**d**(7)	**24**		
	2	*25(/**ac**1)		(Nadab)
	3	1	(2/**ac**)	Nadab (Baasha)
	4	2		
	5	1		Baasha
	~	~		
	25	21		
	26	22		
	27	23		
	28	24		
	(**20**)29	**ac**1		Elah
	30	2		

	(22^L)31	(ac^L)/ac1	Zimri(/Omri^L)
	~	~	
Jehoshaphat	41/ac	11	
	1	12	
	2	**ac1**	Ahab
	~	~	
	22	21	
	23	22	
	24	**ac1**	Ahaziah
	25	2	
Jehoram	1(**2**)	**ac1**	Joram
	2	2	
	3	3	
	4	4	
	(**ac**)5	**5**	
	6	6	
	7	7	
	8	8	
	9	9	
	10	10	
Ahaziah	**ac1**	**11**	
Athaliah	1	12	
	2	**ac1**	Jehu

The chronological data of MT fit into a fairly coherent scheme which is probably more or less identical to the scheme produced by the Priestly chronological revision. There are, however, three discrepancies which clearly result from conflation with the chronology found in LXX and are therefore secondary. These discrepancies, which have already been discussed (p. 92f.), are Omri's accession date (1K 16.23: Asa's 31st year), Joram's alternative accession date (2K 1.17: Jehoram's 2nd year), and Ahaziah of Judah's alternative accession date (2K 9.29: Joram's 11th year). We may also note that MT's date for Abijam's accession reflects non-inclusive antedating and must therefore derive from the post-Priestly revision which introduced this dating system; the original Priestly scheme presumably dated Abijam's accession to Jeroboam's 17th year, with his first regnal year postdated to Jeroboam's 18th year (compare Asa's and Jehoshaphat's accession dates in MT's chronology).

A fourth discrepancy in MT's chronology, which was noted earlier in passing, is of rather more significance since it cannot be explained through conflation with the chronology found in LXX, and may therefore be regarded as a possible survival from pre-Priestly chronology. Ahaziah of Israel is said to have become king in Jehoshaphat's 17th year and to have reigned for 2 years (1K 22.52), and this agrees with the statement that his successor, Joram, became king in Jehoshaphat's 18th year (2K 3.1), provided Ahaziah's reign is inclusively antedated. But it fails to agree with MT's chronology up to this point, according to which Jehoshaphat's 17th year ought to correspond with Ahab's 21st year (see previous table); since Ahab is ascribed a reign length of 22 years (1K 16.29) this means that Ahaziah's accession is dated 1 year before the end of Ahab's reign. Ahaziah's and Joram's accession dates are equally incompatible with MT's chronology beyond this point: if Joram became king in Jehoshaphat's 18th year, Joram's 12th year (in which Ahaziah of Judah is said to have become king) has to correspond with Jehoram's 5th or 6th year, with the result that Ahaziah of Judah's accession falls 2 or 3 years before the end of his predecessor's reign.

A simple way of accounting for the discrepancy between Ahaziah of Israel's accession date and MT's chronology up to this point is to suppose that Ahab originally reigned for only *21 years. This leaves the discrepancy with MT's subsequent chronology unaccounted for; but if we rearrange MT's chronology so that all reigns are inclusively antedated and adopt *21 years as the length of Ahab's reign, it turns out that Israelite and Judean totals for the period from the division of the kingdom to Jehu's revolt are exactly equivalent, as the following table demonstrates.[32]

32. The correspondence between MT's Israelite and Judean reign lengths on this dating system was first noted by Rühl (1894/5:48f.), who attempted to resolve the remaining 1-year discrepancy in MT's totals by subtracting a 1-year overlap from the end of Joram's reign *without* subtracting a similar overlap from the end of Ahaziah of Judah's reign. Andersen (1969:76f.) offers an alternative solution: in his view Ahaziah of Judah probably reigned for 2 years originally, since a 1-year reign is anomalous within a set of inclusively antedated reigns (any reign which extends beyond the first new year from accession automatically enters its 2nd year in an antedating system, while any reign which terminates before the first new year from accession is normally stated in fractions of a year). However, the anomaly of Ahaziah's 1-year reign is more satisfactorily accounted for by noting that Athaliah's reign was evidently deemed to be illegitimate (she is not accorded any of the usual regnal formulae); Ahaziah, despite having been murdered before the end of his first

Rehoboam	17-1 years	Jeroboam	22-1 years
Abijam	3-1 years	Nadab	2-1 years
Asa	41-1 years	Baasha	24-1 years
Jehoshaphat	25-1 years	Elah	2-1 years
Jehoram	8-1 years	Zimri	7 days
Ahaziah	1 year	Omri	12-1 years
		Ahab	*21-1 years
total	95-5 years	Ahaziah	2-1 years
		Joram	12 years
		total	97-7 years

This overlooks one rather important point. MT's chronology reflects Priestly schematization (which reduced the reign lengths of Abijam and Jehoram to create a 430-year interval from the foundation of the temple to its destruction), so we cannot reconstruct the original chronology of this period simply by arranging MT's reigns on the basis of inclusive antedating and reducing Ahab's reign to *21 years. We must begin by attempting to reconstruct the pre-Priestly (Deuteronomistic) chronology of this period, and proceed from there to an attempted reconstruction of the original, pre-schematic chronology.

It was pointed out in the last chapter that LXX's Judean chronology preserves evidence of a pre-Priestly schematism giving 480 years from David's accession to the exile. Judean reign lengths given by LXX^{BL} differ from MT's reign lengths in three (or two and a half) instances: the two main differences are that Abijam is ascribed a reign of 6 years in LXX^{BL} (as against 3 years in MT), while Jehoram is ascribed a reign of 10 years in LXX^L (as against 8 years in MT); LXX^{AB}'s figure of 40 years for Jehoram's reign is clearly impossible on any chronology.[33] The third instance where LXX and MT differ over Judean reign lengths is in Rehoboam's case: LXX^B gives Rehoboam's reign length as 12 years in 1 Kings 12.24a (LXX^L has '17 years', and the verse is lacking in MT), but in 1 Kings 14.21 LXX^{BL} and MT are agreed in ascribing

regnal year, might therefore be credited with a complete year, as there was no other legitimate monarch to whom this year could be assigned.

33. Rahlfs (*Septuaginta*, ad loc.) suggests graphic confusion of *H'* (the Greek symbol for '8') and *M'* (the Greek symbol for '40') as the source of this reading, but it is possible that it reflects a deliberate alteration that was intended to lengthen LXX's world chronology by 30 years (see p. 239f.).

Rehoboam a reign of 17 years. I have argued above (p. 38) that
LXX[B] has in fact preserved the original LXX figure in 1 Kings
12.24a, but this is obviously not the original Biblical figure for
Rehoboam's reign length, since '12 years' is in direct contradiction
to all other chronological data in Kings. In Jehoram's case, LXX[L]'s
figure of 10 years is at variance with the fact that Joram's
accession is synchronized with Jehoram's 2nd year (2K 1.18a); this
accession date clearly presupposes that Jehoram reigned for *11
years (see following table), and since it is otherwise impossible to
account for Joram's accession date we may regard this as being the
original figure for Jehoram's reign. In this earlier version of the
chronology now given by LXX, Jehoram became king in the *2nd
year of Ahaziah of Israel and reigned for *11 years before being
succeeded by Ahaziah of Judah in Joram's 11th year.

Jehoshaphat	**24**	ac1	Ahaziah
Jehoram	25/ac1	2	
	2	ac1	Joram
	3	2	
	4	3	
	5	4	
	6	5	
	7	6	
	8	7	
	9	8	
	10	9	
	*11	10	
Ahaziah	**ac1**	**11**	

The fact that this chronology presupposes inclusive antedating of
Jehoram's reign (as in MT's chronology) offers a possible
explanation of why it was altered. LXX's chronology of Kings
generally presupposes non-inclusive dating (mostly non-inclusive
antedating), but the editor responsible for most of this chronology
was apparently unwilling to alter Jehoram's original reign length in
order to remove this one instance of inclusive antedating; subsequently, a later editor who was not concerned to preserve the
original schematic totals removed this inconsistency by reducing
Jehoram's reign from *11 to 10 years.[34] This second editor either

34. The editor who made this reduction was quite possibly also responsible for
reducing Rehoboam's reign length to 12 years in 1 Kings 12.24a: coupled with a

forgot to readjust Joram's accession date, or else he did adjust it but his adjusted date (*1st year of Jehoram) was subsequently lost through secondary conflation with the earlier chronology.

LXX[BL]'s figures for the reign lengths of Israelite kings from Nadab to Joram are identical with MT's figures, leaving aside LXX[B]'s peculiar figures for 'Zimri', which are discussed below. On the other hand LXX[BL] fail to state the duration of Jeroboam's reign, 1 Kings 14.1–20 having been omitted in the original LXX text.[35] However, Jeroboam's reign length has to be longer than 22 years in LXX's chronology: Asa's accession is synchronized with Jeroboam's 24th year, and later synchronisms presuppose a reign length of *25 years (see table on p. 126f.). Accession synchronisms for Nadab and Baasha reflect inclusive antedating, but they are disregarded in LXX's subsequent chronology, which clearly presupposes non-inclusive dating of Nadab's and Baasha's reigns. This discrepancy between the accession dates of Nadab and Baasha and LXX's subsequent chronology suggests that the former were either taken over unchanged from the original chronology, or have secondarily replaced adjusted accession dates through conflation with chronological data from other textual traditions.

LXX accession dates for Israelite kings after Baasha generally presuppose non-inclusive antedating. A number of discrepancies exist, but these are of secondary origin and cannot be used to reconstruct earlier forms of the chronology. Jehoram's accession date (5th year of Joram) is obviously incompatible with other chronological data in LXX and has evidently resulted from conflation with the chronological scheme presented by MT. Accession dates ascribed to Elah in LXX[BL] and Zimri in LXX[L] are equally incompatible with the rest of LXX's chronology, as can be seen from the table given above (p. 126f.) Other chronological data in LXX point to Asa's 29th year for Elah's accession date, and LXX[BL]'s figure (20th year of Asa) must almost certainly be seen as

1-year reduction in Jehoram's reign length, this 5-year reduction in Rehoboam's reign length had the effect of bringing the chronology now found in LXX into conformity with the Priestly scheme of 430 years from the foundation of the temple to the Babylonian exile.

35. The passage is restored in LXX[A] and other hexaplaric manuscripts. LXX differs from MT on a redactional level at this point: the story of Jeroboam's sick child (1 Kings 14.1–18 in MT) is given in a different form in 1 Kings 12.24g–n (absent from MT).

a secondary corruption of this: the omission of units from compound numerals is, as was noted earlier (p. 109), one of the most commonly attested forms of numerical corruption (the same type of corruption is probably also reflected in Josephus's synchronism for Omri's accession—30th year of Asa).[36]

LXX[L]'s synchronism for Zimri's accession (22nd year of Asa) has clearly resulted from the addition of 2 years (the duration of Elah's reign) to the corrupt synchronism for Elah's accession, and was doubtless intended to make good the previous absence of a synchronism for Zimri's accession in 1 Kings 16.15. The omission of this synchronism in LXX[B] and most other non-Lucianic manuscripts (excluding LXX[A] and hexaplaric manuscripts), is doubtless connected with the fact that LXX[B] and other non-Lucianic manuscripts have confused Zimri ($\zeta\alpha\mu\beta\rho\iota$) and Omri ($\dot{\alpha}\mu\beta\rho\iota$), effectively eliminating the latter; as a result of this confusion LXX contained a second accession date for Zimri (formerly Omri) in 1 Kings 16.23, and this understandably led to the omission of Zimri's original accession date in 1 Kings 16.15.[37] LXX[B]'s statement in 1 Kings 16.15 that Zimri reigned for 7 years (rather than 7 days) in Tirzah may probably be ascribed to the same confusion, and was possibly inspired by the statement in LXX[B]'s text of 1 Kings 16.23 that Zimri (formerly Omri) reigned for a total of 12 years, including *6 years in Tirzah*.

Apart from these secondary discrepancies, LXX's chronology presents a scheme that is remarkably clear and consistent. But this consistency was gained at a price, which in addition to the near-total rewriting of Israelite-Judean synchronisms also involved the removal of at least one pre-Priestly reign length in Israelite chronology. The Priestly chronological revision subtracted 6 years from Judean chronology (reducing Abijam's reign from 6 to 3 years and Jehoram's reign from *11 to 8 years), and must almost certainly have compensated for this by removing 6 years from Israelite chronology also. However, only 3 of these 6 years are

36. This obviously corrupt synchronism for Elah's accession forms the cornerstone of Miller's reconstruction of Israelite and Judean chronology for the early monarchy, even though he also follows Thiele in supposing that '20th year of Asa' was simply an 'estimate' made in the absence of more specific information (Miller 1967:282f.).

37. The Lucianic distinction between Zimri and Omri must in this case be viewed as a secondary restoration, which naturally created the need for a new synchronism for Zimri's accession.

accounted for in LXX's chronology, which presupposes that Jeroboam reigned for *25 years (but fails to say so explicitly). Subsequent Israelite reign lengths are identical to those of MT, if we disregard LXX^B's alteration of Zimri's reign length, although one of these was presumably 3 years longer than its present duration in earlier versions of Israelite chronology. There are no direct indications of where this 3-year reduction may have occurred, but since the removal of 3 years from the reign of Abijam was compensated for by a 3-year reduction in the reign of Abijam's Israelite contemporary (Jeroboam), it is not unlikely that the removal of 3 years from Jehoram's reign will have been compensated for by a corresponding reduction in the reign of one of Jehoram's Israelite contemporaries or near-contemporaries, thus minimizing any disruption to existing Israelite-Judean synchronisms. Joram, who is Jehoram's closest contemporary, must certainly be ruled out, as 12 years is the maximum possible length for Joram's reign on Assyrian evidence (see p. 183ff.), and we may also doubt that Ahaziah's apparently insignificant reign was originally longer than 2 years. This then brings us to Ahab, who may be suspected on other ground of having lost 3 years at the hands of Priestly chronologists. In shortening Judean chronology the Priestly school removed 6 years from two Judean kings who are particularly noted for their wickedness (1K 15.3 and 2K 8.18), and it is reasonable to suppose that they will have looked for Israelite kings with similar qualifications when they removed 6 years from Israelite chronology. The two most distinguished candidates in this respect were undoubtedly Jeroboam, who first 'caused Israel to sin' (1K 14.16 etc.), and Ahab, who 'did more evil in Yahweh's sight than any of his predecessors' (1K 16.30); and we have already seen that Jeroboam's reign was reduced by 3 years in Priestly chronology. We may therefore conclude that Ahab's reign was probably 3 years longer in pre-Priestly chronology than its present length in MT and LXX, and that it was reduced from *25 to 22 years in compensation for the removal of 3 years from Jehoram's reign. We still need to explain how this Priestly figure of 22 years for Ahab's reign came to be included in LXX's chronology, which has otherwise preserved pre-Priestly reign lengths. A probable explanation is that when Israelite reigns were redated by non-inclusive antedating, the consequent removal of 1-year overlaps presupposed by the earlier chronology, in which the majority of these reigns had been inclusively antedated (as in MT's chronology), must inevitably have resulted in an increase in the overall length of Israelite chronology: the adoption of 22 years in place of *25 years for Ahab's reign may therefore be seen as a way of compensating for this increase.

The removal of 3 years from Abijam's and Jeroboam's reigns necessitated only minimal alterations to existing synchronisms, so that MT (with its essentially Priestly chronology) and LXX^{BL} (with an essentially pre-Priestly chronology at this point) give identical synchronisms for Nadab's and Baasha's accessions, although MT necessarily gives a reduced figure for Asa's accession date. LXX synchronisms beyond this point reflect late chronological reworking and are therefore of little significance. But since the removal of 3 years from Abijam's and Jeroboam's reigns required few alterations in subsequent synchronisms, MT's (Priestly) chronology from Nadab's accession to the reign of Ahab may be regarded as broadly identical with pre-Priestly chronology for this period (except for Omri's accession date, which was imported from the chronology now found in LXX). However, the removal of 3 years from Ahab's reign will have necessitated a reduction of 3 years in the accession dates of Ahaziah of Israel and of Joram, and a corresponding increase of 3 years in Jehoram's accession date, before the original balance between Israelite and Judean chronology was restored with the removal of 3 years from Jehoram's reign. Pre-Priestly chronology down to Jehu's revolt may therefore be reconstructed by reversing these Priestly alterations in MT's chronology and by disregarding accession dates which reflect non-inclusive antedating (and were taken from the scheme found in LXX); in the case of Abijam and Omri, for whom alternative accession dates are not given, pre-Priestly accession dates may be reconstructed as being identical with the last regnal year of their respective predecessors, as is regularly the case with post-dating and inclusive antedating. The following table presents a reconstruction of pre-Priestly Deuteronomistic chronology down to Jehu's revolt that has been worked out on this basis; synchronisms which are preserved in MT's chronology are indicated by bold print.

Rehoboam	I	I	Jeroboam
	~	~	
Abijam	17/ac	17	
	I	18	
	2	19	
	3	20	
	4	21	
	5	22	
Asa	ac/6	23	
	I	24	
	2	*25/**ac**I	Nadab
	3	**d**2/**ac**I	Baasha
	4	2	
	~	~	
	24	22	
	25	23	
	26	**ac**I/24	Elah
	27	**ac**I/**ac**2	Zimri/Omri
	~	~	
	37	11	
	38	12/**ac**I	Ahab
	39	2	
	40	3	
Jehoshaphat	41/**ac**	**4**	
	I	**5**	
	~	~	
	11	15	
	12	16	
	13	17	
	14	18	
	15	19	
	16	20	
	17	21	
	18	22	
	19	*23	
	20	*24(/**ac**I)	(Ahaziah)
	21	*25 (2/ac)	(Joram)
	22	I	Ahaziah
	23	2	
	24	I	Joram
Jehoram	**ac**I/25	2	
	2	3	
	3	4	

	4	5	
	5	6	
	6	7	
	7	8	
	8	9	
	9	10	
	10	11	
Ahaziah	*11/ac1/1	12/1	Jehu
/Athaliah			

We are now confronted once again with a discrepancy between Ahaziah of Israel's accession date and Ahab's reign length which is similar to the discrepancy noted earlier; and here it may be suggested that the explanation given previously (p. 128) was substantially correct, except that it failed to take account of Priestly modifications to the chronology. This leads to the conclusion that Ahab's original reign length was (not *21 years but) *24 years, and that this was increased to *25 years by the exilic Deuteronomistic chronologist. A plausible reason for this increase is that it was carried out in order to harmonize Israelite and Judean chronology following alterations to Judean reigns so that—up until Jehoram's accession—they reflected postdating rather than inclusive ante-dating (the latter being incompatible with the non-inclusive reckoning required by Deuteronomistic chronological schematism). However, in making this adjustment the Deuteronomistic chronologist evidently forgot to readjust the accession dates of Ahaziah of Israel and Joram, and the resulting discrepancy was carried over into the Priestly chronological revision when a Priestly chronologist mechanically reduced Ahaziah of Israel's and Joram's accession dates by 3 years in order to compensate for the removal of 3 years from Ahab's reign.

The failure of Priestly chronologists to correct this discrepancy is perhaps less surprising than the apparent carelessness shown by the exilic Deuteronomistic chronologist. However, the reconstruction of Deuteronomistic chronology set out in the previous table evidences a rather ad hoc method of revising Israelite-Judean synchronisms. The Deuteronomistic chronologist, in conformity with his non-inclusive reckoning of Judean reign lengths, appears initially to have set about revising Judean accession dates so that they reflected postdating, while leaving Israelite accession dates, which were irrelevant to his overall synchronism, reflecting inclusive antedating (albeit with minor modifications to make them conform with his revised Judean dates). Having got as far as Jehoram (2K 8.16) it seems that he then realized that this procedure would fail to synchronize the deaths of Ahaziah of Judah and Joram of Israel, and therefore reversed his practice, leaving the Judean reigns of Jehoram and Ahaziah reflecting inclusive antedating while counting the Israelite reigns of Ahaziah and Joram non-inclusively (and also adding another year to Ahab's reign). At this point he ought logically to have gone back and revised Ahaziah of Israel's and Joram's accession dates (1K 22.52 and 2K 3.1), but this he failed to do. A more systematic approach to Israelite-Judean synchronisms could easily have eliminated all instances of inclusive dating in Judean chronology by introducing non-inclusive dating at an earlier point in Israelite chronology, which would also have obviated the need to lengthen Ahab's reign. However, the revision of Israelite-Judean synchronisms was really of secondary importance to the exilic Deuteronomistic chronologist, whose main concern was to construct a schematic chronology expressed through Judean reign lengths.

Apart from the minor modification to Ahab's reign length which we have just discussed there is no other evidence of Deuteronomistic alterations to Israelite or Judean reign lengths in this part of the chronology of Kings, so we may probably conclude that schematic alterations by the (exilic) Deuteronomistic chronologist were primarily concentrated on the period after Jehu's revolt. This conclusion allows us to reconstruct a pre-schematic version of the chronology of this period from the reconstruction of Deuteronomistic chronology given above: to this end we need only reduce Ahab's reign from *25 to *24 years and rearrange Israelite and Judean reigns so that they reflect inclusive antedating. The following table reconstructs the original chronology on this basis.

Rehoboam	1	1	Jeroboam
	~	~	
Abijam	17/ac1	17	
	2	18	
	3	19	
	4	20	
	5	21	

Asa	ac1/6	22	
	2	23	
	3	24	
	4	*25/ac1	Nadab
	5	d2/ac1	Baasha
	~	~	
	25	21	
	26	22	
	27	23	
	28	ac1/24	Elah
	29	ac1/ac/2	Zimri/Omri
	~	~	
	39	11	
	40	12/ac1	Ahab
Jehoshaphat	41/ac1	2	
	~	~	
	21	22	
	22	*23	
	23	*24/ac1	Ahaziah
	24	2/ac1	Joram
Jehoram	ac1/25	2	
	2	3	
	3	4	
	4	5	
	5	6	
	6	7	
	7	8	
	8	9	
	9	10	
	10	11	
Ahaziah /Athaliah	*11/**ac1**/1	1/**12**	Jehu

4.2.2. *From Jehu's revolt to the fall of Samaria*

The chronology of the period from Jehu's revolt to the fall of Samaria presents a rather different set of problems from those encountered above. In contrast to their divergent chronologies of the early monarchic period MT and LXX contain largely identical chronologies for the period after Jehu's revolt. This is essentially because the late chronological reworking which is reflected in

LXX's chronology of the early monarchy was incorporated into the textual traditions behind LXX *and* MT from the time of Jehu's revolt (or, more precisely, from Joash's accession in Jehu's 7th year), as is shown by the large number of non-inclusively antedated reigns (the characteristic feature of this revision) which occur in this part of the chronology.[38] Priestly modifications to the chronology found in MT, which prevented the textual tradition behind MT from adopting this revised chronology, with its non-Priestly figures for Abijam and Jehoram, in the early monarchic period (or, more precisely, in the period from Abijam to Joash), are confined to the period of the early divided monarchy. On the other hand, in contrast to the general agreement between MT and LXX in their chronology of the period under discussion, there are a number of significant chronological variants for this period in Josephus's *Jewish Antiquities*, which largely agreed with MT in its chronology of the early monarchy. Finally, in contrast to the presence of relatively few serious internal discrepancies in MT's and LXX's chronologies of the early monarchy, we are now confronted with a series of major internal discrepancies between Israelite and Judean chronology, and MT's Judean chronology is some 22 years longer than its Israelite chronology. In LXX, where Pekahiah is ascribed a reign of 10 years (MT's figure is 2 years), Judean chronology is 14 years longer than Israelite chronology.

The following list presents the chronological data of MT, LXX, and Josephus for the period from Jehu's revolt to the fall of Samaria.[39] LXX^L is cited as our best witness to the original LXX chronology; other LXX texts, including LXX^B, contain the Kaige recension at this point (note, however, that LXX^A agrees with LXX^L regarding Pekahiah's reign length).

38. Non-inclusive antedating is clearly reflected in MT's and LXX's accession dates for Jehoahaz, Pekahiah, Pekah, and Jotham, and is consistent with accession dates for Amaziah and Hoshea. Other accession dates mostly reflect postdating, probably as the result of secondary conflation with earlier versions of the chronology, or are anomalous on any dating system.

39. See appendix B for references to the relevant passages in *Antiquities*. It should be noted that there are only six kings of this period for whom Josephus gives accession dates (these are Jehoahaz, Jehoash, Amaziah, Jeroboam, Azariah, and Hezekiah), and that he also omits to say by how many years Amaziah outlived Jehoash (2K 14.17) or in which year of Hezekiah's reign Samaria was besieged (2K 18.9). On the other hand Josephus provides additional information in stating that Jehoash's defeat of Amaziah occurred in the 14th year of Amaziah's reign (*Ant* 9.203).

2K 10.36	Jehu reigns for 28 (MT, L) / 27 (Jos.) years < becoming king in Athaliah's 2nd year (L) > .
2K 11.4	Athaliah is removed in the 7th year (of her rule).
2K 12.2	Joash becomes king in Jehu's 7th year and reigns for 40 years.
2K 12.7	Temple repairs are inaugurated in Joash's 23rd year.
2K 13.1	Jehoahaz becomes king in Joash's 23rd (MT, L) / 21st (Jos.) year and reigns for 17 years.
2K 13.10	Jehoash becomes king in Joash's 37th year and reigns for 16 years.
2K 14.1–2	Amaziah becomes king in Jehoash's 2nd year and reigns for 29 years.
2K 14.17	Amaziah lives for 15 years after the death of Jehoash.
2K 14.23	Jeroboam becomes king in Amaziah's 15th year and reigns for 41 (MT, L) / 40 (Jos.) years.
2K 15.1–2	Azariah becomes king in Jeroboam's 27th (MT, L) / 14th (Jos.) year and reigns for 52 years.
2K 15.8	Zechariah becomes king in Azariah's 38th year and reigns for 6 months.
2K 15.13	Shallum becomes king in Azariah's 39th year and reigns for 1 month.
2K 15.17	Menahem becomes king in Azariah's 39th year and reigns for 10 years.
2K 15.23	Pekahiah becomes king in Azariah's 50th year and reigns for 2 (MT, Jos.) / 10 (AL) years.
2K 15.27	Pekah becomes king in Azariah's 52nd year and reigns for 20 years.
2K 15.30	Hoshea becomes king in Jotham's 20th year (MT).
2K 15.32–3	Jotham becomes king in Pekah's 2nd year and reigns for 16 years.
2K 16.1–2	Ahaz becomes king in Pekah's 17th year and reigns for 16 years.
2K 17.1	Hoshea becomes king in Ahaz's 12th year and reigns for 9 years.
2K 17.6	Samaria is captured in Hoshea's 9th year.
2K 18.1–2	Hezekiah becomes king in Hoshea's 3rd (MT, L) / 4th (Jos.) year and reigns for 29 years.
2K 18.9	Samaria is besieged in Hezekiah's 4th year = Hoshea's 7th year.
2K 18.10	Samaria is captured in Hezekiah's 6th (MT, L) / 7th (Jos.) year = Hoshea's 9th year.

This may be set out as follows.

	MT	LXX	**ac**		
Athaliah	1	2	**ac**1		Jehu
	2	3	2		
	3	4	3		
	4	5	4		
	5	6	5		
	6	7	6		
Joash	7/**ac**1		**7**		
	~		~		
	21		27/**ac**$^{Jos.}$		Jehoahaz
	22		28	1	
	23		**ac**1	2	Jehoahaz
	~		~	~	
	33		11	12	
	34		12	13	
	35		13	14	
	36		14	15	
	37		15	16	
	38(**37**)		16	17/**ac**	Jehoash
	39		17	1	
Amaziah	**ac**1$^{Jos.}$/40(**37**)		**ac**1	2	Jehoash
Amaziah	2	**ac**1	**2**	3	
	~	~	~	~	
	12	11	12	13	
		↘12	13↙		
	13		14		
	14		15		
	15		16/**ac**		Jeroboam
	16		1		
	~		~		
	26		11		
	27		12		
	28		13		
Azariah	**ac**$^{Jos.}$/29		**14**		
Azariah	1	**ac**1	(**27**)15		
	~	~	~		
	21→21		35		
	22		36		
	23		37		
	24		38		
	25		39		
	26		40		

Judah King	Judah	Israel	Israel	Israel King
	27	41		
	28	*42		
	~	~		
	38	**ac**/*52		Zechariah
	39	**ac**/**ac**/*1		Shallum
	40	1		/Menahem
	41	2		
	42	3		
	43	4		
	44	5		
	45	6		
	46	7		
	47	8		
	48	9		
	49	10		
	50	**ac**1		Pekahiah
	51	2		
	52	3^{LXX}/**ac**1		Pekah
Jotham	**ac**1	4^{LXX}	**2**	
	2	5^{LXX}	3	
	3	6^{LXX}	4	
	4	7^{LXX}	5	
	5	8^{LXX}	6	
	6	9^{LXX}	7	
	7	10^{LXX}	8	
	8	1	9	Pekah
	9	2	10	
	10	3	11	
	11	4	12	
	12	5	13	
	13	6	14	
	14	7	15	
	15	8	16	
Ahaz	**ac**/16	9	**17**	
	1 17^{MT}	10	18	
	2 18^{MT}	11	19	
	3 19^{MT}	12	20	
	4 **20** ^{MT}	13	**ac**1	Hoshea
	5	14		
	6	15		
	7	16		
	8	17		
	9	18		

	10	19	
	11	20	
	12	**ac**1	Hoshea
	13	2	
Hezekiah	14/**ac**	**3**	
	15 1(**ac**^Jos.)	**4**	
	16 2	5	
	3	6	
	4	**7**	Siege of Samaria
	5	8	
	6(**7**^Jos.)	**9**	Capture of Samaria

Four major discrepancies between Israelite and Judean chronology emerge clearly from this table. In comparison with Judean chronology Jeroboam's reign is 11 years too short, since Zechariah's accession date presupposes that Jeroboam reigned for *52 years. Zechariah himself is said to have reigned only 6 months, but following accession dates presuppose a *1-year reign. Thirdly, MT's 2-year reign for Pekahiah is 8 years short of the total required by Hoshea's accession date in 2 Kings 17.1, although in this case the missing 8 years turn up in LXX^AL, where Pekahiah is said to have reigned for 10 years. And finally, Hoshea's reign is apparently 2 years too short in comparison with Judean chronology: on existing synchronisms there is a 2-year overlap between the reigns of Ahaz and Hezekiah.

There are various ways in which we might attempt to account for these discrepancies, which amount to a difference of 22 years between MT's Israelite and Judean chronologies; but since I have argued earlier that a number of years must have been added to Judean chronology in order to produce the Deuteronomistic schematism of 480 years for the Davidic monarchy, we may most naturally explain these discrepancies as a consequence of this schematizing process: MT's reign lengths for Jeroboam, Zechariah, Pekahiah, and Hoshea are too short in relation to Judean chronology because they represent pre-schematic figures which were not increased in accordance with Deuteronomistic modifications to Judean chronology.

If this explanation is correct, then the discrepancy between Israelite and Judean chronology appears at first sight to be the result of an oversight by the Deuteronomistic chronologist. But it

is difficult to believe that this is in fact the case when Zechariah's
and Shallum's accession dates obviously presuppose increased
figures for Jeroboam's and Zechariah's reign lengths. And if the
Deuteronomistic chronologist forgot to increase Pekahiah's reign
length how are we to account for the fact that LXX[AL] apparently
contain the appropriate schematized figure? A late corrector would
hardly have inserted 8 extra years at this point in the chronology,
for Pekah's accession date (in MT *and* LXX) allows only 2 years
for Pekahiah's reign.[40] The logical conclusion to be drawn is that
the reign lengths of Jeroboam, Zechariah, Pekahiah, and Hoshea
were originally increased in accordance with Deuteronomistic
schematization, but that schematic reign lengths for these kings
were subsequently replaced by pre-schematic figures from the
original chronology. This would simply be another example of the
tendency for data from different versions of the chronology of
Kings to be secondarily conflated.

This conflation of schematic and pre-schematic Israelite reign
lengths could conceivably have been largely accidental. Certainly
there are other instances of chronological conflation (MT's
synchronism for Omri's accession is one example) for which no
obvious reason can be detected; and the fact that this conflation
was apparently restricted to Israelite chronology can be explained by the fact that alterations to Israelite chronology did
not affect the overall schematism expressed by Judean chronology, and were therefore less likely to be noticed or corrected.
But it is also possible that pre-schematic reign lengths for a
number of Israelite reigns were deliberately selected in order to
create a secondary overall schematism within *Israelite* chronology. Krey's theory that Israelite reign lengths given in MT
produce an overall total of 240 years for the duration of the
Israelite monarchy has already been discussed and rejected
(p. 115); on MT's figures Israelite reign lengths for this period
add up to 241 years, not 240 years. However, Krey had a
predecessor who also calculated a total of 240 years for the
duration of the Israelite monarchy: according to Josephus (*Ant*
9.280), 240 years 7 months and 7 days elapsed between the

---

40. The appropriate point at which to insert 8 extra years in MT's and LXX's
chronologies is at the end of Pekah's reign (see previous table). It is therefore no
surprise to find that in 6 minuscules cited by the Cambridge Septuagint Pekah's
reign is indeed extended from 20 to 28 years.

division of the kingdom and the fall of Samaria.[41]

Curiously, the total number of regnal years and fractions of a year stated by Josephus in chronological notices on individual Israelite kings works out at only 239 years 7 months and 7 days. Josephus's figures for the reigns of Israelite kings are identical to MT's figures, with two exceptions: Jehu is ascribed a reign of 27 years (*Ant* 9.160) instead of 28 years, and Jeroboam II is ascribed a reign of 40 years (*Ant* 9.205, 215) instead of 41 years. This second variant almost certainly results from accidental omission of the unit in '41',[42] and may therefore be ascribed to textual corruption in *Antiquities* or in Josephus's source. The first possibility requires us to posit a double corruption since the figure is cited twice in Josephus's account of Jeroboam's reign, but it has the advantage of accounting for the fact that Josephus's total presupposes an extra year in Israelite chronology;[43] in any case one would naturally expect that if textual corruption affected one number this would either be corrected in accordance with the second number or the latter would be altered to agree with the first. On the other hand, Josephus's figure for Jehu (which is also given by the Old Latin translation of the Septuagint) is corroborated by Josephus's synchronisms for Jehu's successors (see below) and may therefore be accepted as a genuine variant.

Josephus's original figures for Israelite reigns were thus identical with MT's figures except in the case of Jehu, for whom Josephus's reign length was 1 less than MT's. And since there is no reason to suppose that Josephus deliberately reduced MT's figure (there is actually good evidence that he did not; see below, p. 148), we may conclude that Josephus's chronology is derived from a Biblical text which gave 27 years as Jehu's reign length but which otherwise agreed with MT in its Israelite reign lengths. On this chronology the duration of the northern kingdom of Israel works

41. Josephus, in common with other Hellenistic historians, erroneously includes reigns of less than a year when calculating chronological totals; reigns which terminate before the first new year from accession have no chronological significance in a dating system in which regnal years are equated with calendar years.

42. Other examples of this common type of numerical corruption have been noted above; see pp. 109 and 131f.

43. See p. 153 for a similar instance where numerical corruption in one of Josephus's Judean reign lengths appears to have created a discrepancy with Josephus's stated total for the duration of the Davidic monarchy.

out, by non-inclusive reckoning, at exactly 240 years, and the schematic nature of this total suggests that it was deliberately contrived. This provides us with a plausible explanation for the conflation of schematic and pre-schematic reign lengths in the Israelite chronology of Kings: a post-Deuteronomistic chronologist selected pre-schematic figures for five Israelite kings (Jehu, Jeroboam II, Zechariah, Pekahiah, and Hoshea) in order to achieve a schematic total of 240 years for the duration of the Israelite monarchy; and further conflation between this modified chronology and the earlier schematized chronology has resulted in the existing chronologies of MT (with pre-schematic figures for Jeroboam, Zechariah, Pekahiah, and Hoshea) and LXX (with pre-schematic figures for Jeroboam, Zechariah, and Hoshea).

There is of course one rather obvious objection to this hypothesis, for the argument that Israelite chronology was deliberately reduced to a schematic total of 240 years could also be used to circumvent my earlier argument that the short reign lengths ascribed to certain Israelite kings are pre-schematic. If the 240-year total for Israelite chronology was deliberately contrived, why should we suppose that this was achieved by selecting pre-schematic figures? Could it not have been attained just as easily by purely arbitrary reductions in Israelite reign lengths, in which case the short and supposedly pre-schematic reign lengths ascribed to Jehu and others would be even less original than the schematic figures presupposed by Israelite-Judean synchronisms? If this were so, we should probably have to conclude that the original chronology of Kings for this period is irretrievably lost to us, and any historical reconstruction of Israelite and Judean chronology of this period would have to depend primarily on non-Biblical evidence. There are, however, a number of significant counter-arguments against this objection.

We may begin by noting that LXX's figure of 10 years for Pekahiah's reign appears to be overtly schematic in a way that MT's figure of 2 years is not, and this is corroborated by the fact that a 10-year reign by Pekahiah is historically impossible.[44] In this instance there is therefore a reasonable case for thinking that MT has preserved Pekahiah's original reign length; and there are

44. See p. 198ff. We know from Assyrian sources that Pekahiah's father, Menahem, was still on the throne in 738 BC, while his successor, Pekah, had become king by 733 BC at the latest.

probably few scholars who have ever suggested otherwise. But it has to be admitted that this argument is not conclusive, for a late editor who was intent on shortening Israelite chronology by a series of arbitrary reductions need not necessarily have been concerned to retain round figures in this chronology; and it is not inconceivable that in reducing various reign lengths he might fortuitously have brought Pekahiah's reign length within the bounds of known historical possibility.

A second argument concerns Zechariah's reign, which is given as 6 months in all textual witnesses, but which would appear to have lasted for a complete year according to Israelite-Judean synchronisms. In this case it seems to me to be entirely reasonable to suppose that the exilic Deuteronomist increased Zechariah's reign from 6 months (effectively zero as far as chronological totals are concerned) to *1 year in order to gain an extra year in Israelite chronology. But it may be doubted that a later editor would have naturally chosen to reduce so short a reign from *1 year to 6 months in order to lose a year at this point, unless '6 months' already existed as a textual variant. Why not take an extra year away from Jeroboam's reign instead, bringing this down to a round total of 40 years?

A third line of argument provides what I consider to be fairly conclusive evidence that the short reigns associated with Jehu and other Israelite kings are genuinely pre-schematic, and not simply the arbitrary invention of a late editor. As the following table demonstrates, Josephus's accession date for Jehoahaz (21st year of Joash) is in agreement with his figure of 27 years for Jehu's reign length. Similarly MT and LXX's accession date for Jehoahaz (23rd year of Joash) agrees perfectly with *their* figure of 28 years for Jehu's reign length. Beyond this point MT, LXX, and Josephus all agree that Jehoahaz reigned for 17 years and was succeeded by Jehoash in the 37th year of Joash's reign. But this date is incompatible with MT and LXX's previous chronology, whereas it agrees perfectly with Josephus's previous chronology provided that Jehoahaz's reign is inclusively antedated.

Joash	1	7	Jehu
	~	~	
	21	ac1/27	Jehoahaz
	~	~	

31	11	
32	12	
33	13	
34	14	
35	15	
36	16	
37	17/**ac** 1	Jehoash

This chronology cannot be Josephus's invention, for we have seen that Josephus counted reigns non-inclusively. But equally, and for the same reason, it cannot be the invention of an editor who sought to produce a schematic total of 240 years for Israelite chronology. We may therefore conclude that the table given above very probably represents the original chronology of this period, and that '27 years' is the original, pre-schematic figure for Jehu's reign. In which case, unless there is good evidence to the contrary, we may reasonably assume that the short reign lengths associated with Jeroboam, Zechariah, Pekahiah, and Hoshea are also pre-schematic.

The probability that Jehoash's accession date (37th year of Joash) is derived from the original, pre-schematic chronology has important consequences for Judean as well as Israelite chronology. MT, LXX, and Josephus are agreed that Joash reigned for 40 years and was succeeded by Amaziah in the 2nd year of Jehoash—which is clearly impossible if Jehoash became king in Joash's 37th year. If Jehoash's and Amaziah's accession dates are original, and if (as the previous table suggests) Israelite and Judean reigns of this period were originally inclusively antedated, Joash cannot have reigned for more than 38 years.

Joash	**37**	**ac** 1	Jehoash
Amaziah	**ac** 1/38	**2**	

There can be little doubt that this is more likely to be the original figure for Joash's reign—40 years is a schematic round figure which recurs throughout Deuteronomistic chronology. The obvious parallel with the 40-year reigns of David and Solomon may well be intentional: according to the Biblical account Joash inaugurated repairs to the Solomonic temple, and his accession restored the Davidic dynasty after it had been practically terminated by Athaliah's purges.

Israelite and Judean chronology runs smoothly from Amaziah's accession as far as Azariah's accession. Jehoash is said to have reigned for 16 years, and this fits perfectly with the fact that Jeroboam's accession is dated to Amaziah's 15th year. But since Amaziah is said to have reigned for 29 years the synchronism given by MT and LXX for Azariah's accession (27th year of Jeroboam) is obviously impossible. Josephus's synchronism (14th year of Jeroboam) is more acceptable, but Josephus's chronology (like that of MT and LXX) requires Jeroboam's reign to be postdated (see table on p. 141f.) and is therefore unlikely to be original; despite limited contacts with Assyria during Jehoash's reign it is improbable that postdating was adopted in Israel at this stage.[45] Now if Jeroboam's reign is inclusively antedated, then it is clear that we must either increase Azariah's accession date by 1 year (to Jeroboam's *15th year) or reduce Amaziah's reign length by 1 year (to *28 years). Since Josephus appears to give original accession dates for Jehoahaz, Jehoash, Amaziah, and Jeroboam, there is reasonable cause for supposing that his accession date for Azariah is also original, in which case we must assume that Azariah's reign length, like Joash's, was secondarily increased (from *28 to 29 years) for the purposes of Deuteronomistic schematism. This suggestion is strengthened by the fact that there appears to be a deliberate chronological parallelism between the reigns of Amaziah and Hezekiah, which was presumably intended to underline other similarities between their reigns (these include noteworthy military successes, and policies which later resulted in foreign invasion and defeat): both kings are said to have reigned for 29 years, having acceded to the throne in their 25th year (2K 14.2; 18.2),[46] and both are associated with a period of 15 years by which they survive a near-fatal illness (2K 20.6) or the death of their main military adversary (2K 14.17).[47] Taking *28 years as Amaziah's original

45. There is actually no good reason to suppose that postdating was ever adopted in the northern kingdom of Israel; see below, p. 181.

46. Hezekiah's accession age is incompatible with chronological data on Ahaz, and has probably been deliberately assimilated to Amaziah's accession age; see p. 224n.

47. It is worth noting that Amaziah and Hezekiah are the only two Judean kings, after David, whose reigns are subdivided in this way. The parallelism at this point may also be closer than I have suggested. 2 Kings 20.6 links Hezekiah's illness with Sennacherib's invasion of Judah, and 2 Kings 19.37 has sometimes been taken to imply that Sennacherib died shortly after this invasion (e.g. by Josephus in *Antiquities* 10.23; Sennacherib actually died long after this event). On this

reign length the pre-schematic chronology of this period may be reconstructed as follows.

Amaziah	**ac1**	**2**	Jehoash
	~	~	
	11	12	
	12	13	
	13	14	
	14	15	
	15	**ac1/16**	Jeroboam
	~	~	
	25	11	
	26	12	
	27	13	
Azariah	**ac1/28**	**14**	

This leaves us with the problem of accounting for MT's and LXX's accession date for Azariah (27th year of Jeroboam). '27th' is not, at first sight, a likely corruption of '14th'; but it may plausibly be explained as a misplaced textual variant to '38th' in Zechariah's accession date—this agrees with existing Biblical chronology to the end of Jeroboam's reign (see table on p. 141f.), in which Jeroboam's 41st year is equivalent to Azariah's 27th year. It may therefore be argued that Zechariah's accession date was corrected to the 27th year of Azariah in certain manuscripts following the reduction of Jeroboam's reign from *52 to 41 years,[48] and that the resulting textual variation between '38th' and '27th' in Zechariah's accession date (2K 15.8) led to the mistaken correction of '14th' to '27th' in Azariah's accession date (2K 15.1). In the original chronology Zechariah's accession would have been dated to Azariah's 28th year—so long as Azariah's original reign length was not shorter than 28 years.

In fact one cannot assume that Azariah reigned as long this, even though he is credited with a reign of 52 years in existing

interpretation, which could also have been the view of the exilic Deuteronomistic chronologist, Amaziah and Hezekiah both lived for 15 years after the death of their main adversary.

48. A similar correction, except that it presupposes non-inclusive antedating or the sequential dating system used in c_2 (see p. 120f.), is found in LXX[N] and 11 minuscules cited in the Cambridge Septuagint; according to these manuscripts Zechariah became king in the *28*th year of Azariah.

Biblical chronologies. We have seen that the Judean chronology of this period in Kings is considerably too long by historical standards. Judean reigns from Jehu's revolt to Ahaz's accession total 140 years by inclusive reckoning (7-1 + 40-1 + 29-1 + 52-1 + 16), which is over 30 years in excess of the historical interval between Athaliah's usurpation of the throne and Ahaz's accession (Ahaz is mentioned in an Assyrian tribute list of 734 BC, while other evidence indicates that Jehu's coup d'état, and Athaliah's usurpation of the Judean throne, occurred in 841 BC).[49] The reductions in Joash's and Amaziah's reigns proposed above account for only 3 of these 30 + years, which leaves 30 years or so to be deducted from Azariah's and Jotham's combined reigns. We may therefore conclude that Azariah's original reign length was somewhere in the vicinity of 20 to 30 years, depending on whether, and by how much, Jotham's reign is also reduced. There is little internal evidence to help us here, but we cannot reduce Azariah's reign too greatly without creating a discrepancy between Azariah's accession age (16 years) and Jotham's accession age (25 years)—if Azariah's reign were reduced to 20 years we would have to suppose that he was only about 11 years old when Jotham was born. Conversely, too great a reduction in Jotham's reign length will only create a similar discrepancy between Jotham's and Ahaz's accession ages.[50]

Israelite chronology becomes equally difficult to reconstruct from internal evidence at around this point. Zechariah's accession may be dated to the 28th year inclusive from Azariah's accession (whether or not the latter was still on the throne), and since I have argued that '6 months' is the original figure for Zechariah's reign, Shallum's and Menahem's accessions may be dated to the same year. But it cannot be taken for granted that Menahem originally reigned for 10 years, as stated in 2 Kings 15.17, since the same round figure was also used for Pekahiah's schematic reign length (now preserved in LXX[AL]). Pekah's 20-year reign must obviously raise similar doubts, which in this instance are confirmed by historical evidence from Assyrian inscriptions showing that Pekah's reign was considerably shorter than this.[51] On the other

49. See below, pp. 183ff. and 202.
50. See below, p. 220.
51. See below, p. 183ff. Pekah was deposed in either 732 or 731 BC, but came to the throne after 738 BC, when Menahem is recorded as having paid tribute to Tiglathpileser III.

hand Pekahiah's reign length, as stated in MT and Josephus, and Hoshea's reign length (in all witnesses) appear to be genuinely pre-schematic: Pekahiah's reign was increased from 2 to 10 years by the exilic Deuteronomistic chronologist, and Hoshea's reign length was apparently increased from 9 to *11 years (his existing reign length is 2 years too short by comparison with Judean chronology).[52]

Israelite-Judean synchronisms, which were a crucial element in my reconstruction of the original chronology of Kings from Jehu's revolt to the reigns of Jeroboam and Azariah, offer little help in reconstructing Israelite and Judean chronology beyond this point. Azariah is the last king before Hezekiah whose accession date is given by Josephus; while MT's and LXX's accession dates for subsequent kings presuppose schematic reign lengths and are therefore secondary or even tertiary. A tertiary series, linking schematic and pre-schematic reign lengths, begins with Pekah's accession-date (52nd year of Azariah); this presupposes that Pekahiah reigned for 2 years (as in the original chronology), but it also presupposes schematic figures for Jeroboam, Zechariah, and Azariah (see table on p. 141f.). This tertiary chronology, which is in stark conflict with LXX's (schematic) figure for Pekahiah's reign, is continued in MT's and LXX's accession dates for Jotham and Ahaz, but is thereafter discontinued in LXX, which reverts to the original schematic chronology (modified slightly to reflect non-inclusive antedating) for Hoshea's accession date (12th year of Ahaz). The same date is also given in MT, but the latter provides an alternative synchronism whereby Hoshea's accession is dated to Jotham's 20th year (2K 15.30). This agrees perfectly with previous tertiary dates, but whoever calculated this figure apparently forgot that Jotham was supposed to have reigned for only 16 years!

A second series of tertiary synchronisms begins with Hezekiah's accession. The siege and capture of Samaria will presumably have been dated to Hoshea's *9th and *11th years in Deuteronomistic schematic chronology (in which Hoshea was ascribed a reign of *11

52. This increase in Hoshea's reign length was possibly intended to create a schematic parallel between Hoshea, last king of Israel, and Zedekiah, last king of Judah. We have previously noted similar instances of apparent schematic parallelism between Joash, and David and Solomon (p. 148), and between Amaziah and Hezekiah (p. 149).

years), and Hezekiah's accession must accordingly have been dated to Hoshea's *5th year.

Ahaz	12	1	Hoshea
	13	2	
	14	3	
	15	4	
Hezekiah	16/ac	5	
	1	6	
	2	7	
	3	8	
	4	9	Siege of Samaria
	5	10	
	6	11	Capture of Samaria

Subsequently, with the readoption of 9 years as Hoshea's reign length, all dates in Hoshea's reign were necessarily reduced by 2 years, thus creating the existing 2-year overlap between the reigns of Ahaz and Hezekiah. It is worth noting that the Ethiopic translation of Kings does in fact date the capture of Samaria to Hoshea's 11th year—despite having previously ascribed Hoshea a reign of only 9 years—and may possibly have preserved an early textual variant at this point; it is unlikely that this reading is merely a secondary correction intended to remove the 2-year overlap between Ahaz and Hezekiah, for this overlap is also present in the chronology of the Ethiopic translation, where Hoshea's 11th year is equated with Hezekiah's *8th* year.[53]

The following table draws together previous tables in recon-

---

53. Josephus's variants are of less significance, and are also contradictory. His accession date for Hezekiah (4th year of Hoshea) was possibly intended to identify Hezekiah's accession year with his first regnal year by lowering the Biblical date for Hezekiah's accession (3rd year of Hoshea). But this is curiously inconsistent with the fact that Josephus dates the capture of Samaria to Hezekiah's *7th* year, suggesting an alternative scheme in which Hezekiah's first regnal year was put back to the Biblical date for his accession year. This discrepancy possibly reflects alternative ways in which Josephus attempted to deal with what he perceived as an inconsistency in Biblical chronology. Anyone who was unfamiliar with the conventions of postdating would naturally assume that the year in which a king came to the throne was also his first regnal year. On this assumption, if Hezekiah's 6th regnal year was equivalent to Hoshea's 9th regnal year, Hezekiah must have come to the throne in Hoshea's 4th regnal year; conversely, if Hezekiah's accession was dated to Hoshea's 3rd regnal year, one might reasonably suppose that Hoshea's 9th year was equivalent to Hezekiah's 7th year.

structing the original chronology of Kings from Jehu's revolt
to the accession of Menahem. Original synchronisms preserved by
MT, LXX, or Josephus are indicated by bold print.

Athaliah	1	1	Jehu
	2	2	
	3	3	
	4	4	
	5	5	
	6	6	
Joash	**ac1/7**	7	
	~	~	
	21	**ac1/27**	Jehoahaz
	~	~	
	31	11	
	32	12	
	33	13	
	34	14	
	35	15	
	36	16	
	37	**17/ac1**	Jehoash
Amaziah	**ac1/38**	**2**	
	~	~	
	11	12	
	12	13	
	13	14	
	14	15	
	15	**ac1/16**	Jeroboam
	~	~	
	25	11	
	26	12	
	27	13	
Azariah	**ac1/28**	**14**	
	~	~	
		34	
		35	
		36	
		37	
		38	
		39	
		40	
		ac1/ac/ac/41	Zechariah/Shallum /Menahem
		~	

4.2.3. *From the fall of Samaria to the Babylonian exile*

Our reconstruction of the original chronology of Kings for the period preceding the fall of Samaria (which is set out in the previous table) was based on a combination of textual evidence from MT, LXX, and Josephus, and literary-historical evidence provided by internal chronological discrepancies. The absence of Israelite-Judean synchronisms for the period from the fall of Samaria to the Babylonian exile, and the virtual absence of textual variants for reign lengths of this period, consequently prevents us from continuing this reconstruction beyond the fall of Samaria. The present subsection is therefore limited to a presentation of the chronological data and discussion of variant figures where these exist. Biblical data for this part of the chronology of Kings, including variant figures from Josephus and from parallel passages in Jeremiah, Chronicles, and 1 Esdras, are as follows.

2K 18.13	Sennacherib invades Judah in the 14th year of Hezekiah.
2K 21.1	Manasseh reigns for 55 years.
2K 21.19	Amon reigns for 2 years.
2K 22.1	Josiah reigns for 31 years.
2K 22.3	Josiah makes arrangements for temple repairs in the 18th year of his reign ⟨in the 8th (BL) / 7th (AN) month⟩.
2K 23.23	The Passover is celebrated in Jerusalem in the 18th year of Josiah's reign.
2K 23.31	Jehoahaz reigns for 3 months ⟨and 10 days (Jos.)⟩.
2K 23.36	Jehoiakim reigns for 11 years.
2K 24.8	Jehoiachin reigns for 3 months ⟨and 10 days (2C 36.9; 1 Esd 1.42; Jos.)⟩.
2K 24.12	Jehoiachin is taken captive in the 8th year of Nebuchadrezzar's reign.
2K 24.18	Zedekiah reigns for 11 years.
2K 25.1	Jerusalem is besieged in the 9th year of Zedekiah, in the 10th month ⟨on the 10th day (MT; Je 52.4; Jos.)⟩.
2K 25.2–3	Jerusalem is captured in the 11th year of Zedekiah, ⟨in the 4th month, (Je 39.2; Je 52.5–6(MT); Jos.)⟩ on the 9th day.
2K 25.8	Jerusalem is destroyed and its inhabitants deported in the 5th month, on the 7th day (MT, ABN) / 9th day (L) / 10th day (Je 52.12) / new moon (Jos.), this being Nebuchadrezzar's 19th year.

2K 25.25   Gedaliah is assassinated in the 7th month.
2K 25.27   Jehoiachin is released from prison in the 37th year of his
            exile, in the 12th month, on the 27th (MT, LXX) / 25th
            (Je 52.31, MT) / 24th (Je 52.31, LXX) day, in the year
            of Evil-merodach's

{ reign/accession (בשנת מלכו) (MT; Je 52.31, LXX). }
{ reign (בשנת מלכתו) (LXX; Je 52.31, MT). }

Most of the variants listed here are fairly trivial as far as the overall
chronology of this period is concerned. There are two minor
variants in reign lengths: Jehoiachin is credited with a reign of 3
months and 10 days in Chronicles, 1 Esdras, and Josephus, and
Jehoahaz is ascribed the same reign length in Josephus (Kings has
'3 months' in both cases). Both variants are almost certainly
secondary. In Jehoiachin's case the phrase 'and 10 days' (ועשרת
ימים) probably originated as a misplaced correction to Jehoiachin's accession age, which is given as '8 years' (שמונה שנים) in
2 Chronicles 36.9 as against '18 years' (שמנה עשרה שנה) in 2
Kings 24.8 (cf. *BHS* ad loc.). Chronicles' reign length for
Jehoiachin was subsequently taken over by 1 Esdras and
Josephus (*Ant* 10.98), and the latter apparently ascribes the same
reign length to Jehoahaz (*Ant* 10.83). However, Josephus's total
of 514 years 6 months and 10 days for the Davidic monarchy is
incompatible with *two* reigns of 3 months and 10 days, so that it
is likely that this second variant is a secondary corruption which
originated through assimilation to Jehoiachin's reign length in
the text of *Antiquities*.

Textual variation over dates associated with the siege and
capture of Jerusalem is equally insignificant for the overall
chronology. The absence of 'in the 4th month' in 2 Kings 25.3 and
LXX's text of Jeremiah 52.6 is clearly an accidental omission,
since a reference to the month of Jerusalem's capture is required by
the following phrase, 'on the 9th (day) of the month'; and the
absence of 'on the 10th day' in LXX's text of 2 Kings 25.1 and in
Jeremiah 39.1 is probably another accidental omission. The
original date of the destruction of Jerusalem and its temple is likely
to have been the 7th day of the 5th month, as in MT's and
LXX[ABN]'s text of 2 Kings 25.8; LXX[L]'s date, the 9th day of the
5th month, is explicable as the result of accidental assimilation to
the date of Jerusalem's capture ('the 9th (day) of the month', 2K

25.3),[54] while the date given in Jeremiah 52.12, the 10th day of the 5th month, probably reflects accidental assimilation to the date on which the siege commenced ('the 10th (day) of the month', Je 52.4).

The precise day of Jehoiachin's release from prison is also of little chronological importance,[55] but greater significance attaches to the question of whether he was released 'in the year of (Evil-merodach's) accession' (בשנת מלכו) or 'in the year of (Evil-merodach's) reign' (בשנת מלכו/מלכתו). A number of scholars have, for chronological reasons, preferred the second possibility, which they interpret as meaning 'in the first year of his reign'.[56] But this is hardly a legitimate interpretation: בשנת מלכו, or בשנת מלכתו, can no more be taken to mean 'in the first year of his reign' than they can be taken as meaning 'in the 2nd year of his reign' or 'in (any other) year of his reign'. The only interpretation along these lines which is linguistically possible is that Evil-merodach released Jehoiachin 'in the only year of his reign'—and this is contradicted by the historical fact that Evil-merodach reigned for 2 years (in addition to his accession year). We therefore have no option but to translate בשנת מלכו as 'in the year of his accession' and to reject בשנת מלכתו as historically meaningless.[57]

One final chronological variant occurs in 2 Kings 22.3. According to both MT and LXX Josiah made arrangements for the repair of the temple, and was told of the discovery of 'the book

54. It is also possible that the date was deliberately altered because Titus's destruction of the second temple occurred on the 9th of Ab (Montgomery and Gehman 1950: 567; Gray ³1977: 766).

55. On text-critical grounds it may be suggested that the original figure is preserved in LXX's text of Jeremiah 52.31, according to which Jehoiachin was released on the 24th day of the month. '27th' (עשרים ושבעה) in 2 Kings 25.27 may then be explained as a corruption of '24th' (עשרים וארבעה): graphic confusion of וארבעה and ושבעה was made easier by the previous occurrence of וישבע within the same verse (Jehoiachin is released in the 37th year of his exile). The other variant, '25th' (עשרים וחמשה) in MT's text of Jeremiah 52.31, may be explained as a partial assimilation to '745' (שבע מאות ארבעים וחמשה) in the preceding verse.

56. See Lewy (1924: 27), Albright (1932: 101–102), Vogelstein (1944: 8,26–27), and Finegan (1964: 210). The latter contravenes elementary rules of Hebrew grammar by interpreting את ראש as an adjectival modifier of בשנת מלכו (it is of course the object of נשא).

57. It is also worth noting that the Phoenician equivalent of בשנת מלכו occurs in a Sidonian inscription of the 5th century BC (CIS I: 4 = Cooke 1903: 40)—בירח מפן[ע] בשת מ[לכן]י מלך בדעשתרת| מלך צדנם ('in the month Mopha in the accession year of Bodashtart, king of the Sidonians').

of the law', in the 18th year of his reign, but LXX also tells us more specifically that this happened in the 8th (LXX[BL]) or 7th (LXX[AN]) month of that year. Whichever month date is preferred in LXX it might reasonably be argued that text-critical considerations favour the originality of LXX's longer text over MT's shorter text: either month date is, or would appear to be, in direct contradiction to the fact that Josiah's subsequent celebration of the Passover is also dated to the 18th year of his reign, and it is therefore easy to see why a later editor might have chosen to suppress a month date at this point, but less easy to account for its later insertion (Begrich 1929a:75). However, literary considerations make it more probable that the shorter text is original (see below, p. 176n.). As far as the inner-Greek variation over the month number is concerned, it is probably easier to assume that '8th month' was changed to '7th month' in order to associate the covenant ceremony which followed the discovery of the lawbook with the Feast of Booths, than to explain a reverse alteration of '7th month' into '8th month'. This last reading possibly originated as a corrupt variant or dittography of the preceding year-date ('in the 18th year of King Josiah').

5

THE HISTORICAL CHRONOLOGY OF
ISRAEL AND JUDAH

5.1 *Calendars and dating systems*

External chronological evidence relating to the historical chronology of Israel and Judah is provided by Mesopotamian and (to a
lesser extent) Egyptian sources. In order to make proper use of this
information it is necessary to have some understanding of the
calendars and dating systems used in Mesopotamia and Egypt, and
also of the calendars and dating systems used by Israel and Judah
during the period of the monarchy. As far as Mesopotamia is
concerned the facts are relatively straightforward. During the first
millennium BC the Assyrians and Babylonians followed a lunisolar
calendar in which cycles of twelve lunar months (354 days) were
adjusted to correspond with the solar year and its cycle of seasons
by periodic insertion of an intercalary month; the first month of
this calendar was Nisan, corresponding to March/April of the
Julian calendar.[1] During the same period Assyrian and Babylonian
reigns were postdated, so that a king's first regnal year was
identified with the calendar year which began on Nisan 1 after his
accession.[2] In order to distinguish Mesopotamian years from
Julian years it is convenient to use the abbreviation 'Nis.' (for
'Nisan calendar'): thus '612 BC (Nis.)' refers to the Babylonian or

---

1. On this and other Mesopotamian calendars, such as the Middle Assyrian
calendar of the second millennium BC, see Hunger 1976–80. The modern Gregorian
calendar, introduced by Pope Gregory XIII in 1582 AD, is a slightly modified
version of the Julian calendar introduced by Julius Caesar in 45 BC. Historians
normally use the Julian calendar rather than the Gregorian calendar to refer to dates
earlier than 1582 AD, except when calculating the dates of seasonal events in remote
antiquity; see Bickerman ²1980:10f.
2. See p. 85.

Assyrian year which began in Nisan of 612 BC and ended in Adar of 611 BC.[3]

In Egypt a solar calendar was used for civil purposes.[4] This divided the year into twelve months of 30 days each plus five epagomenal days at the end of the year. But unlike the Julian calendar, with its system of leap years, the Egyptian calendar made no provision for the fact that the true solar year is fractionally longer than 365 days, with the result that the Egyptian new year (Thoth 1) retreated progressively through the seasons by one day in every four Julian years. In 26 BC, when Augustus reformed the Egyptian calendar by introducing a system of leap years, Thoth 1 corresponded to August 29. However, in the sixth century BC the Egyptian year began in January, while in the tenth century BC it began in April of the Julian calendar. Unfortunately we do not know whether the regnal years ascribed to Egyptian rulers during the Third Intermediate Period (from the eleventh century to the mid-seventh century BC) were identical with civil calendar years, or whether, as in the New Kingdom, they were reckoned from the actual date of accession (Kitchen 1973a:74n.). All we know is that at some point between the end of the New Kingdom and the start of the Saite Dynasty (in 664 BC) the New Kingdom dating system was abandoned in favour of the earlier system of antedating, in which a king's first regnal year was identified with the calendar year which began on Thoth 1 preceding his accession.[5]

The major calendrical/dating problem in reconstructing Israelite and Judean chronology concerns the nature of the calendar(s) and dating system(s) that were used in pre-exilic Israel and Judah. The official Judean calendar of post-exilic times was more or less identical with the Babylonian calendar, except that months were initially numbered rather than named.[6] But we clearly cannot assume that the same calendar was necessarily used in pre-exilic Israel and Judah, although it would obviously simplify the task of

3. See appendix E for a list of Babylonian/Jewish month names and their modern calendrical equivalents.

4. See Parker 1950; Bickerman [2]1980:40–43.

5. See p. 86f. for a discussion of Egyptian dating systems.

6. The use of Babylonian month names (as in the modern Jewish calendar) does not appear to have become widespread in Judean circles until comparatively late in the post-exilic period, although they were used for official purposes under the Persian empire, and they are also used by Nehemiah (a Persian official) in the so-called 'Nehemiah Memoir'. See de Vaux 1961:185.

correlating Mesopotamian and Israelite-Judean data if this were the case.

There is in fact a wide spectrum of scholarly opinion concerning the pre-exilic Israelite-Judean calendar, which is variously supposed to have been a lunisolar, solar, or lunar calendar beginning in either autumn or spring. One point on which there is fairly general agreement is that the original Israelite-Judean calendar was probably broadly identical with the Canaanite-Phoenician calendar, in view of the fact that month names which are attested in Phoenician inscriptions also occur in the account of the construction and dedication of the temple in 1 Kings 6–8; the months in question are 'Ziv, which is the second month' (1K 6.1, 37), 'Bul, which is the eighth month' (1K 6.38), and 'Ethanim, which is the seventh month' (1K 8.2). This view is disputed by Kugler (1922:12–17) and Gandz (1954:627), who argue that the use of Canaanite month names in these passages may be explained on the assumption that there was an abortive attempt by Solomon to introduce Phoenician month names in place of the allegedly earlier system of numbering months, which was promptly reintroduced after Solomon's death.[7] But this theory is improbable, for there is little doubt that Abib, which is mentioned in several passages in Exodus and Deuteronomy (Ex 13.4; 23.15; 34.18; Dt 16.1), belongs to the same series of month names, even if it is as yet unattested in Phoenician. Kugler's contention that חדש האביב is merely a description ('the month of ripening barley ears') and not a proper month name, is hardly convincing, since the month names used in 1 Kings 6–8 have precisely the same descriptive character: Ziv (זו) is the month of 'flowers', Ethanim (האתנים) the month of 'permanent streams' (i.e. the month when only permanent streams were still flowing), and Bul (בול) the month of 'rain' or 'produce'.

On the question of whether the ancient Israelite-Judean calendar was lunisolar, solar, or lunar, it may be noted that a majority of scholars have generally favoured the first alternative.[8] However, Koenig (1906) argued that Israel and Judah originally

---

7. Few modern scholars will be convinced by Kugler's opinion that the antiquity of this system is demonstrated by Joshua 4.19 (a Priestly note on the date of Israel's entry into Canaan). The use of ordinal numbers to identify months is in fact restricted to passages that are, for the most part, clearly exilic or post-exilic (the month numbers in 1 Kings 6–8 are probably late glosses).

8. Proponents of this view include Kugler (1922:2–12), Mowinckel (1952:20–25), Segal (1957), and de Vaux (1961:188–190).

followed a solar calendar, and this theory was later restated and developed by Morgenstern in a series of long articles on the subject.[9] Finally Gandz (1954) has argued that the ancient Israelite-Judean calendar was a purely lunar calendar (like the Islamic calendar) in which no effort was made to adjust the lunar year of 354 days to the solar year of $365\frac{1}{4}$ days.

Gandz's theory has significant chronological consequences which set it apart from the lunisolar and solar theories of other scholars. The lunar year is $11\frac{1}{4}$ days shorter than a solar year, and 100 lunar years are therefore equivalent to only 97 solar years, so that if Israel and Judah originally followed a lunar calendar it will be necessary to subtract 3 years for every 100 years of Israelite-Judean chronology before we can relate this to Mesopotamian or Egyptian chronology. However, Gandz's theory must certainly be rejected. An unadjusted lunar calendar wanders progressively back through the cycle of seasons, making it impossible for seasonal festivals to be dated to a particular calendar month or to other specific points in the calendar. The alleged lunar character of the ancient Israelite-Judean calendar is therefore refuted by the existence of seasonal festivals which *were* dated in this way—the Feast of Unleavened Bread, dated to Abib (Ex 13.4 etc.), and the Feast of Ingathering at 'the end/turn of the year' (Ex 23.16; 34.22). Gandz attempts to counter these objections by arguing that Abib is not really a proper month name (see above), and that שנה ('year') in Exodus 23.16 and 34.22 denotes the agricultural cycle rather than the calendar year (Gandz 1954:631, 635). Neither of these arguments is convincing; the first has been rejected above, and the assumption that Israel and Judah distinguished between agricultural years and calendar years is of doubtful validity (see below, p. 167f.).[10]

9. See Morgenstern 1962 for a summary article with a bibliography of his earlier studies. Morgenstern's views are also summarized and endorsed by Finegan (1964:35–37).

10. A further argument that is sometimes adduced in favour of the solar or lunisolar nature of the Israelite-Judean calendar is the seasonal character of the month names Abib, Ziv, Ethanim, and Bul (see above). But this argument, being essentially etymological, is not necessarily relevant to the historical nature of the Israelite-Judean calendar during the monarchic period. It is not inconceivable that an originally lunisolar calendar with seasonal month names might develop into a purely lunar calendar through the abandonment of a system of intercalary months. Compare the analogous development of the Middle Assyrian calendar in the second millennium BC: available evidence suggests that this calendar, which was a lunar

It is less important for our purposes that we should decide between solar and lunisolar calendrical theories, since 100 solar years are more or less exactly equivalent to 100 lunisolar years. But it may be noted that what limited evidence there is tends to favour the second alternative, although we must certainly discount the oft-repeated argument that the lunar character of the Israelite-Judean month is demonstrated by the fact that Hebrew words for 'month' (חֹדֶשׁ, יֶרַח) are similar or identical to words meaning 'moon' (יָרֵחַ) or 'new moon' (חֹדֶשׁ)[11]—the etymological connection between 'month' and 'moon' in English and other European languages does not alter the fact that there is no correlation between months and moons in the solar calendar used by modern western societies. Equally unconvincing is Gandz's a priori argument that evolutionary development from a solar calendar to a lunisolar calendar is without parallel in other cultures (Gandz 1954:626), since the point at issue is not evolutionary development but the possible replacement of a solar calendar with a lunisolar calendar.[12] On the other hand there is some force in the argument that a lunar or lunisolar calendar is suggested by the importance of the new moon festival in pre-exilic Israel and Judah (Gandz 1954:632). And since the ancient Israelite-Judean calendar was evidently similar if not identical to the Phoenician calendar, it may also be noted that Phoenician calendar months apparently *were* tied to phases of the moon (Kugler 1922:7), and that references to מפע

---

calendar in the sense that months were not adjusted to keep in step with the cycle of seasons, developed from an earlier calendar in which some form of seasonal adjustment *was* carried out (Hunger 1976–80:299).

11. This argument is used by Mowinckel (1952:22), Gandz (1954:630), and de Vaux (1961:183), among others; it is worth noting that Mowinckel, unlike Gandz and de Vaux, does not fall into the trap of confusing יֶרַח ('month') and יָרֵחַ ('moon').

12. A parallel may be found in Ptolemaic Egypt, where in the 3rd century BC the Macedonian (lunisolar) calendar replaced the Egyptian (solar) calendar for official and religious purposes (Bickerman ²1980:38f.). It is also worth noting that Gandz's notion of a uniform progression from lunar to lunisolar to solar calendar is belied by the development of the Middle Assyrian (semi-lunar) calendar from the Old Assyrian (lunisolar) calendar. [See n. 10; the Middle Assyrian calendar was lunisolar to the extent that it operated with lunar months and a solar year, but unlike a true lunisolar calendar it made no attempt to correlate these two calendrical units, so that different years began with different months. This is not unlike the situation which exists in our own calendar, which does not attempt to correlate months and weeks, with the result that different months and years begin on different days of the week.]

לפני or 'first Mopha' in Punic inscriptions (*KAI* 110.3; 137.5) provide evidence of the lunisolar character of the Punic calendar, assuming that this designation is correctly interpreted as indicating an intercalary month (like 'first Adar' in the Babylonian-Jewish calendar).[13]

A final argument in favour of the lunisolar character of the ancient Israelite calendar may be taken from 1 Kings 12.32–33, which accuses Jeroboam of having wilfully altered the date of the autumn festival from the seventh to the eighth month. This has been interpreted by J. B. Segal (1957:257–259) as evidence that Jeroboam intercalated an extra month in that particular year, but it is more likely that the passage describes a permanent alteration in the date of the autumn festival, since it is cited as an act of wilful perversity comparable with Jeroboam's institution of the calf-idols at Dan and Bethel (1K 12.28–30), his construction of shrines at the 'high places' (1K 12.31), and his appointment of non-levitical priests (1K 12.31). It is, however, historically improbable that Jeroboam would have gratuitously altered the month in which the festival was held, since this could only have diminished its effectiveness as a rival to the Judean festival. But it is also unlikely that the story is a complete fabrication, for the accusation that Jeroboam altered the date of the autumn festival is a curious accusation for the Deuteronomistic writer of this passage to have invented, especially since—unlike the previous charges against Jeroboam—it does not actually contravene Deuteronomic legislation. It may therefore be suggested that in later times the autumn festival was indeed celebrated a month later in the north than in the south, and that this circumstance was put to apologetic use by the author of 1 Kings 12.32–33, who traced it back to an act of wilful perversity by Jeroboam. There is no reason, though, to suppose that the date of this festival was in fact altered by Jeroboam or by anyone else, and a more probable explanation is that the north Israelite calendar had in later times fallen a month behind the Judean calendar, with the result that the Israelite month in which the festival was celebrated was now equivalent to the following month of the Judean calendar. The most probable reason for this

13. See Berliner (1916), who argues that 'first Mopha' cannot be a regular calendar month such as 'first Tishri' or 'first Kanun' in the Syrian calendar, because the month name 'Mopha' is also attested without an accompanying qualifier.

shift is that it occurred through the insertion of an additional intercalary month in the northern kingdom (or the omission of an intercalary month in the south).[14] Similar shifts in the correlation of different calendars are known to have happened on other occasions, one instance being the shift in correlation between the Macedonian and Syrian/Babylonian calendars which occurred during the first half of the first century AD (Finegan 1964:61–73; Bickerman [2]1980:25).

Having established that the pre-exilic Israelite-Judean calendar was probably lunisolar, and that it was certainly not a purely lunar calendar, we may turn to the question of the point at which the calendar year was reckoned to begin. Here the Biblical evidence would appear to be quite unambiguous. Certain texts, which are normally regarded as late, clearly presuppose a calendar that began in the spring; thus, for example, Exodus 12.2 (P), which places divine authority behind a spring calendar in which the Passover month (Abib/Nisan) is counted as the first month. On the other hand certain other texts, including texts which are normally regarded as early, apparently presuppose a calendar which began in the autumn. Among these are Exodus 23.16 and Exodus 34.22, which state that the Feast of Ingathering (later known as the Feast of Booths) was to be celebrated at the 'end' or 'turn' of the year: the Hebrew expressions are בצאת השנה, 'at the going out of the year' (Ex 23.16), and תקופת השנה, 'at the going round of the year' (Ex 34.22).[15] Similarly legislation requiring that the land be left fallow

14. Contrast Talmon (1958), who cites 1 Kings 12.32–33 as evidence that the Israelite calendar began one month later than the Judean calendar, but ascribes this difference to a deliberate calendrical alteration by Jeroboam.

15. There has previously been some dispute over the significance of these expressions. However, Kutsch (1971) has convincingly refuted the theory that בצאת השנה denotes the *beginning* of the year (Begrich 1929a:80–81); this notion primarily depends upon a false analogy with the use of יצא and related nominal forms to refer to the rising of celestial bodies. An alternative explanation of תקופת השנה is offered by Vogelstein (1944:30–31), who follows Begrich (1929a:80) in arguing that תקופה in Psalm 19.7 denotes the mid-point of the sun's circuit (the point at which the sun 'turns back' to travel underneath the earth), and concludes that תקופת השנה in Exodus 34.22 must be taken to denote the *middle* of the year (LXX: μεσοῦντος τοῦ ἐνιαυτοῦ). But it is much more probable that תקופה in Psalm 19.7 denotes the *end-point* of the sun's *celestial* circuit—the 'course' referred to in verse 6—and that LXX's translation of Exodus 34.22 merely reflects the fact that the Feast of Booths occurred halfway through the year in the spring calendar of post-exilic Judaism; contrast 2 Chronicles 24.23, where לתקופת השנה refers to the spring, and is accordingly translated as μετὰ τὴν συντέλειαν τοῦ ἐνιαυτοῦ, 'after

every 7th and every 50th year (Ex 23.10–11; Lv 25.1–22) only really makes sense if the year began in the autumn, since a year starting in the spring cuts across two agricultural cycles. Again, the instruction that a trumpeter should be sent out on the Day of Atonement to proclaim the 50th year as a jubilee year (Lv 25.8–12) makes excellent sense in the context of an autumn calendar in which the Day of Atonement came a few days after the new year, but is less satisfactory within the context of the spring calendar which the text in its present (post-exilic) form clearly presupposes (Leviticus 25.9 dates the Day of Atonement to the tenth day of the seventh month, with the result that the jubilee year is apparently proclaimed six months in advance). One final piece of evidence which appears to point to an autumn calendar is the fact that the (10th century) Gezer Calendar (*KAI* 182) begins its list of agricultural activities with two months of ingathering (אסף).

The obvious conclusion to be drawn from these facts is that the ancient Israelite-Judean calendar began in the autumn, and that this was subsequently replaced by a spring calendar resembling the Babylonian calendar.[16] There are, however, a significant number of scholars who dispute this view, maintaining that Israel and Judah followed a spring calendar throughout the monarchic period,[17] or that the spring calendar was used in Israel but not in Judah,[18] or conversely that the spring calendar was used in Judah but not in Israel.[19] The theory that Israel and Judah each employed different calendars during the period of the divided monarchy is essentially a device for harmonizing minor discrepancies in the chronology of Kings; there is no independent evidence which supports this hypothesis,[20] and the evidential value

the end of the year'. (συντέλεια is also used as the Greek equivalent of תקופה in Sirach 43.7, where it occurs in an obscure passage dealing with the phases of the moon.) Further evidence that תקופה denotes the completion of a circuit or cycle is provided by Job 1.5, where the cognate verb הקיף ('go around') is used to refer to the end of a week-long cycle of feast days.

16. Wellhausen 1885:108–109; Begrich 1929a:69–90; Mowinckel 1932:174–176; Auerbach 1952; de Vaux 1961:190–193, and others.

17. Mahler 1916:210–220; Kugler 1922:136–150. Clines (1974) leans towards this view, but argues that the evidence is inconclusive.

18. Coucke 1928:1252; Vogelstein 1944:17f.; Thiele ³1983:51–54; Pavlovský and Vogt 1964:323–324.

19. Kleber 1921:15; Tadmor 1962:265–267.

20. Cf. Thiele ³1983:53: 'For Israel there seems to be no scriptural evidence as to the time of the beginning of the regnal year. However, when a Nisan-to-Nisan

of chronological discrepancies which might be resolved in this way is vitiated by the existence of numerous discrepancies which require more drastic methods of harmonization. In any case one would naturally expect that two kingdoms which shared close cultural ties and had been politically united under David and Solomon would have initially used the same calendar. It is unlikely that Jeroboam would have adopted a spring calendar simply because he had become aquainted with the Egyptian wandering calendar—which at that time began in the spring—during the period of his political exile in Egypt (Coucke 1928:1952; Thiele ³1983:53).

The theory that Israel and Judah followed a spring calendar throughout the monarchic period has tended to be espoused by scholars who have sought to deny the late date which Wellhausen and others ascribed to P (which uses a spring calendar). The central argument put forward by supporters of this theory is that evidence which apparently favours an autumn calendar is simply irrelevant, since it relates to the agricultural year, which was not necessarily identical with the civil calendar year. Clines (1974) puts the case against an autumn calendar as follows. Exodus 23.14–17 and 34.18–23 describe a series of agricultural festivals ending, appropriately, with the Feast of Ingathering, when each year's agricultural work was completed (Clines 1974:26–27). The sabbath and jubilee years are likewise agricultural years (Clines 1974:30). The Gezer Calendar is arranged according to the activities of the farmer's year, and is in any case inconsistent with Exodus 23.14–17 and 34.18–23 in that it attests a year which *begins* (rather than ends) with ingathering (Clines 1974:38).

This argument is at first sight quite plausible, in view of the agricultural associations of the texts used to argue for an autumn calendar, but it loses its plausibility on closer inspection. For a start, it is hardly legitimate to describe the sabbath and jubilee years as (merely) 'agricultural years', when as well as being years of agricultural inactivity they were also years of 'release' (שמטה) or 'liberation' (דרור), in which debts were to be remitted (Dt 15.7–11), Israelite debt-servants released (Dt 15.12–18; Lv

regnal year is used for Israel together with a Tishri-to-Tishri year for Judah, the perplexing discrepancies disappear and a harmonious chronological pattern results.' Other devices by which Thiele achieves this 'harmonious chronological pattern' were discussed in the previous chapter.

25.39–55), and property outside cities was to revert to its
original owners (Lv 25.25–34). There is also significant evidence
that in early post-exilic times the sabbath year was not regarded as
an agricultural year, even though the spring calendar year of that
period obviously did not correspond to the cycle of agricultural
seasons. Leviticus 25.3–4 states that Israelites are permitted to sow
and harvest for six years but that in the seventh year the land is to be
left fallow. Leviticus 25.20–22 then deals with the problem of what
the Israelites are to eat in the seventh year, and the answer—rather
surprisingly—is that God will ensure that the sixth year produces
enough food for *three* years, and that the Israelites will therefore be
able to eat the produce of that year until the harvest of the *ninth* year
provides a new supply of food. What, we may ask, happened to the
harvest of the eighth year, when agricultural activities were once
more permitted? The only satisfactory explanation is that for the
writer of Leviticus 25.20–22 the sabbath year began in the spring,
thus preventing the harvesting of crops sown in the autumn of the
sixth year and also the sowing of crops to be harvested in the
summer of the eighth year, with the resultant loss of two
consecutive harvests; only in the second half of the eighth year
could crops be sown once again, producing a harvest for the ninth
year.[21] The fact that the writer of Leviticus 25.20–22 thereby failed
to distinguish between calendar years and agricultural years, even
though this distinction would have rescued his legislation from the
realms of utopian impracticality, must make it rather doubtful that
such a distinction would have been recognized by earlier writers
either. It should be noted that Leviticus 25.20–22 is clearly a
secondary reinterpretation of legislation which originally envisaged
the loss of a single harvest and which therefore presupposed a year
which began in the autumn. Finally, it must be said that the Gezer
Calendar cannot be dismissed as a catalogue of activities listed
according to the agricultural cycle, since this fails to account for the
fact that the Calendar begins with ingathering, which is the final
activity of this cycle.[22]

21. The same explanation has previously been given by Morgenstern (1935:83–
86).

22. One other piece of evidence which supports an original autumn calendar is
cited by Clines (1974:39–40) as positive evidence in favour of an original spring
calendar. The only agricultural festival which is dated to a specific calendar month
in pre-Priestly legislation is the Feast of Unleavened Bread in the month Abib
(Ex 23.15; 34.18; Dt 16.1). Clines is undoubtedly right in claiming that some

Having now considered and rejected the 'agricultural year' theory, we must look a little more closely at the apparent discrepancy, noted by Clines, between the Gezer Calendar and the festal calendars of Exodus: the Gezer Calendar clearly presupposes a year which began with ingathering,[23] whereas the Exodus calendars date the Feast of Ingathering to the 'end' or 'turn' of the year. Taken in isolation these passages might reasonably be taken to indicate that the Feast of Ingathering was celebrated in the final month of the autumn calendar year, and since this festival is elsewhere dated to Ethanim, or the seventh month of the spring calendar (1K 8.2; 12.32; Lv 23.34), this leads naturally to the conclusion that Ethanim was the final month of the autumn calendar.[24] Other evidence, however, suggests that Ethanim was regarded as the *first* month of the autumn calendar. This is indicated by the fact that the list of agricultural seasons given by the Gezer Calendar appears to correspond with a calendar beginning in September/October,[25] and also, more clearly, by the fact that the Day of Atonement on the tenth day of the seventh month (Lv 16.29) logically has the character of a new year's ritual designed to expiate sins and impurities incurred during the previous year;[26] the new year associations of the Day of Atonement

explanation of this month-date is called for, but it is not very likely that Abib is mentioned simply 'because it is a more significant month than the other months in which the harvest and ingathering festivals fall, i.e. because it is the first month of the year of months.' A more probable explanation is that Abib is mentioned precisely because it was *not* the first month of the year: the Feast of Ingathering was dated to the 'end' of the autumn year and consequently did not need a specific month-date, but the Feast of Unleavened Bread occurred halfway through the autumn calendar year, and was therefore dated specifically to the month Abib.

23. It is doubtful that ingathering as an agricultural activity really occupied two whole months, which is the period allotted to 'ingathering' in the Gezer Calendar, but the term is probably intended as the description of a season in which there was relatively little other farming activity.

24. Auerbach 1952:334–335. Cf. Kutsch 1971:20–21 and Day 1985:19–20.

25. Donner and Rollig ³1971–6:II:182.

26. Note the occurrence of a similar ritual in Babylonia on Nisan 5, the fifth day of the Babylonian new year (de Vaux 1961:508; ANET p.333f.). Against the view that the Day of Atonement was not instituted before post-exilic times (Wellhausen 1885:108; de Vaux 1961:509–510) it must be said that in this case it is hard to account for the fact that this ritual was not performed until the *seventh* month of the post-exilic calendar (contrast Ezekiel 45.18–20, which provides for an atonement ritual on the first day of the first month). It does not seem to me that much weight can be attached to the silence of pre-exilic sources: the Day of Atonement, as it is

are also reflected in the fact that it provided the occasion for the proclamation of jubilee years (Lv 25.9). Finally, some account should also be taken of the fact that the present Jewish calendar, which has reverted to an autumn new year in disregard of Exodus 12.2, counts Tishri (= Ethanim) as the first month of the year.[27]

Cumulatively this evidence suggests that we should reexamine the assumption that Exodus 23.14–17 and 34.18–23 require the Feast of Ingathering to be celebrated in the final month of the year. This assumption presupposes that the Hebrew expressions בצאת השנה ('at the end of the year') and תקופת השנה ('at the turn of the year') indicate the period *immediately preceding* the end of the calendar year. But since the Mishnaic Hebrew expression מוצאי שבת ('the end [going out] of the sabbath) denotes the day *after* the sabbath,[28] it may reasonably be asked whether the Biblical expressions cited above do not denote the period immediately after the end of the calendar year; this is also supported by the fact that LXX translates לתקופת השנה in 2 Chronicles 24.23 as μετὰ τὴν συντέλειαν τοῦ ἐνιαυτοῦ, 'after the end of the year.' There is in this case no inconsistency between the Exodus passages and other evidence: the Feast of Ingathering is celebrated in the first month after the end of the year, and Ethanim (= Tishri) is consequently identified as the first month of the autumn calendar.

Evidence that Israel and Judah originally followed an autumn calendar raises the important question of when the Judean community adopted the Babylonian spring calendar. The most obvious possibility of course is that this occurred during the Babylonian exile, as is suggested by the fact that most or all of the passages which presuppose a spring calendar are either exilic or post-exilic in date (Wellhausen 1885:109; Mowinckel 1932:175f.). It obviously cannot be argued from Exodus 12.2 (P) that the spring calendar dates back to the time of Moses; but neither can one argue from the month dates in Jeremiah 36 and 2 Kings 25 (and parallel

described in Priestly legislature, is not a feast day, and is therefore naturally absent from the festal calendars of Exodus and Deuteronomy.

27. This calendar is not explicitly attested before the Mishnah, though it presumably existed from an earlier date. The impracticality of relating sabbath and jubilee years to the spring calendar may have been one reason for the readoption of an autumn calendar.

28. See Jastrow 1903:746 and Kutsch 1971:19; similarly the Mishnaic Hebrew expression מוצאי שביעית ('the end of the seventh year') denotes the year *after* the seventh year.

passages) that the spring calendar was introduced in pre-exilic times (contra Begrich 1929a:70–72). There is no doubt that Jeremiah 36 presupposes a spring calendar, for the ninth month, in which Jeremiah's scroll was read to Jehoiakim, is clearly identified as a winter month by the fact that Jehoiakim is depicted as sitting in front of a brazier in his winter palace. Nor is there any doubt that the dates associated with the fall of Jerusalem reflect the same spring calendar: Jerusalem was destroyed in the fifth month according to 2 Kings 25.8, and we know from Jeremiah 40.10 and 41.8 that this occurred during the summer. But since the book of Jeremiah and the final chapters of Kings were both composed during the Babylonian exile, and almost certainly in Babylonia rather than Palestine,[29] this proves only that the authors of these passages expressed month dates according to the spring calendar with which their readers were familiar.

There are, however, a number of indications which suggest that the spring calendar was in fact adopted somewhat earlier than the exilic period. In the first place it is surely curious, if the spring calendar was first adopted in Babylonia, that Babylonian month names were not adopted at the same time. The standard explanation, that these names were initially avoided because of their pagan associations (de Vaux 1961:185), is hardly convincing in view of the fact that later Judaism had no such scruples about adopting them.[30] In any case it is only Tammuz which shows obvious pagan associations, and similar associations are also evident in the Babylonian personal names carried by a number of prominent exiles.[31] A more probable explanation of the fact that the Judean

29. Nicholson 1970:116–135. A Palestinian origin for the final chapters of Kings is (in my opinion) virtually inconceivable in view of the fact that 2 Kings 25 seeks to assert that southern Palestine was totally depopulated during the exile: Nebuzaradan is said to have deported almost the entire population of Judah (2K 25.11–12), after which the remaining population fled *en masse* to Egypt following the murder of Gedaliah (2K 25.26). Such an account could hardly have been written by a Palestinian author, but may reasonably be viewed as the work of a Babylonian exile who sought to prove that the community of Babylonian exiles were the true remnant of the Judean nation.

30. See p. 160n. The fact that Nehemiah uses Babylonian month names in the 'Nehemiah Memoir' is clear proof that pious Jews were unconcerned about the pagan associations of these names long before they entered into general circulation.

31. E.g. Shenazzar, Sheshbazzar, and Mordecai (1C 3.18; Ezr 1.18; 2.2), whose names are compounded with the divine names Sin, Shamash (Shash), and Marduk. Note also 'Shawash-sharezer' (שושראצר), a Judean exile mentioned on a 6th-century seal (Avigad 1965:228).

community did not initially use Babylonian month names for the months of the spring calendar is that this calendar was originally adopted in Palestine during the pre-exilic period when these names would have been unfamiliar to most Judeans.

A second indication that the spring calendar was adopted in pre-exilic times is provided by the fact that Jehoiakim's 11-year reign is incompatible with Babylonian chronological data unless it is reckoned according to a spring calendar. We know from evidence provided by the Babylonian Chronicle that Josiah was killed in or shortly before Tammuz of 609 BC (Nis.), and also that Jehoiakim replaced Jehoahaz in or shortly after Elul of the same year (see below, p. 225f.). Jehoahaz is ascribed a reign of only 3 months (2K 23.31), and must therefore have been deposed in favour of Jehoiakim before the end of the Judean year in which Josiah was killed,[32] which is either 609 BC (spr.) or 610 BC (aut.) according to whether Judah followed a spring calendar or autumn calendar at this date. The end of Jehoiakim's reign may also be dated with similar precision, for we know from the Babylonian Chronicle that Jehoiachin, his successor, was deposed in Adar of 598 BC (Nis.) (see p. 228); Jehoiachin, who like Jehoahaz reigned for only 3 months (2K 24.8), must accordingly have succeeded Jehoiakim in either the second half of 598 BC (spr.) or the first half of 598 BC (aut.). We therefore have three possible sets of Judean dates for Jehoiakim's reign: 610 BC (aut.) to 598 BC (aut.), 610 BC (aut.) to 598 BC (spr.), or 609 BC (spr.) to 598 BC (spr.).[33] However, it is only the second and third sets of dates which are compatible with the 11-year reign which 2 Kings 23.36 ascribes to Jehoiakim, for if the latter reigned from 610 BC (aut.) to 598 BC (aut.) he must necessarily be ascribed a reign of either 12 regnal years (counted non-inclusively) or 13 regnal years (counted inclusively). On the other hand a reign which began in 609 BC (spr.) and ended in 598 BC (spr.) works out at 11 regnal years if these are counted non-inclusively, while a reign which began in 610 BC (aut.) and ended in 598 BC (spr.) works out at 11 regnal years (counted

32. With either postdating or antedating, reign lengths are not stated in fractions of a year unless they began and ended within the same calendar year (any king whose reign spanned the first new year from his accession was automatically credited with at least one regnal year).

33. Hypothetically one might add a fourth set of dates, 609 BC (spr.) to 598 BC (aut.), but no one believes that Judah changed from spring calendar to autumn calendar in the course of Jehoiakim's reign.

non-inclusively) if it is also supposed that the change from autumn to spring calendar involved lengthening the year preceding the change by six months or thereabouts (see below, p. 178f.). The obvious conclusion to be drawn from this is that Judah adopted the spring calendar before or during Jehoiakim's reign, for while it is reasonable to suppose that an exilic writer may have replaced original month names by their equivalent numbers in the spring calendar it is much less likely that he would have carried this calendrical revision to the extent of altering original reign lengths.

A number of scholars have nevertheless attempted to defend the view that Judah followed an autumn calendar throughout the pre-exilic period by arguing that Jehoiakim came to the throne at the beginning of 609 BC on this calendar.[34] This is untenable, however, for it requires us to suppose *either* that Jehoahaz's reign extended from 610 BC (aut.) to 609 BC (aut.) *or* that there was an interval of days or weeks between the removal of Jehoahaz in 610 BC (aut.) and Jehoiakim's accession in the following calendar year, 609 BC (aut.). The first of these alternatives requires Jehoahaz to be ascribed 1 regnal year, non-inclusively dated (or 2 years by inclusive dating), and thus conflicts with his stated reign length of only 3 months (see n. 32). And the second is excluded by virtue of the fact that if Jehoiakim came to the throne in the calendar year following the removal of Jehoahaz, this would necessarily have been counted either as Jehoahaz's last regnal year (although the latter was no longer on the throne)—in which case we are once again saying that Jehoahaz's (official) reign extended from 610 BC (aut.) to 609 BC (aut.)—or as Jehoiakim's first regnal year, which produces a total of 12 years for Jehoiakim's reign.[35] To suppose that 609 BC (aut.) was counted as Jehoiakim's zero accession-year, even though Jehoahaz's reign ended in 610 BC (aut.), would be to do violence to the basic principles of postdating, in which zero accession-years were used to avoid 1-year overlaps between

34. Malamat 1956; 1968:140–141; 1975:127; Thiele [3]1983:182); Horn 1967; Freedy and Redford 1970:464–467.

35. An analogous situation in Mesopotamian chronology is provided by the circumstances of Tiglathpileser III's accession on 13th Iyyar 745 BC, after a period of anarchy which began in the previous calendar year. Later chronologists responsible for the Assyrian Kinglist counted 745 BC (Nis.) as the final year of Tiglathpileser's predecessor's reign, even though he was no longer in effective control, and may have already been deposed; Tiglathpileser, on the other hand, counted 745 BC (Nis.) as the first year of his own reign.

successive reigns, *not* to create 1-year gaps in the chronology.[36]

There is, then, a strong case for thinking that the spring calendar was adopted in Judah during pre-exilic times, and that this occurred before or during the reign of Jehoiakim. A *terminus post quem* for the change from autumn to spring calendar is provided by the fact that the latter was almost certainly adopted under Mesopotamian influence and is therefore unlikely to have been introduced before the reign of Ahaz, when Judah first came into direct contact with the expanding Assyrian empire under Tiglathpileser III. This gives us seven Judean reigns during which the spring calendar was possibly adopted, these being the reigns of Ahaz, Hezekiah, Manasseh, Amon, Josiah, Jehoahaz, and Jehoiakim.

Scholars who have held that the spring calendar was adopted during pre-exilic times have generally interpreted this as a direct consequence of Assyrian or Babylonian suzerainty. Thus Begrich (1929a:157) and Jepsen (1964:28, 36) argue that since Judah became a vassal-state of Assyria during the reign of Ahaz, the spring calendar was most probably introduced along with the Assyrian system of postdating at the accession of Ahaz's successor, Hezekiah.[37] A similar line of reasoning is followed by Andersen (1969:100–102), except that Andersen prefers to date the calendar change to the period following Hezekiah's capitulation to Sennacherib, most probably at the accession of his successor, Manasseh.

36. Other arguments against the chronological reconstructions of Malamat *et al.* are presented by Clines (1972). The most serious of these is that if we date Jehoiakim's first regnal year to 608 BC (aut.), the battle of Carchemish in the summer of 605 BC (Nis.) must then be equated with Jehoiakim's 3rd regnal year, 606 BC (aut.), whereas according to Jeremiah 46.2 it occurred in Jehoiakim's *4th* regnal year. Thiele (²1965:161–163, ³1983:183) attempts to get round this difficulty by arguing that although Kings uses an autumn calendar for Judean (and Babylonian) dates, the book of Jeremiah uses a Nisan calendar—except in the case of passages which are paralleled in Kings!

37. A change from antedating to postdating would almost certainly have been effected at the beginning of a reign, as it would hardly have been practical to renumber regnal years retrospectively. There is, however, no obvious reason why a calendar change could not have been introduced at any time. Begrich argues that the adoption of the spring calendar during the middle of a king's reign would have introduced a possible confusion in the numbering of regnal years, since the year preceding the change might either have been lengthened or shortened by six months; but the decision to begin a new regnal year six months early or late would presumably have been the subject of an official decree, so that it is unlikely that this would have caused any real confusion at the time.

A third possibility is argued by Auerbach (1952:336; 1959), who has been followed by de Vaux (1961:185, 191–192) and Finegan (1964:200–203). Auerbach claims that Biblical evidence demonstrates that the autumn calendar was still in use during the reign of Josiah, and that the spring calendar must therefore have been introduced in the course of Jehoiakim's reign, when Judah became a vassal-state of the Babylonian empire.[38]

Auerbach's principal argument for asserting that the autumn calendar was still in use during Josiah's reign is based on the fact that the account of events in Josiah's 18th year which is given in 2 Kings 22–23 seems to be incompatible with a calendar which began in the spring (cf. Wellhausen 1885:108). According to this account Josiah was told of the discovery of 'the book of the law' after making arrangements for temple repairs during the 18th year of his reign (2K 22.3). After listening to the book being read and having consulted Huldah the prophetess he then convened a special assembly of the Judean people in order to conclude a covenant with Yahweh. Josiah is then said to have carried out a series of religious reforms in both Judah and Samaria, finally returning to Jerusalem and arranging a special celebration of the Passover, also dated in the 18th year of his reign (2K 23.23). It is clearly impossible that all these events can have occurred within the two-week period between the start of the spring calendar year and the date of the Passover (14th Nisan), and Auerbach infers from this that Josiah's 18th year began in the autumn. In which case, since it is unlikely (in Auerbach's opinion) that Josiah would have subsequently introduced the Mesopotamian calendar at a time when he was asserting Judean independence from Assyria, and since it is also unlikely that the spring calendar was introduced during the short reign of Jehoahaz, we come down to Jehoiakim's reign as the earliest—and latest—date for the introduction of the new calendar. More specifically, it is argued by Auerbach that the new calendar was adopted in recognition of Babylonian suzerainty during the summer of 604 BC (Nis.), when (according to Auerbach) Jehoiakim went to offer his submission to Nebuchadrezzar in company with other Syro-Palestinian rulers (*ABC* 5.obv.15f.).[39]

---

38. Pavlovský and Vogt (1964:344–346) combine these last two positions by arguing that the spring calendar was first introduced during the reign of Manasseh and then reintroduced during Jehoiakim's reign.

39. Evidence discussed below (p. 227n.) suggests that Jehoiakim did not in fact

This argument is superficially attractive, but it is based upon an uncritical reading of 2 Kings 22–23. In the first place it should be noted that the account of the reforms given in 2 Kings 23.4–20 has undoubtedly undergone considerable secondary expansion, as is shown by the marked concentration of non-classical syntactic constructions.[40] More important, however, is the fact that this entire section has clearly been secondarily inserted into its present context, since it interrupts the obvious narrative connection between 2 Kings 23.3 (Josiah and 'all the people' conclude a covenant with Yahweh) and 2 Kings 23.21 (Josiah commands 'all the people' to keep the Passover).[41] Without this secondary insertion there is no difficulty in supposing that the Passover was celebrated within two weeks of the discovery of the 'book of the law', in which case the dates given in 2 Kings 22–23 are compatible with either a spring or an autumn calendar.[42]

A more important clue to the date at which the spring calendar was introduced is provided by the festal calendar of Deuteronomy 16.1–17, which, interestingly, is cited by both Begrich and Auerbach in support of mutually incompatible conclusions. Two features of this passage are of relevance. One is that Deuteronomy

offer his submission until the autumn of 604 BC (Nis.).

40. These include the use of Unconverted Perfects after the conjunction Waw (ונשא, והשבית, ונתץ, וטמא, והשליך, ושבר, ושרף: 2K 23.4, 5, 8, 10, 12, 14, 15), and the apparent use of the definite article with construct noun forms (הגג עלית אחז, הקבר איש האלהים, and המזבח בית אל: 2K 23.12, 17, 17).

41. Cf. Kugler (1922:139–141), who argues that the reforms described in this section were actually carried out in Josiah's *12th* year, as stated in 2 Chronicles 34.3–7. However, the Chronicler's account is almost certainly a secondary rewriting of the account given in Kings, and cannot therefore be used as independent historical evidence (Williamson 1982:397f.). 2 Kings 23.4–20 was probably moved from an earlier position after 2 Kings 23.23 in order to absolve Josiah of charges of impropriety in having celebrated the Passover before the temple had yet been purified.

42. Note, however, that LXX's text of 2 Kings 22.3 states that Josiah made arrangements for temple repairs in the 8th (or 7th) month of his 18th year, and that this can only be reconciled with 2 Kings 23.23 (dating the Passover to the same year) if it is assumed that '8th month' is given as the later equivalent of Bul, the second month of the old autumn calendar (or that '7th month' is given as the later equivalent of Ethanim). But LXX's month date is almost certainly secondary, since it requires us to suppose that five (or six) whole months elapsed between the time that Josiah learned of the discovery of the lawbook and his subsequent celebration of the Passover; the original narrative of 2 Kings 22–23 (in which 2 Kings 23.3 was followed directly by 2 Kings 23.21) indicates a much shorter period of no more than a few days or weeks.

16.1 follows Exodus 23.15 and 34.18 in dating the Feast of Unleavened Bread (here amalgamated with the Passover) to the old Canaanite month Abib, which suggests that Deuteronomy in its original form was written before the introduction of the spring calendar and its system of numbering months (cf. Auerbach 1952:336). On the other hand Deuteronomy 16.13–15, in contrast to Exodus 23.16 and 34.22, conspicuously omits any statement that the Feast of Booths (or Feast of Ingathering) was to be celebrated at the 'end' or 'turn' of the year, and would therefore appear to offer evidence that Deuteronomy was written *after* the spring calendar had replaced the old autumn calendar (Begrich 1929a:89). A satisfactory interpretation of Deuteronomy 16 should clearly take account of both points, and it may therefore be suggested that the author of this passage wrote while the old calendar was still in use (hence the reference to Abib) but consciously chose not to endorse the old autumn new year. This in turn suggests that the spring calendar was adopted not because it was imposed by either the Assyrians or the Babylonians (there is no evidence that either power imposed its calendar on vassal nations),[43] but rather because the Deuteronomic school favoured the adoption of this calendar as part of its programme of eliminating Canaanite influences in Israelite religion. There is no doubt that the spring calendar was well-suited to this purpose, as it effectively severed the original connection between the Feast of Booths and the Canaanite new year (with its attendant rituals) while giving increased prominence to Passover and the Feast of Unleavened Bread, which the Deuteronomic programme combined and transformed into the most important of the three annual festivals. If this is correct we may conclude that the spring calendar was most probably introduced, along with other Deuteronomic reforms, in the reign of Josiah.[44] The silence of 2 Kings 22–23 on this matter is not

43. It is worth noting that Assyria apparently adopted the Babylonian lunisolar calendar in the reign of Tiglathpileser I (1115–1076 BC), when Assyria was most definitely not a Babylonian vassal-state (see Weidner 1935–6:27–29).

44. Morgenstern (1935:6–7) also argues that the introduction of the Babylonian-Assyrian calendar was one of the Deuteronomic reforms implemented by Josiah. However, in Morgenstern's view this calendar reform consisted in the replacement of an old solar calendar which began in the autumn with a new lunisolar calendar which also began in the autumn, but paradoxically numbered its months from the spring (!); this new calendar, being lunisolar rather than solar, dissociated the Feast of Booths from its original equinoctial date and thus enabled it to be divested of alleged solar trappings which had been taken over from Canaanite religion.

particularly surprising, since this is clearly a selective (and idealized) account of Josiah's reform. But it would be hazardous to argue that the new calendar was actually introduced in Josiah's 18th year. The historical authenticity of this date must be seriously questioned in any case: it belongs to a series of schematic dates, and works out, in Deuteronomistic chronological schematism, at exactly 365 years from the division of the kingdom (see p. 78f.).

Judah's adoption of the spring calendar poses two further questions which must be considered briefly, the first being whether we should posit a similar calendrical change for the northern kingdom of Israel. The only scholar to have suggested this (to my knowledge) is Jepsen (1964:28, 36), who makes the logical assumption that if Judah adopted the spring calendar when she became a vassal-state of Assyria the same is likely to have happened in Israel. Conversely, if I am right in arguing that the Assyrians did not impose their calendar on Judah, there is little reason to suppose that they will have imposed it on Israel either. In which case we have no grounds for thinking that the kingdom of Israel did not use the old autumn calendar throughout its existence.

The second question concerns the manner in which the new calendar was introduced. The change from autumn calendar to spring calendar will necessarily have entailed lengthening or shortening the last year of the old calendar by six months or thereabouts. Auerbach (1959:120) argues that the spring calendar was introduced during the reign of Jehoiakim, and suggests that Jehoiakim's 5th year was lengthened by five months so that it extended from Marheshvan of 605 BC (Jul.) to Nisan of 603 BC.[45] On the other hand Andersen (1969:101–102), who dates the introduction of the spring calendar to Manasseh's accession, argues that Manasseh's accession year was shortened by six

According to Vogelstein (1944:7) the spring calendar was *re*introduced in Josiah's reign (see below). More recently, Hayes and Hooker (1988:85–88) have independently concluded that the spring calendar was introduced in the 18th year of Josiah's reign as part of his religious reform. Rather strikingly, they also claim that the law book on which this reform was based was not (the core of) Deuteronomy but some form of P; their main argument is that P, in contrast to Deuteronomy, specifically requires a spring calendar (Ex 12.2). My own view on this is that Exodus 12.2 endorses an existing calendar against earlier Priestly traditions which presupposed an autumn calendar (see p. 168).

45. In Auerbach's opinion the autumn calendar began in Marheshvan, not Tishri; see p. 169 above.

months, so that it lasted from Tishri of 697 BC (Jul.) to Nisan of 696 BC.[46] Purely practical considerations would appear to favour the second of these procedures: it would presumably have been confusing to have had a year in which the first five or six months were repeated at the end of the year.

Some scholars, however, have noticed that the first procedure (lengthening the year in which a calendar change occurred), if repeated several times in a series of calendar changes, would have the effect of reducing the total number of Judean regnal years in a given period, and have accordingly concluded that this provides a convenient way of accounting for minor deficits in Judean chronology. Vogelstein (1944:7), faced with an apparent 2-year deficit in Judean regnal years from the fall of Samaria (in Hezekiah's 6th year) to the death of Josiah,[47] proposes an ad hoc series of calendar changes in the reigns of Hezekiah (introduction of spring calendar), Manasseh (reintroduction of autumn calendar), and Josiah (reintroduction of spring calendar). Pavlovský and Vogt propose a similar series of changes in the reigns of Manasseh (introduction of spring calendar), Josiah (reintroduction of autumn calendar), and Jehoiakim (reintroduction of spring calendar). Little credibility attaches to either of these proposals, which may be catalogued with other harmonistic devices employed by modern Biblical chronologists.

Turning from calendrical matters, we must also consider the related matter of the dating system(s) used in Israel and Judah during the monarchic period. It is clear from literary-historical evidence in Kings (and Josephus) that Israelite and Judean reigns were inclusively antedated for much of the period of the divided monarchy.[48] But it is also virtually certain that postdating had been introduced in pre-exilic Judah by the beginning of Jehoiakim's reign. One indication of this is the fact that direct Hebrew equivalents of *rēš šarrūti* ('beginning of reign'), which was used in

46. This presupposes of course that Manasseh did not become king until the second half of the autumn calendar year (between Nisan and Tishri), although there is no evidence to support (or refute) this assumption.

47. The fall of Samaria is commonly dated to 722 BC (Nis.), 113 years before the death of Josiah in 609 BC (Nis.), whereas there are only $(23 + 55 + 2 + 31 =)$ 111 Judean years from Hezekiah's 6th year to Josiah's 31st year. This discrepancy is increased to 3 years if the fall of Samaria is dated to 723 BC (Nis.): see p. 206ff.

48. See last chapter. The different types of dating system used in the ancient near east have also been discussed on p. 85ff.

Mesopotamia as a technical term for the period between a king's accession and his first regnal year, occur in four chronological notices associated with Jehoiakim and Zedekiah (see p. 86f.; two of these notices are textually suspect, but this leaves two notices associated with Jehoiakim and Zedekiah which are not suspect). This indication falls short of proof, however, since it is possible but unlikely that the Hebrew expressions (ממלכת ראשית and variants) are used in a general sense to refer to the early part of Jehoiakim's and Zedekiah's reigns, without carrying the specific sense of *rēš šarrūti* in Babylonian texts.[49] A more significant indication is therefore to be found in the fact that Jehoiakim's 11-year reign is incompatible with Babylonian chronological data unless Jehoiakim's regnal years are counted *non-inclusively* on either a spring calendar or on an autumn calendar for the first part of Jehoiakim's reign but on a spring calendar thereafter (see above, p. 171f.). Additional proof that Jehoiakim's reign was postdated rather than non-inclusively antedated is provided by the fact that the battle of Carchemish, which occurred in 605 BC (Nis.), is dated in Jeremiah 46.2 to Jehoiakim's 4th year; this presupposes that Jehoiakim's first regnal year was the year *after* his accession in 609 BC (Nis.).[50]

Postdating, like the spring calendar, was almost certainly adopted through Mesopotamian influence and is therefore unlikely to have been introduced in Judah before the reign of Ahaz, which effectively means that Hezekiah's accession is the earliest occasion at which it could have been implemented (it is unlikely that the changeover was implemented during the course of Ahaz's reign, since this would have required Ahaz's earlier years to be renumbered retrospectively).[51] There is no direct Biblical evidence

49. See p. 86n. It should be said that *rēš šarrūti* is sometimes used in a non-technical sense in *Assyrian* inscriptions, and it is possible that this Assyrian usage also occurs in Nabonidus's Sippar Cylinder (Tadmor 1965:353).

50. It makes no difference to the argument at this point whether Jehoiakim's accession year was 609 BC (spr.), as is the case if the spring calendar was introduced by Josiah, or 610 BC (aut.).

51. Contrast Coucke (1928:1251f.), Thiele (³1983:47–50), Schedl (1962a:94), and Pavlovský and Vogt (1964:323), who assume that postdating was used in Judah from the time of the division of the kingdom (except for an interlude in which antedating was adopted). It is undoubtedly true that figures given in existing Biblical chronologies (in particular that of MT) presuppose postdating for a number of early Judean reigns—though with less consistency than these scholars suppose—but this almost certainly reflects the activity of the exilic Deuterono-

which would allow us to date the introduction of postdating more precisely within the period between Hezekiah's accession and Jehoiakim's accession; but since postdating and the spring calendar were both introduced from Mesopotamia, it is not unreasonable to conjecture that they were both adopted simultaneously (Jepsen 1964:28; Andersen 1969:101)—or rather that the decision to introduce postdating was taken at the same time as the decision to introduce the spring calendar. If, as I have argued, the spring calendar was probably adopted during Josiah's reign, it follows that postdating was most probably introduced at the accession of Josiah's successor, Jehoahaz (this being the earliest point at which a decision taken during Josiah's reign could be practically implemented). This conclusion is supported by a detailed consideration of Judean chronology from Hezekiah's accession to the fall of Jerusalem (see below, p. 222ff.).

One final question which must be considered is whether postdating was ever adopted by the northern kingdom of Israel.[52] It must be said that there is no direct evidence that postdating was or was not adopted in Israel, but the most probable assumption is that it was not adopted. Those who argue to the contrary generally assume that the introduction of postdating, like the introduction of the spring calendar, was a necessary consequence of Assyrian suzerainty; but there is little reason to suppose that the Assyrians imposed either their calendar or their dating system on vassal nations.

The main conclusions of the previous discussion may now be summarized as follows.

1. The original Israelite-Judean calendar was probably lunisolar and began in the autumn, with Ethanim (= Tishri) as the first month.

2. Judah later adopted the Babylonian-Assyrian calendar, but initially replaced Babylonian-Assyrian month names with ordinal numbers; this calendar, which was also lunisolar but began in the spring, was probably adopted during the reign of Josiah.

mistic chronologist, who presupposed non-inclusive dating in his schematization of Judean chronology (see pp. 90f., 136f.).

52. The following scholars have argued that postdating *was* adopted in Israel: Lewy (1927:16), Coucke (1928:1256–1259), Begrich (1929a:113), Vogelstein (1944:21), Thiele (³1983:59–60), Jepsen (1964:28, 34), and Pavlovský and Vogt (1964:344).

3. Judah also adopted the Mesopotamian system of post-dating in place of the earlier Israelite-Judean system of (inclusive) antedating; this probably happened at the accession of Josiah's successor, Jehoahaz.

5.2 *A historical reconstruction of Israelite and Judean chronology*

5.2.1 *From the division of the kingdom to Jehu's revolt*

The primary source of external evidence relating to Israelite and Judean chronology are the historical records of Assyria and Babylonia. We are therefore fortunate in having an accurate chronological framework for Assyrian and Babylonian history during the first millennium BC.[53] This framework, which is based upon Mesopotamian chronographic texts (kinglists, eponym lists, and chronicles), is securely related to Julian chronology through the Ptolemaic Canon, a kinglist compiled by Alexandrian astronomers for use in astronomical calculations.[54] However, since the

53. There is a slight degree of uncertainty concerning Assyrian chronology before the eponymy of Ninurtanasir in 783 BC (Nis.), which arises from the fact that one out of six eponym lists for this period gives six eponyms from Silli-ishtar to Ninurtanasir (inclusive), whereas the remaining five lists have only five eponyms at this point. [The situation is actually a little more complex than this. Four lists (Cb2, Cc, Ca6, STT 1.47) agree, with some variation in names, on essentially the same sequence of eponyms: *Ṣilli-ištar*, *Nabûšarruṣur*, *Adaduballiṭ*, *Mardukšarruṣur*, *Ninurtanāṣir*. A fifth list (STT 1.46) omits *Nabûšarruṣur* but compensates by inserting the name of *Ṣilli-ištar*'s predecessor (*Adadmušammer*) between *Mardukšarruṣur* and *Ninurtanāṣir*. The sixth list (Ca3) places *Nabûšarruṣur* between *Mardukšarruṣur* and *Ninurtanāṣir*, and inserts a sixth eponym, *Balāṭu* (possibly a hypocoristic form of *Adaduballiṭ*), in the position occupied by *Nabûšarruṣur* in the first four lists.] Assyriologists since Forrer (1915:5f.) have generally taken the view that the shorter tradition is original, and have therefore dated Silli-ishtar's eponymy to 787 BC (Nis.); but Shea (1977:240–242) has argued in favour of the longer tradition, and accordingly dates Silli-ishtar's eponymy to 788 BC (Nis.). However, Shea's arguments are conclusively refuted by Brinkman (1978:173–175), who points out that Shea fails to take account of the two eponym lists from Sultantepe (STT 1.46, 47), and also makes an elementary miscalculation in working out Shalmaneser III's accession date from figures given by the Assyrian Kinglist. These figures, when added correctly, plainly support the shorter chronology against the longer chronology advocated by Shea.

54. See Ginzel 1906:138f. and Bickerman ²1980:81–82, 109–111. The Ptolemaic Canon gives reign lengths and continuous totals for successive Babylonian, Persian, Ptolemaic, and Roman rulers beginning with Nabonassar (748–734 BC). The accuracy of this information has been established by means of dated

Mesopotamian calendar began in the spring, whereas the Israelite-Judean calendar originally began in the autumn, it is obvious that Mesopotamian calendar years cannot be equated with Israelite or Judean calendar years (except during the final period of the Judean monarchy, when Judah had adopted the Mesopotamian spring calendar): each Mesopotamian calendar year corresponds to the last six months (or so) of the Israelite-Judean year which began in the previous autumn, plus the first six months (or so) of the following Israelite-Judean year. 841 BC (Nis.), for example, is equivalent to the last six months of 842 BC (aut.) plus the first six months of 841 BC (aut.).

841 BC (Nis.) is in fact the date of a key synchronism between Assyrian and Israelite chronology, corresponding to the 18th year of the reign of Shalmaneser III, when the latter conducted an inconclusive campaign against 'Hazael of Aram' and received tribute from various rulers including 'Jehu the Omrite'[55] (Shl

astronomical phenomena recorded in Ptolemy's Almagest; for example, the total lunar eclipse which is recorded as having occurred on the night of Thoth 29/30 in the first year of Merodachbaladan is astronomically datable to March 19 721 BC (Ginzel 1906:143). The earlier part of the Canon overlaps with Mesopotamian chronographic literature, thereby confirming the basic accuracy of this literature (which was evidently one of the primary sources of chronological data in the Canon). Additional confirmation is provided by the fact that the Assyrian Eponym Chronicle records the occurrence of a solar eclipse in the month Sivan of the eponymy of Bursagale—coinciding with a solar eclipse which is astronomically datable to June 15 763 BC.

55. *ᴵIA-ú-a* (var. *ᴵIA-a-ú*) *mār* *ᴵḪu-um-ri-i*—the designation *mār Ḫumrî* is gentilic rather than patronymic, indicating that Jehu was ruler of *Bīt Ḫumrî* (the common Assyrian name for Israel); similarly the rulers of *Bīt Agūsi, Bīt Adīni, Bīt Dakūri* etc. are designated *mār Agūsi, mār Adīni, mār Dakūri* and so forth (Tadmor 1973:149). McCarter's theory that *ᴵIA-ú-a/ᴵIA-a-ú* is not Jehu but *Joram* (McCarter 1974) must be considered highly improbable. McCarter argues that *ᴵIA-a-ú* is an Assyrian representation of **Yaw*, which is allegedly an (otherwise unattested) hypocoristic of **Yawrām* (= Joram), while the variant (and usual) spelling *ᴵIA-ú-a* supposedly represents **Yawa'*, i.e. **Yaw* plus the hypocoristic ending **-a'*. But hypocoristic names consisting solely of a theophoric element, or of a theophoric element plus *-a'* are rare in Semitic, and Yahwistic hypocoristica of this type are unattested. It may also be noted that McCarter's argument for interpreting *ᴵIA-a-ú* as **Yaw* is based on the assumption that the *ᴵAz-ri-ia-a-ú* who is mentioned in the annals of Tiglathpileser III is the same person as Azariah of Judah, whose name appears as עזיו on two pre-exilic seals; but we now know that this is almost certainly not the case (see below, p. 195.) By contrast ᴷᵁᴿ*IA-ú-du/di*, which is the Assyrian writing of **Yahūd* (= Judah), provides clear support for the conventional view that *ᴵIA-ú-a* is the Assyrian spelling of Jehu (**Yēhū'a* (?); *IA* may be read as *ia, ie, ii,* or *iu*, and for **-hū'a* as a variant of **-hū* compare הואה = הוא in Qumran manuscripts.) For further discussion see Weippert (1978), who is probably

22.1–26; 32.III.45–IV.5; 33.B; Kurb 21–30). Since Assyrian campaigns almost invariably began in the spring it is probable that Jehu's payment of tribute occurred in the late summer of 841 BC, in which case he must presumably have come to the throne either during or before the Israelite year 842 BC (aut.).[56] But we also know that Jehu cannot have come to the throne much before 842 BC (aut.). Shalmaneser III's previous campaign in the west was in the 14th year of his reign, 845 BC (Nis.), when he fought against a coalition of twelve Syro-Palestinian states led by Hadadezer of Aram and Irhuleni of Hamath (Shl 5.I.14–24; 33.91–92; Bull 99–102). Hadadezer, referred to as 'Benhadad' in the Bible, was subsequently murdered by Hazael (2K 8.7–15; cf. Shl 5.I.25–27), who must therefore have become king in 846 BC (aut.) at the earliest. And since the book of Kings places Hazael's accession before that of Jehu, this means that 846 BC (aut.) is also the earliest date at which Jehu could have become king. Jehu's accession may therefore be dated within a possible range of five Israelite years, from 846 BC (aut.) at the earliest to 842 BC (aut.) at the latest.

Further Assyrian evidence would appear to provide us with a way of arriving at a precise date for Jehu's accession. In 853 BC (Nis.), in the 6th year of his reign, Shalmaneser III fought for the first time against the twelve-state coalition headed by Hadadezer and Irhuleni, which on this occasion is said to have included forces led by 'Ahab of Israel'[57] (Shl Mon II.78–102; cf. Shl 33.54–66 and Shl Bull 67–74). This battle, which was fought at Qarqar on the Orontes, almost certainly occurred during the summer of 853 BC (Shalmaneser set out from Assyria on Iyyar 14: Shl Mon II.78) and may therefore be dated to the Israelite year which began in the autumn of 854 BC. Ahab, then, was still on the throne in 854 BC (aut.), 12 years before the latest possible date for Jehu's accession. Now the chronology of Kings assigns reign lengths of 2 and 12 years respectively to Ahab's successors, Ahaziah and Joram, and

right in suggesting that the isolated occurrence of ʾ*IA-a-ú* is a scribal error for ʾ*IA-ú-a*.

56. Even if Jehu paid tribute in the autumn of 841 BC, i.e. at the beginning of the Israelite year 841 BC (aut.), it is doubtful that his accession may be dated any later than 842 BC (aut.). The single regnal year ascribed to Ahaziah is evidence that the latter was assassinated before the first new year of his reign (see p. 172n.); unless we date Ahaziah's entire reign within the first few weeks of 841 BC (aut.), we must therefore conclude that Ahaziah was assassinated by Jehu in or before 842 BC (aut.).

57. ʾ*A-ḫa-ab-bu* ^KUR*Sir-ʾi-la-a-a*.

these two reign lengths total precisely 12 years in all when allowance is made for 1-year overlaps produced by inclusive antedating. Unless, therefore, we dismiss the Biblical figures as unreliable, we must necessarily conclude that 854 BC (aut.) was the last year of Ahab's reign, and 842 BC (aut.) the first year of Jehu's reign. Ahab cannot have ended his reign after 854 BC (aut.), since this would require us to date Jehu's accession after 842 BC (aut.). Conversely, Jehu cannot have begun to reign before 842 BC (aut.), for in this case Ahab's death is pushed back before 854 BC (aut.), when Ahab participated in the battle of Qarqar.

The possibility of establishing absolute dates for Ahab's death and Jehu's accession on the evidence presented above has been pointed out many times since Rühl (1894/5:45–50) first realized that Israelite and Judean reigns of the early monarchic period were originally dated inclusively. However, several scholars have also pointed out problems with this chronology. One of these arises in connection with the date of Ahab's death: according to 1 Kings 22 Ahab died while fighting the Arameans at Ramoth-Gilead; but in the second half of 854 BC (aut.) Ahab was fighting *alongside* the Aramean army at Qarqar. A similar though less widely recognized problem concerns the date of Jehu's accession: according to 2 Kings 9.14–15 the Israelite army was defending Ramoth-Gilead against Hazael when Jehu staged his revolt; but in 842 BC (aut.) Hazael was occupied in fighting the Assyrians. If we assume that the Biblical narratives of 1 Kings 22 and 2 Kings 9 are historically reliable, we must apparently conclude that the Biblical figures for the reigns of Ahaziah and Joram (of Israel) are historically unreliable.

A number of scholars have come to precisely this conclusion; and since there is little scope for reducing Ahaziah's 2-year reign they propose that Joram's reign should be reduced by up to 6 years. Various justifications are offered in support of these reductions, the simplest of which is given by Begrich (1929a:108f.) and Jepsen (1964:41). Their argument is as follows. According to 2 Kings 1.17 Joram became king in the 2nd year of Jehoram of Judah. The latter is said to have reigned for 8 years according to MT (2K 8.17). Jehoram's 8th year, which was also the first and only year of Ahaziah of Judah, was therefore equivalent to Joram's 7th year. And since Ahaziah of Judah and Joram of Israel were both assassinated at the same time it follows that Joram can have reigned for no more than *7 years, not 12 years. However, this seemingly plausible argument is actually based upon a conflation of chronological data from separate and disparate chronological systems. The synchronism given in 2 Kings 1.17 does not properly belong within MT's chronology and can only be fitted into this chronology if one resorts to a series of procrustean alterations or hypothetical coregencies. It is identical, however, with the synchronism given by LXX[L] in 2 Kings 1.18a, and fits (almost) perfectly into LXX's chronology, showing that it is simply one of several synchronisms in MT which were taken over from the chronology found in LXX;[58]

Other proposals for reducing Joram's reign length have been put forward by Lewy (1927:26), Mowinckel (1932:260–261), Albright (1945:20,21), and Miller (1967:287–288). There is no point in discussing each of these in detail, as none is very convincing. But some consideration may be given to the views of Albright and Miller in view of the degree of influence exerted by their respective chronologies. Albright's chronology of the early monarchy is founded on the assumption that chronological data in Chronicles are at least as reliable as chronological data in Kings (Albright 1945:18–19). According to 2 Chronicles 16.1 Baasha attacked Judah in the 36th year of Asa's reign. Allowing for 1-year overlaps produced by inclusive antedating this is the 54th year from the division of the kingdom ((17-1) + (3-1) + 36 = 54). However, according to figures for Israelite reign lengths, Baasha died in the 46th year from the division of the kingdom ((22-1) + (2-1) + 24 = 46). Albright accordingly concludes that we must reduce Rehoboam's reign by 'at least 8, probably 9 years' (p. 20), and proceeds to compensate for this by making corresponding reductions in the reigns of Omri and Joram (both reduced from 12 to *8 years). But it is hardly legitimate to base a whole series of major corrections to the chronology of Kings on a single piece of chronological data given by the Chronicler, who may simply have invented this figure along with other dates in Asa's reign (see Rudolph 1955:239f.). Albright offers no evidence to support the authenticity of Chronicles' data over against the chronology of Kings, apart from asserting that the historical value of material in Chronicles which is not paralleled in Kings is being established by

58. See above, p. 92. The true synchronism for Joram's accession within MT's chronology is given in 2 Kings 3.1.

(unspecified) 'archaeological discoveries' (Albright 1945:18).

The weakness of Albright's proposals is noted by Miller (1967:278f.), who attempts to replace them with a set of similar reductions based on chronological data from the Lucianic text of the Septuagint. Unfortunately Miller fails to notice that LXX[L] gives 10 years (not 8 years) as Jehoram's reign length (see p. 123n.), so that his argument that Joram's reign length must be reduced to 8 (or 7) years[59] is in fact based upon an unintentional conflation of chronological data from MT (Jehoram's reign length) and LXX[L] (Joram's accession date). This is effectively Begrich's argument in a slightly different guise: Joram became king in Jehoram's 2nd year (LXX's chronology); Jehoram reigned for 8 years (MT's chronology); therefore Joram reigned for *8 years, comprising 7 years of Jehoram's reign plus Ahaziah's single year (Miller, unlike Begrich, does not equate this with Jehoram's last regnal year). The other reductions which Miller proposes (Baasha 24 → *18 years; Asa 41 → *31 years) are based upon an uncritical acceptance of LXX's (corrupt) synchronism for Elah's accession (see p. 132n.).

Having rejected these various proposals for reducing Joram's reign we must clearly reconsider the historical reliability of 1 Kings 22 and 2 Kings 9. There are good reasons for doubting the historical accuracy of 1 Kings 22:

1. 1 Kings 22 describes an attempt by Ahab to recover Ramoth-Gilead from the Arameans, but Ramoth-Gilead appears to have remained in Israelite possession until after Joram's death; according to 2 Kings 9.14–15 the latter was wounded while defending Ramoth-Gilead (cf. 2 Kings 10.32–33, which dates the loss of Gilead to Jehu's reign).

2. According to Assyrian annals Israel and Aram were members of a 12-state alliance which confronted Shalmaneser III not only in 853 BC (Nis.), but again in 849 BC (Nis.), 848 BC (Nis.), and 845 BC (Nis.); it is therefore improbable that the battle described in 1 Kings 22 could have occurred during this period.

3. 1 Kings 22.26 refers to 'Joash the king's son' (i.e. the

---

59. On p. 287 of his study Miller states that Joram's reign must be reduced from twelve to 'nine years', but this is apparently an error for 'eight years': on the following page Joram's reign is dated from 851/849 to 844/842 (i.e. 8 years inclusive).

crown prince; see p. 104), but Ahab's successor was Ahaziah, not Joash.

There is therefore a strong case for thinking that 1 Kings 22 has been secondarily associated with Ahab, as is argued by Jepsen (1942), Whitley (1952), and Miller (1966; 1968); the latter is probably correct in arguing that the narrative originally concerned Jehoahaz of Israel, whose son and successor was indeed named Joash.[60]

It is less easy to demonstrate that 2 Kings 9 is not an accurate account of events associated with Jehu's revolt. However, the example of 1 Kings 22 should make us wary of emending the chronology of Kings, which is ultimately based on historical records, to make it conform with narratives that are essentially legendary (or folk-historical) in character, and Astour (1971) has put forward an alternative and plausible reconstruction of events which does not contradict the chronological data of Kings. In 841 BC (Nis.) Israel was indeed confronted with a serious military

---

60. A further argument against the historicity of 1 Kings 22 is of dubious validity. It is often stated that the expression used in 1 Kings 22.40 ('and Ahab slept with his fathers') presupposes that Ahab died a natural death. But this is most probably a stereotyped death-formula, which was usually omitted when the circumstances of a king's death were described in any detail (as in most cases of violent death), but which does not of itself refer to non-violent death, as argued by Alfrink (1943) and others. The strongest argument against this theory is provided by the circumstances of Jehoiakim's death. Jeremiah 22.18–19 asserts that Jehoiakim will lie unlamented and unburied: 'They shall not lament for him ... with the burial of an ass he will be buried, dragged and thrown aside outside the gates of Jerusalem.' Similarly Jeremiah 36.30 predicts, 'His corpse will be thrown aside to the heat by day and the frost by night.' On the other hand 2 Kings 24.6, which fails to provide any details of Jehoiakim's death, states simply that 'Jehoiakim slept with his fathers.' The common assumption that the prophecies of Jehoiakim's death in Jeremiah were unfulfilled, and that Jehoiakim actually died a peaceful death, is in my view hardly credible. Whatever erroneous predictions Jeremiah may have made, it is highly unlikely that an obvious prophetic failure of this magnitude would have been included (twice!) by the Deuteronomistic redactors of the book of Jeremiah, particularly in view of the Deuteronomistic belief that inaccurate predictions were the mark of a false prophet (Dt 18.22; Je 28.5f.). It is therefore much more probable that the Jeremiah prophecies are actually fulfilled predictions, or *vaticinia ex eventu*, which accurately reflect the circumstances of Jehoiakim's death. We know from 2 Kings 24.2f. that Jehoiakim died while Judah was being attacked by Babylonian and allied forces; if the Jeremiah passages are to be believed, we may probably infer that he died while fighting outside Jerusalem, and the Judean army failed to recover his dead body. It is worth noting that Jehoiakim is one of only two Judean kings, not counting those who died in exile, whose burial is not mentioned in Kings (the other, curiously, is Hezekiah).

threat to her northern borders, but this threat came not from Hazael and the Arameans but from the Assyrian army of Shalmaneser III. According to Assyrian inscriptions Shalmaneser concluded his campaign of this year by marching south from Damascus to the Hauran region—where he destroyed 'innumerable towns'—and then west to Mt. Ba'li-ra'si, which should probably be identified with Mt. Carmel (Shl 22.1–25; 32.III.45–IV.15).[61] Astour argues that Joram was wounded at Ramoth-Gilead while attempting to block Shalmaneser's march across northern Israelite territory, and that this was later remembered in Israelite folk tradition as a battle against the Aramean forces of Hazael, who made repeated incursions into Israelite territory during later years. This explanation also offers a plausible explanation of Hosea's reference to the destruction of Beth-Arbel by 'Shalman' (Ho 10.14): Beth-Arbel lay directly in the way of Shalmaneser's march from Hauran to Carmel and was therefore an obvious target for Assyrian reprisals. This in turn gives us a convincing *political* motive for Jehu's revolt, which may logically be regarded as a pro-Assyrian move intended to appease Shalmaneser and prevent further Assyrian reprisals.

Having seen that there is no good reason to alter the chronology of Kings to make it conform to the (folk-historical) narratives of 1 Kings 22 and 2 Kings 9, we may reasonably accept the chronological evidence that Ahab died in 854 BC (aut.), and that Jehu came to the throne in 842 BC (aut.). This evidence is of major importance for the reconstruction of Israelite and Judean historical chronology, in that it allows us to translate our earlier reconstruction of the original chronology of Kings into an absolute chronology of Israelite and Judean history. The table given below presents a reconstruction of Israelite and Judean history from the division of the kingdom to Jehu's revolt; it is identical with the table given on p. 137f., with the addition of absolute dates calculated backwards from 842 BC (aut.).

Rehoboam	1	937	1	Jeroboam
	~	~	~	
Abijam	17/ac1	921	17	
	2	920	18	
	3	919	19	

---

61. Cf. Aharoni ²1979:341.

Judah	Judah yr	BC	Israel yr	Israel
	4	918	20	
	5	917	21	
Asa	ac1/6	916	22	
	2	915	23	
	3	914	24	
	4	913	*25/ac1	Nadab
	5	912	d2/ac1	Baasha
	~	~	~	
	25	892	21	
	26	891	22	
	27	890	23	
	28	889	ac1/24	Elah
	29	888	ac1/ac/2	Zimri/Omri
	~	~	~	
	39	878	11	
	40	877	12/ac1	Ahab
Jehoshaphat	41/ac1	876	2	
	~	~	~	
	21	856	22	
	22	855	*23	
	23	854	*24/ac1	Ahaziah
	24	853	2/ac1	Joram
Jehoram	ac1/25	852	2	
	2	851	3	
	3	850	4	
	4	849	5	
	5	848	6	
	6	847	7	
	7	846	8	
	8	845	9	
	9	844	10	
	10	843	11	
Ahaziah /Athaliah	*11/**ac1**/1	842	1/**12**	Jehu

There are, unfortunately, no external synchronisms between Israelite/Judean chronology and Mesopotamian chronology during the earlier part of this period. Ahab was evidently the first Israelite or Judean king to encounter the armies of Assyria, and his involvement in the battle of Qarqar is consequently our earliest synchronism between Israelite and Mesopotamian chronology. But we do have a previous synchronism between Judean and

Egyptian chronology. In the 5th year of Rehoboam's reign, according to 1 Kings 14.25f., Shishak king of Egypt marched against Jerusalem and successfully extracted a large payment of tribute. Shishak, alias Shoshenq I, founder of the 22nd (Libyan) Dynasty, has also left his own record of this campaign in the form of a triumphal relief and accompanying list of conquered territories, which was inscribed on one of the walls of the temple of Amun at Karnak. This inscription unfortunately does not tell us in which year of Shoshenq's reign the campaign occurred; but since there is evidence that Shoshenq began quarrying stone for his Karnak building programme in the 21st year of his reign (Caminos 1952) it is commonly assumed that his Palestinian campaign was conducted shortly before this date. Hornung (1964:24, 29) argues that it should probably be dated between Shoshenq's 18th and 21st years, most probably in the 20th year of his reign; while Kitchen (1973a:73–74) maintains that Shoshenq is unlikely to have waited for as long as three years before commissioning the relief, and that the campaign may therefore be dated to Shoshenq's 20th or 21st year.

This appears to provide an (almost) exact synchronism between Egyptian and Judean chronology, against which we may hope to test our historical reconstruction of Judean and Israelite chronology. According to this reconstruction Rehoboam's first year was 937 BC (aut.), and his 5th year, 933 BC (aut.); so Shoshenq's 20th year should be roughly equivalent to 932 BC (Jul.).[62] This puts Shoshenq's first year in approximately 951 BC (Jul.). By contrast, most Egyptologists, including Hornung and Kitchen, have agreed with Breasted (1906:I:45) in dating Shoshenq's reign from 945 BC to 924 BC, which is in line with earlier reconstructions of Israelite and Judean chronology—beginning with Rühl 1894/95, and including Thiele ³1983 and Andersen 1969—in which the start of Rehoboam's reign is dated to 931 BC or thereabouts. Thiele (³1983:80) observes that Breasted's date for Shoshenq's Palestinian campaign (*c.* 926 BC) is 'in almost complete accord' with his

---

62. This presupposes that Shoshenq's Palestinian campaign is more likely to have occurred in spring or summer (during the last nine months or so of 933 BC (aut.)) than in winter. The Egyptian civil calendar at this period began in April of the Julian calendar, but it is not known whether the 22nd Dynasty correlated regnal years with calendar years (by antedating), or whether they followed the New Kingdom practice of counting regnal years from the actual date of accession.

own reconstruction of Israelite and Judean chronology. What he failed to realize, however, is that this seemingly impressive agreement results from the fact that Egyptian chronologists, without always admitting it, have commonly based their chronology of this period on the *Biblical* synchronism for Shoshenq's invasion. Thus Kitchen (1973a:72f.) remarks that 'neither the 20th nor the 21st Dynasty can so far offer us any information from which one may calculate their absolute dates BC', and then proceeds to use *Thiele's* date for Rehoboam's 5th year as a fixed point in working out the chronology of the Third Intermediate Period. In a similar fashion Hornung (1964:24–29), who also follows Thiele fairly closely in matters of Biblical chronology, uses the same Biblical synchronism as a fixed point in reconstructing New Kingdom chronology. Breasted almost certainly used the same synchronism in dating Shoshenq's reign, though he does not admit to this. He was certainly aware of the Biblical date for Shoshenq's campaign (Breasted 1906:IV:348), and it is hardly a coincidence that his dating of Shoshenq's reign, which is purportedly based on dead reckoning from the Persian invasion of Egypt in 525 BC, is in close agreement with Rühl's earlier reconstruction of Israelite and Judean chronology (most of Breasted's chronology of the intervening period has since been heavily modified).

Egyptian chronology is therefore of little use to modern reconstructions of Israelite-Judean chronology in this instance. By contrast, Biblical chronology is apparently crucial to current reconstructions of Egyptian chronology for this period, so that if my reconstruction of Israelite and Judean chronology is correct —and if Shoshenq's Palestinian campaign has been correctly dated within the reigns of Shoshenq and Rehoboam—Egyptian chronologists will have to revise their calculations to take account of a 6-year increase in the dates of Shoshenq's reign. Such an increase would not appear to pose serious problems in Egyptian chronology, and might even be desirable, if Kitchen (1973b:231–232) is correct in asserting that the currently accepted dates (945–924 BC) are minimal by earlier and later Egyptian chronology. Albright's low chronology of the Third Intermediate Period (Albright 1953; 1956), in which Shoshenq's reign is dated from 935 to 914 BC, does not appear to have gained much acceptance in Egyptological circles, and is also essentially dependent upon his low chronology of the early divided monarchy in Israel and Judah (Albright 1953:6f.).[63]

Two caveats should be added to this discussion. In the first place it must be said that not all Egyptologists agree that Shoshenq's Palestinian campaign is to be dated in the final years of his reign. Thus G. R. Hughes (Epigraphic Survey 1954:vii) has stated that the Egyptian evidence shows only that the campaign occurred some time before the tenth month of Shoshenq's 21st year, while Redford (1973:10) has argued that the campaign most probably occurred fairly early in Shoshenq's reign. It should also be noted that the Biblical evidence for the date of Shoshenq's campaign is less strong than it might appear. The book of Kings gives equally precise dates for Shalmaneser V's conquest of Samaria ('in the 6th year of Hezekiah', 2K 18.10) and for Sennacherib's invasion of Judah ('in the 14th year of king Hezekiah', 2K 18.13), implying an interval of only 8 years between these events (or 10 years from the start of the siege of Samaria). We know, however, from Assyrian and Babylonian evidence that the conquest of Samaria (in 723 or 722 BC (Nis.)) preceded Sennacherib's invasion of Judah (701 BC (Nis.)) by over 20 years, so that the Biblical date for one (or both) of these events is demonstrably incorrect. One cannot assume that the Biblical date for Shoshenq's campaign is necessarily any more reliable. These dates belong to a series of dates which seems to have been schematically arranged so that events occur at multiples of 5 years from the division of the kingdom (see p. 77f.).

5.2.2. *From Jehu's revolt to the fall of Samaria*

The period from Jehu's revolt to the fall of Samaria is without doubt the most historically problematical period of Israelite and

63. Kitchen (1973a:181; 1973b:232) is particularly scathing of Albright's chronology, although it should be noted that Redford (1973:13) dates Shoshenq's death to c. 906 BC (see below), which is 8 years after Albright's date. Albright's identification of an alleged lunar eclipse in Takeloth II's 15th year with an eclipse which occurred in 822 BC has not been accepted by Egyptologists; see Kitchen (1973a:181), who asserts that this is chronologically impossible, and argues with most contemporary Egyptologists, that the Chronicle of Prince Osorkon, which supposedly refers to this eclipse, actually refers to the *non-occurrence* of a lunar eclipse. More recently, Barta (1980) has argued that the Chronicle *does* refer to the occurrence of a lunar eclipse, which he identifies with an eclipse that occurred in 850 BC. See Baer 1973, Kitchen 1982, Barta 1984, and Krauss 1985:174–177 for further discussion of this (non-?)event.

Judean chronology. If my earlier conclusions are correct, the cause of these problems may be attributed to the fact that Deuteronomistic modifications to the original chronology of Kings were mostly concentrated in this part of the chronology. Nevertheless, the original chronology of this period is not entirely irretrievable, but may be partially reconstructed from literary-historical evidence provided by internal discrepancies in the existing chronology of Kings and variant figures given by Josephus. The results of such a reconstruction have been summarized in the table on p. 154, which spans the period from Jehu's revolt to the reigns of Menahem and Azariah, but breaks off at the point where there is insufficient literary-historical evidence to continue a full reconstruction. This provides us with a literary-historical basis for the historical reconstruction of Israelite and Judean chronology of this period, which may then be checked against external chronological evidence and supplemented with the help of such evidence in places where there is insufficient evidence for literary-historical reconstruction.

We may begin by using the absolute date for Jehu's accession which was established above in order to translate our reconstruction of the original chronology of Kings from Jehu's revolt to the reigns of Menahem and Azariah into an absolute historical chronology of this period. The following table is identical to the table given on p. 154, with the addition of absolute dates calculated forwards from 842 BC (aut.).

Athaliah	1	842	1	Jehu
	2	841	2	
	3	840	3	
	4	839	4	
	5	838	5	
	6	837	6	
Joash	ac1/7	836	7	
	~	~	~	
	21	816	ac1/27	Jehoahaz
	~	~	~	
	31	806	11	
	32	805	12	
	33	804	13	
	34	803	14	
	35	802	15	

	36	801	16	
	37	800	17/ac1	Jehoash
Amaziah	ac1/38	799	2	
	~	~	~	
	11	789	12	
	12	788	13	
	13	787	14	
	14	786	15	
	15	785	ac1/16	Jeroboam
	~	~	~	
	25	775	11	
	26	774	12	
	27	773	13	
Azariah	ac1/28	772	14	
	~	~	~	
		752	34	
		751	35	
		750	36	
		749	37	
		748	38	
		747	39	
		746	40	
		745	ac1/ac/ac/41	Zechariah/ Shallum/Menahem

There are no external synchronisms with Egyptian chronology during the period covered by this table; and in the case of Judean chronology there are no external synchronisms with Mesopotamian chronology either, since putative references to 'Azriyau the Judean' in the annals of Tiglathpileser III are now known to be illusory.[64] There are, by contrast, two Israelite kings of this period,

64. See Na'aman (1974), who shows that a fragment formerly ascribed to Tiglathpileser III and thought to refer to 'Azriyau (or Izriyau) of Judah' (K 6206 = 'Tgl An 103–119') joins on to a second fragment (BM 82-2-23, 131), formerly ascribed to Sargon II. As a result of this join it is now clear that a line which was previously read as [*I*]z-ri-ia-u ᴷᵁᴿIa-u-di (and translated—ungrammatically—as 'Izriyau of Judah') should be read ...ina bi-ri[t mi-i]ṣ-ri-ia (or á]š-ri-ia) u KUR Ia-u-di, 'between my [bo]rder (or [te]rritory) and the land of Judah' (Na'aman 1974:26; Borger 1979:134). In Na'aman's opinion the name found in lines 4 and 11 of the combined text is to be restored as ⌜*I*Ha⌝[-za-qi-i]a-a-u (Hezekiah), and the document ascribed to Sennacherib; but this is disputed by Borger (1979:134–135), who rejects Na'aman's restoration (without suggesting an alternative) and also argues that the combined text might still be ascribed to Sargon II. It is clear, however, that the text is entirely unrelated to

in addition to Jehu, who are mentioned in Assyrian inscriptions; the two kings are Jehoash (or Joash) and Menahem.

5.2.2.1 Israelite chronology

Jehoash is named in the Rimah stele of Adadnirari III, which was published in 1968 by Stephanie Dalley. In this inscription Adadnirari claims to have subjugated the lands of Amurru and Hattu (i.e. north Syria) 'in a single year' (cf. Dalley [Page] 1969:458.), and records having received tribute from 'Mari of Aram', 'Joash of Samaria',[65] and the Tyrians and Sidonians.[66] However, Adadnirari's claim to have subjugated north Syria in a single year, though repeated in the Sheikh Hammad stele, is evidently an exaggeration, for the Eponym Chronicle lists no less than three consecutive campaigns against northern Syria from 805 to 803 BC (Nis.) (a fourth is possibly recorded for 802 BC (Nis.));[67] and we may therefore be wary of accepting the Rimah stele's apparent claim that the conquest of northern Syria also occasioned the payment of tribute by Aram and other central or southerly Syro-Palestinian states including Israel. It is true that the Saba'a stele also links Adadnirari's campaign against Damascus with his conquest of north Syria, which it dates to Adadnirari's 5th regnal year (806 BC (Nis.)),[68] but the chronological evidence of this stele is

passages in Tiglathpileser's annals which refer to a certain Azriyau of unknown nationality. The latter is mentioned in connection with an anti-Assyrian alliance of north-Syrian states, and was possibly the ruler of Hamath (see below, p. 198n.); another north-Syrian ruler with a Yahwistic name was Yaubi'di of Hamath, who is mentioned in the annals of Sargon II.

65. ^{I}IA-'a-su ^{KUR}Sa-me-ri-na-a-a. IA should probably be read iu, as was first suggested by Malamat (1971). Note that Assyrian <s> regularly corresponds with Hebrew (and West Semitic) <š> in first millennium loanwords and transcriptions: Dalley [Page] 1968:148; Kaufman 1974:140f.

66. The Calah Slab records the imposition of tribute on 'Hattu, the whole of Amurru, Tyre, Sidon, Israel, Edom, and Philistia' (Adn Cal 11–14).

67. The Eponym Chronicle lists a campaign 'against the sea' (a-na UGU tam-tim) for this year. This has sometimes been taken to refer to the Mediterranean coast (Dalley 1968:147), but it is more probable that it refers to Sealand in southern Mesopotamia (Brinkman 1968:217).

68. This is probably an error for '6th year', since according to the Eponym Chronicle the Assyrian army campaigned against the Mannaeans in 806 BC (Nis.)—the cuneiform signs for '5' and '6' are similar in form. Note that Pa-la^{r}-aš-tú^{1}, 'Philistia', in older editions and translations of the Saba'a stele (line 12) is a misreading of Hat-te ^{r}GAL-te^{1}, 'great Hattu', or (simply) Hat-te-^{r}-e^{1}, 'Hattu' (Tadmor 1969; 1973:145).

put into doubt by the fact that it too, like the Rimah stele, condenses the three-year conquest of north Syria into a single year's campaign. There are, in any case, serious chronological problems in dating Jehoash's accession as early as 806 (or 805) BC (Nis.).[69] It may be noted that all existing inscriptions of Adadnirari III belong to the literary category of 'summary inscriptions' (also known as 'display inscriptions'); and it is a recognized feature of this category that events of varying dates are arranged on an essentially geographical basis rather than in strict chronological sequence (Tadmor 1973:141). We should also note that the Rimah stele apparently combines two separate documents, one of which is written in the first person and recounts the conquest of north Syria, while the other is written in the third person and lists tribute received from various countries (Tadmor 1973:141–144). It cannot be taken for granted that the two documents necessarily refer to the same campaign (or series of campaigns).

It is therefore possible that Adadnirari's conquest of Damascus, and his receipt of tribute from Jehoash of Israel, occurred some years after his conquest of north Syria, which was completed in 803 (or possibly 802) BC (Nis.). This is in fact a necessary assumption on most reconstructions of Israelite chronology (Jehoash's accession is usually dated after 802 BC),[70] but it is also

69. None of the currently accepted reconstructions of Israelite chronology puts Jehoash's accession this early, although in Mowinckel's chronology Jehoash's accession was in fact dated to 805 BC (aut.). However, Mowinckel arrived at this date in a rather curious fashion. Having excluded Athaliah's 7-year reign from his calculations (in his opinion Athaliah was merely queen regent during the minority years of Joash of Judah), Mowinckel proceeded to compensate for this reduction in Judean chronology by subtracting 5 years from Jehu's reign, but was apparently unaware of having done so: on p. 242 Jehu is credited with a reign of 28 years (and it is clear from Mowinckel's subsequent remarks that this is not a typographical error) but the dates assigned to him, 843–821 BC (aut.), clearly presuppose a reign of only 23 years inclusive. More recently Shea (1978a) has (independently?) arrived at strikingly similar conclusions in his attempt to harmonize the chronology of Kings with the chronological statements of the Saba'a and Rimah stelae; the only material difference is that Shea compensates for his deletion of Athaliah's reign by subtracting 7 years from the reign of Jehoahaz. [Shea (1985a:13) has since discarded this proposed reduction in Jehoahaz's reign in favour of Cody's theory of a coregency between Jehoahaz and Jehoash (Cody 1970:333f.).]

70. Begrich (1929a) and Jepsen (1964) date Jehoash's accession to 802 BC (aut.); and Jepsen (1970) has since argued that this date is vindicated by the evidence of the Rimah stele. But it is far from certain that Adadnirari was actually in the west in 802 BC (Nis.); (he was more probably campaigning in southern Mesopotamia (see above, p. 196n.).

supported by Assyrian evidence, since Tadmor has shown that Adadnirari's campaign against Damascus must probably be identi-fied with the expedition to Mansuate recorded in the Eponym Chronicle for 796 BC (Nis.) (Millard and Tadmor 1973:61–64).[71] Jehoash's payment of tribute may therefore be dated to either 797 BC (aut.) or 796 BC (aut.) by the Israelite calendar; according to the reconstructed chronology given in the previous table this will have been Jehoash's 4th or 5th regnal year.

The next Israelite king after Jehoash to receive a mention in Assyrian historical records is 'Menahem of Samaria',[72] who is named in the annals of Tiglathpileser III alongside 'Rezin of Aram' as one of a number of Syro-Palestinian and Anatolian rulers who are said to have paid tribute at the end of a campaign involving Azriyau in northern Syria (Tgl An 123–157).[73] Because of the fragmentary state of Tiglathpileser's annals[74] this campaign

71. Tadmor argues that Mansuate, an ancient Syrian city, was located in the Beqa valley, where he suggests Adadnirari may have set up his base camp for the campaign against Damascus. Another possibility, argued by Lipiński (1970), is that *Manṣuate* should be identified with presentday *Maṣyat* (alternatively known as *Maṣyad* or *Maṣyaf*), about 28 miles west-south-west of Hamath.

72. ¹*Me/Mi-ni-ḫi-im-me* ᵁᴿᵁ/ᴷᵁᴿ*Sa-me-ri(-i)-na-a-a* (Tgl An 150; Iran 11.5).

73. Azriyau is commonly supposed to have been the leader of the anti-Assyrian coalition against which this campaign was directed. But there is little to support this assumption now that K 6206 (= 'Tgl An 103–119') has been reassigned to Sargon or Sennacherib (see above, p. 195n.). The only relatively unbroken passage in the annals which mentions Azriyau speaks of '19 districts of Hamath together with the towns in their vicinity on the coast of the western sea' *ša i-na ḫi-iṭ-ṭi u gul-lul-ti a-na* ¹*Az-ri-ia-a-ú e-ki-i-mu* (Tgl An 130–131). The final clause of this excerpt is usually translated: 'which had unlawfully defected to [or: sided with] Azriyau'; but this presupposes an otherwise unattested meaning of *ekēmu*, or that *e-ki-i-mu* is a scribal error for another (unidentified) verb. However, *ekēmu ana* in its only attested meaning ('take away from') makes perfectly good sense: 'which they (the rebels) had unlawfully taken away from Azriyau.' In this case, as Tadmor (1961:268) remarks, 'we must conclude that this act towards Azriyau was considered by Tiglath-Pileser as a rebellion against Assyria, and that Azriyau was in fact Tiglath-Pileser's ally.' (Tadmor himself rejects this interpretation on the grounds that 'the text ... seems to imply (line 111) that Azriyau was a foe, not an ally'—but this is part of K 6206, which is no longer ascribed to Tiglathpileser.) If one combines this conclusion with Tadmor's suggestion that Hamath, which is not listed as one of the rebellious states, remained loyal to Assyria (cf. Weippert 1973:44), a possible inference is that Azriyau was ruler of Hamath—although in this case it must be supposed that he died (or was assassinated) in the course of the revolt: the tribute list which concludes this section of the annals names '*Eniel* of Hamath' as a tributary (Tgl An 151–152).

74. See Tadmor 1967 for a discussion of the surviving textual evidence. The annals were inscribed on stone slabs (also bearing reliefs) which were originally

is undated, but since the tribute list which concludes this section of the annals is followed immediately by a dated heading (Tgl An 157) introducing the events of Tiglathpileser's 9th year, 737 BC (Nis.), there is little doubt that it occurred in Tiglathpileser's 8th year, 738 BC (Nis.). Confirmation of this dating is provided by the Eponym Chronicle, which records the capture of Kullani (Biblical Calneh/Calno) in north Syria for this year, and which also states that Ulluba (in Urartu), which was one of the places to which Tiglathpileser deported Syrian populations at the end of the Azriyau campaign (Tgl An 133), was captured in the previous year.[75] This view is disputed by Thiele (³1983:142–159), who claims that Tiglathpileser's annals were not arranged in chronological sequence (in contrast to the normal arrangement of Assyrian annals), and that Menahem might therefore have paid tribute as early as 743 BC (Nis.), when according to the Eponym Chronicle the Assyrian army was campaigning in the vicinity of Arpad.[76] But Thiele's claims are rejected by most Assyriologists,[77]

incorporated in Tiglathpileser's palace at Calah (Nimrud). But this was abandoned not long after Tiglathpileser's death and was subsequently plundered for building materials by Esarhaddon, who re-used the reliefs in his own (unfinished) palace. The fragmentary nature of the surviving text of the annals, and the problems involved in arranging the existing sources in their correct sequence, have not always been properly appreciated by Biblical scholars, presumably because the consecutive line-numbering of Rost's edition gives a misleading impression of completeness and continuity; thus Shea (1978b:45f.) speaks of 'glaring omissions', without apparently realizing that these occur in portions of text which are no longer preserved.

75. Thiele (³1983:150) argues that a previous campaign against Ulluba might have occurred in 743 BC (Nis.). But his evidence for this is derived from 'summary inscriptions', which are usually arranged on geographical rather than chronological principles.

76. According to lines 83–91 of Tiglathpileser's annals (which probably do form a connected sequence, although lines 83–89 and 90–91 are preserved on separate fragments) it was 'in Arpad' (*ina qabal* ^{URU}*Ar-pad-da*) that Tiglathpileser received tribute from various Syro-Palestinian and Anatolian rulers. However, Thiele's assumption that Tiglathpileser was already inside the city of Arpad in 743 BC (Nis.) is based on a mistranslation of the Eponym Chronicle's entry for this year. Luckenbill (ARAB 2 § 1198) translated this as follows: 'in the city of Arpadda. A massacre took place in the land of Urartu (Armenia).' But the correct translation (Tadmor 1961:253) is 'a defeat on Urartu was inflicted in Arpad' (i.e. in the territory of Arpad)—the Eponym Chronicle records that Tiglathpileser spent the following three years campaigning against Arpad before it was captured. One should also question Thiele's assumption that the tribute list in lines 83f. of the annals is a parallel version of the list given in lines 150f. (similarly Tadmor 1961:256); it is more probable that the two lists refer to two separate payments of tribute (Tadmor 1967:179f. See below, p. 200f.).

and are essentially a product of the fact that his own reconstruction of Israelite chronology, in which Menahem's last regnal year is dated to 742 BC (Nis.), is at variance with Assyrian evidence as this is usually interpreted.

Further Assyrian evidence of Israelite-Assyrian contacts during Menahem's reign is provided by a stele found in Iran and published by Levine in 1972.[78] This includes a list of tributaries (Tgl Iran II.3–19), which, aside from differences of order, is virtually identical with the list given in lines 150–154 of Tiglath-pileser's annals. There are, however, two significant differences between the two lists: the Iran stele omits Eniel of Hamath from its list and names Tubail (Ittobaal) rather than Hiram as king of Tyre. Whatever the reason for the omission of Hamath in the Iran stele, the logical inference to be drawn from the fact that the king of Tyre is named differently is that the two lists refer to tribute paid on separate occasions. Since the Iran stele appears to have been erected during Tiglathpileser's campaign against the Medes in 737 BC (Nis.), Levine (1972a:15) concluded that the tribute list given by this text records the payment of tribute in 737 BC (Nis.), with Hiram having recently been succeeded by Tubail. But it has since been pointed out (Cogan 1973; Katzenstein 1973:205) that Hiram is mentioned in Tgl ND 4301 + in connection with events which occurred in 734–732 BC (Nis.).[79] The tribute list given by the Iran stele must therefore predate the list given in lines 150–154 of Tiglathpileser's annals, and Cogan plausibly suggests that the former refers to the payment of tribute which occurred in 740 BC (Nis.) following Tiglathpileser's capture of Arpad (cf. Tgl An 83–91).[80] This will presumably have been the occasion referred to in 2 Kings 15.19: Israel's status as an Assyrian vassal-state had

77. See Tadmor 1961:258f. for a convincing refutation. Tadmor notes that Thiele's arguments are seriously weakened by the fragmentary nature of the annals, and that the main argument for dating Menahem's payment of tribute to 743 BC (Nis.) is based on a mistranslation of the Eponym Chronicle (see previous note).

78. Levine 1972a. The relevant passage is also quoted and discussed in Levine 1972b and Weippert 1973.

79. See Tgl ND 4301 + rev.5f., which describes measures taken against '[Hi]ram of Tyre, who had made [an alliance] with Rezin.'

80. The Eponym Chronicle lists three consecutive campaigns against Arpad in 742 to 740 BC (Nis.). Curiously, though, a statement that Arpad was captured 'after three years' (*a-na 3 MU-MEŠ*) is attached to the second of these campaigns. Tadmor (1961:254) is probably correct in arguing that the statement is misplaced, but see Weippert 1973:36.

apparently lapsed during the period of Assyrian weakness which followed the death of Adadnirari III, and Menahem, confronted with a renewed display of Assyrian power, evidently thought it prudent to renew Israel's allegiance in order to avoid the fate that had befallen Arpad.

Menahem's payment of tribute in 740 and 738 BC (Nis.) provides us with two important fixed points in Israelite chronology, which clearly invalidate any chronological scheme in which the end of Menahem's reign is dated earlier than 739 BC (aut.).[81] Both dates are compatible with the reconstruction of Israelite chronology given above. On this reconstruction Menahem's first year is 745 BC (aut.). Menahem will therefore have paid tribute in the 5th or 6th year of his reign (741 or 740 BC (aut.)) and again in his 7th or 8th year (739 or 738 BC (aut.)), which is within the reign length of 10 years ascribed to him in 2 Kings 15.17. The fact that Menahem must therefore have reigned for a minimum of 7 years suggests that the Biblical figure of 10 years may well be correct, despite the use of 10 and 20 as schematic round numbers for the reigns of Pekah and Pekahiah; it is unlikely that Menahem's original reign length was greater than 10 years, as Deuteronomistic schematization of the chronology of Kings was designed to lengthen this chronology rather than shorten it. If this assumption is correct and 10 years is in fact the original figure, Menahem's reign may be dated from 745 to 736 BC (aut.).

Menahem's successor, Pekahiah, reigned for only 2 years according to MT, which has clearly preserved the original figure against LXX[AL]'s schematic figure of 10 years. Pekahiah's reign may therefore be dated from 736 to 735 BC (aut.), in which case Pekah's assassination of Pekahiah in 735 BC (aut.) must have occurred at approximately the same time that Tiglathpileser was campaigning in Philistia—the Eponym Chronicle records that the Assyrian army campaigned 'against Philistia' in 734 BC (Nis.). Pekah's usurpation of the Israelite throne was almost certainly an anti-Assyrian move, which quite possibly had Aramean backing, since (on these dates) it was followed more or less immediately by the formation of an anti-Assyrian alliance between Aram, Israel, and Tyre (Tyrian involvement is stated in Tgl ND 4301 + rev.5f.;

81. This includes the chronologies of Thiele (³1983), Schedl (1962a), Pavlovský and Vogt (1964), and Andersen (1969), which date Menahem's last year to either 742 or 743 BC (aut./Nis.).

see n. 79 above). This alliance was apparently initiated and led
by Rezin of Aram, and resulted in a two-year Assyrian campaign
'against Damascus' in 733 and 732 BC (Nis.) (Ep Chr). One might
also suppose that the Philistine campaign of 734 BC (Nis.)
represented the first stage of Tiglathpileser's response to this
revolt (Begrich 1929b); but there is little support for this view in
the Assyrian texts, although it is compatible with the chronology
given above. The Philistine campaign was apparently directed
against Hanno of Gaza, who initially fled to Egypt but subsequently returned and was reinstated by Tiglathpileser (Tgl K1
8–15; ND 400 14–19; ND 4301 + rev.13–16). However, none of
the inscriptions which describe this campaign give any indication
that Hanno was acting in concert with Rezin. The one Philistine
ruler who certainly was implicated in Rezin's alliance appears to
have remained loyal to Assyria during 734 BC (Nis.): Mitinti of
Ashkelon is said to have rebelled against Tiglathpileser, and to
have died (committed suicide?) after learning of Rezin's defeat
(Tgl An 235–236); but the tribute list given in Tgl K 3751 7f.
mentions him alongside 'Jehoahaz (Ahaz) of Judah'[82] as one of the
rulers who paid tribute to Tiglathpileser in 734 BC (Nis.).[83] It is
worth noting that this list conspicuously fails to mention Aram,
Israel, and Tyre,[84] which suggests that the anti-Assyrian alliance

82. *Ia-ú-ḫa-zi* ^{KUR}*Ia-ú-da-a-a* (Tgl K 3751 11).
83. This date is established by the following considerations.
    1. Judah and other southern states included in this list are not included in
       tribute lists dating to 740 and 738 BC (Nis.).
    2. Mitinti of Ashkelon was a member of Rezin's anti-Assyrian alliance in
       733–732 BC (Nis.).
This leaves 734 BC (Nis.) as the only possible date for the payment of tribute
recorded in this inscription (Assyrian attention was directed elsewhere in 737–735
BC (Nis.)). Cf. Tadmor and Cogan 1979:505.
84. It is unlikely that these are to be restored in the break at the end of line 7
(Weippert 1973:53), since this presupposes a radical departure from the order of
tributaries in Tgl An 150–154, whereas a comparison of the two lists suggests that
with one exception (Urik of Que and Shipitbaal of Byblos are reversed in K 3751)
they follow the same order.

Annals	K3751
150 Kustaspi of Kummuh	7 Kustaspi of Kummuh
Rezin of Aram	
Menahem of Samaria	
151 Hiram of Tyre	
Shipitbaal of Byblos	Urik of Que
Urik of Que	Shipitbaal of [Byblos]
Pishirish of Carchemish	[Pishirish of Carchemish?]

of these states was formed in direct response to Tiglathpileser's invasion of Philistia in 734 BC (Nis.), and that Mitinti of Ashkelon, having paid tribute to Tiglathpileser in that year, was shortly afterwards persuaded to join the alliance. It was presumably at this time also that Aram and Israel tried unsuccessfully to bring Judah into the alliance through an attack on Jerusalem that was intended to topple the Davidic dynasty (2K 16.5f.; Is 7.1f.).[85]

The exact course of the Assyrian campaign 'against Damascus' in 733 and 732 BC (Nis.) is unclear from the fragmentary state of Tiglathpileser's annals; but it is evident from Assyrian and Biblical texts that it culminated in the capture of Damascus and the annexation of Aramean and northern Israelite territory, and that Rezin and Pekah both lost their lives as a consequence of this

152	Eniel	of Hamath	8	[Eni]el of Hamath
	Panammu of Sam'al		Panammu of Sam'al
	Tarhulara of Gurgum		Tarhulara of Gurgum
	Shulumal of Melid		Shul[umal of Melid]
153	Dadil	of Kashka		[Dadil of Kashka?]
	Washurme of Tabal	9	[Wa]shurme of Tabal
	Us-hit of Tuna		Us-hit of Tuna
	Urpalla of Tuhana		Urpalla of Tuhana
	Tuhamme of Istunda		Tuham[me of Istunda]
154	Urimme of Hubisna		[Urimme of Hubisna?]
	Zabibe queen of Arabia		
		10	[M]atanbaal of Arvad
			Shanip of Beth Ammon
			Shalaman of Moab
			[ ]
			[ ]
		11	[M]itinti of Ashkelon
			Jehoahaz of Judah
			Qausmalak of Edom
			Muse[ ]
			[ ]
		12	[H]anno of Gaza

85. If this reconstruction of events is correct, Ahaz (who paid tribute along with Mitinti and other rulers at the end of Tiglathpileser's Philistine campaign) was already an Assyrian vassal when he appealed to Tiglathpileser for help against Pekah and Rezin (2K 16.7-9). This contradicts the usual assumption that it was Ahaz's appeal to Tiglathpileser which brought Judah into a vassal relationship with Assyria (Herrmann 1975:248; Donner 1977:427; Jagersma 1982:159; Soggin 1984:228), but it agrees with the Biblical account, which suggests that Ahaz's appeal was made on the basis of an existing vassal relationship ('I am your servant and your son'). Oded's attempt to show that the 'Syro-Ephraimite' attack on Jerusalem was a purely local affair which was unrelated to the wider political situation (Oded 1972) is in my opinion quite unconvincing.

campaign: Rezin appears to have been executed by the Assyrians after Tiglathpileser had captured Damascus (2K 16.9), while Pekah was assassinated in a political coup which followed Tiglathpileser's annexation of northern Israelite territory (Tgl An 227–228; K1 15–19; 2K 15.29–30). It is unfortunate that the annals fragment which appears to describe Pekah's assassination is badly damaged and therefore undated, but since the relevant passage also makes reference to 'former campaigns (*girrēteya maḥrâte*) in which Israelite towns and cities had been attacked—presumably in 734 and 733 BC (Nis.)—it most probably describes events which occurred in 732 BC (Nis.).[86] Further evidence for the date of Pekah's assassination has been provided by a recent study (Borger and Tadmor 1982) in which it is pointed out that a corrected reading of Tgl ND 4301+ indicates that Pekah's successor, Hoshea, travelled or sent messengers to Sarrabanu in southern Mesopotamia in order to offer his submission to Tiglathpileser.[87] Tiglathpileser is known to have campaigned in this area in 731 BC (Nis.) and again in 729 BC (Nis.) (Ep Chr; *ABC* 1.i.19–23), and there is little doubt that Hoshea's payment of tribute should be dated to the first of these occasions. Now if Pekah had been succeeded by Hoshea as early as 733 BC (Nis.), we should clearly have expected the latter to have offered his submission in 732 BC (Nis.) in Damascus (along with Ahaz of Judah: 2K 16.10). The only plausible reason why this did not happen is that Pekah was assassinated after or shortly before Tiglathpileser's return to

86. Begrich 1929a:99f.; Tadmor 1967:180. Borger and Tadmor (1982:249) consider 731 BC (Nis.) to be a possible date for Pekah's assassination; but it can hardly be dated as late as 730 BC (aut.), as Schedl (1962a:101) and Andersen (1969:97) suppose.

87. The relevant passage is Tgl 4301 + rev.9–11 (cf. rev.25 and K1 15–19).

(9)[...]⌜*a-na gi*⌝[-*mir-ti-šú* ... *a-di mar-š*]*i-ti-šú-nu a-n*[*a* ...](*10*)[... ¹*A-ú-si-ʾ a-na LU*]*GAL-ú-ti ina UGU-šú-n*[*u aš-kun*...](*11*)[... *a-na e-peš ARAD-ú-te a-na* ^URU^*S*]*ar-ra-ba-ni a-di maḥ-ri-ia*[...]

'(9)[... A]ll [Israel ... together with] their [pos]sessions [I deported] to [Assyria ...](10)[... Hoshea I made k]ing over them[...](11)[... to render servitude ... to S]arrabanu before me [...]'

Wiseman (1956:124, 126) read *ka-ra-ba-ni* for *S*]*ar-ra-ba-ni*, and translated this as 'pleading to my presence.' But *S*]*ar-ra-ba-ni* is confirmed by collation (Borger and Tadmor 1982:246), and is also supported by the parallel in rev.25, referring to an unknown ruler said to have sent/brought tribute to Tiglathpileser in Calah.

Assyria.[88] Pekah's assassination and Hoshea's accession may therefore be dated in the second half (probably) of 732 BC (Nis.), which is equivalent to the first half of the Israelite year which began in the autumn of 732 BC. Pekah's entire reign will thus have occupied a period of only 4 years (inclusive) from 735 BC (aut.) to 732 BC (aut.), in contrast to the schematic figure of 20 years given in Kings. It is of interest to note that a schematic increase from 4 to 20 years is exactly proportional to the schematic increase from 2 to 10 years in the case of Pekahiah's reign, where both schematic and pre-schematic figures are preserved as textual variants.[89]

Hoshea's accession to the Israelite throne inaugurated the final chapter in the history of the northern kingdom, which came to an abrupt end shortly afterwards with the Assyrian siege and capture of Samaria. According to the Biblical account (2K 17.3–6; 18.9–11), Hoshea had asserted Israelite independence from Assyria by withholding his yearly payment of tribute, and had also sought Egyptian support by sending messengers to 'So, king of Egypt'.[90] Tiglathpileser's successor, Shalmaneser V, reacted by launching a military campaign against Hoshea, at which point the latter apparently decided to abandon his revolt, and went to offer

88. If one accepts Tiglathpileser's claim to have 'appointed' Hoshea (Tgl K1 17–18) the most probable inference is that Pekah was assassinated shortly before Tiglathpileser's departure, and that Hoshea gained immediate Assyrian recognition of his succession on condition that he send tribute to Mesopotamia in formal token of his allegiance. Compare the fact that Hezekiah is said to have sent tribute to Nineveh after Sennacherib's Syro-Palestinian campaign (Sn Pr III.37–49).

89. Wellhausen (1875:630–631) proposed to resolve the discrepancy between Assyrian and Biblical chronology at this point by identifying Pekah with Pekahiah and ascribing him a reign of 2 years (MT's figure for Pekahiah's reign) rather than 20 years. But this solution, which has recently been rediscovered by Reade (1981:5), is hardly justified by the fact that Pekah and Pekahiah have nearly identical names ('Pekah' is a hypocoristic of 'Pekahiah'). The fact that Pekah is almost always referred to as 'Pekah ben Remaliah' in Biblical texts (and simply as 'ben Remaliah' in Isaiah 7.9) is an indication that the Biblical writers (and pre-Deuteronomistic tradition in Isaiah 7.9) were careful to distinguish the two rulers.

90. Probably Osorkon IV (Kitchen 1973a:372f.). Hoshea most probably revolted immediately after Tiglathpileser's death in 727 BC (Nis.), the death of an Assyrian ruler being the regular occasion of revolts by Assyrian provinces and vassal-states. An excerpt from Menander's translation of the annals of Tyre which is preserved by Josephus (*Ant* 9.283–287) appears to indicate that Tyre and other Phoenician cities also revolted at this time (see Katzenstein 1973:220f.).

his submission and pay tribute.[91] This rather belated offer of submission failed to satisfy Shalmaneser: Hoshea was arrested and Shalmaneser proceeded to lay siege to Samaria, which fell after a three-year siege in Hoshea's 9th regnal year. Throughout this three-year period (counted inclusively from Hoshea's 7th regnal year) Hoshea apparently remained in Assyrian custody, and Samaria was presumably governed by its council of elders (cf. 2K 10.1).[92]

Hoshea came to the throne in 732 BC (aut.) according to evidence presented above; his 9th regnal year, counted inclusively from 732 BC (aut.), is therefore 724 BC (aut.), and the siege of Samaria is to be dated as having lasted from 726 BC (aut.) to 724 BC (aut.). These dates are in close agreement with the fragmentary evidence of the Eponym Chronicle (Cb3), which reports that Shalmaneser V came to the throne in 727 BC (Nis.) and undertook

91. The Biblical account might conceivably be interpreted as indicating two Assyrian campaigns, the first of which induced Hoshea to renew his allegiance to Assyria by paying tribute (2K 17.3), whereas the second resulted in the siege and capture of Samaria (2K 17.4–6). But Katzenstein (1973:225f.) is on weak ground in arguing that Shalmaneser first campaigned in the west in 727 BC (Nis.), shortly before he succeeded Tiglathpileser on the Assyrian throne. It is true that Luckenbill's translation of the Eponym Chronicle states clearly that the Assyrians campaigned 'against Damascus' in that year (*ARAB* 2 § 1198; cf. Thiele [3]1983:224 for an adaptation of Luckenbill's translation, to which Katzenstein refers). However, Olmstead's reconstruction of the Eponym Chronicle, which forms the basis of Luckenbill's translation, gives *a-na* $^{URU}Di[-maš-qi]$ (note the brackets), with a note that 'the *Di*, omitted by later editors, was evidently clear in the time of G.Smith *Trans. Soc. Bibl. Arch.* II 321f.' (Olmstead 1914/15:357, 336). This is inaccurate: Smith failed to read anything more than *a-na* $^{URU}[$ in the Eponym Chronicle's entry for 727 BC (Nis.), and the *Di* to which Olmstead refers is given by Smith as the last visible sign in the Eponym Chronicle's entry for *728* BC (Nis.) (Schrader 1875:342 read *D[i* at this point). We do not in fact know where the Assyrians campaigned in 727 BC (Nis.), and there is no evidence that this campaign (wherever it was directed) was not conducted by Tiglathpileser himself.

92. A number of Biblical scholars have sought to avoid this conclusion by arguing that 2 Kings 17.3–6 contains two parallel accounts derived from the royal annals of Israel and Judah (cf. Jones 1984:542f.): in the Israelite account (verses 3–4) we are told that Hoshea was imprisoned, but 'reference to the fall of Samaria and the deportation of its inhabitants is discreetly avoided' (Jones 1984:546), whereas the Judean version mentions the 'unpalatable facts' of the siege and deportation (Jones, ibid.). But there is little justification for identifying separate sources, and it is surely far-fetched to suppose that the Israelite annals could have attempted to conceal the fact of Samaria's capture. Judean sources were far less reticent in reporting the Babylonian capture of Jerusalem in 598 and 587 BC (Nis.).

the first campaign of his reign in 725 BC (Nis.). This campaign, which presumably began in the spring (i.e. in the second half of 726 BC (aut.)),[93] was followed by two further campaigns in 724 and 723 BC (Nis.). In each case the name of the place or places against which these campaigns were directed is no longer preserved; but since the three years of military campaigns listed in the Eponym Chronicle coincide in date with the three-year siege of Samaria on Biblical evidence, and since the Babylonian Chronicle records the capture of Samaria as the one notable achievement of Shalmaneser V's reign (*ABC* 1.i.28),[94] there are strong grounds for accepting Olmstead's proposal to restore 'Samaria' in the Eponym Chronicle's entries for this period (Olmstead 1904/5). In this case the fall of Samaria may be dated to the first half of 723 BC (Nis.), or the second half of 724 BC (aut.).

Against this date it must be noted that the majority of Assyriologists put the fall of Samaria a year later, in 722 BC (Nis.), and that this second date is commonly cited by Biblical scholars as an established fact.[95] However, the main evidence for this later dating has now been discarded. For a long time it was taken for granted that the fall of Samaria could be dated to 722 BC (Nis.) by the fact that Sargon II claims to have captured Samaria during his accession year (Sg Kh 10–17; Cal IV.25–41). But this claim contradicts both the Biblical account, which implies that Shalmaneser V was responsible for the capture of Samaria,[96] and also the Babylonian Chronicle, which says so unambiguously (*ABC* 1.i.28). Consequently, since Tadmor's important discussion of the matter (Tadmor 1958:31–40), almost all Assyriologists now accept that Sargon's claim to have captured Samaria in his

93. This was traditionally the season in which Assyrian military campaigns were undertaken.

94. There is no longer any serious doubt that $^{URU}Ša$-*ma-ra-a'-in* is to be identified with Samaria. See Tadmor 1958:39–40.

95. Albright (1945:17) considered this to be 'the only date [in pre-exilic Israelite and Judean chronology] which is absolutely certain.' Similarly, according to Andersen (1969:97n.), 'muss es als gesichert angesehen werden, dass Samaria im Jahre Tisri 722/21 fiel.' But Olmstead's date for the fall of Samaria is accepted by Thiele (³1983:163–168) and Jepsen (1964:33; 1968:43).

96. 2 Kings 17.3–6 states that 'Shalmaneser, king of Assyria' came against Hoshea (v. 3), and that 'the king of Assyria' then laid siege to Samaria (v. 5), and captured it after 3 years (v. 6). Only by forced exegesis can it be maintained that the 'king of Assyria' who captured Samaria may be distinguished from the 'king of Assyria' who laid siege to the city.

accession year is historically inaccurate. This claim was apparently one of several attempts, made late in Sargon's reign, to conceal the fact that the first few years of Sargon's reign were marked by widespread internal revolts that prevented him from undertaking external military campaigns until his 2nd regnal year (Tadmor 1958:31). However, Sargon was in fact responsible for *re*capturing Samaria, which revolted upon the death of Shalmaneser V along with a number of other western provinces and vassal-states (Sg Kh 23f.; LD 33f.; AC 16f.).[97]

Tadmor's rejection of Sargon's claims to have captured Samaria during his accession year was in many ways a vindication of Olmstead's earlier discussion (Olmstead 1904/5). But having demolished the main evidence for dating the fall of Samaria to 722 BC (Nis.), Tadmor nevertheless attempted to retain this date by arguing that Samaria must have been captured shortly before Shalmaneser V's death in Tebeth 722 BC (Nis.). Two main arguments are advanced (Tadmor 1958:37n.). (1) An interval of more than one year between the fall of Samaria and the death of Shalmaneser would have given the latter sufficient time to have deported the Samarians and set about reorganizing Samaria as an Assyrian province. (2) If Samaria was captured only a few weeks before Sargon's accession Sargon's claim to have taken Samaria in his accession year 'would not be entirely unjustified.' But it is not at all obvious why Sargon's appropriation of his predecessor's achievement is any more justified if Samaria was captured a few months before his accession than if it was captured just over a year before his accession. And Tadmor's first argument begs the question of how we know that Shalmaneser V did *not* deport the Samarians and set about reorganizing Samaria as an Assyrian province. Shalmaneser's annals have not survived, and Sargon's claim to have deported the Samarians and turned Samaria into an Assyrian province is not self-evidently any more reliable than his claim to have been responsible for capturing Samaria in the first place; having claimed responsibility for the initial capture of Samaria Sargon obviously had to claim responsibility for these subsequent activities. Furthermore, if Sargon was not responsible for capturing Samaria, then his claim to have deported its inhabitants is in direct contradiction to the Biblical account:

97. This revolt, which was organized by Yaubi'di (also called Ilubi'di) of Hamath, was suppressed in Sargon's 2nd year, 720 BC (Nis.).

according to 2 Kings 17.6 the same 'king of Assyria' who captured Samaria in Hoshea's 9th year was also responsible for deporting the Israelites to Assyria.

Two further comments are in order. Firstly is should be remarked that Forrer's proposal to restore 'Sam'al', 'Que', and 'Hilakku' in the Eponym Chronicle's entries for 725 to 723 BC (Nis.) (Forrer 1920:71) is not a satisfactory alternative to Olmstead's restoration of these entries (contra Tadmor 1958:33n.), since it is based on the assumption that Samaria was captured by *Sargon* at the end of a one-year (!) campaign which began in the last year of Shalmaneser's reign. Secondly, Tadmor's date for the capture of Samaria cannot easily be reconciled with the 9-year reign length which Kings ascribes to Hoshea, unless Hoshea's accession is dated impossibly late, or it is argued that Hoshea's reign ended with his arrest shortly before the siege of Samaria (Tadmor 1958:37; 1962:287)—which is in direct contradiction to the Biblical statement that the siege of Samaria began in Hoshea's *7th* year (2K 18.9).[98] Hoshea's regnal years were evidently counted up to the capture of Samaria even though he was apparently under Assyrian arrest during the siege; the fact that he was not replaced by another king suggests that he was still regarded as the legitimate ruler.

5.2.2.2 Judean chronology

Judean chronology from Jehu's revolt to the fall of Samaria poses an even more difficult set of historical problems than Israelite chronology of the same period. I have argued that there is sufficient literary-historical evidence to reconstruct the Judean chronology of Kings in its pre-schematic form as far as the reign of Azariah, and that this in turn may be translated into an absolute historical chronology in which Azariah's accession is dated to 772 BC (aut.).[99] Although there is no external historical evidence by which this reconstruction may be tested, it is at least partially corroborated by the fact that it is interdependent with my

98. This theory was first advanced by scholars who accepted Sargon's claim to have captured Samaria in his accession year. See Kugler 1922:160–161, Lewy 1927:15–16, Begrich 1929a:103, Mowinckel 1932:196–197, and Albright 1945:22.

99. See table on p. 194f.

reconstruction of Israelite chronology down to the reign of Menahem, which is itself consistent with Mesopotamian chronology of the same period. But beyond Azariah's accession there is insufficient evidence for a purely literary-historical reconstruction, and little historical evidence to use in its place. All we know for certain is that according to Assyrian evidence noted earlier (p. 202) Ahaz paid tribute to Tiglathpileser in 734 BC (Nis.). This leaves us with an interval of around 38 years between Azariah's accession and Ahaz's payment of tribute; and it is obvious that there is no way in which the reign lengths ascribed to Azariah (52 years) and Jotham (16 years) can possibly be fitted into this period.

In the absence of any direct evidence for dating Azariah's and Jotham's reigns, Judean chronology of this period is best approached by looking at evidence relating to the reigns of Ahaz and Hezekiah. The book of Kings offers us three specific synchronisms between Judean and Assyrian chronology during the reign of Hezekiah. Two of these are connected with the siege and capture of Samaria: according to 2 Kings 18.9–10 Samaria came under siege in Hezekiah's 4th year and was captured in Hezekiah's 6th year. Since we have just established that 723 BC (Nis.) / 724 BC (aut.) is the most probable date of the fall of Samaria, this points to 729 BC (aut.) as the date of Hezekiah's accession.[100] However, 2 Kings 18.13 dates Sennacherib's invasion of Judah to Hezekiah's 14th year, and we know from Assyrian evidence that this occurred in 701 BC (Nis.).[101] On the probable assumption that Sennacherib set out from Assyria in the spring, his invasion of Judah is likely to

100. This assumes that Hezekiah's reign was antedated; this date would be raised to 730 BC (aut.) if postdating were assumed.

101. This date is based upon the following evidence. Sennacherib's military campaigns are numbered but not dated in his annals. However, *termini ante quos* are provided by dated colophons, while those campaigns which were directed against Babylonia are dated in the Babylonian Chronicle according to Babylonian regnal chronology. Sennacherib's first campaign ended with the capture of Hirimmu and Hararatu (Sn Pr 1.54–64) in Belibni's first year as king of Babylon (*ABC* 1.ii.24–25), which was 702 BC (Nis.); and his second campaign was evidently undertaken in the same year, since the Bellino Cylinder, which recounts the first two campaigns, is dated in the eponymy of Nabule'u (Sn Bell colophon), also 702 BC (Nis.). Sennacherib's third campaign, against western rebel states including Judah (Sn Pr II.37–III.49), must therefore have occurred in or after 701 BC (Nis.). But this is also the latest possible date, since Sennacherib's fourth campaign, which ended with the replacement of Belibni by Ashurnadinshumi (Sn Pr III.50–75), is dated in the Babylonian Chronicle (*ABC* 1.ii.26–31) to Belibni's 3rd regnal year (700 BC (Nis.)).

have occurred in the Judean year which began in the autumn of 702 BC, which gives us 715 BC (aut.) as the date of Hezekiah's accession.[102]

One (or both) of these dates is plainly erroneous, but there is disagreement among scholars as to which synchronism, or synchronisms, should be rejected. However, it is generally assumed that one or other of the two sets of synchronisms (those relating to the siege and capture of Samaria, or the synchronism relating to Sennacherib's invasion of Judah) *is* historically reliable, and Biblical chronologists may therefore be divided into two main groups according to whether they date Hezekiah's accession somewhere between 729 BC and 727 BC or whether they date it in 716 or 715 BC (variation over the exact date reflects differing assumptions about calendars and dating systems, or disagreement concerning the date of the capture of Samaria).[103] Various reasons are given for preferring one or other of these dates. Wellhausen (1875:635–636) argued that the fall of Samaria was less important to Judean writers than the deliverance of Jerusalem, and that it was therefore more likely that an inaccurate date would have been attached to the former event than to the latter.[104] Others (e.g. Smith 1873:323) have argued that '14th year of King Hezekiah' in 2 Kings 18.13 should be emended to '24th year of King Hezekiah' (this reduces the discrepancy but fails to eliminate it). Alternatively, it is suggested that some process of scribal or editorial miscalculation has occurred; and one widely held theory is that the date given in 2 Kings 18.13 was secondarily calculated from 2 Kings 20.6, where Hezekiah is promised an additional 15 years of life following his recovery from a near-fatal illness, and 2 Kings 18.2, in which Hezekiah is said to have reigned for 29 years in

---

102. Or 716 BC (aut.) if Hezekiah's reign is postdated.

103. The first group (dating Hezekiah's accession between 729 and 727 BC) includes Lewy (1927:15, 19n.), Coucke (1928:1265–1268), Begrich (1933:74), Vogelstein (1944:2–3), Tadmor (1962:277–279), Schedl (1962a:112–119), Jepsen (1964:29f., 36–38; 1968:44–46), and Pavlovský and Vogt (1964:342–343). The second group (dating Hezekiah's accession to 716 or 715 BC) includes Wellhausen (1875:635–638), Mowinckel (1932:214–220), Albright (1945:22), Thiele (³1983:174), and Andersen (1969:98). Vogelstein attempts to harmonize both sets of synchronisms by positing an 'era of Hezekiah's reform', which allegedly began in 714 BC.

104. Contrast Vogelstein (1944:2), who argues that the fall of Samaria was 'so terrifying' that 'for generations, probably, people were unable to forget that this blow had fallen in the 6th year of Hezekiah.'

total.[105] Proponents of this theory point out that the story of Hezekiah's illness is only loosely connected with the story of Sennacherib's invasion, and might originally have belonged to a quite different historical context. However, this observation may be carried a stage further by noting that 2 Kings 20.6 has the appearance of being a secondary addition to the story of Hezekiah's illness that was inserted precisely in order to create a link between this story and the story of Sennacherib's invasion. It is therefore more likely that the reference to 15 additional years in 2 Kings 20.6 was secondarily calculated from the date in 2 Kings 18.13 than that the latter was calculated from the former.

There are, in fact, strong reasons for thinking that *neither* synchronism is historically authentic. If Hezekiah's accession is dated to 729 BC (aut.) or thereabouts, we are faced with a deficit of 2 to 3 years (or more) in Judean chronology from Hezekiah's accession to the death of Josiah in 609 BC (Nis.), which requires us to lengthen Hezekiah's reign and/or the reigns of one (or more) of his successors by an equivalent amount.[106] If, on the other hand, Hezekiah's accession is dated to around 715 BC (aut.), Ahaz's reign must then be extended by 3 to 4 years (or more) in order to take account of the fact that he is listed as one of a number of Syro-Palestinian rulers who are said to have paid tribute to Tiglathpileser III in 734 BC (Nis.). There is, however, no plausible reason why either of these reigns should have been shortened in the first place; Deuteronomistic schematization of the chronology of Kings sought to lengthen this chronology rather than reduce it.

A further reason for rejecting these synchronisms is that they appear to have been constructed to reflect a schematic pattern of Israelite-Judean history within the overall 1000-year framework of Deuteronomistic chronology (see p. 77f.). If we simply add together the pre-Priestly Judean reign lengths of this chronology we arrive at a total of 400 years from the division of the kingdom to the Babylonian exile, with the fall of Samaria in Hezekiah's 6th year occurring two-thirds of the way through this period, 267 years after the division of the kingdom. In this scheme Sennacherib's

---

105. See Coucke 1928:1266; Tadmor 1962:279; Jepsen 1964:29–32; Pavlovský and Vogt 1964:343.

106. The book of Kings ascribes 29+55+2+31 years to Hezekiah, Manasseh, Amon, and Josiah, giving a total of 114 to 117 years depending on whether postdating or antedating is assumed.

invasion of Judah in Hezekiah's 14th year occurs 275 years after the division of the kingdom (125 years before the fall of Jerusalem), and Shalmaneser's attack on Samaria in Hezekiah's 4th year occurs 265 years after the division of the kingdom, 10 years before Sennacherib's invasion of Judah. The two Assyrian attacks on Israel and Judah have evidently been juxtaposed quite deliberately in 2 Kings 18, and the schematic 10-year interval which separates them serves to reinforce this juxtaposition and underline similarities and dissimilarities between the two occasions.[107]

The schematic nature of these Biblical synchronisms requires us to look elsewhere for evidence which may be used to date the reigns of Ahaz and Hezekiah. Fortunately there is one piece of evidence which lies outside the framework of Deuteronomistic chronology, and which therefore has considerable importance as having presumably escaped Deuteronomistic schematization. Isaiah 14.28–32 contains an oracle against Philistia which is dated to the year of Ahaz's death, but which also incorporates historical allusions which may be dated in relation to Mesopotamian chronology. In view of its chronological importance it is worth quoting the passage in full.

28	בשנת מות המלך אחז היה המשא הזה:
29	אל תשמחי פלשת כלך כי נשבר שבט מכך
	כי משרש נחש יצא צפע ופריו שרף מעופף:
30	ורעו בכורי דלים ואביונים לבטח ירבצו
	והמתי ברעב שרשך ושאריתך יהרג:
31	הילילי שער זעקי עיר נמוג פלשת כלך
	כי מצפון עשן בא ואין בודד במועדיו:
32	ומה יענה מלאכי גוי
	כי יהוה יסד ציון ובה יחסו עניי עמו:

28 In the year that King Ahaz died there came this oracle:

29 Do not rejoice all Philistia, that the rod which struck you is broken,

    for from the snake's root there comes forth a viper, and its fruit is a flying serpent.

30 The firstborn of the poor will graze, and the needy will lie down in safety,

---

107. As evidence of deliberate juxtaposition it may be noted that Shalmaneser's attack on Samaria is also recounted in its appropriate narrative context in 2 Kings 17.3–6.

and/but I (LXX: he) will kill your root (LXX: offspring) with famine, and he (1QIs^a: I) will slay your remnant.

31   Wail, o gate! Cry, o city! Despair, all Philistia!
      For smoke is coming from the north, and there is no straggler in their ranks.

32   And what should one answer the messengers of the nation (LXX: nations)?
      That Yahweh has founded Zion, and in her (1QIs^a: him) the poor of his people will find refuge.

Textual notes

29   שבט מכך: LXX translates this phrase as a construct chain, ὁ ζυγὸς τοῦ παίοντος ὑμᾶς ('the yoke of your smiter'). But despite Isaiah 9.3, with שבט הנגש בו ('the rod of his oppressor'), מכך is more probably an appositional modifier of שבט (cf. Is 14.5–6).

30   והמתי ... יהרג: the awkward juxtaposition of 1st sg. and 3rd sg. may be resolved either by reading *והמית, 'and/but he will kill' (LXX: ἀνελεῖ δέ), in place of והמתי, or by reading אהרג, 'I will slay' (1QIs^a: אהרוג) instead of יהרג.

      שרשך: LXX's τὸ σπέρμα σου ('your offspring') is often thought to reflect a variant *זרעך, but it is probably only a free translation of שרשך; compare ζυγός as a free translation of שבט in the previous verse.

31   בודד, 'straggler': literally 'one who separates himself.' 1QIs^a reads מודד, 'one who measures'—'there is none who can measure their ranks' (?).

32   גוי: LXX has ἐθνῶν, 'nations' (similarly the Peshitta and Targum), but MT is probably more original.
      בה, 'in her': this is preferable to 1QIs^a בו, 'in him', which is probably influenced by Psalm 2.12 and similar passages.

Before we can make use of this passage for chronological purposes we must obviously first consider the question of its authenticity. There is little doubt that verses 29 and 31 belong together as part of a single unit, as is shown by the close syntactic parallelism which exists between them, and by the repetition of 'all Philistia' (פלשת כלך) in both verses. On the other hand verse 30a is almost certainly intrusive, and should probably be regarded as a secondary addition (Wildberger 1978: 586); some scholars (Donner 1964:110; Kaiser 1974:51; Clements 1980a:149) prefer to transpose v. 30a after verse 31 or 32, but this raises the problem of accounting for its initial displacement from that position. Having removed v. 30a it is possible to view v. 30b as the original continuation of the previous verse, provided one reads ‏*והמית‎ ('and he will kill') in place of ‏והמתי‎ ('and I will kill'), following LXX. But it is then difficult to account for the secondary insertion of v. 30a, and a more probable solution is to view the whole of verse 30, which forms a good antithetical couplet, as a fragment inserted on the catchword principle (‏שרש‎ in verse 30b echoes ‏שרש‎ in the previous verse).[108] Verse 32 has also been viewed as secondary by some scholars (e.g. Fullerton 1925/6:95f.), but it provides a suitable conclusion to verses 29 and 31, and should probably be retained as an integral part of the original oracle, which is therefore to be found in verse 29 and verses 31 to 32. This nucleus is entirely appropriate to the political situation of Isaiah's time, and is also consistent with the political message of other Isaianic oracles (see p. 217), so that its own Isaianic authenticity may be safely accepted.[109]

A second question which must be considered concerns the accuracy of the oracle's superscription (v. 28); for even if the basic oracle is Isaianic it may still be argued that the heading is a secondary addition inserted by a late redactor who had no reliable knowledge of the circumstances in which the oracle was originally delivered (Clements 1980a:148; cf. Kaiser 1974:51f.). But this is improbable: the majority of oracles and narratives in Isaiah 1–35 are undated, and it is hard to see why a late redactor should have singled out this particular oracle to be provided with a fictitious date. The theory that this date was inserted because the 'broken rod' of verse 29 was identified with Ahaz is highly unlikely (cf. Gray 1912:266), for there is no record of Ahaz ever having 'struck' the Philistines. Furthermore, Isaiah's commission as a prophet is also dated to the year in which a Judean king died (Is 6.1: ‏בשנת‎

108. This presupposes that ‏שרשך‎ ('your root') rather than *‏זרעך‎ ('your offspring') is the original reading in verse 30b. Against the alleged unsuitability of ‏שרש‎ in this context (Begrich 1933:70 and others) it may be noted that ‏שארית‎ ('remnant'), which parallels ‏שרש‎ in this verse, is used to mean 'descendants' in at least two Biblical passages (Gn 45.7; 2S 14.7), and that ‏שרש‎ is used in parallelism with ‏פרי‎ ('fruit' = 'descendants') in verse 29 and in other passages (Is 37.31; Am 2.9; Ho 9.6; *KAI* 14.11–12).

109. Kaiser (1974:52–53) is one of the few modern commentators to have questioned the Isaianic authenticity of the oracle's nucleus, but this must be set against his general predilection for dating oracles to the Persian or Hellenistic periods.

מות המלך עזיהו, 'in the year that King Uzziah died'), and there is
certainly no reason to question the authenticity of this dating.[110]

Having now established the probable authenticity of the oracle
(excluding v. 30) and its heading we may turn to consideration of
their chronological implications. The oracle itself was evidently
delivered shortly after the death of an Assyrian king, since verse
29b alludes to a succession of (oppressive) rulers,[111] while the
reference to an attack from the north (v. 31) clearly identifies the
enemy as Assyria, and thus excludes the possibility that Ahaz was
the ruler whose death prompted Philistine rejoicing.[112] Now there
are only two Assyrian rulers whose deaths might conceivably have
coincided with the death of Ahaz: Tiglathpileser III, who died in
Tebeth 727 BC (Nis.) (*ABC* 1.i.24), and Shalmaneser V, who died
in Tebeth 722 BC (Nis.) (*ABC* 1.i.29). Since Tebeth was the tenth
month of the Mesopotamian calendar Ahaz's death must therefore
have occurred in either 727 BC (aut.) or 722 BC (aut.).

A majority of scholars have argued in favour of identifying the
dead Assyrian ruler with Tiglathpileser III.[113] There are two main
arguments for this identification. (1) Tiglathpileser III campaigned against Philistine cities in 734 BC (Nis.) and again in
733–732 BC (Nis.),[114] whereas there is no evidence that Shalmaneser V ever campaigned in this area; the phrase שבט מכך ('the rod

110. Kaiser's assertion that the opening words of Isaiah 14.28 'are clearly
based upon 6.1' (Kaiser 1974:51) rather begs the question; why should we
assume that either date is based upon the other? Nobody, so far as I am aware,
argues that the date given in 2 Kings 22.3 (for example) is based upon the date in
2 Kings 18.13 because there are similarities in phraseology.

111. Verse 29bβ is almost certainly in semantic parallelism with verse 29bα;
i.e. the verse refers to a *single* succession involving two rulers (rather than two
successions involving three rulers).

112. This theory has few modern advocates, but has been defended by Irwin
(1927/8), who argues that verse 28 has to be understood as giving not merely the
time but also the occasion of the following oracle. However, if this were the case
we should naturally extend the same understanding to Isaiah 6.1, although, as
Irwin admits (p. 76n.), the causal connection between the death of Uzziah and
the inaugural vision of Isaiah is not entirely obvious. Those who identify the
'broken rod' of verse 29 with Ahaz are also faced the problem mentioned above
of accounting for the fact that Ahaz is not known to have 'struck' Philistia. Irwin
(1927/8:84–85) argues, unconvincingly, that Ahaz was directly responsible for
Tiglathpileser III's invasion of Philistia, and might therefore be regarded as one
who had indirectly struck at Philistia.

113. Coucke 1928:1266–1267; Begrich 1933; Tadmor 1962:278; Pavlovský
and Vogt 1964:342–343; Wildberger 1978:578.

114. See above, p. 201ff.

which struck you') is therefore more appropriately applied to Tiglathpileser than to Shalmaneser. (2) If Ahaz died in 727 BC (Nis.), Hezekiah's 6th year could coincide with the fall of Samaria in 722 BC (Nis.). But this second argument carries little weight, since Samaria probably fell in 723 BC (Nis.),[115] and we have already seen that the Biblical synchronism between Hezekiah's reign and the fall of Samaria is difficult to reconcile with later Judean chronology. The first argument may also be rejected: the 'rod' of verse 29 probably refers not to Tiglathpileser (or any other Assyrian ruler) but to Assyria itself (cf. Isaiah 10.5).[116] The Philistines are cautioned by Isaiah against believing that the death of one Assyrian ruler meant the end of Assyrian rule in the west; that this was the perennial hope of Assyrian provinces and vassal-states is reflected in the series of revolts which almost invariably greeted the deaths of successive Assyrian rulers.

A better case can be made for associating the oracle with the death of Shalmaneser V in 722 BC (Nis.).[117] We know from Sargon's inscriptions that Gaza was one of the Assyrian vassal-states which revolted at this time (Sg Kh 56–58; LD 25–26; Cyl 19), whereas there is no evidence that any Philistine city rebelled in 727 BC (Nis.). Isaiah 14.29–32 is highly appropriate to this situation, and may plausibly be interpreted as Isaiah's response to messengers from Gaza ('the messengers of the nation', v. 32) who were attempting to persuade Judah to join the revolt—other Isaianic oracles show that Isaiah consistently opposed Judean involvement in political intrigues against Assyria, arguing that Judah should rely solely upon Yahweh's supernatural protection (Is 18.1–6; 30.1–5, 15–17; 31.1–5). It must be admitted, however, that with the lack of Assyrian historical evidence for Shalmaneser V's reign one cannot exclude the possibility that some other Philistine city might have revolted in 727 BC (Nis.); and it is also conceivable that a planned Philistine revolt was abandoned before it resulted in direct conflict with Assyria.

115. See above, p. 206ff.

116. Note that this alleviates the 'curious mixture of metaphors' which Fullerton (1925/6:87) and others have commented upon.

117. Donner 1964:111–113; Clements 1980a:148. Fullerton (1925/6) dates the oracle to 720 BC (Nis.) following Sargon's defeat at Der. But it is probably an exaggeration to describe this defeat as a 'disaster' (Fullerton 1925/6:94); and Fullerton's interpretation also fails to take account of the clear reference to a succession of rulers in verse 29b.

Consequently although the oracle in Isaiah 14.29f. is most plausibly associated with the death of Shalmaneser V, it is also possible that it was delivered 5 years earlier following the death of Tiglathpileser III. On this evidence Ahaz's death is most probably to be dated to 722 BC (aut.), but might also be dated to 727 BC (aut.).

Either of these dates is compatible with Judean chronology beyond this point, depending on whether postdating was adopted as early as Hezekiah's reign or at the start of Jehoahaz's reign (see p. 223ff.). There is, however, little doubt that dating Ahaz's death to 722 BC (aut.) fits more easily with Judean chronology up to this point. According to 2 Kings 16.2 Ahaz reigned for a total of 16 years, which brings us back to 737 BC (aut.) or 742 BC (aut.) as the date of Ahaz's accession. But Ahaz is unlikely to have become king as early as 742 BC (aut.): Isaiah 7.14 appears to indicate that he was fairly recently married at the time of the Syro-Ephraimite attack on Jerusalem c. 734 BC (aut.),[118] and it is also improbable that the combined reigns of Azariah and Jotham can be reduced to as little as 31 years (inclusive) from 772 to 742 BC (aut.).[119] Consequently if

118. The 'young woman' (הָעַלְמָה) mentioned in this verse is almost certainly Ahaz's wife, though this is disputed among Biblical scholars. The only other serious possibility is to identify her as Isaiah's wife; but the one positive argument in favour of this identification is that Isaiah had two other children with symbolic names (Shear-yashub and Maher-shalal-hash-baz). However, Shear-yashub was born before the birth of Immanuel was announced, and it is therefore unlikely that Isaiah's wife could still be referred to as a 'young woman': the word עַלְמָה, while it certainly does not mean 'virgin', is probably inapplicable to a woman with children. (Some have attempted to meet this objection by suggesting that Isaiah had more than one wife, or that his first wife had died and he had since remarried. See Gottwald 1958:42–43.) Clements (1980a:86) argues that the young woman cannot be identified with Ahaz's wife on the grounds that this would make Ahaz responsible for the prophetic significance of the child's name. But this objection misses the point, since it is clear from parallel birth annunciations (Genesis 16.11; 17.19 etc.) that the final clause of Isaiah 7.14 is to be interpreted not as a prediction but as an instruction. The young woman 'shall call (is to call) his name Immanuel.' Or, more probably, וְקָרָאת ('and she shall call') should be revocalized as *וְקָרָאתְ ('and you shall call'; LXX: καὶ καλέσεις): compare the 2nd singular forms of קרא in Genesis 16.11 and Genesis 17.19. In this case Ahaz is himself instructed to call the child Immanuel, and must obviously be the child's father. It may also be noted that Isaiah 8.8 ('... will fill the breadth of your land, Immanuel') is more naturally addressed to Ahaz's future heir than to one of Isaiah's sons.

119. See below; a chronology in which Azariah's and Jotham's reigns are reduced to this extent is not compatible with Biblical accession ages for Azariah,

Ahaz's death is dated to 727 BC (aut.), one should probably reduce his reign length by 5 years or so in order to date his accession somewhere in the vicinity of 737 to 734 BC (aut.). This is unnecessary if Ahaz's death is dated to 722 BC (aut.). On this dating Ahaz must evidently have reigned for a minimum of 13 to 14 years, since he is recorded as having paid tribute to Tiglathpileser III in 734 BC (Nis.), and this figure is close to his stated reign length of 16 years. In view of these considerations, Ahaz's reign is most probably to be dated from 737 BC to 722 BC (aut.).[120]

This leaves us with 36 years (inclusive) between Azariah's accession in 772 BC (aut.) and Ahaz's accession in 737 BC (aut.). It is obvious from this that Azariah's reign length must be drastically reduced from the Biblical figure of 52 years, but it is not immediately obvious whether the Biblical figure for Jotham's reign length must also be reduced. Let us begin by assuming that the Biblical figure for Jotham's reign (16 years) is in fact correct. In this case Azariah's reign must be reduced from 52 to *21 years (21 years plus 16 years equals 36 years when allowance is made for a 1-year overlap produced by inclusive antedating), which gives us the following dates for Azariah's and Jotham's reigns: Azariah, 772–752 BC (aut.), and Jotham, 752–737 BC (aut.). There are, however, two main objections to this chronology. The first of these concerns the prophetic ministry of Isaiah, which began in the year of Azariah's (Uzziah's) death (Is 6.1) and ended some time after Sennacherib's invasion of Judah in 702 BC (aut.). If Azariah died in 752 BC (aut.) then Isaiah's ministry will have spanned a period of

Jotham, and Ahaz unless one assumes that Azariah and Jotham fathered their respective heirs at an average age of only 14 years.

120. Kugler (1922:163) gives almost the same dates for Ahaz's reign (736–721 BC (spr.)), and cites 2 Chronicles 30.1–11 as evidence that Hezekiah came to the throne after the fall of Samaria. This passage, which is also cited by scholars who date Hezekiah's accession c. 715 BC (e.g. Thiele [3]1983:175f.) relates how Hezekiah in his first regnal year (2C 29.3) invited the inhabitants of northern Israel to celebrate the Passover in Jerusalem, and appears to presuppose a situation in which the northern kingdom had already fallen. But any attempt to use this passage for chronological purposes is precariously dependent upon the historicity of Hezekiah's Passover celebration (and also on the Chronicler's dating of this putative event). The book of Kings makes no mention of this Passover, and appears to rule out the possibility of its occurrence by the categoric assertion that 'no such Passover [as Josiah's] had been kept since the days of the judges who judged Israel, during all the days of the kings of Israel and of the kings of Judah' (2K 23.22).

over 50 years, which is possible but perhaps excessive, especially as there are relatively few Isaianic oracles which can plausibly be dated to the period before the Syro-Ephraimite attack on Jerusalem in *c.* 734 BC (aut.).[121] A second and more serious problem concerns Azariah's and Jotham's accession ages, which are 16 and 25 years respectively according to 2 Kings 15.2 and 15.33. If these figures are historically correct, and if Azariah reigned for only *21 years, the latter was only (16 + 21 =) 37 years old when he died, and (37 - 25 =) 12 years old when Jotham was born, which is quite improbable.[122] Yet if Azariah's reign is increased from *21 to *31 years in order to avoid this problem, and Jotham's reign is reduced accordingly from 16 to *6 years, we are then faced with an even worse discrepancy between Jotham's and Ahaz's accession ages. According to 2 Kings 16.2 Ahaz was 20 years old when he became king; thus if Jotham's reign is reduced to *6 years it follows that the latter was (25 + 6 =) 31 years old when he died, and (31 - 20 =) 11 years old when Ahaz was born.[123]

121. Clements' assertion that there are *no* Isaianic oracles from this period (Clements 1980a:73) is based upon his acceptance of Jepsen's chronology, in which Azariah's death is dated to 736 BC (aut.) (and Jotham's death is dated 5 years earlier!). But the Isaianic nucleus of Isaiah 2–5, with its attacks on social injustice and its largely unspecific threats of future punishment, fits the situation before 734 BC (aut.) rather well; compare the content of Amos's prophecies, which date from the reign of Jeroboam II (785–745 BC (aut.)) according to the chronology set out above.

122. This calculation is only approximate, since a person's age was presumably calculated (as a rule) from his/her actual date of birth, whereas regnal years in this period were counted from the new year preceding a king's accession. Thus a king might be 16 years old at his accession, but only 15 years old at the start of his first regnal year (i.e. at the new year preceding his accession). If this is taken into account in calculating Azariah's age at Jotham's birth we end up with a margin of error of 1 year either way:

$$16\,(-1) + 21 = 37\,(-1)$$
$$37\,(-1) - 25\,(-1) = 12 \pm 1$$

There is one further complication. By our system of reckoning a person is 12 years old in the *13th* year of their life (one celebrates one's 12th birthday at the end of 12 complete years). However, in Hebrew age reckoning a person was 12 years old in the *12th* year of their life: compare Genesis 7.6 with Genesis 7.11 (Noah is 600 years old in the 600th year of his life), and Genesis 17.12 with Leviticus 12.3 (a child is 8 days old on the 8th day of his life). Hebrew ages must therefore be reduced by 1 year to arrive at a modern equivalent: if Azariah was only 12 ± 1 years old by Hebrew reckoning when he fathered Jotham, this is equivalent to 11 ± 1 years old by our reckoning.

123. Taking account of the factors discussed in the previous note it would be more accurate to say that on these figures Jotham was 11 ± 1 years old when Ahaz

In view of the genealogical problems which arise if Azariah's age is set as low as *21 years or as high as *31 years, the most reasonable course open to us is to increase our original estimate of Azariah's reign length from *21 to *26 years, and to reduce Jotham's reign accordingly from 16 to *11 years. On these figures Azariah was (16 + 26 =) 42 years old when he died, and (42 - 25 =) 17 years old when Jotham was born; while Jotham was (25 + 11 =) 36 years old when he died, and (36 - 20 =) 16 years old when Ahaz was born.[124] Taking this as a reasonable approximation, Azariah's reign may be dated from 772 to 747 BC (aut.), and Jotham's reign from 747 to 737 BC (aut.). But it must be emphasized that this is only an approximation: if we assume that 14 years is the minimal age for either king to have fathered his successor (see previous note), the date at which Jotham succeeded Azariah might be raised by up to 3 years or lowered by up to 2 years.

The following chart incorporates the results of the preceding discussion into a synchronistic chronology of Israelite and Judean history from Azariah's accession to the death of Ahaz, and completes the table given on p. 194f.[127]

was born, by Hebrew reckoning, or 10 ± 1 years old by our system of age reckoning.

124. Once again, we should allow a margin of error of 1 year either way, and then subtract 1 year to arrive at the equivalent ages in our system of age reckoning. Compare the ages suggested above with Amon's age on fathering Josiah, which works out at (22 + 2 - 8 =) 16 ± 1 years (Hebrew reckoning), or Josiah's age on fathering Jehoahaz, which also comes to (8 + 31 - 23 =) 16 ± 1 years old (Hebrew reckoning). Josiah's age on fathering Jehoiakim, which works out at only (8 + 31 - 25 =) 14 ± 1 years (Hebrew reckoning) is probably the minimal age at which any king is likely to have fathered an heir. It may be noted that Josiah was only 8 years old when he came to the throne, and is likely to have married at an early age in order to maintain the dynastic succession.

125. According to this chronology Ahaz came to the throne 2 years before Pekah. This is in contradiction to 2 Kings 15.37, where we are told that Rezin and Pekah began to attack Judah during Jotham's reign ('in those days Yahweh began to send Rezin king of Aram and Pekah the son of Remaliah against Judah'). However, 2 Kings 15.37 is contradicted by Isaiah 7, according to which news of the Syro-Ephraimite conspiracy reached Jerusalem during Ahaz's reign, and may therefore be disregarded as a later addition. The insertion of this verse is possibly connected with the fact that Pekah's reign length was increased from *4 to 20 years: the Deuteronomistic chronologer responsible for lengthening Pekah's reign length may also have decided to lengthen the Syro-Ephraimite attack on Jerusalem into a more protracted period of harassment comparable with Hazael's earlier depredations (note the similar phraseology of 2 Kings 10.32–33).

Judah	Judah yr	BC	Israel yr	Israel
Azariah	**ac1**	772	**14**	Jeroboam
	~	~	~	
	21	752	34	
	22	751	35	
	23	750	36	
	24	749	37	
	25	748	38	
Jotham	26/ac1	747	39	
	2	746	40	
	3	745	ac1/ac/ac/41	Zechariah/
	4	744	2	Shallum/Menahem
	5	743	3	
	6	742	4	
	7	741	5	
	8	740	6	
	9	739	7	
	10	738	8	
Ahaz	ac1/11	737	9	
	2	736	10/ac1	Pekahiah
	3	735	2/ac1	Pekah
	4	734	2	
	5	733	3	
	6	732	ac1/4	Hoshea
	7	731	2	
	8	730	3	
	9	729	4	
	10	728	5	
	11	727	6	
	12	726	7	Samaria besieged
	13	725	8	
	14	724	9	Fall of Samaria
	15	723		
Hezekiah	16/ac	722		

5.2.3 *From the fall of Samaria to the Babylonian exile*

The task of reconstructing Judean chronology during this period is complicated by the question of Judah's adoption of the Mesopotamian spring calendar and postdating system. Indirect evidence discussed in the first section of this chapter suggests that the spring calendar was probably adopted during the reign of Josiah; and I have argued that postdating was probably adopted at the same time, and first implemented at the accession of Josiah's successor, Jehoahaz. With regard to the manner in which the spring calendar was introduced I have suggested that purely practical considerations make it more likely that the year preceding the change was shortened by six months than that it was lengthened by this amount (p. 178f.).

According to our reconstruction of Israelite and Judean chronology up to this point Hezekiah came to the throne in 722 BC (aut.), 2 years after the fall of Samaria. The following chronology of the period from Hezekiah's accession to the Babylonian exile is calculated from this date using Biblical figures for the reigns of Judean kings, and is based upon my earlier conclusions about the introduction of the spring calendar and postdating, namely: (1) that the spring calendar was adopted during Josiah's reign; (2) that the year preceding its adoption was shortened by six months; and (3) that postdating was introduced at Jehoahaz's accession.

Hezekiah	(29 years)	722–694 BC (aut.)
Manasseh	(55 years)	694–640 BC (aut.)
Amon	(2 years)	640–639 BC (aut.)
Josiah	(31 years)	639–609 BC (aut./spr.)
Jehoahaz	(3 months)	609 BC (spr.)
Jehoiakim	(11 years)	609–598 BC (spr.)
Jehoiachin	(3 months)	598 BC (spr.)
Zedekiah	(11 years)	598–587 BC (spr.)

There are comparatively few external synchronisms with Mesopotamian or Egyptian chronology during the earlier part of this period. Hezekiah is named in Assyrian texts which describe Sennacherib's third campaign of 701 BC (Nis.),[126] but the Biblical date for this event (2K 18.13) is schematic and historically unreliable (see p. 212f.). It should be noted that the chronology given above is incompatible with the 'two-campaign theory' favoured by the Albright school and recently resuscitated by Shea (1985b), according to which the story of the miraculous deliverance of Jerusalem in 2 Kings 18.17–19.37 relates to a hypothetical

126. Sn Pr II.37–III.49 (and earlier editions of Sennacherib's annals); B1–3 17–22; Neb 13–15. Na'aman (1974) is probably correct in adding K 6206 + BM 82-3-23,131 (see above, p. 195n.).

second Palestinian campaign undertaken by Sennacherib towards the end of his reign. Such a campaign could not have occurred before 690 BC (Nis.), for there is no record of it in the latest edition of Sennacherib's annals, written after his eighth campaign of 691 BC (Nis.).[127] Proponents of this theory must therefore adopt a chronology based upon the (schematic) date in 2 Kings 18.13, which allows Hezekiah's death to be dated *c.* 687 BC. But there are serious problems with this chronology (p. 212), and the discrepancies between 2 Kings 18.13–16 and 2 Kings 18.17f. that have given rise to the two-campaign theory are more satisfactorily accounted for by differences in literary genre (Clements 1980b).[128]

Hezekiah's successor, Manasseh, is mentioned twice in Assyrian texts belonging to the reigns of Esarhaddon and Ashurbanipal. In the first of these (Esrh NinAF v.55) Manasseh is listed as one of twenty-two western vassals who were required to contribute materials for rebuilding the Assyrian palace at Nineveh. Work on the palace was completed in 676 BC (Nis.): copies of Nineveh Prism A are dated to the eponymy of Atarilu, 673 BC (Nis.), but the historical introduction of this text covers only the first 5 years of Esarhaddon's reign; and a copy of Nineveh Prism B, which

127. The Babylonian Chronicle (*ABC* 1.iii.16–18) dates this campaign 'year unknown' (*MU NU ZU*). However, the previous campaign is dated by the Babylonian Chronicle to the first year of Mushezibmarduk of Babylon, 692 BC (Nis.) (*ABC* 1.iii.13–16), and the Taylor Prism, containing the latest edition of the annals, is dated to the eponymy of Belemuranni, 691 BC (Nis.).

128. Hezekiah's accession age of 25 years (2K 18.2) poses serious problems for any chronology that accepts the Biblical figures for Ahaz's reign length and accession age. According to 2 Kings 16.2 Ahaz became king when he was 20 years old and reigned for 16 years, which means that if Hezekiah's accession age is correct, Ahaz was only 11 ± 1 years old (Hebrew reckoning) when Hezekiah was born—10 ± 1 years old by our reckoning (see p. 220n.). This is manifestly impossible, and we may therefore conclude that the Biblical figure for Hezekiah's accession age is most probably incorrect. This conclusion is strengthened by the following considerations. (1) There is an apparently deliberate numerical parallelism between the reigns of Hezekiah and Amaziah, in that both are ascribed identical reign lengths and accession ages. I have argued earlier that Amaziah's reign length was secondarily lengthened to agree with Hezekiah's (p. 149); and it may reasonably be argued that in this case the reverse process has occurred, with Hezekiah's accession age having been altered in conformity with Amaziah's accession age. (2) There is good reason to think that the Immanuel prophecy of Isaiah 7.14f. relates to the birth of Ahaz's eldest son, who should presumably be identified with Hezekiah (see above, p. 218n.). If this is correct, the latter will presumably have been born shortly after the Syro-Ephraimite invasion (c. 734 BC (aut.)), and cannot have been more than 13 years old at his accession in 722 BC (aut.).

contains a parallel but less detailed text, is dated to the eponymy of Banba, 676 BC (Nis.).[129] The second Assyrian text which names Manasseh (Ash PrC 1.25) contains a similar list of twenty-two western vassals who had to provide troops for Ashurbanipal's first Egyptian campaign in 667 BC (Nis.).[130] These references are of only limited value in dating Manasseh's 55-year reign: it is universally agreed that this began well before 676 BC (Nis.) and ended long after 667 BC (Nis.).

A more important synchronism between Mesopotamian and Judean chronology is provided by Josiah's death at the battle of Megiddo (2K 23.29f.). Josiah, unlike Hezekiah and Manasseh, is not mentioned in Assyrian or Babylonian records; but his death is securely dated to the summer of 609 BC by the fact that the 'large Egyptian army' which crossed the Euphrates in Tammuz of Nabopolassar's 17th year, 609 BC (Nis.), (*ABC* 3.66f.) was undoubtedly the same Egyptian army as that which Josiah unsuccessfully attempted to prevent from reaching the Euphrates (2K 23.29f.).[131] This date agrees perfectly with the chronological table given above, and so provides independent confirmation of this chronology, which was calculated from Hezekiah's accession in 722 BC (aut.).[132]

129. Heidel 1956; Borger 1956:125.
130. The date of this campaign is provided by the 'Esarhaddon Chronicle' (*ABC* 14.40–44), which places it in the first year of Shamash-shumukin, king of Babylon.
131. Reade (1981:2) is probably the only recent scholar to have questioned this synchronism, which is incompatible with his reconstruction of Israelite and Judean chronology in which Josiah's death is dated to 608 BC (Nis.). Reade argues that the Babylonian Chronicle mentions movements by the Egyptian army only in years when it came into contact with the Babylonians, and therefore has no relevance to possible Egyptian moves in those years, e.g. 608 BC (Nis.), when the Babylonians campaigned in a different direction. However, the Egyptian army which defeated Josiah is specifically said to have been on route for a rendezvous with the 'king of Assyria', who is also mentioned in the Babylonian Chronicle's entry for 609 BC (Nis.), but who disappeared from the scene after the Egyptians failed to recapture Haran on his behalf in 609 BC (Nis.). This failure brought an end to the last vestiges of Assyrian power, leaving the Babylonians free to turn their attention to the east; there are no further references to Assyria in the Babylonian Chronicle, and no further clashes between Babylonian and Egyptian forces are reported until Nabopolassar's 20th year, 606 BC (Nis.).
132. Note, however, that the same date is also arrived at if we start from 727 BC (aut.), which is a less probable date for Hezekiah's accession (see p. 218f.), and assume that postdating was introduced at the start of Hezekiah's accession (this is the earliest date at which it is likely to have been introduced), and that the adoption

According to 2 Kings 23.31f. Josiah's successor, Jehoahaz, reigned for only 3 months before he was deposed by Necho, who arrested him at Riblah in the land of Hamath. This fits in rather well with the evidence of the Babylonian Chronicle. Josiah's death is likely to have occurred in Sivan of 609 BC (Nis.), for the Egyptian army probably took nearly a month to cover the 650 kilometres from Megiddo to the Euphrates (Clines 1972:30f.; Malamat 1975:125). After crossing the Euphrates the Egyptians proceeded to lay siege to Haran, which held out against them until Elul (*ABC* 3.68f.), when the arrival of the Babylonian army brought the siege to an end (it is not clear whether the Egyptian army was defeated or withdrew without a fight—the Chronicle is broken at this point). The Egyptian army presumably began its return journey more or less immediately, and is therefore likely to have reached Riblah in Elul or Tishri. This gives us a period of 3 to 4 months from Josiah's death in Sivan to Jehoahaz's deposal in Elul or Tishri, which is in close agreement with the Biblical figure of 3 months for Jehoahaz's reign.[133]

Jehoahaz was replaced by Jehoiakim, apparently an elder brother, who reigned for 11 years (2K 23.26). During his reign 'Nebuchadrezzar king of Babylon came up, and Jehoiakim became his servant for 3 years, but subsequently turned back and rebelled against him' (2K 24.1). Jehoiakim's acceptance of Babylonian suzerainty was undoubtedly a result of Nebuchadrezzar's decisive victory over the Egyptians at Carchemish, which left him in effective control of Syria and Palestine, and which occurred in the final year of Nabopolassar, 605 BC (Nis.), shortly before the latter's death on 8th Ab (*ABC* 5.1–11). However, Jehoiakim is unlikely to have submitted to Nebuchadrezzar immediately, and it was

of the spring calendar involved lengthening the previous year by six months. This produces the following chronology for the period from Hezekiah's accession to the death of Josiah.

Hezekiah	(29 years)	727–698 BC (aut.)
Manasseh	(55 years)	698–643 BC (aut.)
Amon	(2 years)	643–641 BC (aut.)
Josiah	(31 years)	641–609 BC (aut./spr.)

133. This should not necessarily be regarded as an exact figure. It is worth noting that the reign lengths of all Israelite and Judean kings who reigned for less than a year appear to be calendrical round numbers: Zimri is said to have reigned for 7 days (a week), Shallum for 1 month, Jehoahaz of Judah and Jehoiachin for 3 months (a quarter), and Zechariah for 6 months.

probably not until 604 BC (Nis.)—when Nebuchadrezzar received tribute from 'all the kings of Hattu'—that he was forced to transfer his allegiance from Egypt to Babylon.[134] The 3-year period of Jehoiakim's vassalship may therefore be dated from Nebuchadrezzar's first regnal year, 604 BC (Nis.); and Jehoiakim's rebellion against Babylonian suzerainty is thereby dated to Nebuchadrezzar's 4th year, 601 BC (Nis.), when a Babylonian attempt to invade Egypt was repulsed with heavy losses on both sides (*ABC* 5.rev.6–7). The extent of the damage incurred by Nebuchadrezzar's army is reflected in the fact that Nebuchadrezzar was forced to spend the following year refitting his horses and chariotry (*ABC* 5.rev.8); it was not until Nebuchadrezzar's 6th year, 599 BC (Nis.), that the latter was able to return to the west, where he is said to have despatched his army on raids against Arab tribes of the Syrian desert (*ABC* 5.rev.9–10).

Reprisals against Judah possibly began in the same year with military action by Chaldean and foreign contingents of Nebuchadrezzar's army (2K 24.2). This was followed by a full-scale siege of Jerusalem, which is described in both Hebrew and Babylonian sources. According to 2 Kings 24.10f. the siege began during *Jehoiachin's* reign and was initially conducted by Nebuchadrezzar's officials, with Nebuchadrezzar arriving once the siege was already underway.[135] At this point Jehoiachin surrendered, and

134. There is evidence to suggest that Jehoiakim waited until the last possible moment before offering tribute. The Babylonian Chronicle is somewhat broken at this point, but it appears that Nebuchadrezzar captured a Syro-Palestinian city, probably Ashkelon (ᵁᴿᵁx-x(-x)-il-lu-nu), in Kislev of 604 BC (Nis.) (*ABC* 5.18–20). This was in all probability the occasion of the national fast which, according to Jeremiah 36.9f., was proclaimed in Judah in the 9th month (Kislev) of Jehoiakim's 5th year (604 BC (spr.)). At this stage it would seem that Jehoiakim had not yet offered his allegiance to Nebuchadrezzar—hence the alarmed reaction to Jeremiah's prediction of a Babylonian invasion (verse 29)—but he will doubtless have submitted shortly thereafter. See Malamat 1956:251–252.

135. This version of events may need to be modified in view of the following textual considerations. In 2 Kings 24.10 MT informs us that 'Nebuchadrezzar's servants' (עבדי נבכדראצר) came up to Jerusalem and laid siege to it, but LXX (supported by the Peshitta and a small number of Hebrew manuscripts) states that 'Nebuchadrezzar' came up to Jerusalem. This conflicts with verse 11, where we are told that Nebuchadrezzar came to Jerusalem when his servants were already besieging the city, but it is probably the original reading, since the consonantal text found in most Hebrew manuscripts has a singular verb presupposing a singular subject (עלה; Qere עלו). If this assessment is correct it is highly unlikely that verse 10 originally preceded verse 11, and we should probably conclude that verses 10 and 11 are textual variants which originally belonged to separate textual traditions

Nebuchadrezzar appointed Zedekiah in his place before taking Jehoiachin into exile along with a significant number of nobles and artisans.[136] The Babylonian Chronicle (*ABC* 5.rev.11–13) confirms the broad outline of this account, and also gives a precise date for the capture of Jerusalem and the arrest of Jehoiachin. Here we are told that Nebuchadrezzar mustered his army and set off for Hattu (Syro-Palestine) in his 7th regnal year in the month Kislev, and that having encamped against 'the city of Judah' he captured it and arrested its king on Adar 2nd; after which he appointed 'a king of his own choice' and returned to Babylon with heavy tribute. This gives us our most precise synchronism between Mesopotamian and Judean chronology: according to Babylonian evidence Jehoiachin's reign ended on Adar 2nd 598 BC (Nis.), and this agrees with the less precise date given in the chronological table on p. 223. Since Jehoiachin is ascribed a reign of only 3 months, this evidence also allows us to date the end of Jehoiakim's reign fairly precisely: bearing in mind that '3 months' may be a round calendrical figure (p. 226n.) it would appear that Jehoiakim met his death in Marheshvan or Kislev of 598 BC (Nis.), at approximately the same time that Nebuchadrezzar is said to have left Babylon. The book of Kings is oddly silent about the circumstances of Jehoiakim's death, but we have seen that there is Biblical evidence

---

—once these variants were combined it is understandable that verse 10 should have been harmonized with verse 11 by the insertion of עבדי ('servants'). Either variant might theoretically be original, but it is more probable that verse 10 is a rewriting of verse 11 (with Nebuchadrezzar's arrival put back to the start of the siege) than that the reverse should be the case. This has one important consequence for the date of the siege. It is only 2 Kings 24.10 which associates the start of the siege with the reign of Jehoiachin; and if this verse is secondary it is equally possible that the siege may actually have begun during Jehoiakim's reign.

136. The precise number varies according to different texts. According to 2 Kings 24.14 Nebuchadrezzar deported 10,000 Judeans at this point. However, 2 Kings 24.16 puts the number of deportees at 7,000, plus 1,000 smiths and craftsmen, while Jeremiah 52.28 gives a more modest figure of 3,023 Judeans. This last figure is probably correct; the Babylonians do not appear to have conducted mass deportations on the scale practised by the Assyrians, and the round numbers given by Kings are unlikely to be historical. In any case 2 Kings 24.14 is probably a late addition, as evidenced by its non-classical use of an Unconverted Perfect after Waw (והגלה). Those who prefer to harmonize Biblical discrepancies wherever possible may follow Malamat (1975:134f.) in postulating two deportations: a main deportation of 7,000 Judeans (2K 24.16) followed by a later deportation of 3,023 Judeans (Je 52.28), making a total of 10,000 deportees in all (2K 24.14). But it is unclear how the 1,000 smiths and craftsmen of 2 Kings 24.16 are to be accounted for on this theory.

which suggests that Jehoiakim came to a violent end (see p. 188n.). If we take the view that the siege of Jerusalem began during Jehoiakim's reign (see above, p. 227n.) it may be argued that Jehoiachin began to negotiate terms of surrender immediately after Jehoiakim's death, and that it was this which prompted Nebuchadrezzar to set out from Babylon and take personal credit for the city's capture.

Biblical evidence for the date of Nebuchadrezzar's second capture of Jerusalem is unfortunately contradictory, and the existing text of the Babylonian Chronicle breaks off several years before this event. In consequence, Biblical scholars have long been divided over whether Jerusalem fell in 587 BC (Nis.) or 586 BC (Nis.).[137] The argument in favour of the second of these dates is fairly straightforward: 2 Kings 25.8 and its parallel, Jeremiah 52.12, date the destruction of Jerusalem and the associated deportation to Nebuchadrezzar's 19th year, which in Babylonian chronology was 586 BC (Nis.). However, the validity of this dating is put in serious doubt by the fact that the book of Kings dates the previous capture of Jerusalem and the arrest of Jehoiachin to Nebuchadrezzar's 8th year (2K 24.12), whereas the Babylonian Chronicle dates these events to Nebuchadrezzar's *7th* year (*ABC* 5.rev.11–13). By contrast, Jeremiah 52.28f. (a postscript to the book of Jeremiah) dates the first deportation of Judeans to Nebuchadrezzar's 7th year, which is in agreement with the Babylonian Chronicle's date for the first capture of Jerusalem, but dates the second deportation to Nebuchadrezzar's *18th* year. Given the agreement which exists between Jeremiah 52.28 and the Babylonian Chronicle over the date of the first capture of Jerusalem and subsequent deportation, there is a strong case for preferring the date of the second deportation given by Jeremiah 52.29 over that given by 2 Kings 25.8 and Jeremiah 52.12. On this evidence the second capture of Jerusalem occurred in 587 BC (Nis.). The Deuteronomistic editors of Kings and (the main body of) Jeremiah evidently miscalculated the length of Nebuchadrezzar's

137. The following scholars have favoured 587 BC (Nis.): Rühl (1894/5), Kugler (1922), Coucke (1928), Begrich (1929a), Mowinckel (1932), Albright (1945), Noth (1958), Kutsch (1959; 1974), Jepsen (1964), Andersen (1969), and Cazelles (1983).

Supporters of the later date, 586 BC (Nis.), include Kamphausen (1883), Lewy (1927), Vogelstein (1944), Thiele (³1983), Malamat (1956; 1968; 1975), Tadmor (1956; 1962), Vogt (1957; 1975), Auerbach (1961), Schedl (1962b), Horn (1967), and Freedy and Redford (1970).

reign and numbered Nebuchadrezzar's years one year too high: compare also Jeremiah 25.1 and 32.1, which wrongly equate Jehoiakim's 4th year with Nebuchadrezzar's first year, and Zedekiah's 10th year with Nebuchadrezzar's 18th year. This miscalculation probably arose because Nebuchadrezzar was mistakenly thought to have become king before the start of 605 BC (Nis.), when he campaigned in the west on his father's behalf, whereas he did not in fact become king until Elul 1st of that year, shortly after the battle of Carchemish (*ABC* 5.10f.); the same mistaken belief may also be reflected in Jeremiah 46.2's anachronistic reference to 'Nebuchadrezzar king of Babylon' as victor at the battle of Carchemish.[138]

Other considerations make it virtually certain that Jerusalem fell in 587 BC (Nis.). We know from the Babylonian Chronicle that Jehoiachin's reign ended on Adar 2nd 598 BC (Nis.),[139] and since Judah used the Mesopotamian system of postdating during this period it follows that Zedekiah's 11-year reign will have lasted from 598 to 587 BC (Nis.). Those who wish to date the fall of Jerusalem to 586 BC (Nis.) have sought to avoid this conclusion by one of two arguments, both of which violate basic principles of the postdating system by assuming that in situations where a king came to the throne shortly after the new year, the remainder of that year might be reckoned as a zero accession-year even if it had not been assigned to his predecessor's reign. Thus Vogt and others have argued that Nebuchadrezzar could have taken several weeks

138. Contrast Freedy and Redford (1970:466), who think that it is the dates in Jeremiah 52.28f. which are mistaken, despite the agreement between Jeremiah 52.28 and the Babylonian Chronicle. Other scholars have looked for various ways of harmonizing Jeremiah 52.28f. with the chronological statements of Kings, one fairly obvious possibility being the suggestion that there were actually four deportations in Nebuchadrezzar's 7th, 8th, 18th, and 19th years (Malamat 1957:77–78; 1968:154); by a curious coincidence the book of Kings mentions only the second and fourth of these deportations, while Jeremiah 52.28f. mentions only the first and third. Alternative and equally improbable suggestions may be found in *Seder Olam Rabba*, chapters 25 and 27, and Vogelstein 1944:12.

139. Vogt (1957:93f.) argues unconvincingly that although Jehoiachin was arrested on Adar 2nd 598 BC (Nis.), he was not officially deposed until Nisan 597 BC (Nis.): Nebuchadrezzar apparently deferred his decision over Jehoiachin's fate because he was initially uncertain whether to replace him or not. Note, however, that if Jehoiachin's reign had extended into Nisan of 597 BC (Nis.) this would necessarily have been counted as his first regnal year under the postdating system. Thus the fact that Jehoiachin is credited with a reign of only 3 months is evidence that he was deposed *before* the end of 598 BC (Nis.).

to organize affairs in Jerusalem following its initial capture on Adar 2nd 598 BC (Nis.), and that as a result Zedekiah may not have been appointed until the start of 597 BC (Nis.); counting this as his zero accession-year brings us to 586 BC (Nis.) for the second capture of Jerusalem in Zedekiah's 11th year.[140] On the other hand Malamat and others argue that Judah followed an autumn calendar throughout the pre-exilic period, so that Zedekiah's first year will have begun in the autumn of 597 BC (Jul.), and Zedekiah's 11th year will have overlapped with Nebuchadrezzar's 19th year, 586 BC (Nis.).[141] This second chronology avoids the need to posit what is effectively a zero calendar-year at the start of Zedekiah's reign— but only because it has already posited a zero calendar-year at the beginning of Jehoiakim's reign (see p. 173f.).

Further evidence that Jerusalem fell in 587 BC (Nis.) and not 586 BC (Nis.) is provided by Ezekiel 33.21, which states that Ezekiel learnt of the capture of Jerusalem on the 5th day of the 10th month of the 12th year of the first exile.[142] The interpretation of this date depends of course upon the starting point from which the years of the first exile were counted, and those who argue that Nebuchadrezzar required several weeks to organize affairs after his initial capture of Jerusalem have cited Ezekiel 33.21 as evidence that the second capture of Jerusalem should be dated to *586* BC (Nis.): if the first deportation occurred early in 597 BC (Nis.), the 12th year (inclusive) from this date is 586 BC (Nis.). Or alternatively, if the first deportation is dated to 598 BC (Nis.) it might still be argued that the first year of this deportation did not begin until the following year, i.e. that it was effectively postdated, by analogy with regnal chronology. In fact, however, there is clear evidence that the first year of the exile of Jehoiachin was 598 BC (Nis.). According to 2 Kings 25.27 and Jeremiah 52.31 Jehoiachin was

140. Vogt 1957:92f.; 1975; Auerbach 1961; Schedl 1962b.

141. Malamat 1956;1968:140–141; 1975:127; Thiele ³1983:190–191; Horn 1967; Freedy and Redford 1970:464–467.

142. Some scholars have followed LXX^L and the Peshitta in reading '11th year' rather than '12th year', since this resolves a discrepancy between Ezekiel 33.21 and Ezekiel 26.1, where an oracle alluding to the fall of Jerusalem is dated to the 11th year of Jehoiachin's exile (thus Zimmerli 1983:191, among others). But a better solution is to follow LXX^A in reading '12th year' (שנה עשרה בשתי*) instead of '11th year' (שנה עשרה בעשתי) in Ezekiel 26.1. The book of Ezekiel elsewhere uses שנה עשרה אחת for '11th year' (Ezk 30.20; 31.1); and the only other instance of עשתי עשרה in Ezekiel (Ezk 40.49) is clearly a corruption of עשרה שתי (LXX δώδεκα; see Zimmerli 1983:342).

released from prison in the 37th year of his exile, in the accession
year of Evil-merodach.[143] The latter came to the throne in 562 BC
(Nis.), and since this is equated with the 37th year of Jehoiachin's
exile it follows that Jehoiachin's first year of exile was 598 BC
(Nis.). Thus Ezekiel learnt about the capture of Jerusalem from a
survivor 5 months after its destruction and the deportation of its
inhabitants (dated to the 7th day of the 5th month by 2 Kings
25.8f.), which is a reasonable interval considering the source of his
information; according to Ezra 7.9, Ezra took 4 months to make the
reverse journey from Babylonia to Jerusalem in what are described
as favourable circumstances ('with Yahweh's favourable hand
upon him').

143. בשנת מלכו; the variant בשנת מלכתו ('in the year of his reign'), which is
given in MT's text of Jeremiah 52.31 and implied by LXX's translation of 2 Kings
25.27, is historically meaningless since Evil-merodach reigned for more than a
single year (see p. 157).

6

FROM P TO USSHER

Previous chapters of this book have traced the development of Biblical chronology in reverse to uncover a series of different chronologies. In the preceding chapter, the earliest of these was used as a basis for reconstructing the historical chronology of Israel and Judah. This chapter returns to the point we started from, and surveys the development of Biblical chronology in the opposite direction: from P to the chronologies of MT, SP, and LXX, and from here to the chronologies of later Jewish and Christian interpreters.

6.1 *Revised Biblical chronologies*

6.1.1 *MT*

The Masoretic text has to a large extent preserved the original figures of Priestly chronology. Apart from the ambiguous addition of a 2-year period between the flood and the birth of Arpachshad, MT's postdiluvian chronology is essentially the same as the original Priestly chronology. In the antediluvian period, there are three instances where MT's chronology diverges from the original Priestly chronology: MT's figure for Jared's age of begetting is 100 years higher than the original Priestly figure, Methuselah's age of begetting is 118 years higher than the original Priestly figure, and Lamech's age of begetting is 129 years higher than the original Priestly figure (see table on pp. 44–5). These alterations were discussed above (p. 13f.), where I argued that MT or the textual tradition behind MT adopted higher figures for these three antediluvians to ensure that they died before the flood.

But there may also have been other reasons for these alterations. The Samaritan Pentateuch contains modified antediluvian figures which were also designed to prevent Jared, Methuselah, and Lamech from surviving the flood, but in this case the overall chronology was not affected, since chronological modifications were applied to the lifespans of these three ancestors rather than to their ages of begetting. The fact that modifications to MT's antediluvian figures also altered the overall chronology raises the possibility that this reflects a deliberate revision of the original Priestly chronology.

The following table sets out MT's chronology in years from creation. Because of the ambiguity surrounding the date of Arpachshad's birth (discussed above: p. 18f.), there are two possible sets of figures for postdiluvian chronology.

Flood	1656 AM
Abraham	1946/8 AM
Entry into Egypt	2236/8 AM
Exodus	2666/8 AM
Foundation of temple	3146/8 AM
Destruction of temple	3576/8 AM

One date stands out from other dates in this table. It has often been pointed out that if we ignore the 2-year period between the flood and the birth of Arpachshad, MT's date for the exodus is two-thirds of the way through a 4000-year era. If this is a deliberate feature of the chronology, then one of the effects of this revision of MT's chronology is to give greater prominence to the exodus and the events at Sinai, and this agrees with the importance of these events in later Judaism.

There is another more intriguing feature of MT's chronology. If this was devised to place the exodus two-thirds of the way through a 4000-year era, then it is striking to note that the 3999th year of this era is also the year of the Maccabean rededication of the temple in 164 BC: on MT's chronology there are 323 years from the destruction of the temple to the year 3999, and there are also 323 years from the destruction of the temple in 587 BC to the Maccabean rededication of the temple in 164 BC. If we apply the postdating system used in the original version of Priestly chronology, the first year of the rededicated temple is exactly 4000 years from the creation of the world.[1]

1. This association between the year 4000 AM and the rededication of the temple was pointed out by Murtonen (1954:137) and Johnson (1969:32) and has been

The obvious inference to be drawn from this is that MT's chronology was created in the Maccabean period and was devised to portray the Maccabean rededication of the temple as the start of a new era of history. But there is a problem which must be considered. This interpretation presupposes that the authors of MT's chronology had access to accurate chronological information for the period from 587 to 164, whereas evidence from other ancient sources suggests that Jewish writers of the Greco-Roman period had a rather inaccurate notion of postexilic chronology. The most celebrated example is provided by the rabbinic tractate *Seder Olam Rabba*, which allows a total of 52 years for the entire duration of the Persian period. Other examples include Josephus (*Ant* 20.234), who calculated a period of 414 years from the end of the exile (538 BC) to the accession of Antiochus Eupator (164 BC), and the Hellenistic chronographer Demetrius (fragment 6), who apparently reckoned a period of 338 years and three months from Nebuchadrezzar's deportation of the inhabitants of Jerusalem (587 BC) to the accession of Ptolemy IV (in 222 BC). Within the Bible, the author of Daniel calculated an interval of 490 years for the period from 587 BC to 164 BC (Dn 9.24–27).

The example from Daniel can be dismissed immediately. 490 (seventy times seven) years is a schematic figure which had to match the seventy years of Jeremiah's prophecy (Dn 9.2), whether the author knew of the true duration of this period or not. The same objection applies to the 52-year period of *Seder Olam Rabba*, for this is another schematic figure, which was also designed to fit into a 490-year period from Nebuchadrezzar's destruction of the first temple to Titus's destruction of the second temple (see below, p. 257). And Josephus's period of 414 years is part of a larger calculation which allows a round total of 950 years from the foundation of the first temple to the Maccabean rededication of the second temple: 466 years from the foundation of the temple to its destruction, 70 years exile, and 414 years to the rededication of the temple.[2]

discussed by Thompson (1974:15) and Hayes (1979:25). Johnson calculates 3756 years to the exile, 50 years for the exile, and 374 years from the edict of Cyrus (538 BC) to 164 BC to arrive at a total of 4000 years instead of 3999 years; but the interval between 587 BC and 538 BC is 49 years rather than 50 years.

2. Elsewhere, Josephus calculates a period of 470 years from the foundation of the temple to its destruction (*Ant* 10.147), which is equivalent to the 430 years of

This leaves us with Demetrius's 338-year period from the fall of Jerusalem to the accession of Ptolemy IV. In contrast to other examples of chronological inaccuracy this cannot be dismissed as schematic. On the face of it, it seems that Demetrius under-estimated the interval between 587 BC and 222 BC by 27 years. But matters are actually less straightforward than this. Demetrius fragment 6 contains three chronological calculations: 128 years and six months from Sennacherib's (!) captivity of the northern tribes to Nebuchadrezzar's captivity of Jerusalem, 573 years and nine months from the captivity of the northern tribes to the time of Ptolemy IV, and 338 years and three months from the second captivity to the time of Ptolemy IV. Apart from the fact that Demetrius has evidently confused Shalmaneser's capture of Samaria with Sennacherib's invasion of Judah,[3] there is clearly something wrong with his arithmetic or with the text as it stands. 338 years and three months plus 128 years and six months does not add up to 573 years and nine months; and the interval between Sennacherib's invasion of Judah and the fall of Jerusalem is 125 years and six months according to Biblical figures. In all proba-bility, '128 years' is a textual corruption of *125 years, and '573 years' is a corruption of *473 years, in which case the 338-year period must also be emended to *348 years (473 - 125 years). This is still incorrect historically, but the error is reduced from 27 to 17 years.

the Masoretic text plus an extra 40 years for Solomon (whom Josephus credits with an 80-year reign).

3. Bickerman (1975:80–84) assumes that Demetrius is referring to three sep-arate events: the captivity of the northern tribes, Sennacherib's invasion of Judah, and Nebuchadrezzar's captivity of Jerusalem. But what the text actually says is this: 'In his book *Concerning the Kings in Judah* Demetrius says that the tribes of Judah, Benjamin, and Levi were not taken captive by Sennacherib, but that from this captivity to the last captivity which Nebuchadrezzar took from Jerusalem there were 128 years and six months. From the time when the ten tribes were taken captive from Samaria to Ptolemy IV there 573 years and nine months; from the time that the captivity from Jerusalem occurred there were 338 years and three months.' Now although Demetrius does not say in so many words that Sennacherib deported the northern tribes, this is clearly implied by the fact that he refers to a captivity under Sennacherib ('from this captivity to the last captivity') in which the southern tribes (Judah, Benjamin, and Levi) were not deported, and then goes on to speak of the captivity of the ten (northern) tribes. It is manifestly absurd to suppose that Demetrius envisaged a separate captivity under Sennacherib, in which no tribes were actually deported, and then counted the number of years between this non-captivity and the final captivity of Jerusalem.

Why then did Demetrius miscalculate the period from 587 BC to 222 BC by 17 years? One possibility is that he did not have access to accurate chronological information. But there is also another possibility. 17 years is the exact number of years which elapsed between the initial foundation of the second temple in the second year of Cyrus (537 BC: Ezr 1.1; 3.8) and its subsequent refoundation in the second year of Darius (520 BC: Hg 1.1). If Demetrius confused these two events, as he seems also to have confused Shalmaneser's capture of Samaria with Sennacherib's invasion of Judah, this would automatically create a 17-year discrepancy in his calculations at this point. If this explanation is correct, Demetrius's sources for postexilic chronology must have been completely accurate, and there is no reason to suppose that the authors of MT's chronology could not also have had access to accurate chronological sources. One obvious possibility is that Demetrius and the MT chronologists derived their information directly or indirectly from temple records.

6.1.2 *SP*

I argued in chapter 2 that SP has largely preserved the original Priestly chronology of the antediluvian period, but that it has departed from the original chronology by adopting increased ages of begetting for postdiluvian ancestors in Genesis 11, and by modifying the 430-year period of Exodus 12.40 to cover the period in Egypt together with the previous 215 years in Canaan. This had the effect of adding 435 years to Priestly chronology in the period from the flood to the exodus. The following table sets out SP's chronology for this period.

Flood	1307 AM
Abraham	2247/9 AM
Entry into Egypt	2537/9 AM
Exodus	2752/4 AM

There are two points which may be noted about this chronology. The first is that it dissociates the year 2800 AM from the foundation of the Jerusalem temple (the Samaritans had their own sanctuary at Gerizim), and the second is that it brings the date of the settlement (2752/4 plus 40 years: Ex 16.35) to within a few years of the same date. Now according to a Samaritan tradition which is preserved in the Tolidah chronicle (Bowman 1977:44), the conquest of Canaan extended over a 7-year period.[4] If we disregard the 2-year interval between the flood and the birth of Arpachshad and assume that the Samaritan chronology uses postdating, the first year of the conquest is 2793 AM,[5] and the seventh year of the conquest is 2799 AM. According to the Tolidah chronicle (Bowman 1977:44), this was also the year in which Phinehas calculated the correct intervals of the Samaritan calendar 'according to the breadth of Mount Gerizim'.[6] SP's chronology therefore associates the year 2800 AM with the first year of the Samaritan calendar, which is probably also the first year of the Gerizim sanctuary (the year after its foundation).[7]

6.1.3 *LXX*

The Septuagint contains a longer chronology than either MT or SP, which results from the fact that antediluvian and postdiluvian ancestors in Genesis 5 and 11 have consistently high ages of begetting (there is also an extra postdiluvian ancestor, Kenan II). This increase is partially offset, however, by the fact that LXX chronology changes the 430 years spent in Egypt to a period of 430 years in Canaan and Egypt.

The following table presents LXX chronology from creation to the exile. See pp. 44–5 for the figures on which this is based, and note that postdiluvian figures incorporate the 2-year period from the flood to the birth of Arpachshad, while the interval from the foundation of the temple to the exile incorporates the lower LXX figure for Rehoboam's reign (see page 38f. for discussion of this last point).

Flood	2242 AM
Abraham	3314 AM

4. See also Joshua 14.10.

5. Strictly speaking, the exodus should also be postdated to 2753 AM, since it occurred at the start of the year.

6. However, in another passage (Bowman 1977:41), the establishment of the calendar is dated to the *first* year of the conquest.

7. This was first argued by Jepsen (1929), except that Jepsen uses a slightly different set of calculations to place the *foundation* of the Gerizim sanctuary in the year 2800 AM.

Entry into Egypt	3604 AM
Exodus	3819 AM
Foundation of temple	4259 AM
Destruction of temple	4689 AM

This shows evident signs of chronological schematism. If LXX chronology uses a non-inclusive dating system such as postdating or non-inclusive antedating, the first year of the exodus is 3820 AM, the temple's first year is 4260 AM, and the first year after the destruction of the temple is 4690 AM. If we then add 70 years to the rebuilding of the second temple (Zc 1.12), the first year of the rebuilt temple is 4760 AM, which is 240 years before 5000 AM. This raises the obvious question: what (if anything) happened in 5000 AM? 240 years from the foundation of the second temple in 520 BC brings us down to 280 BC, which is interesting when one considers that the Letter of Aristeas dates the translation of the Pentateuch to the reign of Ptolemy II (282–247 BC). However, the chronology found in LXX probably existed in Hebrew texts used by the translators (see below), in which case it cannot originally have been meant to commemorate the LXX translation. Another possibility is that 5000 AM was associated with the conquests of Alexander the Great in 333 BC onwards or with the division of his empire after 323 BC: 240 years is, after all, a schematic figure which may be no more accurate than Daniel's 490-year period. A third possibility is that nothing happened in 5000 AM. The chronology may have been created in the years preceding 5000 AM by people who had witnessed the dissolution of the Persian empire and looked forward to the inauguration of a new world era which would presumably see the restoration of an independent Jewish kingdom.

There is also evidence of a second LXX chronology which adds 40 years to the original LXX chronology to place the first year of the second temple (or the first year of the postexilic period) in 4800 AM. This chronology is attested in Codex Vaticanus (LXX[B]), which reckons 435 years for the period in Canaan and Egypt (Ex 12.40), and then adds 30 years to Jehoram's reign (2K 8.17) to give a total of 465 years from the foundation of the temple to its destruction (counting 17 years for Rehoboam's reign). LXX[B]'s figure for Jehoram's reign is corroborated by LXX[A], but stands in striking disagreement with accession synchronisms and is clearly a secondary alteration, which may have originated as a scribal error (see p. 129). The same chronology could also have existed in LXX manuscripts which added 40 years to the period from the exodus to the foundation of the temple by adopting MT's figure of 480 years for this period, although this is not true of existing Lucianic manuscripts which read '480 years', since these require a 435-year total for the duration of the first temple, with Rehoboam's 12-year reign (1K 12.24a) increased to 17 years in line with 1 Kings 14.21.

The two main features which distinguish LXX's chronology from the chronologies of MT and SP are that it has consistently adopted higher ages of begetting for the pre-Abrahamic period, and that it also gains an additional 130 years by inserting an extra postdiluvian ancestor (Kenan II) and assigning him the same ages as Shelah. In most cases the higher age of begetting is 100 years greater than the corresponding low figure, but this is reduced to a 50-year difference in the case of Nahor, and increased to a 135-year difference in the case of Lamech. I argued earlier that the 135-year increase in Lamech's age of begetting represents a secondary alteration of an original 100-year increase (see p. 15). If we disregard this secondary addition of 35 years to Lamech's figure, the consequence of adding 100 years to fifteen pre-Abrahamic ages of begetting from Adam to Lamech and from Arpachshad to Serug (Noah's and Shem's ages are unvarying), with a further 50 years for Nahor and 130 years for Kenan II, is to increase the original Priestly chronology by 1680 years. This produces the chronological scheme shown in the following table (the original Priestly totals are given in brackets).

Flood	2209/7 AM	(1309/7 AM)
Abraham	3279 AM	(1599 AM)
Entry into Egypt	3569 AM	(1889 AM)
Exodus	4000 AM	(2320 AM)
Foundation of temple	4479 AM	(2799 AM)
Destruction of temple	4909 AM	(3229 AM)

The most interesting feature of this chronology may be seen in the fact that the exodus is dated to 4000 AM. This gives the exodus, and the events of Sinai, a much greater degree of chronological significance than in the original Priestly chronology: in the original chronology the exodus was dated 720 years after the birth of Abraham in 1599 AM and 480 years before the foundation of the temple in 2799 AM, whereas in this chronology the exodus is the key event to which all other events are related. This is a significant ideological shift, which may be seen as a deliberate correction of the original Priestly ideology.

This revised version of Priestly chronology should be regarded as the ancestor of LXX chronology. It was this which resulted in the transmission of two distinct chronological traditions giving shorter and longer chronologies for the period from Adam to Abraham. Both traditions are also reflected in MT and SP to some degree. It should be noted, however, that MT's figure for Lamech's age of begetting (126 years higher than the original Priestly figure) appears to be derived from the LXX figure (increased by 135 years) rather than the earlier, 100-year higher figure (see above, p. 15). If this assessment is correct, it follows that the original LXX chronology was probably created within the Hebrew textual tradition which lies behind the Septuagint translation, rather than being an innovation of the Septuagint translators.

6.2 *Postbiblical chronologies*

6.2.1 *Jewish chronologies*

6.2.1.1 Demetrius

Some of the chronological calculations of the Hellenistic Jewish historian Demetrius have been discussed already (see above, pp. 235–7, and p. 35f.). Demetrius wrote in Greek during the reign of Ptolemy IV (222–205 BC). In fragment 2, Demetrius calculates a period of 3624 years from creation to the entry into Egypt, and 1360 years from the flood to this event (Demetrius 2.18), which was followed by a period of 215 years spent in Egypt (Demetrius 2.19). This last total agrees with LXX chronology, as does the 1360-year interval from the flood to the entry into Egypt. On the other hand, the 3624-year interval from creation to the entry into Egypt is 20 years higher than the original LXX total, and presupposes a figure of 187 years (as in MT) rather than 167 years for Methuselah's age of begetting.

If Demetrius's original chronology incorporated 187 years for

Methuselah's age of begetting, this could have implications affecting the date of MT's chronology. For if Demetrius borrowed this
figure from the chronology found in MT, that chronology would
necessarily have to be earlier than the Maccabean date suggested
above. Alternatively, MT and Demetrius may be drawing on an
independent chronological tradition. There is also a third possibility: '187 years' is found as a secondary reading in a number of
LXX manuscripts, and it is possible that Demetrius's chronology
was corrected to agree with this later version of LXX chronology.

Demetrius's chronology of the period after the exodus is not
preserved in existing fragments. However, indirect evidence of
Demetrius's chronology for this period may possibly be found in a
comment by Clement of Alexandria (*Stromata* 1.113), who noted
that some authorities allowed a period of 595 years from the death
of Moses to the accession of Solomon, whereas others allowed 576
years (Clement himself prefers 523 years and seven months).
Elsewhere, Clement contrasts Demetrius's chronology with the
chronologies of Philo the Elder and Eupolemus. Wacholder
(1974:63–4) has inferred from this that the totals given in *Stromata*
1.113 are taken from the chronologies of Demetrius on the one
hand, and Eupolemus and Philo the Elder on the other. If we add
40 years in the wilderness to the first total, and then add the first
four years of Solomon's reign (to the foundation of the temple), the
number of years from the exodus to the foundation of the temple is
639 years, which should possibly be increased to 639 years and six
months by allowing an extra six months for David's reign (cf. 2
Samuel 5.5).[8] This is 200 years higher than LXX's figure of 440
years from the exodus to the temple, and may be regarded as a
correction to the LXX figure which was designed to allow
sufficient time for the chronological periods specified in Judges
and Samuel.

6.2.1.2 Eupolemus

Eupolemus was a Palestinian Jewish historian who wrote in Greek
in the middle of the second century BC. In one of the surviving
fragments of his work (fragment 5) he is said to have calculated a
period of 5149 years from creation to the 5th year of the reign of

8. Josephus's figures for this period total 591 years and six months (see appendix
B), which Josephus rounds up to 592 years (*Ant* 8.61).

'Demetrius'—which is synchronized with the 12th year of 'Ptolemy of Egypt'—and 2580 years from the exodus to the same date; the second figure is almost certainly a scribal error for *1580 years.

The identity of the Seleucid ruler Demetrius to whom Eupolemus refers is disputed by scholars. Earlier scholars identified him with Demetrius II (145–140 BC), but modern scholars favour Demetrius I (162–150 BC) because this fits the Ptolemaic synchronism better (Wacholder 1974:41). However, the grounds for this identification are now weakened by the fact that Wacholder (following Gutschmid) has shown that the synchronism with Ptolemaic chronology was inserted by a later editor, who also inserted a note which continued the chronology for 120 years after Eupolemus's date. This editor clearly identified Demetrius with Demetrius I, but this identification should not automatically be accepted as being correct.

Eupolemus's chronology for the period from creation to the exodus apparently differed from all other surviving chronologies. 5149 minus *1580 brings us to 3569 AM (or 3570 AM) for the date of the exodus, which is 250 years lower than LXX's date for this event (3819 AM) and 903 years higher than MT's date (2666 AM). What is more interesting is the fact that 1580 is clearly a schematic figure. If we now return to the second of Clement of Alexandria's totals for the period from the death of Moses to the accession of Solomon, which was probably derived from Eupolemus's chronology (see above, p. 242), it can be seen that this fits neatly into a 1580-year period. 576 years from the death of Moses to the accession of Solomon, plus 40 years in the wilderness, plus 4 years of Solomon's reign,[9] adds up to 620 years for the period from the exodus to the foundation of the temple, leaving 960 years from the foundation of the temple to the 5th year of Demetrius's reign. Now 960 years divides equally into two periods of 480 years, of which the first 480 years are accounted for by the period between the foundation of the first temple and foundation of the second

9. Fragment 2b of Eupolemus's history states that Solomon became king when he was 12 years old and began work on the temple when he was 13 years old, which appears to contradict the Biblical statement that the temple was founded in the 4th year of Solomon's reign. In fact, however, Eupolemus's chronology is in agreement with *LXX's* account of the foundation of the temple, which states that the task of preparing stones and timbers for the temple had been underway for 3 years before the temple was actually founded in Solomon's 4th year (1K 5.27–6.1, LXX).

temple.[10] So Eupolemus calculated a round schematic figure of 480 years from the foundation of the second temple to the 5th year of Demetrius, exactly mirroring the 480-year period from the foundation of the first temple to the foundation of the second temple.

Why did he do this? The only reasonable explanation is that the 5th year of Demetrius was marked by an event which Eupolemus considered to be comparable in its significance to the foundation of the first and second temples. One would be hard pressed to find an event in the 5th year of Demetrius I (158 BC) which could fit this description. On the other hand, the 5th year of Demetrius II (141 BC) witnessed the Maccabean liberation of Jerusalem (through the expulsion of the Seleucid garrison) and the emergence of an independent Jewish state with Simon (brother of Judas Maccabaeus) as high priest.[11] Eupolemus is known to have had close Maccabean associations, since he is normally identified with 'Eupolemus the son of John, son of Accos' whom Judas Maccabaeus sent to Rome as part of a mission 'to establish friendship and alliance, and to free themselves from the yoke' (1M 8.17–18).

6.2.1.3 Jubilees

The book of Jubilees (written in about the middle of the second century BC) contains a distinctive jubilee chronology in which dates are expressed in years, weeks of years, and jubilees (weeks of weeks of years) from the world's creation. The overall chronology is overtly schematic, with the interval from creation to the settlement in Canaan being an exact total of fifty jubilees, or 2450 years (Jub 50.4). Jubilees' original chronology for the antediluvian period was apparently identical with the original Priestly

10. This 480-year period is part of the original Priestly chronology, and is also preserved by later Jewish chronological tradition in *Seder Olam Rabba*. See below, p. 256.

11. Cf. 1 Maccabees 13.50–52: 'Then (the garrison) cried to Simon to make peace with them, and he did so. But he expelled them from there and cleansed the citadel from its pollutions. On the twenty-third day of the second month, in the one hundred and seventy-first year [of the Seleucid era, = 141 BC], the Jews entered it with praise and palm branches, and with harps and cymbals and stringed instruments, and with hymns and songs, because a great enemy had been crushed and removed from Israel. And Simon decreed that every year they should celebrate this day with rejoicing.'

chronology, but its present antediluvian chronology has been modified to bring it closer to SP's chronology (see pp. 22–6).

The postdiluvian chronology of Jubilees contains large numbers of discrepancies, and has probably been worked over by several different editors. For example, Jubilees 11.15 dates the birth of Abraham to 1876 AM, and this agrees with the date given by Jubilees 12.12 for Abraham's 60th year (1936 AM). But it fails to agree with dates which are given for Abraham's migration (1953 AM: Jub 12.28f.), the birth of Ishmael (1965 AM: Jub 14.24), the birth of Isaac (1987 AM: Jub 16.15), and Abraham's death (2057 AM according to Jubilees 21.1f., or 2109 AM according to Jubilees 22.1).[12] However, these discrepancies do not affect the overall scheme of 50 jubilees from creation to the settlement.

There are two other points that may be made with regard to the chronology of Jubilees. Firstly, Jubilees includes the extra postdiluvian ancestor (Kenan II) found in LXX's chronology. Secondly, the postdiluvian ages of begetting which are implied by Jubilees' chronology are higher than the original Priestly figures (given by MT), but lower than the increased ages of begetting found in SP and LXX: on average, Jubilees' implied ages are 30 years higher than MT's figures. The inclusion of Kenan II is significant, since it strengthens the case for thinking that Kenan II existed in Hebrew texts of Genesis before the Septuagint translation was produced (see p. 240f.): Jubilees was almost certainly written in Hebrew, and Hebrew fragments have been found at Qumran.

6.2.1.4 Josephus

Chronological data from Josephus has been used in previous chapters to reconstruct earlier forms of Biblical chronologies where the Biblical evidence appeared to be incomplete or defective. Josephus's two main works, the *Jewish War* and the *Antiquities of the Jews* (written during the last decades of the first century AD), provide a wealth of chronological information which draws on Biblical and non-Biblical traditions. Besides giving lifespans and

---

12. It is true that Jubilees does not state how old Abraham was when he left Haran, but we are told Abraham's age at the births of Ishmael and Isaac (86 years and 100 years: Jub 14.24; 15.17), and his age when he died (175 years: Jub 21.2), and these agree with Biblical figures.

reign lengths (etc.) which resemble Biblical notices, but sometimes contain divergent figures, Josephus also punctuates his narratives with chronological summaries stating year totals for extended periods such as the durations of the northern and southern kingdoms (*Ant* 9.280; 10.143) or the interval from the foundation of the temple to its destruction by Titus (*War* 6.269). In some cases these summaries were evidently calculated by Josephus from chronological data in his own narrative: for example Josephus's chronological notices for the period from the exodus to the temple add up to 591 years and six months (see appendix B), and Josephus gives the total duration of this period as 592 years (*Ant* 8.61). Significantly, this total takes no account of the duration of Abdon's period of rule, which is not stated in Josephus's narrative.

In other cases, chronological totals may have been taken over from Josephus's sources. For example, *Jewish War* 6.269 states that the period from the foundation of the temple to its destruction by Titus was 1130 years, and the period from the rebuilding of the temple in Cyrus's second year to its destruction by Titus was 639 years. The period from the foundation of the temple to its destruction by Titus therefore breaks down into a period of 491 years to the foundation of the second temple plus 639 years to its destruction. Now 491 years is one year greater than a schematic total of 490 years, and 639 years is a year short of a round total of 640 years, which makes it appear as if Josephus has disguised an originally schematic chronology by redividing it into two non-schematic periods. Alternatively, the original chronology may have specified a 490-year period from the foundation of the temple to the *return from exile* (in Cyrus's first year) followed by 640 years from the return to the destruction of the second temple. Either way, it is unlikely that Josephus would have created a schematic chronology which he then went on to conceal, so a more probable explanation is that he took over and adapted these totals from one of his sources.

Josephus's use of sources may also account for the existence of major discrepancies between different chronological statements. We have seen that in *Antiquities* 8.61 Josephus calculates an interval of 592 years from the exodus to the foundation of the temple. Elsewhere, however, Josephus allows 612 years for the period from the exodus to the temple (*Ant* 20.230; *Ap* 2.19). Similar discrepancies occur in other places: Saul is said to have reigned for 40 years in *Antiquities* 6.378, but in *Antiquities* 10.143 his reign is given as 20 years. There are various ways in which these discrepancies may be explained,[13] but the most straight-forward explanation may be that Josephus had access to various conflicting sources of chronological information, and did not always take care to check that his calculations for a particular period agreed with calculations that he had stated elsewhere. One should also allow for the possibility that Josephus may have changed his mind in certain cases. It is worth noting that chronological discrepancies of this type do not normally occur within the space of a single book (this contrasts with the situation in Kings or Jubilees, where chronological discrepancies occur within the space of a few chapters or verses): Josephus's longest work (the *Antiquities*) spans twenty books and was presumably written over an extended period of time.

Josephus gives three different chronologies for the period from creation to the exodus. The first of these is found in books 1 and 2 of the *Antiquities* (1.80–88, 148–154; 2.318–319), and is similar to LXX chronology. According to *Antiquities* 1.82, there were 2262 years from Adam to the flood, which is identical to the figure given in LXX manuscripts which have borrowed MT's figure for Methuselah's age of begetting (187 years).[14] Josephus's figures for antediluvian ages of begetting and total lifespans are shown in the following table.

Adam	$230+(700) = 930$
Seth	$205+(707) = 912$
Enosh	$190+(715) = 905$
Kenan	$170+(740) = 910$
Mahalalel	$165+(730) = 895$
Jared	$162+(800) = 962$
Enoch	$165+(200) = 365$
Methuselah	$187+(782) = 969$
Lamech	$188+(519) = 707$
Noah	
age at flood	$600+ 350 = 950$

13. Von Destinon (1880) argues that Josephus's chronology has suffered from scribal and editorial corruptions, and was originally consistent.

14. 2262 years is the total found in the best manuscript of the *Antiquities* at this point (R), but other manuscripts (SPL) have 2656 years, which seems to be partially assimilated to MT's total and does not agree with Josephus's figures for antediluvian ages of begetting. See Niese 1885–95:i:xxxv and Thackeray 1930:38.

Apart from the fact that Josephus agrees with the secondary LXX
figure for Methuselah's age of begetting, the only other case of
disagreement between Josephus and LXX chronology concerns
Lamech's total lifespan, where Josephus's figure of 707 years is
reminiscent of MT's figure of 777 years (the LXX figure is 753
years).

Josephus's postdiluvian chronology in *Antiquities* 1.148–154 is
similar but not identical to LXX chronology. The stated total of
992 years (*Ant* 1.148)[15] is actually 80 years less than LXX's figure;
this is because Josephus does not include Kenan II, who
contributes 130 years to LXX's chronology, but adds an extra *50
years to Nahor's age of begetting.[16] Josephus's ages of begetting
for this period are shown in the following table.

years from flood	12
Arpachshad	135
Shelah	130
Eber	134
Peleg	130
Reu	130
Serug	132
Nahor	120
Terah	70

One significant point about these figures is that they actually add
up to 993 years, which is one year higher than Josephus's stated
total. This discrepancy is almost certainly to be attributed to the
fact that Nahor's age of begetting has been accidentally reduced
from *129 by scribal omission of the original units. Nahor's
original figure was therefore 100 years higher than MT's figure,

15. This is the figure found in manuscripts R and O; other manuscripts (SPL)
have 292 years at this point, which disagrees with Josephus's individual figures and
is evidently assimilated to MT's total (the same manuscripts have partially
assimilated Josephus's antediluvian total to MT's total). See Thackeray 1930:72–
73, and contrast Wacholder 1968:452n., who follows von Destinon in arguing that
292 is the original figure. Wacholder's position is curious, since he accepts R's
figure of 2262 years for the antediluvian period, but criticizes Niese for following
RO in *Antiquities* 1.148–154. Von Destinon, by contrast, argued that Josephus's
entire chronology for the pre-Abrahamic period was originally identical with MT's
chronology, thereby harmonizing the chronology of *Antiquities* 1 with chronological data in *Antiquities* 10.147 (discussed below).

16. The figure found in existing manuscripts (120 years) is 41 years higher than
LXX's figure, but this is almost certainly a scribal error for '129' (see below).

which is also the case with other postdiluvian ages of begetting, except that the units in Reu's and Serug's ages of begetting are switched around in Josephus's chronology. This also explains another curious feature of Josephus's postdiluvian chronology, which is the 12-year interval between the flood and the birth of Arpachshad (MT, SP, and LXX have 2 years at this point): this is probably a scribal correction of '2 years', which was intended to compensate for the loss of 9 years from Nahor's age of begetting.

Josephus's postdiluvian chronology continues with a statement that Abraham was 75 years old when he left Haran (*Ant* 1.154), and is later taken up with a statement that the exodus occurred 430 years after Abraham's migration to Canaan, which was also 215 years after the entry into Egypt (*Ant* 2.318). This is identical with LXX's chronology for this period. Josephus's overall chronology in the first two books of the *Antiquities* is given in the following table.

Flood	2262 AM
Abraham	3254 AM
Entry into Egypt	3544 AM
Exodus	3759 AM

A quite different chronology for this period is to be found in *Antiquities* 8.61–62. This gives the numbers of years which elapsed from the exodus, from Abraham's migration, from the flood, and from creation to the foundation of the temple. The stated figures are as follows: 592 years from the exodus to the foundation of the temple, 1020 years from Abraham's migration to the foundation of the temple, 1440 years from the flood, and 3102 years from creation. This produces the following chronology for the period from creation to the exodus.

Flood	1662 AM
Abraham's migration	2082 AM
Exodus	2510 AM

The interval from creation to the flood is 6 years greater than MT's total for this period, which is most easily explained if we suppose that this chronology presupposes LXX's figure for Lamech's age of begetting (188 years as against 182 years in MT), but otherwise follows MT's antediluvian chronology. From the flood to Abraham's migration there are 420 years, which is 55 years more than in MT's chronology,[17] and from Abraham's migration to the exodus there are 428 years, which contrasts with 645 years in MT and 430 years in LXX. The interval from creation to the exodus is 100 years greater than in Jubilees' chronology.

A third chronology is found in *Antiquities* 10.147, which states the number of years from the foundation of the temple to its destruction, and the number of years from the exodus, from the flood, and from creation, to the same event. The figures are: 470 years from the foundation of the temple to its destruction, 1062 years from the exodus to this event, 1957 years from the flood, and 3513 (variant: 4513) years from creation. This gives the following chronology for the period from creation to the exodus.

Flood	1556 AM
Exodus	2451 AM

This produces a date for the exodus which is identical to MT's chronology if one reduces the period in Egypt from 430 years to 215 years in accordance with the exegetical tradition that the 430 years of Exodus 12.40 were to be counted from Abraham's entry into Canaan. Curiously, however, the date for the flood is 100 years less than in MT's chronology, while the interval from the flood to the exodus is 100 years greater than in MT's chronology (with a 215-year reduction to the period in Egypt). The simplest way of explaining this is to suppose that the figure of 1957 years from the flood to the destruction of the temple is a scribal corruption of *1857 years.

6.2.1.5 Pseudo-Philo

Pseudo-Philo's Book of Biblical Antiquities (*Liber Antiquitatum Biblicarum*) was probably written in Hebrew towards the end of the first century AD, and survives in Latin translation. It contains various items of chronological data, including a set of antediluvian figures which resemble figures from the Septuagint (*LAB* 1.1–22; 5.8). These are shown in the following table.

17. This possibly reflects the addition of Kenan II: Jubilees' chronology allows 57 years from the birth of Kenan II to the birth of Shelah (Jub 8.1, 5).

Adam	$(230) + 700 = (930)$
Seth	$105 + 707 = (812)$
Enosh	$180 + 715 = (895)$
Kenan	$520 + 730 = (1250)$
Mahalalel	$165 + 730 = (895)$
Jared	$172 + 800 = (972)$
Enoch	$165 + 200 = (365)$
Methuselah	$187 + 782 = (969)$
Lamech	$182 + 585 = (767)$
Noah	300
age at flood	$600 + 350 = 950$

Numbers which are shown in brackets are not stated in the text; Adam's age of begetting is inferred to be 230 (as in LXX) from the fact that the number of his remaining years agrees with the LXX figure (MT has $130 + 800$ at this point).

For the most part, this chronology agrees with LXX chronology in giving ages of begetting which are 100 years or so higher than the ages of begetting found in SP. But there are three striking anomalies. Firstly, Seth's age of begetting is the same as SP's and MT's figure, which is 100 years less than the figure found in LXX. Secondly, Kenan's age of begetting is 350 years higher than the LXX figure. And thirdly, Noah's age of begetting is 200 years lower than the figure found in MT, SP, and LXX. The difference in Noah's age of begetting is curious (and hard to explain), but Kenan's age of begetting is probably a scribal error for '170 years' (reading 'CLXX' for 'DXX'), and Seth's age of begetting may also be an error for '205 years' (reading 'CCV' for 'CV').[18] There are also two other cases where the figures given by Pseudo-Philo are unmatched by Biblical figures, but these differences have the effect of cancelling each other out: Enosh's age of begetting is 10 years lower than the LXX figure, while Jared's age of begetting is 10 years higher than in LXX.

If these corrections to Seth's and Kenan's ages of begetting are adopted, Pseudo-Philo's chronology for the antediluvian period is 14 years longer than LXX's chronology (the flood occurs in 2256 AM). This is because *LAB* incorporates two of MT's figures: Methuselah's age of begetting is 187 years (167 years in LXX), and Lamech's age of begetting is 182 years (188 years in LXX).

18. Cohn 1898:281.

However, according to *LAB* 3.6, the flood occurred 1652 years after creation, which is 590 years less than LXX's original total, and 4 years less than MT's figure. So how can we explain this discrepancy? One possibility is that 3.6 is a secondary addition to the text (Harrington *et al.* 1976:II:87–88), but it is also possible that 3.6 contains the original total, and that the chronology in chapter 1 has been modified to agree with Septuagint chronology (Cohn 1898:282).

There are some indications which appear to favour this second alternative. Firstly, although Pseudo-Philo does not give a full set of chronological figures for postdiluvian ancestors from Shem to Abraham, those figures which are given are closer to MT's figures than to LXX's (*LAB* 4.12–15). These are shown in the following table.

Reu	+ 119
Serug	29 + 67
Nahor	34 + 200
Terah	70

LAB's figures differ from those of MT and LXX (and some of them look as if they are assigned to the wrong person: Serug lives 30 + 200 years in MT, and Nahor lives for 29 + 119 years), but Serug's age of begetting is 101 years less than in LXX, and Nahor's age of begetting is 45 years less than the LXX figure. The fact that *LAB* resembles MT's chronology more closely than LXX's chronology at this point may therefore suggest that its antediluvian chronology would also have been closer to MT's chronology, but was later altered. The fact that *LAB*'s postdiluvian chronology was not altered in this way could then be explained by supposing that an editor who modified *LAB*'s antediluvian chronology did not trouble to alter *LAB*'s postdiluvian figures because *LAB* does not contain a complete chronology of the postdiluvian period.

Pseudo-Philo's chronology of the patriarchal period is identical to the chronology found in *Seder Olam Rabba*, which is based on the Masoretic Text:[19] the Israelites are in Egypt for 210 years (*LAB* 8.14), and the 350-year period from God's promise to Abraham to the birth of Moses (*LAB* 9.3) presupposes a 430-year

19. The chronology of *Seder Olam Rabba* is discussed below on p. 255f.

period from God's promise to the exodus, since Moses was 80 years old when this happened (*LAB* 9.3 also mentions a 130-year period from the start of the Egyptian period to the birth of Moses, which is 80 years less than the total period in Egypt).

LAB 10.7 and 19.5 follow standard Biblical tradition in allowing 40 years for the wilderness period, and Pseudo-Philo gives various items of chronological data for the period of the judges, but he also omits items which would allow one to construct a continuous chronology for this period. One interesting piece of chronological information is revealed to Moses shortly before his death. In *LAB* 19.7 God says to Moses, 'I will show you the place where they will serve me for 740 years. And after this it will given into the hands of their enemies, and they will destroy it, and foreigners will surround it.' It is usually thought that this refers to the destruction of the first temple by Nebuchadrezzar (although some scholars also argue that the calendar date given in the same verse—the 17th day of the 4th month—is derived from a date which was associated with the siege of the *second* temple).[20] But 740 years is a far longer period than any other chronology allows for the duration of the first temple, and it is therefore more natural to suppose that this figure represents the combined durations of the first and second temples. However, this creates an opposite problem, since 740 years is rather a short interval for the period from the foundation of the first temple to the destruction of the second temple: *Seder Olam Rabba* allows 410 years for the duration of the first temple, 70 years destruction, and 420 years for the duration of the second temple, giving an overall total of 900 years.

There are various possible solutions to this problem. If 740 is the correct figure, it is easier to suppose that Pseudo-Philo assumed a comparatively short period for the duration of the second temple than that he added over 300 years to the Biblical total for the period of the first temple. But it is also possible that 740 is not the correct figure. Cohn (1898:327) suggested that 740 (DCCXL) was to be emended to 850 (DCCCL), since this agrees with *Seder Olam Rabba*'s chronology for the period from the settlement to the Nebuchadrezzar's destruction of the first temple. Cohn's suggestion assumes that the 'place where they will serve me' is the land of Israel rather than the temple, whereas the

20. See Cohn 1898:327; this is denied by Harrington *et al.* 1976:II:67-70.

passage clearly describes the destruction of a city or building; but if DCCXL (740) can be emended to DCCCL (850), one might also consider adopting DCCCC (900) as the original reading.

This suggestion may or may not be correct, but if it is correct, it would imply that Pseudo-Philo's overall chronology was similar to the chronology of *Seder Olam Rabba*. According to this chronology, the second temple was destroyed in 3828 AM. This is interesting for the following reason. *LAB* 28.8 gives the total duration of the present world as either 4000 years (according to one family of manuscripts) or 7000 years (according to another family), and the most recent edition of *LAB* (Harrington *et al.* 1976:II: 163–164) argues that 4000 years is the correct reading. It is probably easier to suppose that 4000 years was changed to 7000 years than to suppose that the reverse happened. The idea that the world would last for 7000 years became the dominant view of Christian interpretations of Biblical chronology (which were based on Septuagint figures),[21] but is much less strongly attested in Jewish writings. It is found in the long recension of 2 Enoch (33.1–2), and there is also a reference to 7000 'ages' in recension B of the Testament of Abraham (7.16). By contrast, the Testament of Moses dates the death of Moses to 2500 AM (TMos 1.2), and calculates 250 'times' (weeks of years) from the death of Moses to the Messiah (10.12), making a total of 4250 (2500 + 1750) years from creation to the Messiah. And according to the Babylonian Talmud (T. b. *Abodah Zarah* 9a; T. b. *Sanhedrin* 97b), the 'school of Elijah' reckoned 4000 years from creation to the Messiah and a further 2000 years for the Messianic age.

There is one final complication to this discussion. According to *LAB* 19.15, God replies to Moses's request for information on the duration of the world by saying 'Four and a half have passed and two and a half remain'. If this is a cryptic reference to a 7000-year era (the unspecified units of time are millennia), it could be argued that '7000 years' is the original reading in *LAB* 28.8. But there is a serious problem with this interpretation, because no other ancient writer dated the death of Moses as late as 4500 years after creation (on LXX's chronology Moses died in 3859 AM). Moses's death was most commonly dated in the middle of the third millennium from creation—in 2500 AM according to the Testament of Moses, 2450

21. See p. 258f.

AM according to Jubilees, or 2488 AM according to the chronology of *Seder Olam Rabba*. However, there is no unit of time which can be multiplied by $4\frac{1}{2}$ to give a result which is close to 2500 ($4\frac{1}{2}$ sevenths of 4000 is $2571\frac{1}{2}$, but why would Pseudo-Philo have used units of $571\frac{1}{2}$ years?).

In my view, *LAB* 19.15 *does* presuppose a 7000-year era, but this does not necessarily prove that '7000 years' is the original reading in *LAB* 28.8. The manuscript variation between '4000' and '7000' in *LAB* 28.8, and the discrepancy between the antediluvian figures of *LAB* 1 and the antediluvian total of *LAB* 3.6, are evidence of two competing chronologies: a short (original?) chronology which resembles *Seder Olam Rabba*'s interpretation of MT's chronology, and a longer chronology which is similar to Christian interpretations of LXX chronology. The $4\frac{1}{2} + 2\frac{1}{2}$ scheme of *LAB* 19.15 agrees with this longer (secondary?) chronology, except that it suggests an unusually high date for Moses's death.

6.2.1.6 *Seder Olam Rabba*

Seder Olam Rabba, traditionally ascribed to Jose ben Halaphta (2nd century AD), is a rabbinic tractate which is devoted to the subject of Jewish chronology from the time of creation to the end of the Biblical period and beyond. Twenty-nine chapters are devoted to the subject of Biblical chronology, and a final chapter sketches Jewish chronology from the end of the Biblical period to the destruction of the second temple. This chronology also forms the basis of the Jewish world era, in which dates are stated in years from creation, and year 1 corresponds to 3761 BC.

Seder Olam Rabba's account of Biblical chronology combines an interest in midrashic expansion—adding details such as the calendar date on which Moses broke the tablets of the law—with a concern for chronological harmonization which is continued by many modern Biblical scholars. One point of interest is that *Seder Olam Rabba* interprets the 430-year period of Exodus 12.40 as applying to the period spent in *Canaan and* Egypt (*SOR* 1), despite the fact that MT (in contrast to SP and LXX) makes no reference to Canaan, and gives this as the duration of Israel's period in Egypt. The finer details of this chronology (*SOR* 1, 3) are as follows. The 430-year period of Exodus 12.40 incorporates the 400-year period mentioned in Genesis 15.13. This second period is counted from the birth of Isaac when Abraham was 100 years old. According to figures given in Genesis, Isaac was 60 years old when Jacob was born, and Jacob was 130 years old when he entered Egypt, which leaves 210 years for the period in Egypt. (This period of 210 years is also equated with Job's lifespan, which is inferred from Job 42.16, 'after this Job lived 140 years', and Job 42.10, 'and the Lord gave Job twice as much as he had previously [70 years]'). This leaves an obvious difficulty: if the 400-year period of Genesis 15.13 began in Abraham's 100th year, the 430-year period of Exodus 12.40 must be dated from Abraham's 70th year, which is 5 years before Abraham left Haran for Canaan (according to Genesis 12.4 Abraham was 75 when he left Haran). *Seder Olam Rabba* confronts this problem with impeccable logic: Abraham left Haran for an initial visit to Canaan when he was 70 years old, and then returned to Haran for 5 years before migrating to Canaan in his 75th year!

Within the monarchic period, *Seder Olam Rabba* reduces the interval from the foundation of the first temple to its destruction from 430 years (MT) to 410 years (*SOR* 28), thereby removing a 20-year surplus in Judean chronology for the period from the division of the kingdom to the fall of Samaria (in MT there are 261 Judean years but only 241 Israelite years for this period).[22] Despite this 20-year reduction in the duration of the first temple, the interval between the foundation of the first temple and the foundation of the second temple is 480 years (as in the original Priestly chronology): *Seder Olam Rabba* 28 counts 410 years for the duration of the first temple and 70 years from the first temple's destruction to the foundation of the second temple.

Seder Olam Rabba's outline of postexilic chronology is overtly schematic, being fitted into an overall scheme of 490 years from the destruction of the first temple to the destruction of the second temple. This is derived from Daniel's prophecy of seventy weeks of years (*SOR* 28). Chapter 30 divides the overall period of 490 years into five smaller periods:

---

22. This is effected by having a 7-year overlap between Jehoshaphat and Jehoram and a 15-year overlap between Amaziah and Uzziah (*SOR* 17; 19. See pp. 100 and 105). This removes 22 years from MT's total, but an extra year is added by counting *inclusively* from Solomon's 4th year, and another year may have been obtained by adding together the 3-month reign lengths of Jehoahaz and Jehoiachin and then rounding up the 6-month total to a whole year.

1. 70 years from the destruction of the first temple to the foundation of the second temple; this is further divided into 52 years of exile and 18 years from the return to the foundation of the second temple (*SOR* 29).
2. 34 years of the Persian kingdom after the foundation of the second temple (giving 52 years for the entire duration of the Persian empire).
3. 180 years for the kingdom of Greece.
4. 103 years for the Hasmonean kingdom.
5. 103 years for the 'kingdom of Herod'.

The historical absurdity of *Seder Olam Rabba*'s 52-year period for the duration of the Persian empire (which actually lasted for over two centuries) has been noted by other scholars, but the significant point in this is that '52 years' is an inherently schematic number (see page 37n.), which is used here as part of a larger schematic total. Within this total, the 52 years of the Persian kingdom follow 52 years of Babylonian exile, and this symmetry is repeated with 103 years of the kingdom of Herod following 103 years of the Hasmonean kingdom. Another element of chronological schematism is to be seen in the fact that Nebuchadrezzar is ascribed a reign of 45 years (*SOR* 28: he actually reigned for 43 years), which breaks down into 19 years preceding the destruction of the temple (2K 25.8) and 26 years after the destruction of the temple; the 52 years of Babylonian exile are thus equally divided into 26 years under Nebuchadrezzar and 26 years under his successors. To round matters off, there are 18 years from the time that Judah came under Babylonian dominion to the Babylonian exile,[23] making a total of 70 years from the start of Babylonian dominion to the end of the exile (*SOR* 28; compare Jeremiah 25.11; 29.10).

6.2.2 *Christian chronologies*

6.2.2.1 The New Testament

The apostle Paul appears to have had a minor interest in matters of Biblical chronology. In Acts 13.19–21, Paul gives a chronological

23. This happened in Nebuchadrezzar's 2nd year according to *SOR* 24, and there are 18 years (counting inclusively) from this year to Nebuchadrezzar's 19th year.

summary of events from the exodus to the time of David. This comprises 40 years in the wilderness, followed by 450 years from the settlement to the time of Samuel, and another 40-year period for the reign of Saul. The combination of 450 and 40 years is interesting in view of the significance attached to 490-year periods in Daniel and elsewhere; in Paul's chronology there are 490 years from the exodus to the reign of Saul, and the same number of years from the settlement to the reign of David.

In a second passage (Galatians 3.17), Paul states that the Mosaic law was introduced 430 years after God's promise to Abraham. This agrees with Septuagint and Samaritan chronology, but is in conflict with (a natural interpretation of) MT's chronology for this period. However, one cannot infer that Paul was necessarily following Septuagint (or Samaritan) chronology at this point, since rabbinic exegesis (in *Seder Olam Rabba* and elsewhere) calculated the same number of years from Masoretic evidence. It may be noted that this figure, whatever its origin, adds on to the 530-year total of Acts 13 to give 960 (2×480) years from Abraham's migration to the reign of David.

6.2.2.2 Eastern Christianity

Early Christian interpretations of Biblical chronology after the 1st century AD were strongly influenced by the belief that the history of the world would last for six millennia corresponding to the six days of the world's creation, and that this would be followed by a seventh sabbatical millennium paralleling the day on which God rested from his creation (compare the eschatological millennium in Revelation 20.2, which possibly derives from an early formulation of this scheme, and certainly influenced its later development).[24] One result of this analogy between the creation of the world and its subsequent history was that the birth of Christ was normally dated to the sixth millennium of world history, because Adam, who prefigured Christ (according to Christian doctrine), was created on the sixth day of the world's creation. Since this belief agreed rather well with the chronological data of the Septuagint, the earliest

24. *Epistle of Barnabas* 15.4–5; Irenaeus, *Contra Haereses* V:28.2–4; John Malalas, *Chronographia* X; Hippolytus, *In Danielem* IV:24. The following survey of patristic and mediaeval Christian chronologies is based on studies by A. D. v. den Brincken (1957a, 1957b) and V. Grumel (1958).

Christian fathers were agreed that the birth of Christ could be dated more or less exactly in the middle of the sixth millennium. Theophilus of Antioch, writing in or soon after 180 AD, calculated a period of 5698 years from the death of Adam to the death of Marcus Aurelius in that year (*Ad Autolycum* 3.28), and Clement of Alexandria (born c. 150 AD) calculated 5784 years from Adam to the death of Emperor Commodus in 192 AD (*Stromata* 1.2). Julius Africanus (c. 164 to 240), who wrote an influential world chronicle synthesizing Biblical and non-Biblical history, calculated that there were exactly 5500 years to the birth of Christ (he also calculated 3000 years—half of 6000 years—to the death of Peleg, whose name means 'half' or 'division').

Various motivations underlie early Christian interest in chronology. One of these was apologetic: Christian writers sought to reject the accusation that Christianity was a recent superstition by claiming that Christianity was the legitimate continuation of Jewish religion, and by using Biblical chronology to prove that Moses and the prophets antedated Greek writers and philosophers by several centuries. But their interest in chronological schematism shows that they also used chronology to express their belief that history manifested a divine purpose which could be traced from creation to the end of the present era. This belief had one further consequence. If one could calculate how long ago the world had been created, and if it was agreed that the present era was to last for six millennia, one could presumably also calculate the date at which the present era would end. Actually, most Christian writers were careful to *avoid* offering explicit calculations on this point (which might contravene New Testament passages such as Mark 13.32 or Acts 1.7); and they also took care to leave a respectable interval between their own time and the year 6000, which presumably helped to discourage popular expectations of an immediate eschaton.

6.2.2.3. Eusebius

The most important Christian chronographer after Julius Africanus was Eusebius (c. 260–340 AD), who produced a synchronistic chronicle of world history to his own time, in which the events of different nations were arranged in parallel columns and dated in

years from the birth of Abraham.[25] In the first book of his
Chronicle Eusebius also offers a general discussion of the chronologies of each nation: the section on Hebrew chronology discusses
chronological differences between the Septuagint, Samaritan
Pentateuch, and Masoretic Text, and presents various arguments
in favour of Septuagint chronology (although it is worth noting
that Eusebius—and Africanus previously—disregarded Kenan II
in his calculations). Eusebius argued for a shorter chronology than
had previously been accepted, and dated the birth of Christ to 5199
AM (one year short of a schematic total of 5200 years). Eusebius's
Chronicle was translated into Latin and extended to 378 AD by
Jerome, and this chronology subsequently gained general acceptance in the west. On the other hand, eastern Christianity continued
to use the earlier, longer chronology (the Byzantine world era
began in September 5509 BC).

6.2.2.4 Bede

Western Christianity appears initially to have taken little notice of
the fact that the Eusebian chronology transmitted by Jerome and
later western chroniclers conflicted with the chronological figures
contained in Jerome's Vulgate translation of the Hebrew Biblical
text (presumably because these figures did not support traditional
belief in a 6000-year era of the world). This resulted in a popular
expectation that the world would end in around 800 AD. However,
Bede, writing in the early part of the 8th century, calculated from
the Vulgate that there were only 3952 years from creation to the
birth of Christ. This caused Bede to be accused of heresy, but his
chronology was subsequently adopted by the western church,
particularly after the expected end of the world failed to material-
ize, and Bede's date for the creation of the world remained the
accepted date for over eight centuries in the west.

6.2.2.5 Luther

The Protestant Reformation witnessed a new interest in Biblical
chronology, in which schematic considerations were once again
prominent. Martin Luther (1483–1546) published his own

---

25. See the study of Eusebius's *Chronicle* by Mosshammer (1979).

calculations in a work entitled *Supputatio annorum mundi*, which first appeared in 1541.[26] According to Luther's chronology, there were 3960 years from creation to the birth of Christ, which is hardly different from Bede's figure. But the significant feature of Luther's chronology is that it was designed to associate the beginning of the Christian era with the year 4000 AM. Luther dated the death and resurrection of Christ to 34 AD (= 3994 AM), which was also the start of the final 7-year week of Daniel's seventy weeks of years in Luther's chronology. This final week accordingly ended in 4000 AM, and halfway through this period (in Luther's chronology) there occurred the Apostolic council of Acts 15. This council had momentous significance for Luther, since he believed that it had publicly abolished the Mosaic law and inaugurated a new age of grace.

Luther also had a particular reason for wishing to associate the year 4000 AM with the start of the Christian era. According to the Babylonian Talmud, the Rabbinic 'school of Elijah' calculated that the world would last for a total of 6000 years: 'the first 2000 years are to be void, the next 2000 years are the period of the Law, and the following 2000 years are the period of the Messiah' (T. b. *Abodah Zarah* 9a; T. b. *Sanhedrin* 97b). This saying was well-known to the reformers. Luther learnt of it through Carion and Melanchthon, and worked out his chronology to fit this scheme. Ironically, he was unaware of the fact that the saying came from the Talmud, and seems to have thought that it derived from the Biblical prophet Elijah.

6.2.2.6 Ussher

James Ussher (1581–1656), Archbishop of Armagh from 1625, is famous for the fact that he dated the creation of the world to October 23rd 4004 BC.[27] The exegetical route by which Ussher

26. Luther's chronology is discussed in detail by Barr (1989).

27. Ussher's chronological works include the *Annales Veteris Testamenti*, a chronological digest of events from creation to the Maccabean period, which appeared in 1650, *Annalium Pars Posterior* (its sequel), which appeared in 1654, and *Chronologia Sacra*, which presents an argued defence of the chronology set out in the *Annals*, and was published posthumously in 1660. An English translation of the *Annals* was published in 1658. Ussher's chronological calculations later gained quasi-canonical status through their insertion into the margins of English Bibles published after 1701.

arrived at this date has been discussed by James Barr (1984), who also draws attention to the fact that Ussher's chronology is deliberately schematic (Ussher makes the same point in his own preface to the *Annals*). In Ussher's scheme of things, Christ is born in 4 BC (shortly before the death of Herod the Great), the Jerusalem temple is completed 1000 years earlier in 1004 BC, and the world is created 3000 years before that, making a total of 4000 years from creation to the birth of Christ (this agrees with the Rabbinic tradition that there would be 4000 years from creation to the age of the Messiah). In this respect Ussher stood in direct line from the original Biblical chronologists, who used similar patterns of chronological schematism to express their own (pre-Christian) ideologies.

Ussher also combined two other strands of chronological tradition. As a classical scholar, he followed Eusebius in seeking to incorporate Biblical and classical data in a universal chronicle of human history. He also continued the strong Jewish-Christian tradition of attempting to harmonize chronological discrepancies in the Biblical text. Ussher pursued this last objective with an attention to chronological detail which went beyond that of his predecessors, and it was probably this aspect of his work which caused his chronology to be incorporated into the margins of English Bibles from 1701 till the early part of this century.

There is one other feature of Ussher's chronology which deserves comment. Ussher was not the first person to have dated the creation of the world to 4004 BC. Forty years before the first volume of the *Annals* appeared, Thomas Lydiat had published a chronological study entitled *Emendatio temporum*, in which the creation of the world was dated to the same year. This appeared in 1609, when Ussher was in England, acquiring books for the library of Trinity College, Dublin. During this visit Ussher was introduced to Lydiat and invited him to stay with him in Dublin, where Lydiat apparently assisted Ussher in his own chronological researches. Comparison of Lydiat's study with Ussher's work reveals a number of clear similarities, and Ussher's chronology could almost be described as a revision of Lydiat's. This is shown in the following table, which is based on Ussher's table in *Chronologia Sacra*, p. 1, with the addition (in brackets) of figures from Lydiat's chronology.

	yrs	mos	days	[yrs]
1 Creation to flood	1656	0	0	[1656]
2 Flood to Abraham's migration	426	6	14	[422]
3 Abraham's migration to exodus	430	0	0	[430]
4 Exodus to foundation of temple	479	0	17	[479]
5 Foundation of temple to its destruction	424	3	8	[429]
6 Destruction of temple to birth of Christ	583	3	25	[590]

But the differences are no less important than the similarities. Ussher's chronology is more detailed and more precise than Lydiat's chronology. The original edition of the *Annals* comprises 1356 pages in two folio volumes, whereas Lydiat's book was a mere 334 pages of octavo. Ussher's overall scheme of chronology was also different from Lydiat's. Both scholars dated the creation of the world to 4004 BC; but Lydiat dated the birth of Christ in 4007 AM (= 3 AD), whereas Ussher dated it seven years earlier in 4000 AM, thereby correcting a weak point in Lydiat's chronology (Herod the Great had died in 4 BC) while also achieving an appropriate round figure for the birth of Christ.

7

CONCLUSION

A major part of this study has been concerned with the task of reconstructing the original pre-schematic chronology of the book of Kings and using this to construct a historical chronology of the Israelite and Judean kingdoms. Previous attempts to construct a historical chronology of Israel and Judah have mostly failed to recognize the schematic nature of Biblical chronology, and have therefore started from a false set of principles. One group of scholars have used a variety of harmonistic devices in an attempt to demonstrate that the chronology of Kings is (for the most part) internally consistent and historically accurate, while other scholars have argued that the chronology has been corrupted through an accidental process of editorial misunderstandings or scribal corruptions. Both positions are mistaken: the chronology of Kings is historically inaccurate, but it is not corrupt. The reason it is inaccurate is that the Biblical writers were more interested in chronological schematism than in historical accuracy. Biblical chronology is essentially mythical.

This does not mean that it is historically worthless. Large parts of Biblical chronology are indeed worthless from a historical perspective, but this is not true of the chronology of Kings. In its present form, the chronology of Kings is no less schematic than the chronology of Genesis or Judges, but it differs from these chronologies in having been constructed from an originally non-schematic chronology. The historical reconstruction of Israelite and Judean chronology which was presented in chapter 5 is based on a literary-historical analysis of the chronology of Kings (chapter 4), in which I argued that textual variants and internal discrepancies can be used in a partial reconstruction of an original pre-schematic form of this chronology.

From a narrow historical viewpoint, the schematic nature of the chronology of Kings is a nuisance which has to be recognized and dealt with. But there is another way of looking at this. The fact that the Biblical writers valued mythical schematism more highly than historical fact so far as chronology was concerned suggests that the 'historical' books of the Bible may be more appropriately categorized as myth than as history. Some of the events described in these books are purely fictitious (the flood, for example), while others, such as Sennacherib's invasion of Judah, are historical events that have (to varying degrees) been fictionalized. For the Biblical writers, the historicity of an event (or date) was less important than its meaning. This is not to say that mythical events and dates were regarded as non-historical by the Biblical writers or their contemporaries, any more than Ussher saw his own (schematic) chronology as fictitious. Mythical creativity is largely a matter of selecting and reshaping elements from earlier traditions.

The mythical purpose of chronological schematism is that it serves to express a belief that history is governed by a divine plan. Events which occur at regular intervals are not the result of chance: chronological schematism shows the hand of God in history, just as cosmic order shows the hand of God in creation. The precise nature of the divine plan varies according to different schemes. In Deuteronomistic chronology, God's plan concerned Israel's occupation of the land of Canaan, whereas in Priestly chronology the plan is centred on Abraham and the temple. In Christian schemes of chronology, the divine plan is naturally centred on Christ. Some versions of Biblical chronology incorporate an eschatological element. The early Christian scheme of seven millennial ages looked forward to the inauguration of God's kingdom on earth at the end of the sixth millennium, followed by the final eschaton a thousand years later. This does not seem to have been a significant concern of the original Biblical writers. The original Priestly chronology was probably fitted into a 4000-year era. But in Priestly chronology the end of the present era does not seem to have been a matter of significant interest, and the year 4000 lay in the distant future, 720 years after the foundation of the second temple. The Deuteronomistic scheme of 1000 years in Canaan does not allow one to predict God's plan for the next 1000 years, although the fact that God's plan for Israel had been inextricably linked with the land of Canaan in the past could presumably be taken as grounds for hoping that this might also be true in the future.

Schematism is really a natural human activity. The twentieth century has its own versions of chronological schematism. There are fundamentalist groups which see history as a succession of 'dispensations' or ages, and there are others who believe that events are controlled by stars or planets, and that we are currently living in the 'age of Aquarius'. These are fringe beliefs which are not taken seriously by most people. But the division of history into centuries and millennia is itself schematic. And most academic disciplines (including Biblical scholarship) are highly schematic in the way they categorize their subject matter. From this perspective, chronological schematism is simply one of the ways in which people have sought to categorize and make sense of the universe.

APPENDIX A

BIBLICAL CHRONOLOGICAL DATA

The following tables give ages of begetting (for ancestors and patriarchs), periods of rule, and other significant chronological intervals. Unstated totals are given in parentheses, and data which are not directly attested in the Biblical text (or Josephus) have been starred. Curly brackets indicate that a number is not included in a following total.

A.1 *Priestly chronology:*
from creation to the foundation of the second temple

		MT	LXX	SP	(Priestly)
(Gn 5.3)	Adam	130	230	130	130
(Gn 5.6)	Seth	105	205	105	105
(Gn 5.9)	Enosh	90	190	90	90
(Gn 5.12)	Kenan	70	170	70	70
(Gn 5.15)	Mahalalel	65	165	65	65
(Gn 5.18)	Jared	162	162	62	62
(Gn 5.21)	Enoch	65	165	65	65
(Gn 5.25)	Methuselah	187	167	67	*69
(Gn 5.28)	Lamech	182	188	53	53
(Gn 5.32)	Noah	{500}	{500}	{500}	{500}
(Gn 7.6; 9.28)	age at flood	600	600	600	600
(Gn 11.10)	Shem	{100}	{100}	{100}	{100}
	(total)	(1656)	(2242)	(1307)	(1309)
(Gn 11.10)	flood to Arpachshad	2	2	2	*—
(Gn 11.12)	Arpachshad	35	135	135	35
(Gn 11.13)	Kenan	—	130	—	—
(Gn 11.14)	Shelah	30	130	130	30
(Gn 11.16)	Eber	34	134	134	34
(Gn 11.18)	Peleg	30	130	130	30
(Gn 11.20)	Reu	32	132	132	32
(Gn 11.22)	Serug	30	130	130	30
(Gn 11.24)	Nahor	29	79	79	29

(Gn 11.26)	Terah	70	70	70	70
	(total)	(290/2)	(1070/2)	(940/2)	(290)
(Gn 21.5)	Abraham	100	100	100	100
(Gn 25.26)	Isaac	60	60	60	60
(Gn 47.9)	Jacob, age on entering Egypt	130	130	130	130
	(total)	(290)	(290)	(290)	(290)
(Ex 12.40)	Israel in Egypt	430	(215)	(215)	430
	Israel in Canaan and Egypt		430	430	
(1K 6.1)	Exodus to temple	480	440		480
(Kings)	1st temple period	(430)	(430/5)		(430)
	'Exile'				*(50)

A.2 *Deuteronomistic chronology: from the settlement to the Babylonian exile*

		MT	LXX	Jos.	(Dtr)
(Ju 3.8)	Mesopotamian oppression	8	8	8	*7
(Ju 3.11)	Period of tranquillity	40	50	40	40
(Ju 3.14)	Moabite oppression	18	18	18	18
(Ju 3.30)	Period of tranquillity	80	80	(81)	80
(Ju 4.3)	Canaanite oppression	20	20	20	20
(Ju 5.31)	Period of tranquillity	40	40	40	40
(Ju 6.1)	Midianite oppression	7	7	7	7
(Ju 8.28)	Period of tranquillity	40	40	40	40
(Ju 9.22)	Abimelech	3	3	3	3
(Ju 10.2)	Tola	23	23	—	23
(Ju 10.3)	Jair	22	22	22	22
(Ju 10.8)	Ammonite oppression	18	18	18	18
(Ju 12.7)	Jephthah	6	6	6	*7
(Ju 12.9)	Ibzan	7	7	7	7
(Ju 12.11)	Elon	10	—	10	10
(Ju 12.14)	Abdon	8	8	—	8
(Ju 13.1)	Philistine oppression	40	40	40	40
(Ju 15.20; 16.31)	Samson	20	20	20	20
(1S 4.18)	Eli	40	20	40	40
(1S 7.15)	Samuel	—	—	(30)	30
	(total)	(450)	(430)	(450)	(480)
(1S 13.1)	Saul sole rule	2	—	{(40)/20} 22	40
(1K 2.11)	David	40	40	40	40

(1K 11.42)	Solomon	40	40	80	40
(1K 12.24a)	Rehoboam	—	12	—	—
(1K 14.21)	Rehoboam	17	17	17	17
(1K 15.2)	Abijam	3	6	3	6
(1K 15.10)	Asa	41	41	41	41
(1K 22.42)	Jehoshaphat	25	25	25	25
(2K 8.17)	Jehoram	8	10	8	*11
(2K 8.26)	Ahaziah	1	1	1	1
(2K 11.4)	Athaliah	7	7	7	7
(2K 12.2)	Joash	40	40	40	40
(2K 14.2)	Amaziah	29	29	29	29
(2K 15.2)	Uzziah	52	52	52	52
(2K 15.33)	Jotham	16	16	16	16
(2K 16.2)	Ahaz	16	16	16	16
(2K 18.2)	Hezekiah	29	29	29	29
(2K 21.1)	Manasseh	55	55	55	55
(2K 21.19)	Amon	2	2	2	2
(2K 22.1)	Josiah	31	31	31	31
(2K 23.31)	Jehoahaz	{3 mos}	{3 mos}	{3 mos}	{3 mos}
(2K 23.36)	Jehoiakim	11	11	11	11
(2K 24.8)	Jehoiachin	{3 mos}	{3 mos}	{3 mos}	{3 mos}
(2K 24.18)	Zedekiah	11	11	11	11
	(total)	(474)	(474/9)	(514)	(480)

APPENDIX B

CHRONOLOGICAL DATA IN JOSEPHUS

B.1 *From the exodus to the foundation of the temple*

(*Ant* 8.61)	total	592 years
(*Ant* 20.230; *Ap* 2.19)	total	612 years
(*Ant* 4.176, 327)	Moses	40 years
(*Ant* 5.117)	Joshua	25 years
(*Ant* 6.84)	anarchy	18 years
(*Ant* 5.181)	Mesopotamian oppression	{8 years} [see p. 67n.]
(*Ant* 5.184)	'Kenaz'	40 years
(*Ant* 5.187)	Moabite oppression	18 years
(*Ant* 5.197)	Ehud	80 years
(*Ant* 5.197)	Shamgar	1 year
(*Ant* 5.200)	Canaanite oppression	20 years
(*Ant* 5.209)	Barak	40 years
(*Ant* 5.211)	Midianite oppression	7 years
(*Ant* 5.232)	Gideon	40 years
(*Ant* 5.239)	Abimelech	3 years
(*Ant* 5.254)	Jair	22 years
(*Ant* 5.263)	Ammonite oppression	18 years
(*Ant* 5.270)	Jephthah	6 years
(*Ant* 5.271)	Ibzan	7 years
(*Ant* 5.272)	Elon	10 years
(*Ant* 5.273–4)	Abdon	—
(*Ant* 5.275)	Philistine oppression	40 years
(*Ant* 5.316)	Samson	20 years
(*Ant* 5.359)	Eli	40 years
(*Ant* 6.294)	Samuel (sole rule)	12 years
(*Ant* 6.294, 378)	Samuel and Saul	18 years
(*Ant* 6.378)	Saul (sole rule)	22 years (Lat: 2)
(*Ant* 10.143)	Saul	{20 years}
(*Ant* 7.65, 389)	David in Hebron	7 years, 6 months
(*Ant* 7.389)	David in Jerusalem	33 years
(*Ant* 8.61)	Solomon before temple	4 years
	(total)	(591 years, 6 months)

B.2 *Judean kings: from David's accession to the Babylonian exile*

(*Ant* 10.143)	total	514 years, 6 months, 10 days
(*Ant* 7.389)	David in Hebron	7 years, 6 months
(*Ant* 7.389)	David in Jerusalem	33 years
(*Ant* 8.211)	Solomon	80 years
(*Ant* 8.264)	Rehoboam	17 years
(*Ant* 8.285)	Abijam	3 years
(*Ant* 8.314)	Asa	41 years
(*Ant* 9.44)	Jehoshaphat	25 years
(*Ant* 9.104)	Jehoram	8 years
(*Ant* 9.121)	Ahaziah	1 year
(*Ant* 9.143)	Athaliah	7 years
(*Ant* 9.142f., 272)	Joash	40 years
(*Ant* 9.204)	Amaziah	29 years
(*Ant* 9.227)	Uzziah	52 years
(*Ant* 9.243)	Jotham	16 years
(*Ant* 9.257)	Ahaz	16 years
(*Ant* 10.36)	Hezekiah	29 years
(*Ant* 10.46)	Manasseh	55 years
(*Ant* 10.47)	Amon	2 years
(*Ant* 10.77)	Josiah	31 years
(*Ant* 10.83)	Jehoahaz	3 months, 10 days
(*Ant* 10.98)	Jehoiakim	11 years
(*Ant* 10.98)	Jehoiachin	3 months, 10 days
(*Ant* 10.135)	Zedekiah	11 years
	(total)	(514 years, 12 months, 20 days)

Synchronisms:

(*Ant* 8.264)	Abijam's accession	18th year of Jeroboam I
(*Ant* 9.186)	Amaziah's accession	2nd year of Jehoash
(*Ant* 9.216)	Uzziah's accession	14th year of Jeroboam II
(*Ant* 9.260)	Hezekiah's accession	4th year of Hoshea

B.3 *Israelite kings: from the division of the kingdom to the fall of Samaria*

(*Ant* 9.280)	total	240 years, 7 months, 7 days
(*Ant* 8.287)	Jeroboam	22 years
(*Ant* 8.287)	Nadab	2 years
(*Ant* 8.299)	Baasha	24 years
(*Ant* 8.307)	Elah	2 years

(*Ant* 8.311)	Zimri	7 days
(*Ant* 8.312)	Omri	12 years
(*Ant* 8.316)	Ahab	22 years
(*Ant* 9.19)	Ahaziah	2 years
(*Ant* 9.27)	Joram	12 years
(*Ant* 9.160)	Jehu	27 years
(*Ant* 9.173)	Jehoahaz	17 years
(*Ant* 9.177)	Jehoash	16 years
(*Ant* 9.205, 215)	Jeroboam	40 years
(*Ant* 9.228)	Zechariah	6 months
(*Ant* 9.228)	Shallum	30 days
(*Ant* 9.232)	Menahem	10 years
(*Ant* 9.233)	Pekahiah	2 years
(*Ant* 9.234)	Pekah	20 years
(*Ant* 9.258)	Hoshea	9 years
	(total)	(239 years, 7 months, 7 days)

Synchronisms:

(*Ant* 8.287)	Nadab's accession	2nd year of Asa
(*Ant* 8.312)	Omri's accession	30th year of Asa
(*Ant* 9.173)	Jehoahaz's accession	21st year of Joash
(*Ant* 9.177)	Jehoash's accession	37th year of Joash
(*Ant* 9.205)	Jeroboam's accession	15th year of Amaziah
(*Ant* 9.277)	siege of Samaria	7th year of Hoshea
(*Ant* 9.278)	fall of Samaria	9th year of Hoshea
		= 7th year of Hezekiah

APPENDIX C

MESOPOTAMIAN CHRONOLOGY
(FIRST MILLENNIUM)

The following tables are based on Brinkman's chronological appendix in Oppenheim ²1977:335–348, which should be consulted on points of detail. Note, however, that reigns are dated from the year of accession to conform to the way in which I have dated Israelite and Judean reigns; this contrasts with Brinkman's practice of dating reigns from the first regnal year (i.e. the year following an accession year).

C.1 Kings of Assyria

Adadnirari II	(21 years)	912–891 BC (Nis.)
Tukultininurta II	(7 years)	891–884 BC (Nis.)
Ashurnasirpal II	(25 years)	884–859 BC (Nis.)
Shalmaneser III	(35 years)	859–824 BC (Nis.)
Shamshi-adad V	(13 years)	824–811 BC (Nis.)
Adadnirari III	(28 years)	811–783 BC (Nis.)
Shalmaneser IV	(10 years)	783–773 BC (Nis.)
Ashurdan III	(18 years)	773–755 BC (Nis.)
Ashurnirari V	(10 years)	755–745 BC (Nis.)
Tiglathpileser III	(18 years)	745–727 BC (Nis.)
Shalmaneser V	(5 years)	727–722 BC (Nis.)
Sargon II	(17 years)	722–705 BC (Nis.)
Sennacherib	(24 years)	705–681 BC (Nis.)
Esarhaddon	(12 years)	681–669 BC (Nis.)
Ashurbanipal	(42 years)	669–627 BC (Nis.)
Ashuretelilani		
Sinshumulishir		
Sinsharishkun		–612 BC (Nis.)
Ashuruballit II	(3 years)	612–609 BC (Nis.)

C.2 *Babylonian rulers*

Nabonassar	(14 years)	748–734 BC (Nis.)
Nabunadinzeri	(2 years)	734–732 BC (Nis.)
Nabushumukin II	(1 month)	732 BC (Nis.)
Nabumukinzeri	(3 years)	732–729 BC (Nis.)
Tiglathpileser	(2 years)	729–727 BC (Nis.)
Shalmaneser	(5 years)	727–722 BC (Nis.)
Merodachbaladan II	(12 years)	722–710 BC (Nis.)
Sargon II	(5 years)	710–705 BC (Nis.)
Sennacherib	(2 years)	705–703 BC (Nis.)
Mardukzakirshumi II	(1 month)	703 BC (Nis.)
Merodachbaladan II	(9 months)	703 BC (Nis.)
Belibni	(3 years)	703–700 BC (Nis.)
Ashurnadinshumi	(6 years)	700–694 BC (Nis.)
Nergalushezib	(1 year)	694–693 BC (Nis.)
Mushezibmarduk	(4 years)	693–689 BC (Nis.)
Sennacherib	(8 years)	689–681 BC (Nis.)
Esarhaddon	(12 years)	681–669 BC (Nis.)
Ashurbanipal	(1 year)	669–668 BC (Nis.)
Shamash-shumukin	(20 years)	668–648 BC (Nis.)
Kandalanu	(21 years)	648–627 BC (Nis.)
interregnum	(1 year)	627–626 BC (Nis.)
Nabopolassar	(21 years)	626–605 BC (Nis.)
Nebuchadrezzar II	(43 years)	605–562 BC (Nis.)
Evilmerodach	(2 years)	562–560 BC (Nis.)
Neriglissar	(4 years)	560–556 BC (Nis.)
Labashimarduk	(3 months)	556 BC (Nis.)
Nabonidus	(17 years)	556–539 BC (Nis.)

C.3 *Persian rulers*

Cyrus II	(9 years)	539–530 BC (Nis.)
Cambyses II	(8 years)	530–522 BC (Nis.)
Bardiya	(6 months)	522 BC (Nis.)
Darius I	(36 years)	522–486 BC (Nis.)
Xerxes I	(21 years)	486–465 BC (Nis.)
Artaxerxes I	(41 years)	465–424 BC (Nis.)
Xerxes II	($1\frac{1}{2}$ months)	424 BC (Nis.)
Darius II	(19 years)	424–405 BC (Nis.)
Artaxerxes II	(46 years)	405–359 BC (Nis.)
Artaxerxes III	(21 years)	359–338 BC (Nis.)
Arses	(2 years)	338–336 BC (Nis.)
Darius III	(5 years)	336–331 BC (Nis.)

APPENDIX D

ISRAELITE-JUDEAN CHRONOLOGY

D.1 *Kings of Israel*

Jeroboam	(*25 [> 22] years: [LXX])	937–913 BC	(aut.)
Nadab	(2 years)	913–912 BC	(aut.)
Baasha	(24 years)	912–889 BC	(aut.)
Elah	(2 years)	889–888 BC	(aut.)
Zimri	(7 days)	888 BC	(aut.)
Omri	(12 years)	888–877 BC	(aut.)
Ahab	(*24 [> 22] years)	877–854 BC	(aut.)
Ahaziah	(2 years)	854–853 BC	(aut.)
Joram	(12 years)	853–842 BC	(aut.)
Jehu	(27 years: Jos.)	842–816 BC	(aut.)
Jehoahaz	(17 years)	816–800 BC	(aut.)
Jehoash	(16 years)	800–785 BC	(aut.)
Jeroboam	(41 years)	785–745 BC	(aut.)
Zechariah	(6 months)	745 BC	(aut.)
Shallum	(1 month)	745 BC	(aut.)
Menahem	(10 years)	745–736 BC	(aut.)
Pekahiah	(2 years)	736–735 BC	(aut.)
Pekah	(*4 [> 20] years)	735–732 BC	(aut.)
Hoshea	(9 years)	732–724 BC	(aut.)

D.2 *Kings of Judah*

Rehoboam	(17 years)	937–921 BC	(aut.)
Abijam	(6 years: LXX)	921–916 BC	(aut.)
Asa	(41 years)	916–876 BC	(aut.)
Jehoshaphat	(25 years)	876–852 BC	(aut.)
Jehoram	(*11 [> 10: LXX] years)	852–842 BC	(aut.)
Ahaziah	(1 year)	842 BC	(aut.)
Athaliah	(7 years)	842–836 BC	(aut.)
Joash	(*38 [> 40] years)	836–799 BC	(aut.)
Amaziah	(*28 [> 29] years)	799–772 BC	(aut.)
Azariah	(?26 [> 52] years)	772–?747 BC	(aut.)
Jotham	(?11 [> 16] years)	?747–737 BC	(aut.)

Ahaz	(16 years)	737–722 BC (aut.)
Hezekiah	(29 years)	722–694 BC (aut.)
Manasseh	(55 years)	694–640 BC (aut.)
Amon	(2 years)	640–639 BC (aut.)
Josiah	(31 years)	639–609 BC (aut./spr.)
Jehoahaz	(3 months)	609 BC (spr.)
Jehoiakim	(11 years)	609–598 BC (spr.)
Jehoiachin	(3 months)	598 BC (spr.)
Zedekiah	(11 years)	598–587 BC (spr.)

D.3 *Synchronistic table: from the division of the kingdom to the fall of Samaria*

The following table draws together three tables presented earlier (pp. 189f., 194f., and 222.). Synchronisms which are given by MT, LXX, or Josephus are indicated by bold print.

Rehoboam	1	937	1	Jeroboam
	~	~	~	
Abijam	17/ac1	921	17	
	2	920	18	
	3	919	19	
	4	918	20	
	5	917	21	
Asa	ac1/6	916	22	
	2	915	23	
	3	914	24	
	4	913	*25/ac1	Nadab
	5	912	d2/ac1	Baasha
	~	~	~	
	25	892	21	
	26	891	22	
	27	890	23	
	28	889	ac1/24	Elah
	29	888	ac1 /ac/2	Zimri/Omri
	~	~	~	
	39	878	11	
	40	877	12/ac1	Ahab
Jehoshaphat	41/ac1	876	2	
	~	~	~	
	21	856	22	
	22	855	*23	
	23	854	*24/ac1	Ahaziah
	24	853	2/ac1	Joram
Jehoram	ac1/25	852	2	
	2	851	3	

	3	850	4	
	4	849	5	
	5	848	6	
	6	847	7	
	7	846	8	
	8	845	9	
	9	844	10	
	10	843	11	
Ahaziah	*11/ac1/1	842	1/**12**	Jehu
/Athaliah	2	841	2	
	3	840	3	
	4	839	4	
	5	838	5	
	6	837	6	
Joash	**ac1/7**	836	**7**	
	~	~	~	
	21	816	**ac1/27**	Jehoahaz
	~	~	~	
	31	806	11	
	32	805	12	
	33	804	13	
	34	803	14	
	35	802	15	
	36	801	16	
	37	800	17/**ac1**	Jehoash
Amaziah	**ac1/38**	799	**2**	
	~	~	~	
	11	789	12	
	12	788	13	
	13	787	14	
	14	786	15	
	15	785	**ac1/16**	Jeroboam
	~	~	~	
	25	775	11	
	26	774	12	
	27	773	13	
Azariah	**ac1/28**	772	**14**	
	~	~	~	
	21	752	34	
	22	751	35	
	23	750	36	
	24	749	37	
	25	748	38	
Jotham	26/ac1	747	39	
	2	746	40	
	3	745	ac1/ac/ac/41	Zechariah/Shallum
	4	744	2	/Menahem
	5	743	3	
	6	742	4	
	7	741	5	

	8	740	6		
	9	739	7		
	10	738	8		
Ahaz	ac1/11	737	9		
	2	736	10 / ac1		Pekahiah
	3	735	2/ ac1		Pekah
	4	734	2		
	5	733	3		
	6	732	ac1/4		Hoshea
	7	731	2		
	8	730	3		
	9	729	4		
	10	728	5		
	11	727	6		
	12	726	7		Samaria besieged
	13	725	8		
	14	724	9		Fall of Samaria
	15	723			
Hezekiah	16/ac	722			

APPENDIX E

BABYLONIAN/JEWISH MONTH NAMES AND THEIR JULIAN EQUIVALENTS

1 Nisan	(Canaanite Abib)	March/April
2 Iyyar	(Canaanite Ziv)	April/May
3 Sivan		May/June
4 Tammuz		June/July
5 Ab		July/August
6 Elul		August/September
7 Tishri	(Canaanite Ethanim)	September/October
8 Marheshvan	(Canaanite Bul)	October/November
9 Kislev		November/December
10 Tebeth		December/January
11 Shebat		January/February
12 Adar		February/March

BIBLIOGRAPHY

1. *Ancient Texts*

Adadnirari III, Calah Slab (Adn Cal),
    edition: Tadmor 1973:148f.,
    translations: *ANET* p. 281f.; *ARAB* 1 § 738f.; *TUAT* 1 p. 367f.
Adadnirari III, Rimah stele (Adn Rim),
    edition: Dalley 1968,
    translations: Dalley 1984:197f.; *TUAT* 1 p. 368.
Adadnirari III, Saba'a stele (Adn Sab),
    edition: Tadmor 1973:144f.,
    translations: *ANET* p. 282; *ARAB* 1 § 732f.; *TUAT* 1 p. 369.
Adadnirari III, Sheikh Hammad stele (Adn SH),
    edition: Millard and Tadmor 1973:57f.,
    translation: *TUAT* 1 p. 369.
Ashurbanipal, Prism C (Ash PrC),
    edition: Streck 1916:138f.,
    translations: *ANET* p. 294; *ARAB* 2 § 874f.
Assyrian and Babylonian Chronicles (ABC),
    edition: Grayson 1975,
    translations: *ANET* p. 301f., 563f.; *TUAT* 1 p. 401f.
Demetrius, historical fragments,
    editions: Jacoby 1958:666f.; Holladay 1983:51f.,
    translation: *OTP* 2 p. 843f.
Eponym Chronicle (Ep Chr),
    edition: Ungnad 1938,
    translation: *ARAB* 2 § 1198.
Esarhaddon, Nineveh Prisms A [Formerly 'B' or 'C'] and F (Esrh NinAF)
    edition: Borger 1956:36f.,
    translations: *ANET* p. 289f.; *ARAB* 2 § 499f., 688f.; *TUAT* 1 p. 392f.
Esarhaddon, Nineveh Prism B [Formerly 'A'] (Esrh NinB),
    edition: Borger 1956:36f., 125,
    translations: *ANET* p. 290; *ARAB* 2 § 525f.
Eupolemus, historical fragments,
    editions: Jacoby 1958:672f.; Holladay 1983:93f.,
    translation: *OTP* 2 p. 861f.
Josephus, *Contra Apionem (Ap)*,
    edition: Niese 1885–95,
    translation: Thackeray 1926.
Josephus, *Jewish Antiquities (Ant)*,
    edition: Niese 1885–95,

translation: Thackeray 1930, Thackeray and Marcus 1934, Marcus 1937, 1943, Marcus and Wikgren 1963, Feldman 1965.

Josephus, *Jewish War (War)*,
    edition: Niese 1885–95,
    translation: Thackery 1927, Thackery 1928.

Jubilees (Jub),
    edition: Charles 1895,
    translations: Charles 1902; *AOT* p. 1f.; *OTP* 2 p. 35f.

Pseudo-Philo, *Liber Antiquitatum Biblicarum (LAB)*,
    edition: Harrington et al. 1976,
    translation: *OTP* 2 p. 297f.

Sargon II, Ashur Charter (Sg AC),
    edition: Saggs 1975:11f.,
    translations: *ARAB* 2 § 132f.; *TUAT* 1 p. 387.

Sargon II, Calah Prism (Sg Cal),
    edition: Gadd 1954:173f.,
    translation: *TUAT* 1 p. 382.

Sargon II, Cylinder Inscription (Sg Cyl),
    edition: Peiser 1890:38f.,
    translations: *ARAB* 2 § 116f.; *TUAT* 1 p. 386.

Sargon II, Khorsabad annals (Sg Kh)
    edition: Lie 1929,
    translations: *ANET* p. 284f.; *ARAB* 2 § 3f.; *TUAT* 1 p. 378f.

Sargon II, Large display inscription (Sg LD),
    edition: Peiser 1890:52f.,
    translations: *ANET* p. 284f.; *ARAB* 2 § 52f.; *TUAT* 1 p. 383f.

Seder Olam Rabba (SOR),
    edition: Ratner 1897.

Sennacherib, Bellino Cylinder (Sn Bell),
    edition: Luckenbill 1924:55f., 99f.,
    translation: *ARAB* 2 § 268f., 372f.

Sennacherib, Bull inscriptions 1–3 (Sn B1–3),
    edition: Luckenbill 1924:76f.,
    translations: *ANET* p. 288; *ARAB* 2 § 323f.; *TUAT* 1 p. 390.

Sennacherib, Nebi Yunus inscription (Sn Neb),
    edition: Luckenbill 1924:85f.,
    translations: *ANET* p. 288; *ARAB* 2 § 344f.; *TUAT* 1 p. 390f

Sennacherib, Prisms (Sn Pr),
    edition: Luckenbill 1924:23f., 128f.,
    translations: *ANET* p. 287f.; *ARAB* 2 § 232f., 423f.; *TUAT* 1 p. 388f.

Shalmaneser III, Ashur text 5: Basalt Statue (Shl 5),
    edition: Michel 1947:57f.,
    translations: *ANET* p. 280; *ARAB* 1 § 679f.; *TUAT* 1 p. 365.

Shalmaneser III, Ashur text 22: annal fragment (Shl 22),
    edition: Michel 1949:265f.,
    translations: *ANET* p. 280; *ARAB* 1 § 671f.; *TUAT* 1 p. 365f.

Shalmaneser III, Ashur text 32: marble slab (Shl 32),
    edition: Michel 1954:27f.,
    translation: *TUAT* 1 p. 366f.

Shalmaneser III, Ashur text 33: Black Obelisk (Shl 33),

edition: Michel 1955:137f.; 1956:221f.,
   translations: *ANET* p. 278f.; *ARAB* 1 § 553f.; *TUAT* 1 p. 362f.
Shalmaneser III, Bull Inscription (Shl Bull),
   edition: Billerbeck and Delitzsch 1908:144f.,
   translations: *ANET* p. 279f.; *ARAB* 1 § 640f.; *TUAT* 1 p. 363f.
Shalmaneser III, Kurba'il statue (Shl Kurb),
   edition: Kinnier Wilson 1962.
Shalmaneser III, Monolith Inscription (Shl Mon),
   edition: Peiser 1889,
   translations: *ANET* p. 277f.; *ARAB* 1 § 594f.; *TUAT* 1 p. 360f.
Testament of Levi (TLev),
   edition: de Jonge 1978,
   translations: Charles 1908; Hollander and de Jonge 1985; *AOT* p. 505f.; *OTP* 1 p. 775f.
Testament of Moses (TMos),
   edition: Charles 1897,
   translations: *AOT* p. 601f., *OTP* 1 p. 919f.
Tiglathpileser III, Annals (Tgl An),
   edition: Rost 1893:2f.,
   translations: *ANET* p. 282f.; *ARAB* 1 § 761f.; *TUAT* 1 p. 370f.
Tiglathpileser III, Iran stele (Tgl Iran),
   edition: Levine 1972a:11f.,
   translation: *TUAT* 1 p. 378.
Tiglathpileser III, 'Kleinere Inschrift 1' (Tgl K1),
   edition: Rost 1893:78f.,
   translations: *ANET* p. 283f.; *ARAB* 1 § 815f.; *TUAT* 1 p. 373f.
Tiglathpileser III, tablet K 3751 (Tgl K 3751),
   edition: Rost 1893:54f.,
   translations: *ANET* p. 282; *ARAB* 1 § 786f.; *TUAT* 1 p. 374f.
Tiglathpileser III, tablet ND 400 (Tgl ND 400),
   edition: Wiseman 1951:21f.,
   translation: *TUAT* 1 p. 375f.
Tiglathpileser III, tablet ND 4301 + ND 4305 + ND 5422 + K 2649 (+) ND 5419, with duplicate DT 3 (Tgl ND 4301 +)
   texts/editions: Wiseman 1956 (ND 4301 + ND 4305), Wiseman 1964:119f. (ND 5422, ND 5419), *CT* 35 (1920), pl. 39 (K 2649), Rost 1893 pl. 34 (DT 3),
   translations: *ARAB* 1 § 805f. (DT 3); *TUAT* 1,367f.
Tolidah Chronicle,
   texts: Neubauer 1873; Bowman 1954,
   translation: Bowman 1977:37f.

2. *Modern Authors*

Aharoni Y. (1979 [1962]), *The land of the Bible: a historical geography*, ET, 2nd ed.; London: Burns and Oates.
Albright W. F. (1932), 'The seal of Eliakim and the latest preëxilic history of Judah, with some observations on Ezekiel', *JBL* 51, 77–106.
Albright W. F. (1945), 'The chronology of the divided monarchy of Israel',

BASOR 100, 16–22.

Albright W. F. (1953), 'New light from Egypt on the chronology and history of Israel and Judah', *BASOR* 130, 4–11.

Albright W. F. (1956), 'Further light on synchronisms between Egypt and Asia in the period 935–685 BC', *BASOR* 141, 23–27.

Alfrink B. (1942), 'L'expression שכב עם אבותיו', *OTS* 2, 106–118.

Andersen K. T. (1969), 'Die Chronologie der Könige von Israel und Juda', *ST* 23, 69–114.

Astour M. C. (1971), '841 BC: the first Assyrian invasion of Israel', *JAOS* 91, 383–389.

Auerbach E. (1952), 'Die babylonische Datierung im Pentateuch und das Alter des Priester-Kodex', *VT* 2, 334–342.

Auerbach E. (1959), 'Der Wechsel des Jahres-Anfangs in Juda im Lichte der Neugefundenen Babylonischen Chronik', *VT* 9, 113–121.

Auerbach E. (1961), 'Wann eroberte Nebukadnezar Jerusalem?', *VT* 11, 128–136.

Avigad N. (1965), 'Seals of exiles', *IEJ* 15, 222–234.

Baer K. (1973), 'The Libyan and Nubian kings of Egypt: notes on the chronology of Dynasties XXII to XXVI', *JNES* 32, 4–25.

Barta W. (1980), 'Die Mondfinsternis im 15. Regierungsjahr Takelots II. und die Chronologie der 22. bis 25. Dynastie', *RÉ* 32, 3–17.

Barta W. (1984), 'Anmerkungen zur Chronologie der Dritten Zwischenzeit', *GM* 7, 7–12.

Barr J. (1984), 'Why the world was created in 4004 BC: Archbishop Ussher and Biblical chronology' *BJRL* 67, 575–608.

Barr J. (1989), 'Luther and Biblical chronology' *BJRL* 72.

Begrich J. (1929a), *Die Chronologie der Könige von Israel und Juda und die Quellen des Rahmes der Königsbücher* (Beiträge zur Historischen Theologie 3); Tubingen: Verlag von J. C. B. Mohr (Paul Siebeck).

Begrich J. (1929b), 'Der syrisch-ephraimitisch Krieg und seine weltpolitischen Zusammenhänge', *ZDMG* 83, 213–237.

Begrich J. (1933), 'Jesaja 14,28–32: ein Beitrag zur Chronologie der israelitisch-judäischen Königszeit', *ZDMG* 86, 66–79.

Berliner E. (1916), 'Le mois intercalaire du calendrier Punique', *RA* 13, 55–61.

Bickerman E. J. (1975), 'The Jewish historian Demetrios', in J. Neusner (ed.), *Christianity, Judaism, and other Greco-Roman cults* (Studies in Judaism in Late Antiquity 12) 3, 72–84; Leiden: E. J. Brill.

Bickerman E. J. (1980 [1968]), *Chronology of the ancient world*, 2nd ed.; London: Thames and Hudson.

Billerbeck A. and Delitzsch F. (1908), 'Die Palasttore Salmanassars II von Balawat: Erklärung ihrer Bilder und Inschriften ... nebst Salmanassars Stierkoloss- und Throninschrift', *BA* 6:1.

Bimson J. J. (1981 [1978]), *Redating the exodus and conquest*, 2nd ed.; Sheffield: Almond Press.

Bodine W. R. (1980), *The Greek text of Judges: recensional developments* (Harvard Semitic Monographs 23); Chico, California: Scholars Press.

Boling R. G. (1975), *Judges* (Anchor Bible); New York: Doubleday.

Borger R. (1956), *Die Inschriften Asarhaddons Königs von Assyrien* (AfO Beiheft 9); Graz.

Borger R. (1979 [1963]), *Babylonisch-assyrische Lesestücke* (AnOr 54), 2nd ed.; Rome: Pontificium Institutum Biblicum.

Borger R. and Tadmor H. (1982), 'Zwei Beiträge zur alttestamentlichen Wissenschaft aufgrund der Inschriften Tiglatpilesers III', *ZAW* 94, 244–251.

Bowman J. (1954), *Transcript of the original text of the Samaritan chronicle Tolidah*; Leeds: University of Leeds department of Semitic languages.

Bowman J. (1977), *Samaritan documents relating to their history, religion, and life*; Pittsburgh: the Pickwick Press.

Breasted J. H. (1906), *Ancient records of Egypt: historical documents from the earliest times to the Persian conquest*, 5 vols.; Chicago: University of Chicago Press.

Brincken A. D. v. den (1957a), *Studien zur lateinischen Weltchronistik bis in das Zeitalter Ottos von Freising*; Düsseldorf: Michael Trittsch Verlag.

Brincken A. D. v. den (1957b), 'Weltären', *Archiv für Kulturgeschichte* 39, 133–149.

Brinkman J. A. (1968), *A political history of post-Kassite Babylonia, 1158–772 BC* (AnOr 43); Rome: Pontificium Institutum Biblicum.

Brinkman J. A. (1978), 'A further note on the date of the battle of Qarqar and Neo-Assyrian chronology', *JCS* 30, 173–175.

Buccellati G. (1963), 'Nota: in 1 Sam. 13,1 ...', *BibOr* 5, 29.

Burney C. F. (1903), *Notes on the Hebrew text of the books of Kings*; Oxford: Oxford University Press.

Caminos R. A. (1952), 'Gebel es-Silsilah no. 100', *JEA* 38, 46–61.

Cazelles H. (1983), '587 ou 586', *The word of the Lord shall go forth: essays in honour of David Noel Freedman* (edd. Carol L. Meyers and M. O'Connor); Winona Lake: Eisenbrauns.

Charles R. H. (1895), *The Ethiopic version of the Hebrew book of Jubilees*; Oxford: Oxford University Press.

Charles R. H. (1897), *The Assumption of Moses*; London: Adam and Charles Black.

Charles R. H. (1902), *The book of Jubilees translated from the editor's Ethiopic text*; London: Adam and Charles Black.

Charles R. H. (1908), *The Testaments of the Twelve Patriarchs*; London: Adam and Charles Black.

Clements R. E. (1980a), *Isaiah 1–39* (New Century Bible Commentary); London: Marshall, Morgan, and Scott.

Clements R. E. (1980b), *Isaiah and the deliverance of Jerusalem* (JSOTS 13); Sheffield: JSOT Press.

Clines D. J. A. (1972), 'Regnal year reckoning in the last years of the kingdom of Judah', *AJBA* 2, 9–34.

Clines D. J. A. (1974), 'The evidence for an autumnal new year in pre-exilic Israel reconsidered', *JBL* 93, 22–40.

Cody A. (1970), 'A new inscription from Tell al-Rimah and King Jehoash of Israel', *CBQ* 32, 325–340.

Cogan M. (1973), 'Tyre and Tiglath-Pileser III', *JCS* 25, 96–99.

Cohn L. (1898), 'An apocryphal work attributed to Philo of Alexandria', *JQR* (Old Series) 10, 277–332.

Cooke G. A. (1903), *A text-book of North-Semitic inscriptions*; Oxford: Oxford University Press.

Coucke V. (1928), 'Chronologie Biblique', *DBS* 1, 1244–1279.

Cross F. M. (1973) *Canaanite myth and Hebrew epic*; Cambridge, Massachusetts: Harvard University Press.

Dalley [Page] S. (1968), 'A stela of Adad-nirari III and Nergal-ereš from Tell al Rimah', *Iraq* 30, 139–153.

Dalley [Page] S. (1969), 'Adadnirari III and Semiramis: the stelae of Saba'a and

Rimah', *Or* 38, 457–458.

Dalley S. (1984), *Mari and Karana: two Old Babylonian cities*; London and New York: Longman.

Day J. (1985), *God's conflict with the dragon and the sea: echoes of a Canaanite myth in the Old Testament* (University of Cambridge Oriental Publications 35); Cambridge: Cambridge University Press.

Destinon J. von (1880) *Die Chronologie des Josephus*; Kiel.

De Vries S. J. (1962), 'Chronology of the Old Testament', *IDB* 1, 580–599.

Donner H. (1964), *Israel unter den Völkern* (SVT 11); Leiden: E. J. Brill.

Donner H. (1977), 'The separate states of Israel and Judah', *Israelite and Judean history* (edd. J. H. Hayes and J. M. Miller); London: SCM Press.

Donner H. and Röllig W. (1971–6 [1962–4]), *Kanaanäische und Aramäische Inschriften*, 3 vols., 3rd ed.; Wiesbaden: Otto Harrassowitz.

Driver S. R. (1913 [1890]), *Notes on the Hebrew text and the topography of the books of Samuel*, 2nd ed.; Oxford: Oxford University Press.

Epigraphic Survey (1954), *Reliefs and inscriptions at Karnak, vol. 3: the Bubastite Portal* (University of Chicago Oriental Institute Publications 74); Chicago: University of Chicago Press.

Feldman L. H. (1965), *Josephus IX, Jewish Antiquities, books XVIII–XX, index* (Loeb Classical Library); London: William Heinemann.

Finegan J. (1964), *Handbook of Biblical chronology*; Princeton, N. J.: Princeton University Press.

Forrer E. (1915), 'Zur Chronologie der neuassyrischen Zeit', *MVAG* 20/3.

Forrer E. (1920), *Die Provinzeinteilung des assyrischen Reiches*; Leipzig: J. C. Hinrichs'sche Buchhandlung.

Freedy K. S. and Redford D. B. (1970), 'The dates in Ezekiel in relation to Biblical, Babylonian, and Egyptian sources', *JAOS* 90, 462–485.

Fullerton K. (1925/6), 'Isaiah 14.28–32', *AJSL* 42, 86–109.

Gadd C. J. (1954), 'Inscribed prisms of Sargon II from Nimrud', *Iraq* 16, 173–201.

Gandz S. (1954), 'The calendar of ancient Israel', *Homenaje a Millás Vallicrosa* 1, 623–646.

Gardiner A. H. (1945), 'Regnal years and civil calendar in Pharaonic Egypt', *JEA* 31, 11–28.

Gardiner A. H. (1961), *Egypt of the Pharaohs*; Oxford: Oxford University Press.

Ginzel F. K. (1906), *Handbuch der mathematischen und technischen Chronologie*, vol. 1; Leipzig: J. C. Hinrichs'sche Buchhandlung.

Gooding D. W. (1970), Review of Shenkel 1968, *JTS* n.s. 21, 118–131.

Gottwald N. K. (1958), 'Immanuel as the prophet's son', *VT* 8, 36–47.

Gray B. (1912) *Isaiah 1–27* (International Critical Commentary); Edinburgh: T. & T. Clark.

Gray J. (1977 [1964]), *I & II Kings* (Old Testament Library), 3rd ed.; London: SCM Press.

Grayson A. K. (1963), 'Nota: ancora 1 Sam. 13,1.', *BibOr* 5, 86, 110.

Grayson A. K. (1975), *Assyrian and Babylonian chronicles* (Texts from Cuneiform Sources 5); New York: J. J. Augustin.

Green A. R. (1983), 'Regnal formulas in the Hebrew and Greek texts of the books of Kings', *JNES* 42, 167–180.

Grumel V. (1958) *La Chronologie* (Bibliothèque Byzantine: Traité d'Études Byzantines 1); Paris.

Harrington D. J., J. Cazeaux, C. Perrot, and P. M. Bogaert (1976), *Pseudo-Philon*,

Les Antiquités Bibliques (SC 229–230); Paris: Cerf.

Hayes J. (1979), *An introduction to Old Testament study*; London: SCM.

Hayes J. and Hooker P. K. (1988), *A new chronology for the kings of Israel and Judah, and its implications for Biblical history and literature*; Atlanta: John Knox Press.

Heidel A. (1956), 'A new hexagonal prism of Esarhaddon (676 BC)', *Sumer* 12, 9–37.

Helm R. (1956), *Eusebius Werke 7: die Chronik des Hieronymus* (GCS); Berlin: Academie-Verlag.

Herrmann S. (1975 [1973]), *A history of Israel in Old Testament times*, ET; London: SCM Press.

Holladay C. R. (1983), *Fragments from Hellenistic Jewish Authors; vol. 1: historians* (SBL Texts and translations 20, Pseudepigrapha Series 10); Chico, California: Scholars Press.

Holladay W. L. (1986), *Jeremiah 1* (Hermeneia); Philadelphia: Fortress Press.

Hollander H. W. and de Jonge M. (1985), *The Testaments of the Twelve Patriarchs: a commentary* (Studia in Veteris Testamenti Pseudepigrapha 8); Leiden: E. J. Brill.

Horn S. H. (1967), 'The Babylonian Chronicle and the ancient calendar of the kingdom of Judah', *AUSS* 5, 12–27.

Hornung E. (1964), *Untersuchungen zur Chronologie und Geschichte des Neuen Reiches* (Ägyptologische Abhandlung 11); Wiesbaden: Otto Harrassowitz.

Hunger H. (1976–80), 'Kalendar', *RLA* 5, 299–303.

Hurvitz A. (1974), 'The evidence of language in dating the Priestly Code', *RB* 81, 24–56.

Hurvitz A. (1982), *A linguistic study of the relationship between the Priestly source and the book of Ezekiel* (Cahiers de la Revue Biblique 20); Paris.

Irwin W. A. (1927/8), 'The exposition of Isaiah 14.28–32', *AJSL* 44, 73–87.

Jagersma H. (1982 [1979]), *A history of Israel in the Old Testament period*, ET; London: SCM Press.

Jacoby F. (1958), *Die Fragmente der griechischer Historiker*, vol. 3C; Leiden: E. J. Brill.

Jastrow M. (1903), *A dictionary of the Targumim, the Talmud Babli and Yerushalmi, and the Midrashic literature*; New York.

Jepsen A. (1929), 'Zur Chronologie des Priesterkodex', *ZAW* 47, 251–255.

Jepsen A. (1942), 'Israel und Damaskus', *AfO* 14, 154–158.

Jepsen A. (1964), 'Zur Chronologie der Könige von Israel und Juda', *Untersuchungen zur israelitisch-jüdischen Chronologie* (BZAW 88) by A. Jepsen and R. Hanhart, 1–47.

Jepsen A. (1968), 'Noch einmal zur israelitisch-jüdischen Chronologie', *VT* 18, 31–46.

Jepsen A. (1970), 'Ein neuer Fixpunkt fur die Chronologie der israelitischen Könige?', *VT* 20, 359–361.

Johnson M. D. (1969), *The purpose of the Biblical genealogies*; Cambridge: CUP.

Jonge M. de (1978), *The Testaments of the Twelve Patriarchs: a critical edition of the Greek text*, with H. W. Hollander, H. J. de Jonge, and T. Korteweg (Pseudepigrapha Veteris Testamenti Graece 1/2); Leiden: E. J. Brill.

Jones G. H. (1984), *1 and 2 Kings* (New Century Bible Commentary); London: Marshall, Morgan, and Scott.

Kaiser O. (1974), *Isaiah 13–39* (Old Testament Library); London: SCM Press.

Kamphausen A. (1883), *Die Chronologie der hebräischen Könige: eine geschichtlich Untersuchung*; Bonn: Verlag von Max Cohen & Sohn.

Katzenstein H. J. (1973), *The history of Tyre from the beginning of the second millennium BCE until the fall of the Neo-Babylonian empire in 538 BCE*; Jerusalem: the Schocken Institute for Jewish Research.

Kaufman S. A. (1974), *The Akkadian influences on Aramaic* (AS 19); Chicago: University of Chicago Press.

Kaufmann Y. (1960 [1937–56]), *The religion of Israel*, ET; Chicago: University of Chicago Press.

Kinnier Wilson J. V. (1962), 'The Kurba'il statue of Shalmaneser III', *Iraq* 24, 90–115.

Kitchen K. A. (1973a), *The Third Intermediate Period in Egypt (1100–650 BC)*; Warminster: Aris and Phillips.

Kitchen K. A. (1973b), 'Late Egyptian chronology and the Hebrew monarchy', *JANES* 5, 225–233.

Kitchen K. A. (1982), 'Further thoughts on Egyptian chronology in the Third Intermediate Period', *RÉ* 34, 59–69.

Kleber A. M. (1921), 'The chronology of 3 and 4 Kings and 2 Paralipomenon', *Biblica* 2, 1–29, 170–205.

Klein R. W. (1974), 'Archaic chronologies and the textual history of the Old Testament', *HTR* 67, 255–263.

Koch K. (1978), 'Die mysteriösen Zahlen der judäischen Könige und die apokalytischen Jahrwochen', *VT* 28, 433–441.

Koenig E. (1906), 'Kalendarfragen im althebräischen Schriftum', *ZDMG* 60, 605–644.

Krauss R. (1985), *Sothis- und Monddaten: Studien zur astronomischen und technischen Chronologie Altägyptens* (Hildesheimer Ägyptologische Beiträge); Hildesheim: Gerstenberg Verlag.

Krey E. (1877), 'Zur Zeitrechnung des Buches der Könige', *ZWT* 20, 404–408.

Kugler F. X. (1922), *Von Moses bis Paulus: Forschungen zur Geschichte Israels*; Münster: Verlag der Aschendorffschen Verlagsbuchhandlung.

Kutsch E. (1959), 'Zur Chronologie der letzten judäischen Könige (Josia bis Zekekia)', *ZAW* 71, 270–274.

Kutsch E. (1971), '"... am Ende des Jahres": zur Datierung des israelitischen Herbstfestes in Ex 23.16', *ZAW* 83, 15–21.

Kutsch E. (1974), 'Das Jahr der Katastrophe: 587 v. Chr.: kritische Erwägungen zu neueren chronologischen Versuchungen', *Biblica* 55, 520–545.

Lagarde P. A. de (1883), *Librorum Veteris Testamenti canonicorum pars prior Graece*; Göttingen: D. A. Hoyer.

Larsson G. (1983), 'The chronology of the Pentateuch: a comparison of the MT and LXX', *JBL* 102, 401–409.

Levine L. D. (1972a), *Two Neo-Assyrian stelae from Iran* (Royal Ontario Museum, Art and Archeology Occasional Paper 23); Toronto: Royal Ontario Museum.

Levine L. D. (1972b), 'Menahem and Tiglath-pileser: a new synchronism', *BASOR* 206, 40–42.

Lewy J. (1924), 'Forschungen zur alten Geschichte Vorderasiens', *MVAG* 29/2.

Lewy J. (1927), *Die Chronologie der Könige von Israel und Juda*; Giessen: Verlag von Alfred Topelmann.

Lie A. G. (1929), *The inscriptions of Sargon II, king of Assyria; part 1: the annals*; Paris: Librairie Orientaliste Paul Geuthner.

Lipiński E. (1970), 'The Assyrian campaign to Mansuate, in 796 BC, and the Zakir stele', *AION* 30, 393–399.

Luckenbill D. D. (1924), *The annals of Sennacherib*; Chicago: University of Chicago Press.

McCarter P. K. (1974), 'Yaw, son of "Omri": a philological note on Israelite chronology', *BASOR* 216, 5–7.

McCarter P. K. (1980), *1 Samuel* (Anchor Bible); New York: Doubleday.

Mahler E. (1916), *Handbuch der jüdischen Chronologie*.

Malamat A. (1956), 'A new record of Nebuchadrezzar's Palestinian campaigns', *IEJ* 6, 246–256.

Malamat A. (1957), 'A further note on Nebuchadrezzar's Palestinian campaigns', *Judah and Jerusalem* (The twelfth archaeological convention of the Israel Exploration Society), p. 73–78 (Hebrew); Jerusalem.

Malamat A. (1968), 'The last kings of Judah and the fall of Jerusalem: a historical-chronological study', *IEJ* 18, 137–156.

Malamat A. (1971), 'On the Akkadian transcription of the name of King Josiah', *BASOR* 204, 37–39.

Malamat A. (1975), 'The twilight of Judah: in the Egyptian-Babylonian maelstrom', *SVT* 28, 123–145.

Marcus R. (1937), *Josephus VI, Jewish Antiquities, books IX–XI* (Loeb Classical Library); London: William Heinemann.

Marcus R. (1943), *Josephus VII, Jewish Antiquities, books XII–XIV* (Loeb Classical Library); London: William Heinemann.

Marcus R. and Wikgren A. (1963), *Josephus VIII, Jewish Antiquities, books XV–XVII* (Loeb Classical Library); London: William Heinemann.

Mayes A. D. H. (1983), *The story of Israel between settlement and exile: a redactional study of the Deuteronomistic History*; London: SCM Press.

Michel E. (1947), 'Die Assur-Texte Salmanassars III (858–824) (2. Fortsetzung)', *WO* 1/2, 57–71.

Michel E. (1949), 'Die Assur-Texte Salmanassars III (858–824) (3. Fortsetzung)', *WO* 1/4, 255–271.

Michel E. (1954), 'Die Assur-Texte Salmanassars III (858–824) (6. Fortsetzung)', *WO* 2/1, 27–45.

Michel E. (1955), 'Die Assur-Texte Salmanassars III (858–824) (7. Fortsetzung)', *WO* 2/2, 137–157.

Michel E. (1956), 'Die Assur-Texte Salmanassars III (858–824) (8. Fortsetzung)', *WO* 2/3, 221–233.

Millard A. R. and Tadmor H. (1973), 'Adad-nirari III in Syria: another stele fragment and the dates of his campaigns', *Iraq* 35, 57–64.

Miller J. M. (1966), 'The Elisha cycle and the accounts of the Omride wars', *JBL* 85, 441–454.

Miller J. M. (1967), 'Another look at the chronology of the early divided monarchy', *JBL* 86, 276–288.

Miller J. M. (1968), 'The rest of the acts of Jehoahaz', *ZAW* 80, 337–342.

Montgomery J. A. and Gehman H. S. (1951), *Kings* (International Critical Commentary); Edinburgh: T. & T. Clark.

Moore G. F. (1895), *Judges* (International Critical Commentary); Edinburgh: T. & T. Clark.

Morgenstern J. (1935), 'Supplementary studies in the calendars of ancient Israel', *HUCA* 10, 1–148.

Morgenstern J. (1962), 'Year', *IDB* 4, 923–924; New York: Abingdon Press.

Mosshammer A. A. (1979), *The Chronicle of Eusebius and the Greek chronographic tradition*; Lewisburg: Bucknell University Press.

Mowinckel S. (1932), 'Die Chronologie der israelitischen und jüdischen Könige', *AcOr(D)* 10, 161–277.

Mowinckel S. (1952), *Zum israelitischen Neujahr und zur Deutung der Thronbesteigungspsalmen*; Oslo: Jacob Dybwad.

Murtonen A. (1954), 'On the chronology of the Old Testament' *ST* 8, 133–137.

Na'aman N. (1974), 'Sennacherib's "letter to God" on his campaign to Judah', *BASOR* 214, 25–39.

Nelson R. D. (1981), *The double redaction of the Deuteronomistic History* (JSOTS 18); Sheffield: JSOT Press.

Neubauer A. (1873), *Chronique Samaritaine* (extrait no. 14 du Journal Asiatique de 1869); Paris.

Nicholson E. W. (1970), *Preaching to the exiles: a study in the prose tradition of the book of Jeremiah*; Oxford: Basil Blackwell.

Niese B. (1885–95), *Flavii Iosephi Opera* (7 vols.); Berlin: Weidmann.

Noth M. (1958), 'Die Einnahme von Jerusalem in Jahre 597 v. Chr.', *ZDPV* 74, 137–157.

Noth M. (1981 [1943]), *The Deuteronomistic History* (JSOTS 15), ET; Sheffield: JSOT Press.

Oded B. (1972), 'The historical background of the Syro–Ephraimite war reconsidered', *CBQ* 34, 153–165.

Olmstead A. T. (1904/5), 'The fall of Samaria', *AJSL* 21, 179–182.

Olmstead A. T. (1914/15), 'The Assyrian Chronicle', *JAOS* 34, 344–368.

Oppenheim A. L. (1977 [1964]), *Ancient Mesopotamia: portrait of a dead civilization*, 2nd ed., completed by Erica Reiner; Chicago: University of Chicago Press.

Parker R. A. (1950), *The calendars of ancient Egypt* (Studies in Ancient Oriental Civilization 26); Chicago: University of Chicago Press.

Pavlovský V. and Vogt E. (1964), 'Die Jahre der Könige von Juda und Israel', *Biblica* 45, 321–347.

Peiser F. E. (1889), 'Die Monolith-Inschrift III Rawl. 7–8', *KB* 1, 150–174.

Peiser F. E. (1890), 'Inschriften Sargons (722–705 v. Chr.)', *KB* 2, 34–81.

Polzin R. (1976), *Late Biblical Hebrew: toward an historical typology of Biblical Hebrew prose* (Harvard Semitic Monographs 12); Missoula: Scholars Press.

Rahlfs A. (1904), *Septuaginta-Studien 1: Studien zu den Königsbüchern*; Göttingen: Vandenhoeck & Ruprecht.

Ratner B. (1897), *Seder Olam Rabba, die Grosse Weltchronik*; Wilna.

Reade J. (1981), *Mesopotamian guidelines for Biblical chronology* (Syro-Mesopotamian Studies 4/1); Malibu: Undena Publications.

Redford D. B. (1973), 'Studies in relations between Palestine and Egypt during the first millennium BC; II: the Twenty-Second Dynasty', *JAOS* 93, 3–17.

Rendtorff R. (1977), *Das überlieferungsgeschichtliche Problem des Pentateuch* (BZAW 147).

Richter W. (1964), *Die Bearbeitungen des 'Retterbuches' in der deuteronomischen Epoche* (Bonner Biblische Beiträge 21); Bonn: Peter Hanstein Verlag.

Rost P. (1893), *Die Keilschrifttexte Tiglat-Pilesers III.* (2 vols.); Leipzig: Verlag von Eduard Pfeiffer.

Rowley H. H. (1950), *From Joseph to Joshua: Biblical traditions in the light of archaeology* (Schweich Lectures 1948); London: the British Academy.

Rudolph W. (1955), *Chronikbücher* (Handbuch zum Alten Testament); Tubingen: Verlag von J. C. B. Mohr (Paul Siebeck).

Rühl F. (1894/5), 'Chronologie der Könige von Israel und Juda', *DZGW* 12, 44–76, 171.

Saggs H. W. F. (1975), 'Historical texts and fragments of Sargon II of Assyria', *Iraq* 37, 11–20.

Schedl C. (1962a), 'Textkritische Bemerkungen zu den Synchronismen der Könige von Israel und Juda', *VT* 12, 88–119.

Schedl C. (1962b), 'Nochmals das Jahr der Zerstörung Jerusalems, 587 oder 586 v. Chr.', *ZAW* 74, 209–213.

Schrader E. (1875), 'Assyrische-Bibliches', *JPT* 1, 321–342.

Segal J. B. (1957), 'Intercalation and the Hebrew calendar', *VT* 7, 250–307.

Segal M. H. (1927), *A grammar of Mishnaic Hebrew*; Oxford: Oxford University Press.

Shea W. H. (1977), 'A note on the date of the battle of Qarqar', *JCS* 29, 240–242.

Shea W. H. (1978a), 'Adad-nirari III and Jehoash of Israel', *JCS* 30, 101–113.

Shea W. H. (1978b), 'Menahem and Tiglath-pileser III', *JNES* 37, 43–49.

Shea W. H. (1985a), 'Israelite chronology and the Samaria ostraca', *ZDPV* 101, 9–20.

Shea W. H. (1985b), 'Sennacherib's second Palestinian campaign', *JBL* 104, 401–418.

Shenkel J. D. (1968), *Chronology and recensional development in the Greek text of Kings*; Cambridge, Massachusetts: Harvard University Press.

Skinner J. (1930 [1910]), *Genesis* (International Critical Commentary), 2nd ed.; Edinburgh: T. & T. Clark.

Smith G. (1873), 'On a new fragment of the Assyrian Canon belonging to the reigns of Tiglath-Pileser and Shalmaneser', *TSBA* 2, 321–332.

Soggin J. A. (1981) *Judges* (Old Testament Library), ET; London: SCM Press.

Soggin J. A. (1984 [1985]), *A history of Israel from the beginnings to the Bar Kochba revolt, AD 135*, ET; London: SCM Press.

Stenring K. (1965), *The enclosed garden*; Stockholm: Almqvist and Wiksell.

Streck M. (1916), *Assurbanipal und die letzten assyrischen Könige bis zum Untergange Ninevehs* (3 vols.); Leipzig: J. C. Hinrichs'sche Buchhandlung.

Tadmor H. (1956), 'Chronology of the last kings of Judah', *JNES* 15, 226–230.

Tadmor H. (1958), 'The campaigns of Sargon II of Assur: a chronological-historical study', *JCS* 12, 22–40, 77–100.

Tadmor H. (1961), 'Azriyau of Yaudi', *SH* 8, 232–271.

Tadmor H. (1962), 'כרונולוגיה' ('Chronology'), *EB* 4, 245–310.

Tadmor H. (1965), 'The inscriptions of Nabunaid: historical arrangement', *AS* 16, 351–363.

Tadmor H. (1967), 'Introductory remarks to a new edition of the annals of Tiglath-pileser III', *Proceedings of the Israel Academy of Sciences and Humanities* 2/9, 168–187.

Tadmor H. (1969), 'A note on the Saba'a stele of Adad-Nirari III', *IEJ* 19, 46–48.

Tadmor H. (1973), 'The historical inscriptions of Adad-Nirari III', *Iraq* 35, 141–150.

Tadmor H. (1979), 'The chronology of the first temple period: a presentation and evaluation of the sources', *The world history of the Jewish people* 4/1, 44–60, 318–320; Jerusalem: Massada Press (an updated English abridgement of

Tadmor 1962; reprinted as an appendix to Soggin 1984).

Tadmor H. and Cogan M. (1979), 'Ahaz and Tiglath-Pileser in the book of Kings: historiographic considerations', *Biblica* 60, 491–508.

Talmon S. (1958), 'Divergences in calendar-reckoning in Ephraim and Judah', *VT* 8, 48–74.

Tengström S. (1982), *Die Toledotformel und die literarische Struktur der priester-lichen Erweiterungsschicht im Pentateuch* (Coniectanea Biblica; Old Testament Series 17); Lund.

Thackeray H. St. J. (1926), *Josephus I, The Life, Against Apion* (Loeb Classical Library); London: William Heinemann.

Thackeray H. St. J. (1927), *Josephus II, The Jewish War, books I–III* (Loeb Classical Library); London: William Heinemann.

Thackeray H. St. J. (1927), *Josephus II, The Jewish War, books IV–VII* (Loeb Classical Library); London: William Heinemann.

Thackeray H. St. J. (1930), *Josephus IV, Jewish Antiquities, books I–IV* (Loeb Classical Library); London: William Heinemann.

Thackeray H. St. J. and Marcus R. (1934), *Josephus V, Jewish Antiquities, books V–VIII* (Loeb Classical Library); London: William Heinemann.

Thiele E. R. (1951), *The mysterious numbers of the Hebrew kings: a reconstruction of the chronology of the kingdoms of Israel and Judah*; Chicago: University of Chicago Press.

Thiele E. R. (1965 [1951]), *The mysterious numbers of the Hebrew kings: a reconstruction of the chronology of the kingdoms of Israel and Judah*, 2nd ed.; Grand Rapids: W. B. Eerdmans.

Thiele E. R. (1974), 'Coregencies and overlapping reigns among the Hebrew kings', *JBL* 93, 174–200.

Thiele E. R. (1983 [1951]), *The mysterious numbers of the Hebrew kings: a reconstruction of the chronology of the kingdoms of Israel and Judah*, 3rd ed.; Grand Rapids: Zondervan.

Thompson T. L. (1974), *The historicity of the patriarchal narratives* (BZAW 133); Berlin: Walter de Gruyter & Co.

Ungnad A. (1938), 'Eponymen', *RLA* 2, 412–457.

Van Seters J. (1983), *In search of history: historiography in the ancient world and the origins of Biblical history*; New Haven: Yale University Press.

Vaux R. de (1961 [1958/60]) *Ancient Israel: its life and institutions*, ET; London: Darton, Longman, and Todd.

Vogelstein M. (1944), *Biblical chronology I: the chronology of Hezekiah and his successors*; Cincinnati.

Vogt E. (1957), 'Die neubabylonische Chronik über die Schlacht bei Karkemisch und die Einnahme von Jerusalem', *SVT* 4, 67–96.

Vogt E. (1975), 'Bemerkungen über das Jahr der Eroberung Jerusalems', *Biblica* 56, 223–230.

Wacholder B. Z. (1974), *Eupolemus: a study of Judaeo-Greek literature* (Monographs of the Hebrew Union College 3); New York.

Weidner E. F. (1935/6), 'Aus den tagen eines assyrischen Schattenkönigs', *AfO* 10, 1–52.

Weippert H. (1972), 'Die "deuteronomistischen" Beurteilungen der Könige von Israel und Juda und das Problem der Redaktion der Königsbücher', *Biblica* 53, 301–339.

Weippert M. (1973), 'Menahem von Israel und seine Zeitgenossen in einer

Steleninschrift des assyrischen Königs Tiglathpileser III aus dem Iran', *ZDPV* 89, 26–53.

Weippert M. (1978), 'Jau(a) mār Ḫumri—Joram oder Jehu von Israel?', *VT* 28, 113–118.

Wellhausen J. (1871), *Der Text der Bücher Samuelis*; Göttingen: Vandenhoeck & Ruprecht.

Wellhausen J. (1875), 'Die Zeitrechnung des Buchs der Könige seit der Theilung des Reiches', *JDT* 20, 607–640.

Wellhausen J. (1876) Review of G. Smith, *The Assyrian Eponym Canon*, *TLZ* 1, 539–541.

Wellhausen J. (1878), ed., *Einleitung in das Alte Testament*, by F. Bleek, 4th ed.

Wellhausen J. (1885 [1878]), *Prolegomena to the history of ancient Israel*, ET; Edinburgh.

Whitley C. F. (1952), 'The Deuteronomic presentation of the house of Omri', *VT* 2, 137–152.

Wifall W. R. (1968), 'The chronology of the divided monarchy of Israel', *ZAW* 80, 319–337.

Wildberger H. (1978), *Jesaja 13–27* (Biblische Kommentar); Neukirchen-Vluyn: Neukirchener Verlag.

Williamson H. G. M. (1982), *1 and 2 Chronicles* (New Century Bible Commentary); London: Marshall, Morgan, and Scott.

Williamson H. G. M. (1983), 'The composition of Ezra i–vi', *JTS* n.s. 34, 1–30.

Williamson H. G. M. (1985), *Ezra, Nehemiah* (Word Biblical Commentary); Waco, Texas: Word Books.

Wiseman D. J. (1951), 'Two historical inscriptions from Nimrud', *Iraq* 13, 21–26.

Wiseman D. J. (1956), 'A fragmentary inscription of Tiglathpileser III from Nimrud', *Iraq* 18, 117–129.

Wiseman D. J. (1964), 'Fragments of historical texts from Nimrud', *Iraq* 26, 118–124.

Zimmerli W. (1983 [1969]), *Ezekiel 2* (Hermeneia), ET; Philadelphia: Fortress Press.

INDEX OF ANCIENT TEXT REFERENCES

6. Northwest Semitic Inscriptions

INDEX OF SUBJECTS